INA AND MANIPUR

About the Editors

Shukhdeba Sharma Hanjabam (MSW, Ph.D.) is a Professor and Head of the Department of Social Work at Indira Gandhi National Tribal University, Amarkantak, Madhya Pradesh. He completed his Ph.D. from the School of Social Work, Tata Institute of Social Sciences, Mumbai, and his post-doctoral from the University of Florida, Florida, USA (2014-15) as a Fogarty International Centre Fellow. He can be contacted at <hanjabam@gmail.com>

Aheibam Koireng Singh (1978-2022) was an Assistant Professor at the Centre for Manipur Studies, Manipur University, Canchipur, Imphal West District, Manipur. He is formerly the General Secretary of Manipur University Research Club.

Kakchingtabam Ruhinikumar Sharma (MA, Ph.D.) is Head and Assistant Professor, Department of History, Ideal Girls College (Government of Manipur), Akampat, Imphal-East- 795001, Manipur, India. He can be contacted at <kruhinikumar@gmail.com>.

INA AND MANIPUR
An Unforgettable Battle for India's Independence in the Indo-Myanmar Region

Edited by

Shukhdeba Sharma Hanjabam
Aheibam Koireng Singh
Kakchingtabam Ruhinikumar Sharma

Published for

Intellectual Forum of North East—Manipur

CONCEPT PUBLISHING COMPANY PVT. LTD.
NEW DELHI - 110 059

ISBN: 978-93-6344-039-5

First Published 2025

Published and Printed by

Concept
Since 1974

Concept Publishing Company Pvt. Ltd.
A/15-16, Commercial Block, Mohan Garden
New Delhi-110059 (India)
T: +91-11-41101460
E: publishing@conceptpub.com, *W*: www.conceptpub.com

Cataloging in Publication--Courtesy: D.K. Agencies (P) Ltd. <docinfo@dkagencies.com>

INA and Manipur : an unforgettable battle for India's independence in the Indo-Myanmar region / edited by Shukhdeba Sharma Hanjabam, Aheibam Koireng Singh, Kakchingtabam Ruhinikumar Sharma.

pages cm

Contributed articles.

"Published for Intellectual Forum of North East - Manipur."

Includes bibliographical references and index.

ISBN 9789363440395

1. Indian National Army. 2. Manipur (India)--Politics and government--20th century. 3. Manipur (India)--History, Military--20th century. 4. Manipur (India)--History--Autonomy and independence movements. I. Hanjabam, Shukhdeba Sharma, 1983- editor. II. Singh, Aheibam Koireng, editor. III. Sharma, Kakchingtabam Ruhinikumar, editor. IV. Intellectual Forum of North East India (Gauhati, India)

LCC DS485.M48I53 2025 | DDC 954.170359 23

Dedicated to

INA Martyrs and Veterans

&

Aheibam Koireng Singh

A Tribute

Netaji, Azad Hind Fauj and Indian Freedom Struggle*

I humbly pay my homage to Netaji Subhas Chandra Bose on the eve of his 126th birthday. Every year the birth anniversary of Netaji is being observed throughout this country and in many other places in the world. It is fitting that the Government of India declared the 23rd January, the birth anniversary of Netaji as Parakram Divas. And we all know Netaji was the embodiment of *Parakram*, he personifies this. The very utterance of 'Netaji'—Netaji Subhas Chandra Bose electrifies those who speak it out, inspires immediately, and pays homage and tribute to the one most popular leader of our freedom struggle.

Friends…let me share something astonishing that happened some years ago at one deemed university from my home state, Karnataka. It has a name that sounds like 'Manipur'—the Manipal University, well known for its Medical and Engineering Colleges. Shri T.A. Pai who was also the Union Minister for some time and, founded the Manipal Institutes launched a project for Youth leadership. He called it 'Old for Young' and a person was appointed to carry on the project among the youth. Old for young was O.L.D. (Operation Leadership Development) and the person appointed for the job conducted a survey among the youth, particularly the university-going students. And one of the questions was, 'Who do you consider as the youth ideal for yourself? Generally, we think that the students will name some

---

*Public Lecture on NETAJI, AZAD HIND FAUJ, AND INDIAN FREEDOM STRUGGLE by Mananiya Shri Dattatreya Hosabale Ji, Sarkaryavah, Rashtriya Swayamsewak Sangh at Central Hall, GP Women's College, Dhanamanjuri University on 22 January, 2023.

film star, or awesome sportsman (though there is nothing wrong if somebody does), but when the opinion poll was conducted, and the results were published, everyone was astonished and overjoyed. Two great personalities of our country, Swami Vivekananda and Netaji Subhas Chandra Bose topped the chart. So, the university students considered Swami Vivekananda and Netaji Subhas Chandra Bose as their ideals. So, I would like to emphasize here for those people who are elders, those who are above 60 like me, to have immense faith in our youngsters.

Our youth, given the opportunity, will rise. Our youth are not going to defile this country. Our youth will embrace the threats, the opportunities, and the challenges because during the entire history, the youth of this country have come up and risen to the occasion. And so it was during the long-drawn freedom struggle of our country. During the 1000 years of struggle, this nation has seen great adventurous deeds and acts of the young men and women in safeguarding the interests of our nation. The pages of history are full of great sacrifices and renunciation by the youngsters. The annals of our freedom struggle will point to those unsung heroes of Manipur as well as the rest of the country. In Manipur there stands a monument which has the inscription, "we sacrificed our today so that you live your tomorrow." And such young heroes sacrificed their lives so that this nation flourishes. The people of this country will have a great future. And in this galaxy, the shining star is none other than Netaji Subhas Chandra Bose. That is why it is most befitting that the government has chosen to name the birth anniversary of Netaji the 'Parakram Divas.'

About Netaji, I need not go into much detail. Even after so many years, people remember him, respect him, get inspired by his words, and name their children after him as Subhas. In this country, the great heroes live on even today, long after their death. Their names are still there like Shri Ram and Shri Krishna. People in our country, Bharat, name their children as Ram and Krishna. Names of the great warriors and heroes who fought for the nation—like Rana Pratap and Shivaji, are also still there. Parents name their kids as Rana Pratap and Shivaji. Likewise, hundreds and thousands of people in this country even today remember Netaji by calling their son as Subhas. The tradition continues, and the memory continues. The respect is not at all diminished, it is increasing day by day. The reason is that this country has always respected and remembered and eulogized the great men and women who have sacrificed their everything for the cause of the people, for the cause of the nation, and for the cause of Dharma. That is, what we see, people who sacrifice everything, are respected more.

We know of Siddhartha, a prince, who came out one night leaving behind his wife and a small kid. He went in search of the truth and meaning of life and we all know that prince became Gautama Buddha. He sacrificed everything and went in search of 'the supreme knowledge'. One who embraces such life, ready to accept any challenge or sickness not for any selfish reason, but for the emancipation of the people, for the upliftment of the ordinary folks or for the establishment of Dharma is widely respected. Similarly, those who sacrificed to attain the independence of a nation are deeply revered. If Siddhartha was to continue as a prince and die as a prince, who would have remembered him today? There are thousands and thousands of kings and princes in this country. Only those people are remembered who accept the challenges of the time, who organize the people, who are ready to take on the leadership, stand in front, and who are ready to denounce everything. Netaji, as is known by all, was a very bright student. He appeared for the examination of the Indian Civil Service (ICS). In those days, the ICS examination was a very prestigious one, and one who cleared the ICS examination became one of the most powerful officers in the British Empire. All the wealth and happiness would be at his feet. But, here was a young man who had just cleared the examination, and he writes a letter to his brother and having being inspired by the words of Swami Vivekananda, he says, "My life is for Indians and not to become the most obedient servant in the British empire." "I have come in search of a different reason," he says and he sacrifices that ICS prestige. He did not become an ICS though he could have as he had cleared all the examinations but he resigned himself and came out. He said, "Being an Indian I can be equal to the political masters who are ruling over us. But at the same time, I do not consider this as the most important thing in life." That requires guts, that talks of commitment. Unless one is inspired by a nobler cause, by a higher objective in life, he cannot do such a thing.

And Netaji came back to Bharat. He joined the Indian freedom struggle, which he had already participated in. He took out the Tiruvannamalai March in Calcutta. He was arrested by the British police and was sent to jail. Netaji was sent to jail by the British eleven times in his life. Every time the British released him, Subhas was not accepting defeat. Subhas could not be suppressed, nor discouraged. Again and again, he jumped into the fray because the fire was not extinguished, because he considered these hardships and misery and challenges as a suppression.

Bhagat Singh, Sukhdev, and Rajguru were hanged for planning the economic development of India. When we attained independence, naturally, we will have to think and plan for the economic development of our nation. Netaji Subhas Chandra Bose appointed Jawaharlal Nehru as the Chairman of the Planning Committee within the Indian National Congress. And there was an engineer from Mysore, who lived for 101 years and who was later awarded the Bharat Ratna—Sir Mokshgundam Vishveshwarayya. Netaji Subhas Chandra Bose requested him to head the Science and Technology and Engineering Committee under the Indian National Congress. And Subhas Chandra Bose wanted to hand over his presidential chair to someone who would carry on these things. People said there were differences between Gandhiji and Subhas. I am not too smart to comment upon them.

But history shows that ultimately Gandhiji made his appearance at the 1939 Tripuri Congress, when Subhas Chandra Bose wanted to hand over the things that he had started as the President of the Indian National Congress. He said that they should oppose the British, "we should challenge them, this negotiation. The British are not going to accept these things. You must challenge them with force." But, within the Congress, Netaji's thoughts were not acceptable to some people, particularly to leaders like Gandhiji and others. At the 1939 Tripuri Congress, Mahatma Gandhiji chose a candidate—Pattabhi Sitaramayya to represent him at the election. Subhas Chandra Bose was not ready to accept this change and the election for the party president of the Congress was held for the first time. Subhas Chandra Bose, who received over 1500 votes, won the election by over 200 votes. He continued his political work for the Indian National Congress but due to ideological differences, he later resigned and started his own faction without saying a word against anybody.

Netaji tried to awaken the Indian people and organize them through political activism. He wanted to show the power of the people to the British so that they would leave this country and India could attain Independence. Netaji tried it honestly and his leadership was so popular that when he was in jail, his nomination was filed and Netaji got elected for the Kolkata Mayorship. That was his popularity and Netaji thought that the British were not going to budge so simply. By 1939, the political horizon slowly changed as the Second World War was in the offing. Germany, Japan, and others were on one side and the Allied forces were on the other side. The British as an important empire were participants in the world war and all their attention and resources were invested in the war. Netaji's strategy was to strike while the enemy was weak but his colleagues in the Indian National Congress disagreed. They said no, now we shall co-operate with the British so that after the war is over, they will give freedom to us. Netaji did not accept this argument and he went ahead as per his plan.

Netaji, as we all know, was trying to have his contacts and alliances outside India, in the rest of the world. He said that the enemy of the British are our friends because the enemy of the enemy is my friend. In war strategy, such things must be employed and he tried to contact and communicate with such forces, countries, and the leaders of those nations who are on the opposite side of the Allied forces. But in the end, he was arrested and when he fell ill inside the jail, he was supposed to be sent to England for treatment but he did not go. He went to Dalhousie for treatment. When he was in jail and his health deteriorated, the British feared that, if Netaji died in jail, then the British would not be able to face the situation. So, the British doctors said it was better to release him. The British government released him but he was put under house arrest in Calcutta. He was there for months, banned from stepping out and surrounded by the police. We know of the great escape. On 16-17 January, 1941, Netaji escaped wearing a long gown and disguising himself as Ziauddin. He went out of the house without the police recognizing him and took a car and went up to Damoh, later known as Netaji Subhas Chandra Bose station. From there he went to Kesava and then to Russia to meet Mussolini and ultimately met Hitler. When he met them, many people tried to associate Netaji with Nazism and Fascism. Mussolini and Hitler were dictators and their political thoughts like Nazism and Fascism were unpopular at that time, and not acceptable even till the present day. However, Netaji met them for the sake of the freedom struggle of India and was only following war strategy—when you are engaged in a battle against an enemy, you should take the help of the enemy's enemy.

So, for that, I will quote Kunstman's account of the incident when Netaji did not just flatter or praise Hitler when they met. He was brave enough to call a spade a spade on the face of Hitler. In his book, Mein Kampf, Adolf Hitler had abused India in very derogatory terms. When Netaji met Hitler, he had the gumption to say, "These are the things which I do not accept. What you are writing in your book is untruth, not correct. You do not know about India." Netaji's personality was such that Hitler accepted, "Yes, I might have committed some mistakes. I will correct it in my next edition." Netaji had the guts and confidence to say, "I am not begging, if I am seeking help from you, I am seeking it in the great cause of humanity, I will not bow before you and accept what you have done, which was wrong." This is how Netaji safeguarded the respect of our country and the culture of his nation in his heart.

Later, he went to Southeast Asia on two submarines to escape from British surveillance. People from the British intelligence was always shadowing Netaji. When he reached Japan, he talked to General Tojo. The Japanese people had taken some soldiers as prisoners of war during their war with the British. Most of them were Indians who were serving in the British army. So, the people of Japan forgave those Indians, whom they made prisoners of war. This is how the Indian National Army (INA) brought many prisoners of war. Indian National Army or Azad Hind Fauj was founded by Rash Behari Bose. The original idea was by two gentlemen, Captain Mohan Singh, and Nikit Singh. Mohan Singh thought that Indians should join hands with other countries in the world and prepare for a free-spirited struggle outside India. Rash Behari Bose not only accepted the idea of Mohan Singh but agreed to do it and they launched the India National Army. Around

60,000 people were trained in this army. So, the Indian National Army was founded. Since Rash Behari Bose heard the thoughts and activities of Netaji Subhas Chandra Bose, and because of his inspiring personality and words, Rash Behari Bose was ready to hand over the supreme commandership of the Indian National Army to Netaji.

Rash Behari Bose handed over his Azad Hind Fauj to Netaji in Singapore in a big function. Netaji came to be known as the supreme commander of the Indian National Army. Under the leadership of Netaji, about 15,000-18,000 people joined from Manipur and other villages of India. Women also came forward, so Netaji created different regiments in his Indian National Army. When women wanted to join INA, Netaji formed the Jhansi Laxmibai Regiment and publicly announced from Singapore, "We will ask you to come towards Delhi. Give me your blood, I will give you freedom." He sent a letter to Gandhiji saying, "Gandhiji, I am taking many such steps for the liberation of the country. Thousands of young people are moving forward here, ready to sacrifice for their country. They will be marching towards the borders of India, to liberate India." You see, there is neither hatred nor disrespect in the mind of Netaji about Mahatma Gandhi, the person due to whom Netaji left the Congress President in 1939. He said to him, "Gandhiji, I need your blessings and good wishes." What is a wise leader like? The one in whose heart there are glimpses of love, will neither think nor speak with hatred about anyone. I am here trying to talk about spirituality.

Unless a person is spiritually inspired, unless a person is spiritually charged, he will not do such acts. He does not remember the insults to him. In life, there are instances of ups and downs. A leader should never lose heart in the face of ups and downs. You should not lose your confidence. Netaji was a leader and set great examples. When women were in *purdah* in many states of India, Netaji inspired the women, made them wear uniforms, and started the Rani Lakshmi Bai Regiment. There were people from every corner in Netaji's Indian National Army, every part was represented in the Indian National Army. People were there from Tamil Nadu, Kerala, Hyderabad, Rajasthan, and the Northeast. People were there from Manipur in hundreds and hundreds.

In Netaji's Indian National Army, there were Hindus, Muslims, people of Harijans, Sikh Sardars, and Rajputs. In Netaji's Indian National Army, there were not only people who fought with swords and guns but also poets and writers. Consider this song,

> "Kadam Kadam Badhaye Jaa,
> Khushi Ke Geet Gaye Jaa.
> Yeh zindagi hain qaum ki
> Tu qaum pe lootaye jaa."

Think carefully of those who write such songs, they do not take the wrong steps. Those who composed such songs were also part of the Indian National Army. Netaji is a great leader of this youth culture of India and the freedom movement of India—how he travelled the world, brought closeness to his country, and announced the Provisional Government of India.

You know that Japan bombed Manipur twice during the British rule, but Japan's war was not against India. It was against the British. Therefore, Japan took steps to give a warning to the British. Knowing this, the people of Manipur and even the former Chief Minister of Manipur had served in the Indian National Army. Please read about Mr. Koireng Singh. Read the book about the 'Contribution of Manipur in the Freedom Struggle' and 'Unsung Heroes of Manipur'. Contribution of Manipur and North-East in the Indian National Army led by Netaji Subhas Chandra Bose is an inspiring saga for all times to come. The people of Manipur started leaving their villages and cities. But when INA started their marches from Singapore, not one but many people came forward to join the Indian National Army. They knew that this was an uphill task. They knew that they were raising their voice against the most powerful empire on earth. They were not fools but they knowingly accepted this challenge. Colonel Shaukhat Malik of the Indian National Army, spoke in Moirang that by the time they reached there from Singapore, some people had left them and they had lost them. But they knew that from Imphal to Delhi, several people will join in this war—those who have resolved to liberate India by keeping their faith and belief in the attainment of Mother India. "We muster the courage to move forward. The struggle for the motherland would not be easy", he said.

In Singapore, thousands of people donated to the Indian National Army. The people of India—the women, and the mothers of India gave their jewelry items for Netaji's fight, for Netaji's Army. The young men collected money in the streets. They donated in response to Netaji's appeal through radio from Singapore. He liberated the Andaman and Nicobar Islands, and named it "Saheed" and "Swarajya" and hoisted the tricolor flag there. Indian National Army also came to the North East, particularly Moirang of Manipur.

Because he declared the Provincial Government of India, he declared himself as the President, Prime Minister, and Supreme Commander of the Army. The Provincial Government of India established by Netaji Subhas Chandra Bose was recognized by 11 countries. He introduced his currency and established radio and the cabinet. He announced his plans to march to Delhi. Unfortunately, INA had to accept defeat against the British Army. Many people died in the war.

The Japanese Government informed Netaji that they could not move forward as it was the most adverse situation, "If we survive, then we would fight more." So, Netaji came out and flew from there in a plane. His plane crashed on 18th August, 1945. On 23rd August, the government announced that Netaji is no more. We were told this because everyone else died. Netaji, no dead body was found. There are thousands of people in India and in the world who do not believe that Netaji died that day in the plane crash. Many Inquiry Commissions were constituted. But it is difficult to come to any conclusion. The Commission has given its report, all of it is in the public domain.

Bharat has always believed in the values of existence or *Chiranjeevi*. In the history of Bharat, we believe Ashwatthama, Bali, Balaji Hanuman, Singh Charan, Parasurama, etc. as *Chiranjeevi*. They live in some form or the other. It is said that Netaji Subhas Chandra Bose will join these *Chiranjeevi* in this *Kaliyug* as well. Netaji is an indomitable figure in courage and valour. He has given new meaning to 'bravery'. He gave India, a wonderful fragrance and shine.

Netaji's ideas, ideals, and dreams will never perish. He will survive in some form or the other. When ideas, ideals, and dreams are of high quality, and for a noble cause, and are free from any self-aggrandizement, they will be perceptualized, in every heart and soul.

So, I think a wonderful great man like Netaji was born in India, connected India, travelled around the world, and shook the people of the world. Netaji did a wonderful job of connecting devotion with *karma*, leadership, and thought with each other. Let us all dedicate our tribute once again in the memory of Netaji. With these words, I am blessed to have been invited to the programme on Netaji—a Chiranjeev—like persona, with all our friends.

Jai Hind.

Dattatreya Hosabale
Sarkaryavah, Rashtriya Swayamsevak Sangh

Acknowledgements

We want to start by appreciating and acknowledging our esteemed chapter contributors for making valuable contributions in the form of book chapters.

We thank the E-Pao. Net for their permission to reproduce, "Japanese Bombing of Imphal" by M. Ranjit Singh. We show our courtesy to the Golden Jubilee Celebration Committee of the Azad Hind Government, 1993, for their permission to reproduce the articles from their souvenir (21st October, 1992). The articles are: (i) 'INA Headquarters, Moirang, 1944' by Hemam Nilamani Singh and (ii) 'Contribution of the Manipuris in the INA Movement' by Mairembam Koireng.

We also thank Hemam Nilamani Foundation: A Charitable Trust, Moirang, particularly Hemam Nandakumar Singh (Boy), grandson of Hemam Nilamani and Joint Secretary of the Trust for their permission to reproduce the article titled, 'A Pilgrim from Manipur' by M. Jugindro Singh from their Souvenir of 108th Birth Anniversary Celebration of Hemam Nilamani Singh (10th July, 2020).

We acknowledged Professor Shri Prakash Mani Tripathi, Hon'ble Vice Chancellor; and Professor Alok Shrotriya, Dean (Academic) of Indira Gandhi National Tribal University, Amarkantak; Professor Naorem Lokendra Singh, Hon'ble Vice-Chancellor, Manipur University; and Shri Samurailatpam Premananda Sharma, formerly member of the High Level Committee, headed by the Prime Minister Shri Narendra Modi to commemorate the 125th birth anniversary of Netaji Subhas Chandra Bose, for their encouragement during our research and publication of the book.

We are grateful to Smt. Anita Aheibam, Freelance Translator and Media Communicator; Dr. Natasha Elangbam, Department of Mass Communication, Manipur University; and Shri Bishnulatpam Rohit Sharma, PG Student of Manipur University for translating and refining the Public Lecture of Respected Shri Dattatreya Hosabale Ji, Sarkaryavah, Rashtriya Swayamsevak Sangh.

We also would like to put on record our sincere appreciation to our advisers and colleagues of the Intellectual Forum of North East—Manipur and Guwahati for giving us the required moral and intellectual support to complete this book in a time bound manner.

We expressly owe our indebtedness to one and all who are associated in one way or the other in bringing out this book.

Shukhdeba Sharma Hanjabam
Aheibam Koireng Singh
Kakchingtabam Ruhinikumar Sharma

Contents

THEME II
INA AND MANIPUR

Theme III
STORIES OF SELECT INA VETERANS

Theme IV
SECOND WORLD WAR AND MANIPUR

Contributors' Profile

Bramhacharimayum Sadananda Sharma is pursuing an M.Sc. (IT) from the National Institute of Electronics & Information Technology (NIELIT) Akampat, Imphal East, Manipur. He writes on contemporary issues and is a columnist for some leading newspapers based in Manipur.
Email: sadanandasharmabca@gmail.com

Daniel Chabungbam is the Sub-Editor of a leading Manipuri Vernacular Daily Newspaper, Poknafam. He is a recipient of the R.K. Maipaksana Journalist Fellowship 2015 Manipur State Journalist Award, 2017; R.K. Sanatomba Memorial Journalist Award, 2019; and Best Northeast Journalist Award, 2019.

Dattatreya Hosabale (Shri) is Sarkaryavah, Rashtriya Swayamsevak Sangh.

Hemam Nilamani Singh was an active member of the Indian National Army, which fought against the British government. He later became MLA of Moirang and served as Deputy Education Minister of Manipur Government.

Irengbam Mohendra (Dr.) was born at Uripok in Imphal, to Irengbam Gulamjat Singh and Irengbam O Mani Devi. Educated in Imphal, Darjeeling, Bombay, and Nainital, he qualified as a doctor from Agra in 1962. After training in Delhi Hospitals and a stint in Imphal, he left for the UK, where he settled. Married with Margaret, they have a daughter, Anita, and a son, Neil.
Email: imsingh@onetel.com/http://www.drimsingh.co.uk.

James Khangenbam is a journalist and an independent documentary filmmaker. He is a co-founder of the website news portal www.manipurtimes.com. **Email:** jameslaphoi@gmail.com

Kakchingtabam Ruhinikumar Sharma (Dr.) is Assistant Professor, Department of History, Ideal Girls College (Government of Manipur), Akampat, Imphal-East- 795001, Manipur, India.
Email: kruhinikumar@gmail.com

Khelena Gurumayum (Dr.) is an Associate Professor at the Department of Political Science at Manipur University.
Email: khelenag@yahoo.com

Khuraijam Nimaicharan Singh is Sahitya Academy and Sahitya Bhushan Awardee and author of the well-known book, 'The 2nd World War in Manipur & My Childhood'. His present address is Khurai Thoudam Leikai, Ayangpali Road, Imphal.

Khuraijam Surjalal Singh, who goes by the pen name Ink Hands, is a Project Fellow in a Protein Biochemistry and Molecular Biophysics lab at Delhi University. A junior editor and coordinator at Paomi Post Imphal, he is a bibliophile and has an undying passion for the natural world. **Email:** inkhands.yaall@gmail.com

Kongbrailatpam Sarojkumar Sharma is a senior journalist based in Imphal. He has been writing for the *Times of India* since 2003. He began his career in *The Imphal Free Press* since its establishment in 1996 and later joined *The Sangai Express* in 1999. He also regularly contributes to other newspapers and magazines. He was also the former president of the All Manipur Working Journalists' Union (AMWJU) and Secretary of the Manipur Press Club. He teaches journalism as a guest lecturer at the government-run State Institute of Journalism in Imphal. He had also served as a member of the Manipur State Journalists' Welfare Scheme set up by the state government. **Email:** sarojmanipur@gmail.com

Konsam Himalay Singh (Dr.), PVSM, UYSM, AVSM, YSM, retired as a Lt. General of the Indian Army. He is a member of the Consultative Group of Government of Manipur, Naga Peace Talks, and a visiting scholar at the Department of National Security Studies at Manipur University. He was also the former Chairperson of the Manipur Public Service Commission.
Email: himalay27@yahoo.com

Laiphrakpam Nishikanta Singh, VSM & BAR, retired as Lt. General, Indian Army. He served as a Professor at Army War College and the Indian Military Training Team in Bhutan. He was also the former Chairperson of the Manipur Public Service Commission.
Email: nishiby555@gmail.com

Lal Dena (Prof.) retired as Professor of History, Manipur University. He was also the Vice Chancellor of Sangai International University, Churachandpur, Manipur.

M. Jugindro Singh is an Associate Professor & Head, Department of History, Moirang College (Government of Manipur), Moirang, Bushnupur District, Manipur. He attended seminars and contributed papers at State, National, and International levels, mainly on Netaji and INA.

M. Ranjit Singh retired as Lt. Col. (Retd.) of the Indian Army. Presently, he is Vice President, Manipur Horse Riding & Polo Association.

Mairembam Koireng was an active member of the Indian National Army, which fought against the British Government. He later became the Chief Minister of Manipur.

Mairembam Prithviraj Singh was formerly a Member of the Manipur Legislative Assembly (MLA) from Moirang Constituency, Bishnupur District, Manipur.

Manindra Konsam is Senior Journalist and Editor, *Sanathong* (a popular Monthly Magazine) based in Imphal, Manipur.
Email: manindraningthouja@gmail.com

Moirangthem Asnikumar Singh is the founder secretary of Manipur Thinkers Forum, an independent think tank and Chairman, Loktak Development Authority. He is also the State Spokesperson of BJP Manipur Pradesh.

Moirangthem Shanti Devi (Dr.) is Assistant Professor, Department of Political Science, Kha Manipur College, Kakching, Manipur, India.

Mongsatabam Makhonmani (Dr.) is a renowned Film Director based in Imphal and a Sahitya Akademi Awardee for his travelogue in Manipuri—"Chinglon Amadagi Amada". He retired from the Department of Manipuri, Manipur University of Culture, Imphal.

Naorem Lokendra Singh (Prof.) is Vice-Chancellor of Manipur University. **Email:** lokendranaorem2015@gmail.com

Nongmaithem Pramodini (Dr.) is a lecturer at Kakching Higher Secondary School, Government of Manipur.

Pebam Nganthoiba Mangang (Dr.) is working as Social Development Specialist with the Department of MAHUD, Government of Manipur. He earned his Doctoral degree from the School of Social Work, Tata Institute of Social Sciences, Mumbai. **Email:** pebamng@gmail.com

Priyadarshni Maisnam G. (Dr.) is an Assistant Professor at the Department of History, S.K. Women's College (Government of Manipur), Nambol, Bishnupur District, Manipur. She is a Life Member of the Indian History Congress, N.E. India Historical Association, and Manipur Historical Society.

Rajkumar Ranjan Singh (Dr.) is formerly Hon'ble Union Minister of State for External Affairs and Education, Government of India. **Email:** ranjanrk50@gmail.com

Samurailatpam Premananda Sharma, formerly member of the High-Level Committee, headed by the Prime Minister Shri Narendra Modi to commemorate the 125th birth anniversary of Netaji Subhas Chandra Bose, and Formerly Court Member, Central University of Himachal Pradesh.

Sunzu Bachaspatimayum is a filmmaker and a freelance Journalist. **Email:** sunzubm@gmail.com

Sylvia Yambem (Dr.) is a faculty member at the Department of History, Manipur University, and was also an ICSSR Post-Doctoral Fellow (2016-2017). **Email:** sylvia.yambem@gmail.com

Wairokpam Mangol Singh is the author of the well acclaimed book, "Prithivigi Anisuba Lanjao Amasung Manipur Party/ The Second World War and the Manipur Party" (1984), Shri Wairokpam Mangol Singh, Lairik Yengbam Leikai, Imphal, Manipur.

Y. Modhu Singh retired as Associate Professor and former Head of the Department of Political Science at Moirang College. He was also the IQAC Coordinator of Moirang College. He exhibits cultivation in writing several papers on Netaji and INA. He is a motivational counsellor and a faculty of Lions Clubs International

District 322D. Currently, he is working as a Principal at Advanced Intermediate College, Moirang.

Email: modhuyumkhaibam@gmail.com

Yaiphaba Meetei Kangjam (Yai) is a part of Battle of Imphal Tours, which offers Second World War-themed battlefield tours in North East India and Myanmar (Burma). He also organises contemporary tours around Manipur through his venture Imphal Walks, besides being a founding member of the Manipur Association of Tour Operators (MATO). Yai holds a Master's degree in Tourism Management and completed his thesis on Battlefield Tourism, with particular reference to Manipur.

Email: yaiphakangjam@gmail.com

Yumnam Rajeshwor Singh is the Founder and Chairperson of the Second World War Imphal Campaign Foundation. He is sociologist by training.

Email: yrs001@gmail.com; www.imphalcampaignfoundation.com

1

Introduction

Kakchingtabam Ruhinikumar Sharma and
Samurailatpam Premananda Sharma

Because of her strategic position of being sandwiched between India and South East Asia, Manipur even though territorially insignificant in comparison with her neighbours were able to carve out a niche for herself. She had both the fortune and misfortune of experiencing Sinic and Indic cultural influence from early times which on the other hand helped in the evolution of a synthesised and unique culture resulting in Manipur attaining almost a civilisation state. Though situated in the extreme ends of the two cultures she experienced the vicissitudes of history, which sometimes threatened her very existence, yet could re-emerge from the rubbles she was buried in. Her attempt to emerge as a regional power in early eighteenth century was soon eclipsed as she fell prey to the rising Burmese power owing to the changed geo-political scenario in the region as a result of the game of one up-manship among the European powers like the British, French and Portuguese.

The struggle for mastery of the region among the European powers coupled with resurgent Burmese nationalism having expansionist motives caused irreparable damage to Manipur's body polity and Manipur almost becoming a buffer to Burma and British

India. These stories have been told many a times. The three wars between Burma and British India (1824-1826; 1852-1853; 1885) referred to in history as Anglo-Burma Wars, finally resulted in the annexation of Burma to the British Indian Empire, yet Manipur was able to enjoy its independent entity for a few more years till her defeat in the Anglo-Manipur War of 1891. Though Manipur lost her sovereignty, her strategic position remained as earlier. The echoes of World War I was heard in this small hill state in the form of Khongjai Lan as a reaction to the labour recruitment policy indulged in by the colonial administration, which the natives considered unjustified.

Thus when the sounds of air raids and bombing by Japanese airplanes were heard at Imphal for the first time on 10th May, 1942, it was alarmingly clear that Manipur was going to be one of the important theatre of World War II as Imphal holds key to both the opposing fronts in their future scheme. Manipur's strategic importance and the necessity to control or defend it were in fact going to determine the course of the War. Both the Japanese and more so to the Azad Hind Fauz of Subhas Chandra Bose Imphal hold the key to their victory. For Subhas Bose, if Imphal was liberated, his dream of liberating India is almost a certainty and for the Japanese it heralds the demise of British colonial rule in Asia.

It is no wonder that thus Manipur became one of the bloodiest and toughest battles of Second World War in history along with Monte Cassino in Italy and Kohima in Naga Hills of Assam. The natives of Manipur and Naga Hills lived through and experienced the battles which could be epic, epic in the sense that the violence, loss of lives and displacement that the War had brought in. Through these papers, a humble effort is made to reconstruct the life of Manipur during the Second World War and how natives responded to it along with the experiences of individuals who worked or volunteered for Indian National Army (INA) with the hope that in doing so, they were inspired by an idea called *azadi* or freedom; freedom from foreign rule and domination by outsiders of their land.

Keeping this in consideration, this book which altogether consists of 32 chapters is organised into four themes. The **first chapter** is the Introduction by Kakchingtabam Ruhinikumar Sharma & Samurailatpam Premananda Sharma.

The **second chapter**, "Indian National Army (Azad Hind Fauj) During World War II and the Princely Kingdom of Manipur" by Konsam Himalay Singh highlights that prior to the Great War 1944, Manipur was an isolated kingdom. The year 1944 changed all that with the Allied and Japanese forces fighting to gain control of the Imphal Valley in Manipur and Kohima in the Naga Hills in Assam to the north. With the Japanese defeat in Burma in mid-1945, the INA crumbled without ever securing the mass. Moirang in Manipur remains a testimony to the brave soldiers of the INA who unfurled the first Indian National Flag there. Along with the Japanese Peace-museum near Maibam Lokpa Ching enroute to Moirang from Imphal, the memories of the war are vivid in the hearts of the Manipuris.

The **third chapter**, "INA-Japanese Imphal and Kohima Campaign and Local Participation (1942-45)" by Naorem Lokendra Singh deals with the coming of the war in Chin Hills in Burma; the war campaign in Bishenpur, Red Hill, Tamu-Shenam Saddle, Nungshigum, and Shangshak of Manipur; Kohima of erstwhile Naga Hills in Assam; local participation in Manipur by the Meiteis, Kukis, Tangkhul Nagas, and Nagas of Naga Hills; and concludes with the post-war socio-political changes. It highlights that the changes during the wartime provided material as well as ideological basis for strong political movements during 1946-1949 period. It was during such a time of tremendous change that the economic base of the nascent Manipuri and Naga middle class were strengthened through massive investments in transportation, trade, supply and construction works. Ideologically, the Manipuri and Naga middle class was exposed to the national and international political trends and therefore, was on the lookout for opportunities to struggle for broad socio-economic and political changes in their respective states.

The **fourth chapter**, "Manipur in the Geo-Political Mapping of India's Winning Freedom" by Y. Modhu Singh concludes that by geographical compulsions and patriotic temperament of the people of Manipur she became a theatre of liberation war, her soil wetted with the blood of martyrs and unsung heroes, countless innocent people, men, women and children died, flag of freedom hoisted ceremonially on her liberated soil. History has vividly testified that freedom was granted to India in 1947 due to the resultant effects of the Liberation War on the soil of Manipur. Contribution of the people of Manipur and venture of Netaji and the INA for losing the fetters of bondage of 380 million Indian people from the British colonial subjugation leading to the ultimate national freedom is sunken deep in spite of the fact that the Red Fort Trial accelerated the pace of the dawn of India's freedom.

The **fifth chapter**, Indian National Army/Azad Hind Fauj and Imphal Campaign by Shukhdeba Sharma Hanjabam traces the marches of INA and the battles involving INA in the Imphal Campaign. The battle fought by INA in the Imphal Campaign is now completing 78 years. The first action of the INA in the Imphal campaign was seen in the Arakan Sector, Bishnupur Sector, and Kohima Sector. INA first Division, which constitutes Subhas, Gandhi, and Azad Brigades, continued the actions. They remain unsung heroes and are not yet adequately appreciated and acknowledged. The INA heroes who fought in these battles and the battle sites are yet to be systematically documented and investigated. The British and Allied Forces and the Japanese have built memorial sites and even museums in Manipur. But unfortunately, there is no memorial site for INA soldiers where INA veterans, families, friends, students, and youth could offer prayer to these brave soldiers and recall the sacrifice for their motherland. It is suggested that INA memorial sites should be developed at a suitable place in Manipur to engrave the names of the unsung INA Heroes and their stories. The celebration of 75 years of Independence will be incomplete without acknowledging the contribution of the INA, who fought for Indian Independence in the Imphal Campaign.

The **sixth chapter**, "Footprints of Our Noble Sons in the World Turning Event: A Remembrance" by Priyadarshni M. Gangte highlights that INA movement under the leadership of Subhas Chandra Bose was a collective effort against the mighty power. Many people, even from Manipur irrespective of their community fought heroically though it could not be shown as victor directly. She also observes that it is for that reason that, as a mark of respect and acknowledgement to their sacrificial and sincere contribution, people remember them by offering their homage to these Noble Sons.

The **seventh chapter**, "World War II, INA and Manipuri Literature: A Synoptic Survey" by Kakchingtabam Ruhinikumar Sharma highlights that INA occupies an important place in the history of India's struggle for freedom. The world opinion was affected by the exploits of Netaji Subhas Chandra Bose and Indian National Army. Manipuri literature too has not Lagged behind in capturing the World War, especially because Imphal, and for that matter the entire state was in the grip of war for more than a year. When peace gradually returned in Manipur a few literati of the land started picking up their pen recording and recollecting events of the contemporary Manipur. There are many authors who documented the War in Manipur which greatly enriched one's understanding of trials and tribulations of the people of those harrowing days, which portrays beautifully a poignant tale of human suffering and endurances etc. Thus the Second World War stories continue to remain inseparable from the minds of people across the region.

The **eighth chapter**, "The Second World War, Colonial State Building, INA and Local Participation in Manipur" by Sylvia Yambem attempts to locate the diverse socio-political consciousness to people's own lived experience under the colonial state and also the divisive process of colonial state building that created a fragmented Manipur state. Colonial policies that led to events like the 1919 Kuki rebellion or the second Nupi Lan in 1939 as well as the numerous political organizations like the Nikhil Manipur Mahasabha or the Praja Sanmelani were instrumental in creating an environment conducive to the rise of differentiated loyalties. This diverse political consciousness exhibited by the inhabitants of Manipur during the Second World War reflected the wider fragmentation of state-society relationship under British colonialism.

The **ninth chapter**, "Manipur Pauna Independence League and Second World War" by Aheibam Koireng Singh & Hanjabam Shukhdeba Sharma highlights the activities of the league which was formed quite early in advance with the objective of liberating India with Manipur in particular. It worked in close association with Indian Independence League (IIL) and intelligence agencies. As regards the Political arrangement the MPIL wanted Manipur to be put, their leaders stated and put forth the condition which was also agreed upon by the Japanese force that, "Manipur was a princely state but of late we have been under the rule of British colonialism otherwise Manipur have never been under any colonial subjugation. So Manipur would be an independent sovereign state as existed before." They also took part in the war campaign against the allied force. The activities of Manipur party were also completely stopped with the Allied Force taking over of Burma completely on 6th May, 1945.

The **tenth chapter**, "A Flower on Lofty Heights (*Takane No Hana*) and INA in Manipur by Rajkumar Ranjan Singh trace the importance of Imphal, the capital of Manipur, which was popularly remembered by the Japanese as 'Takane No Hana' (A Flower on Lofty Heights), during the Second World War in 1944. The Allied and Japanese forces were fighting to gain control over the land of "Flower on Lofty Heights" and consequently, Imphal was turned into a major theatre of war during the Second World War. The chapter concluded that the INA's endeavours also hastened the process of India's Freedom and the people of Manipur have contributed to the INA campaign.

The **eleventh chapter**, "Three Months of Provisional INA Government in Manipur and Contributions of Local Population" by Laiphrakpam Nishikanta Singh examine the situation in

Manipur post the aerial bombing of Imphal by Japanese aircraft on Sunday 10th May, 1942. The Indian National Army entered Manipur with Japanese support and established its Headquarters at Moirang on 14th April, 1944 from where it administered all the liberated areas of Manipur for three months. The Japanese army lost the five-month-long Manipur war campaign and all the fighting troops operating in Manipur retreated on 20th July, 1944. Thus Imphal has a unique place in the Indian Freedom Struggle because the Manipur Campaign of INA towards its effort to liberate India turned out to be a decisive factor in the fight for Indian independence and hastened up the departure of British from India.

The **twelfth chapter**, "INA Headquarters, Moirang, 1944" by Hemam Nilamani Singh highlights that INA planted the Indian Tri-colour Flag on the 14th April, 1944 at Moirang Kangla, (Manipur) for the first time as a liberated area in the Indian soil and also declaring Moirangas their advance Headquarters. At the battle, the British forces in their attempt to re-capture Moirang Captain Ito and many soldiers of the combined forces lost their lives in the battle and wet Moirang with the blood of Martyrs. Afterwards the combined forces attacked against the British and defeated them. Moirang was again under the control of the INA and Japanese forces. But they were forced to retreat towards Burma. The hardships co-shared by the INA, the Japanese forces and the people of Moirang as well as of Manipur in the line of executing the historic responsibility of liberation from the British responsibility for liberation from the British Imperialism cannot be underestimated.

The **thirteenth chapter**, "Azad Hind Fauz and the Advanced INA Headquarters, Moirang" by Mairembam Prithviraj Singh and Khelena Gurumayum recall that the INA movement led by Netaji Subhas Chandra Bose was a key component that eventually compelled the British to leave India. Even in death, the courage of Netaji inspired all the Indians to resist and challenge the authority of the British. The original Advanced Headquarters of the INA still exists in splendour at Moirang Konjengbam Leikai and has finally, become a site of international significance. It was from this place where the INA and Japanese forces mobilised to attack the British position of the 17th British Column at Bishnupur in its attempt to capture Imphal, the capital of Manipur, which was crucial for the 'Delhi Chalo' mission. Once Imphal is liberated, Netaji could install an effective "Provisional Government of Free India" on Indian soil. The Advanced INA Headquarters, Moirang signifies the courage and sacrifices of the Indo-Japanese forces and their supporters, and inspire everybody towards a selfless and strong sovereign Nation.

The **fourteenth chapter**, "Contribution of the Manipuris in the INA Movement" by Mairembam Koireng Singh concludes by exhorting to acknowledge and give due credit to those who participated in the INA movement and worked together in Manipur Front for three months and went underground. He retrospect that the liberation army dispossessed from the British rule almost all the hills of Manipur, came down to the valley; occupied Pallel in the south-east; Kameng, Sekmai, Kangpokpi and Kanglatombi in the north-east; Torbung and Moirang in the south-west; Bishnupur and Irengbam/Lokpaching (Red Hill) in the heart of the valley. Only a small portion of the Manipur valley could not be liberated. The three Division of Nippon Army and One Brigade of INA would not be able to continue heavy fighting for three months against the mighty Allied forces without the co-operation and involvement of the local people.

The **fifteenth chapter**, "INA's Involvement in the Battle of Imphal" by Kangjam Yaiphaba Meetei highlights that the INA's broad strategy was to join hands with the Japanese Army and fight the British, take the fight towards the India-Burma border, liberate the British occupied areas on their way to Delhi and ultimately unfurl the Indian Tricolour flag at the Red Fort. The biggest objective of the INA before reaching Delhi, however, was to defeat the British forces in Imphal at the India-Burma border. The chapter studies the activities of the INA in Manipur (of which Imphal is the capital) during the Japanese Army's Operation U-Go or Imphal Operation. It analyses how successful Bose's men were in their aim of liberating Imphal and the obstacles they faced in the process. It also throws some light on the different ways in which the people of Manipur engaged with the INA in their homeland.

The **sixteenth chapter**, "Relevance of Manipur in INA Movement" by Moirangthem Shanti Devi highlights that the idea of political consciousness was very strong and the demand for the establishment of a responsible government in Manipur was very high with the experience of INA movement in Manipur. During this movement the British government tried to stop the possible moral and physical support of the people of Manipur in favour of INA. This chapter attempts to give insight to the *modus operandi* and relevance of the Manipuris in the INA movement and examine the impact of INA movement on the socio-economic and political conditions. It brings to light that the majority of the sepoys in the corps was Indian. The captured Indian troops were expected to provide potential recruits for the expansion of the INA. The Nikhil Manipuri also have in consensus shown solidarity to the appeal of Netaji.

The **seventeenth chapter**, "INA's Honour at the Battle of Imphal and its Catalysing Impetus to India's Independence" by Yumnam Rajeshwor Singh basically consists of two parts. The first part deals with the Battle Honour of INA at Mittong Khunou in the Imphal War campaign and the second part highlights the importance and catalysing role of Battle of Imphal in India's Independence. It highlights that the INA was defeated in the Battle of Imphal in March—June, 1944 and left with no option but to surrender. Almost all of them surrendered after their retreat from the Indian Border. The trial was the most ominous event since the Sepoy Mutiny of 1857. Its outcome would produce enormous impact and the Imphal Campaign had brought the INA within reach of Independence. Though the military campaign had ended in a fiasco, the political war of anti-British and pro-Independence agitation as a result of INA brought to victory.

The **eighteenth chapter**, "World War II and its Changing Scenerio in Manipur: An Overview" by Kongbrailatpam Sarojkumar Sharma highlights that the most significant place of the war affairs of the Japanese and INA troops was located at Moirang, in Manipur's Bishnupur district. From Moirang, the INA-Japanese troops chalked out war strategies and operated to fight against the Allied forces. After President V.V. Giri and Ram Nath Kovind is the second Presidents of India to visit the complex. The chapter ends with a quotation of the President Kovind, which he wrote on the visitor's book of the museum on 22nd November, 2017 stating, "I offer my humble tribute to the brave soldiers of the Indian National Army who made supreme sacrifices to liberate Mother India under exemplary leadership of Netaji Subhas Chandra Bose. This monument reminds us of the valour of the INA and makes us commit ourselves to the service of the Nation."

The **nineteenth chapter**, "The Idea of Netaji, Manipur and the INA" by Moirangthem Asnikumar Singh is a simple but heartfelt tribute to Netaji and his ideas. It concludes by emphasising to reinvigorate the ideas of Netaji that it becomes all the more pertinent and necessary that the heroic tales of INA and Netaji ought to be a part of school curriculum for children of all age groups. It is paramount that the young students of this nation recognise and understand the values and ideals of men who sacrificed their lives so that their children could live in a proud, resolute and self-reliant India. Netaji's patriotic values and ideas need to be instilled amongst the hearts and minds of young Indians who will mould the destiny of this nation in the 21st century. It is never too late or too 'out of touch' to look upto our heroes of the past for inspiration, especially when those heroes are men like Netaji.

The **twentieth chapter**, "INA in the Story of an Incomplete Diary" by Makhomani Mongsaba gives a description of the attempt by Late Budhamani, a close friend and classmate of INA veteran, Late Nake Ahmed Choudhury in their school and intermediate days of their education, to write a 'war diary' about the World War II in Manipur. The diary was almost done but could not be completed because there was something amiss in it as Budhamani could not believe anybody other than Nake about the INA flag-hoisting at Moirang for the first time. But with the sudden death of Nake and Budhamani, the diary that the latter had written was still left incomplete with no one to fill it up. Attributing all what he learnt of INA to Nake, Budhamani and others mentioned in this write-up, the author concludes by remembering Nake Ahmed's words, "To win the hearts of the people...! The revolt that people do not support... would be hard to succeed".

The **twenty-first chapter**, "A Pilgrim from Moirang" by M. Jugindro Singh highlights that H. Nilamani willingly reciprocated to the call of Netaji and INA. Shri H. Nilamani Singh was without home, without family but the man of Netaji. To the poorly equipped army who were without money, food and friend in an inhospitable forbidden land, the help and assistance of Shri H. Nilamani Singh was a heaven sent opportunity. On 8th September, 1945, he was arrested by the British Army and imprisoned thereafter in the Rangoon Central Jail for more than 7 (seven) months. After release, Shri H. Nilamani Singh reached Imphal in the morning of 7th May, 1946. He plunged himself into the service of the people after his arrival at Moirang. It was he who prepared the list of the freedom fighters in Manipur. He delivered number of talks furnished with valuable information of historical importance on Netaji at State and National functions.

The **twenty-second chapter**, "Potsangbam Tomal Singh (1903-1999): His Contribution to Political and Socio-Economic Life in 20th Century Manipur" by Aheibam Koireng Singh highlights the outstanding contribution of Potsangbam Tomal Singh who was decorated and honoured with an award of Tamrapatra in 1972 by the Government of India for his outstanding contribution in the fight for freedom of India from the British colonial rule. In addition to his active political life, he was a man with multifaceted personality 'having inventive skill in various fields of crafts and designs'. His name was enshrined as Freedom fighter in the INA Memorial Complex at Moirang. His life spanned almost a century which covers almost all the political events of Modern Manipur. He was one of the makers of Modern Manipur. Notwithstanding his association with the INA, his concern for the interest and welfare of the state of Manipur clearly illustrates his rootedness as the true son of the soil.

The **twenty-third chapter**, "Ringshi Keishing: A Profile of INA Veteran" by Daniel Chabungbam recaps the association of Ringshi Keishing, INA war veteran with Subhas Chandra Bose's INA in the fight against the British. He first serve as a guide of the INA and afterwards rose to the rank of Lieutenant. Ringshi Keishing never met Subhas Chandra Bose but served under Lieutenant Colonel Shah Nawaz Khan who was a close comrade of Subhas Chandra Bose. Nawaz Shah was one of the three defendants in the first of the Indian National Army trials in 1946. As an army man, Ringshi Keishing first fought in a battle at Schakok Camp in Ango Ching hill range. And his second experience of war was at Finch corner then at Kangkhui area and later on at Sangshak. He passed away in January 18, 2015 at the ripe age of 94 years.

The **twenty-fourth chapter**, "Japanese bombing of Imphal" by M. Ranjit Singh highlights that in December 1941, Japan entered Second World War. This last event was at first taken quietly in Manipur, no one realizing how soon Japan would reach the frontiers of Manipur. Japan dropped the first bomb on Imphal on Sunday, the 10th May, 1942 and again on Friday, the 16th May, 1942 heralding the beginning of Second World War in Manipur. The Japanese had complete air superiority in the sky of Burma and Manipur during that fateful month of May 1942. The most fiercely contested battle of the Burma campaign, the battle of Imphal which, if for no other reason, will go down in history as the greatest military defeat ever suffered by the Japanese on land. Japanese 15th Army suffered around 30,000 casualties in Battle of Imphal.

The **twenty-fifth chapter**, "Koirengei Airfield: British's Bulwark Against Japanese Siege" by Sunzu Bachaspatimayum highlights that the nine airfields in Manipur, the Imphal Main was the British bulwark against the Japanese siege (in 1944) of Manipur during the Battle of Imphal/Kohima. It is by now a key part of Manipuri collective memory because of the Manipur State government exercising its wisdom took a series of steps recently to acquire the old airfield at Koirengei from the Ministry of Defence which raises both hope and dread. The chapter ends by emphasizing the opinion of a prominent British war historian Christopher David Johnson to keep intact utilize the Koirengei airfield for war tourism with a fitting memorial to those gallant airmen and defenders of the garrison, stating that the outcome of the whole Burma campaign would have been very different had it not been for the Koirengei airfield, the unique airfield, with two runways perpendicular to each other.

The **twenty-sixth chapter**, "Indo-Japanese Soldiers in the Khuga Valley of Churachandpur, April to August, 1944" by Lal Dena deals with the important historical theme of the Indo-Japanese occupation of the Khuga valley and the nature of the local people's response to it. It highlights the rapid deterioration the Indo-Japanese army fortune in Manipur. One of the top-ranking INA commanders at the time of parting said, "I am so thrilled and particularly grateful to you for what you and your villagers have done for my soldiers. In fact, it is only because of your help and co-operation that my soldiers could survive till today. But now many of them are suffering from malaria and dysentry, we are leaving soon.When India achieves her freedom, you folks will never be forgotten." The next day, the officer went to Thingkangphai and hurriedly left for Burma.Their unfathomable patriotism, their spirit of sacrifice and their long forbearance are still the talk of every household in the Khuga valley of Manipur even today.

The **twenty-seventh chapter**, "Matric Examination in Manipur during Second World War" by Manindra Konsam and translated from Manipuri by Pebam Nganthoiba Mangang recalls the struggle of the teachers and students to give Matric examination (board examination) of 1943 in Manipur during the Second World War. The Examination commenced on Monday, 19th April, 1943, which was conducted by Calcutta University. The paper recalls that whenever the warplanes were seen flying in the sky, the warning sounds of sirens were given to take precautions. The students appearing in the Examination managed to hide, kneeling inside a big pit dug out at the place of the examination by the person in charge, Shri Sougaijam Samarendra's residence. Once the siren stopped, they were moved out from the pit and resumed the writing, giving extra time to make up the time spent at the pit for hiding. The same procedure was continued whenever siren sounds were heard while writing the Examination. Despite taking the Examination in such a horrific environment, all the students passed the Matric examination except the female students.

The **twenty-eighth chapter**, "Second World War in Manipur with Special Reference to Kakching" by Nongmaithem Pramodini highlights that during the Second World War Kakching people met lots of suffering as the village was also a war field. The bombing of Kakching on Tuesday 9th November, 1943, caused a lot of civilian casualties. It concludes that when Kakching was in the state of village life, many villagers became the victims of the Second World War. One of the most remarkable impacts of the war was the progress of formal education in the village. Post war scenario of education in Kakching was in favourable condition. After the Second World War Kakching had been gradually developed with rapid progress of education. The Second World War brought great changes in many spheres of Kakching village. In fact, the post-war Kakching marked the progress of both material and intellectual aspects of this village.

The **twenty-ninth chapter**, "The Second World War in Manipur and my Childhood" by Kh. Nimaicharan Singh is an autobiographical account of the childhood days of the author himself along with his vivid experience of the Second World War period as well as some of the important battles fought in Manipur retold in brief. In his childhood days, he saw and experienced the miserable plight of the period during unforgettable period in the history of Manipur. His father also died in a fierce Japanese Bombing. In the words of noted literateur, N. Kunjamohon Singh, "Of course, it is not very much a personal account but a portrait of the socio-economic life of the state devastated by the war. The book reads like a novel, to be precise, an autobiographical novel with a number of lively anecdotes and episodes—sometimes pathetic and pitiable, sometimes funny and folly."

The **thirty chapter**, "My *Japan Lan* Memoir After Four Score Years" by Irengbam Mohendra Singh observes that Imphal became the nerve centre of the British Commonwealth soldiers fighting the Japanese simultaneously at Imphal and Kohima fronts. Japanlan was the greatest discovery of the world for Manipuris without having to travel. The history of the Japanese cutting off the 4th Corps of the British Army in Manipur from the rest of the world in early 1944, is a gripping tale of their courage and endurance. The war bewitched the Meitei nation. The immediate post-war Imphal was the equivalent of peeling onions, unearthing the generations of hopes and regrets. Manipuris owe a great deal to Japanlan. Without it Manipuris (Indians) might still be struggling for a while for independence. It is a piece of quasi-fiction that the behaviour of the Manipuri youth, who are now in their 80s, formed the first phalanx in a major character upheaval of Meiteis.

The **thirty-first chapter**, "Reverberations of a War before Time" by Khuraijam Surjalal Singh highlights that the Second World War reached and felt in India and Manipur with the Japanese bombing of Imphal on 10th May, 1942. The aggression that the Japanese unleashed in Manipur, greatly affected the life of the natives in Imphal and the far-flung regions of Manipur. Manipur became the part of India that was mostly affected by the war and the Burma campaign of the Axis forces. In the months that followed, Manipur turned into an operation base, and people and soldiers of all sorts of race and religion thronged in. The Forgotten War only remains a thing of human memory and the battlefield where the Goras and Japanese once fought got reclaimed by nature and echoes with the songs of cicadas. The chapter ends with a famous quote of Winston Churchill, "Old men make war, young men fight and die".

The **thirty-second chapter**, "*Japan Lan* and Imphal Peace Museum: A Personal Reflection" by James Khangenbam asserts that the stories of battles are also survival stories that teaches many lessons to the humanity. Encouragingly nations who once fought in Imphal routinely came to shake hands in Imphal at commemorations of Second World War sending a message to avoid war in future. It concludes by pondering whether—the events taking place in Imphal are unique and impactful, Manipur contributing to global peace, the affections by the locals create a warm environment for promoting amity to the participating nations and cementing a healing message to the World, Manipur stands tall in hosting such similar events in future, the impacts of Second World War to Manipur is contemporarily discussed and the war victims are being consoled officially in the present era, there is a dedicated Memorial Centre where homage could be paid to the Second World War civilian victims of Manipur.

The **thirty-third** and **concluding chapter**, "Japan Lan: Life in Kangla Sangomshang and Siphai" by Bramhacharimayum Sadananda Sharma deals with an important place during the period of the great Second World War will ever remain in history even generations after generations. The airfield in Kangla was also a very important one which played a big role in saving Manipur from the clutches of the invading Japanese Army. It highlights that during war time many villagers fled to other neighbouring villages specifically in Tumukhong, Moirangpurel, Sabungkhok, Pukhao etc. and settle there by doing agricultural work for survival. Even though there were many bomb explosions near the village, there was no report of casualty only one cattle was injured in bombing. Amidst war zone life was simple for them few stalls of women vendors could be seen selling *pans*, sweets, cigarettes are being opened. People were generous and kind helping each other sharing things between friends and neighbours were a part of life.

Even among the Manipuris of today's generation many seems to be ignorant about how the Second World War had a bearing on their lives. Confronted by the Nazi threat, Winston Churchill once remarked that "A nation that forgets its past has no future". Maybe, others might share a differing view about nationalism, but this very idea of nationalism brought different nationalities of regions around the globe with multiplicity of language came, fought and died in defence of freedom and dignity of national self. Yet such event of historical significance seems to be given a miss till date by those concerned except for paying occasional lip service. The full story of the war is yet to be told in its entirety. Through these chapters, we hope to make a humble beginning knowing well of our handicaps.

Theme I
INA AND IMPHAL CAMPAIGN

2

Indian National Army (Azad Hind Fauj) during World War II and the Princely Kingdom of Manipur

Konsam Himalay Singh

Prior to the Great War 1944, Manipur was an isolated kingdom, isolated from the British Indian Subcontinent in many ways. Communication system with the outside world was scanty. Only a jeepable track existed between Imphal and Dimapur, the nearest railhead in Assam. Imphal-Tamu Road was a mule track in a different alignment than it exists now. The country was economically independent. People grew their own food and cotton and silk. They wove their own clothes and many sources of entertainment existed at the time. Food was a plenty hence the prices of edible items were low.

The year 1944 changed all that with the Allied and Japanese forces fighting to gain control of the Imphal Valley in Manipur and Kohima in the Naga Hills in Assam to the north. At one stage, it is believed that there were two soldiers to every three Manipuri population during the Great War. Prices of the commodities sky-rocketed during the war. Many Manipuris stayed back in the far-flung villages but a few thousands who could manage to flee to safer Imphal migrated there.

There is a belief in Manipur that when the eastern gate is opened, the kingdom will become "*Huntre khunfam*" the words used in Manipuri polo when the starter throws the ball to open the game of Sagol Kangjei (Polo). The Manipur Puranas believed that a great fight would take place in the Country (Manipur) involving three armies. The Royal astrologers had proclaimed that the year 1944 would be one of great distress to the inhabitants of Manipur. In this year the British and Japanese forces fought one of the most deadly battles during the Great War. Many people also believe that the Great War as prophesied in the Puranasis yet to come in the future for they believed that the army dressed in red will be the winner.

The INA as part of the Japanese forces which was operating to threaten British India revolved around the capture of Imphal and Kohima in order to progress their operations in Bengal and in Assam. INA under Netaji Subhas Chandra Bose took full advantage of the Japanese assistance and aimed to liberate India from the British rule. Netaji calculated that the people of India and the British Indian army soldiers would revolt against the British once INA arrived on the soil of British India.

As the Japanese forces swept through the Malayas, Singapore and Burmese territories, it was felt that it was only a question of time before the Japanese forces would arrive in the Indian Territory along with the INA. The plans chosen by Bose and Masakazu Kawabe, Chief of the Burma area army of the Imperial Army, envisaged the INA being assigned limited but independent sector in the *U-Go* offensive. No INA units were to operate at less than battalion strength. Operation *U-Go* was the Japanese offensive launched in March 1944 against the forces of the British Empire in the Naga Hills and in Manipur.

Advance parties of the *Bahadur* Group also went forward with advanced Japanese units. As the offensive opened in the eastern frontier, the INA's 1st Division, consisting of four guerrilla regiments, was divided between *U-Go* and the diversionary *Ha-Go* offensive in Arakan. A Bahadur Group unit, led by Col. Shaukat Malik, was able to reach Moirang Village in Manipur Valley in early April. The main body of the 1st Division was, however, committed to the *U-Go*, directed towards north Manipur. Led by Shah Nawaz Khan, it successfully protected the Japanese flanks against Chin and Kachin guerrillas as Lt. General Mutaguchi's three divisions crossed the Chindwin river and the Naga Hills, and participated in the main offensive through Tamu in the direction of Imphal and Kohima. The 2nd Division of the INA, under M.Z. Khan, was placed to the right flank of the 33rd Division attacking Kohima. By April 1944, Imphal-Kohima Road axis had been cut off by the Japanese forces with the INA units in support in terms of intelligence gathering, vanguard actions, propaganda operations as well as flank protections of the main force.

Manipur, in the meanwhile had become a battleground of epic proportions. While some Naga affiliated tribes supported and assisted the Allied forces, some Kukis supported the Japanese forces and thereby assisted the INA soldiers. A few Kukis who helped the Japanese Forces and the INA during the period have been given the status of "Freedom Fighters". These Kukis were given preliminary and basic military training by the Japanese forces. However, Chin groups of Burmese tribes were considered a threat by the Japanese forces and deployed the INA to thwart these threats from Chins and the Kachins in Burma.

The Japanese forces and the INA had major logistical drawbacks of being devoid of Air supplies which the British forces enjoyed greatly with three air strips in the Imphal Valley itself. The Japanese air bases were at least 600 miles away. The Japanese forces were not able to evacuate the sick and wounded in time. Lt. General Mutaguchi was still confident that his forces would be in better condition after the capture of the Imphal Plains where he expected plentiful of food and war-fighting equipment. He further pushed his tired and hungry soldiers more and more despite the monsoons looming large just about a month later.

However, by the time Khan's INA forces left Tamu, the offensive had been held, and Khan's troops were redirected to Kohima. After reaching Ukhrul in the Hills of Manipur well short of Kohima, they found Japanese forces had begun their withdrawal from the area after the reverses in the battle of Kohima.

According to Lt. General Evans, after the capture of a hill near Bisenpur by 2/5 Gorkhas, "they found the Japanese soldiers mess tins in which were cooked ordinary grass and large black slugs." Many Japanese soldiers captured after the battle were without hands or legs in many cases. Among them were some of the INA soldiers suffering the same plight.

The INA's forces suffered the same fate as Mutaguchi's army when the siege of Imphal was broken. With little or nothing in the way of supplies, and with additional difficulties caused by the monsoon, Allied air dominance, and Burmese irregular forces, the 1st and 2nd divisions of INA began withdrawing alongside the 15th Army and Burma Area Army. During the withdrawal through Manipur, a weakened Gandhi regiment held its position against the advancing Maratha Light Infantry of the erstwhile British Indian army on the Burma-India road while the general withdrawal was prepared. The 2nd and 3rd INA regiments protected the flanks of the Yamamoto force successfully at the most critical time during this withdrawal to Burma, but wounded and diseased men succumbed to starvation along the route. Commonwealth troops following the Japanese forces found dead INA soldiers along with Japanese troops who had died of starvation. The INA lost a substantial number of men and amount of material in this retreat from the battle of Imphal. A number of units were disbanded or used to feed into new divisions.

Some historians opined that the role of INA not to have had significant impact on the outcome of the war. While many others felt that their contributions in the fight against the British forces have been largely downplayed by the British. The INA also had few differences initially with the Japanese forces as regards the manner of their employment and the weapons and equipment provided to them *vis-à-vis* their Japanese soldiers who were their counterparts. Be that it may, it has been established that within the constraints of the organisation and equipments provided to them, they did play a significant role especially in the Battle of Imphal. The INA soldiers operated as Advance parties and reconnaissance parties of the Japanese forces. They also acted as Psychological warriors by their attempts to influence the British Indian soldiers in the frontline to act against the British but not much were achieved in this front. The Britishers also looked at the deserted Indian soldiers with contempt. Some historians opined that the INA's combat record was undistinguished, and the army arguably achieved its greatest success after the war.

As the war progressed and the Japanese position worsened, so too did that of the INA. With its soldiers dispirited and suffering low morale, the INA joined in the general retreat of Japanese 15th Army as British and Commonwealth forces recaptured Burma in 1944-45. Desertions increased considerably and Bose was obliged to introduce capital punishment in March 1945 to try to address the problem. Yet it was noted, "From April 1945... the INA's retreat, which had hitherto been orderly, became a rout and mass surrenders became frequent." This was the time when the INA along with the Japanese forces were retreating from the onslaught of the British troops.

With the Japanese defeat in Burma in mid-1945, the INA crumbled without ever securing the mass defections from the British Indian army that Bose had confidently predicted. Bose died in an air crash while *en route* to the USSR, where he had hoped to elicit Soviet aid to continue his struggle against the British.

Fay, a famous post war historian, in his 1993 history analyses war-time press releases and field counter-intelligence directed at *Sepoys*. He concludes that the *Jiffs* campaign promoted the view that INA recruits were weak-willed and traitorous Axis collaborators, motivated by selfish interests of greed and personal gain. He concludes that the allegations of torture were largely products of the *Jiffs* campaign. He supports his conclusion by noting that isolated cases of torture had occurred, but allegations of widespread practice of torture were not substantiated in the charges against defendants in the Red Fort trials. Published memoirs of several veterans, including that of William Slim, portray the INA troops as incapable fighters and as untrustworthy. Another historian, Mr. Toye noted in 1959 that individual desertions occurred in the withdrawal from Imphal. Mr. Fay concluded that stories of INA desertions during the battle and the initial retreat into Burma were largely exaggerated. The majority of desertions occurred much later, according to Fay, around the battles at Irrawaddy and later around Popa. Fay specifically discusses Slim's portrayal of the INA, pointing out what he concludes to be inconsistencies in Slim's accounts. Fay also discusses memoirs of Shah Nawaz, where Khan claims INA troops were never defeated in battle. Fay criticises this too as exaggerated. He concludes the opinions held by Commonwealth war veterans such as Slim were an inaccurate portrayal of the unit, as were those of INA soldiers themselves. Harkirat Singh notes that British officers' personal dislike for Subhas Chandra Bose may have prejudiced their judgement of the INA itself.

Although Bose had ensured the INA's participation in the fighting, he was frustrated by the reluctance of the Japanese to employ the INA in anything more than secondary roles. The Japanese, at all levels of IJA command, did not think highly of the Indian soldiers, and this attitude contributed to the INA's poor combat performance. Japanese commanders limited the size of the INA, provided it with inadequate logistical support, and gave it substandard arms and equipment. Initially, the Indian soldiers received captured Allied weapons, much of them in a poor state of repair (including "old and rusty" rifles) with a general paucity of ammunition. However, even these severe restrictions *might* have been overcome had the Japanese possessed the confidence to deploy the INA in tactical operations as a cohesive unit rather than in a dispersed "penny packet" fashion.

Nonetheless, some INA units, such as 1st Battalion, 2nd INA Division, performed well. The Japanese felt that the Tamil troops, recruited exclusively from Malaya, had generally done far better than their ex-Indian army/ex-POW comrades. But despite Bose's assertions that the INA should be above all else a secular organization, there is evidence that conflict between the INA's Muslim and Sikh troops undermined both the effectiveness and the willingness of Muslim troops to fight.

In independent India, the treatment of former INA soldiers by government and omission of the INA and the Red Fort trials from historical records of the period leading up to Indian Independence in 1947 have come in for criticisms. Indian activists like Samar Guha, historians like Kapil Kumar, as well as Indian parliamentarians allege that official histories of the independence movement largely omit events surrounding the INA—especially the Red Fort trials and the Bombay Mutiny.

Moirang in Manipur remains a testimony to the brave soldiers of the INA who unfurled the first Indian National Flag there. Along with the Japanese Peace-museum near Maibam Lokpa Chingen route to Moirang from Imphal, the memories of the war are vivid in the hearts of the Manipuris. The currency notes circulated by the INA among the people of Manipur bears a testimony to the efforts of the INA to free India from the British rule during the period. People of Manipur warmly welcomed the INA leaflets dropped from the Japanese planes asking one and all to rise against the British rule. However, events after the monsoon rains of 1944 changed the course of history when the INA along with the Japanese forces were forced to retreat from Manipur by the Allied forces by October 1944.

3

INA-Japanese Imphal and Kohima Campaign and Local Participation (1942-1945)

Naorem Lokendra Singh

I
COMING OF THE WAR

IA—Chin Hills

After overrunning the Allied forces in South East Asia, the Imperial Japanese Air Force carried out strategic bombing at many vital areas in Rangoon on 23rd December, 1941. The Burmese nationalists supported the Japanese in the initial phase of the war. As a result, the latter could easily establish military control of the region and Rangoon was captured on 7th March, 1942.To counteract the Imperial Japanese military advances, the Allied forces too organised 'local levies' among many ethnic communities, i.e. Shans, Kachins, Nagas and Chins. In May, Sir Reginald Dorman Smith, the Governor of Burma fled to Shimla and set up the Burmese Government in exile there. In August 1943, the Japanese granted Burma the status of independent nation although it continued to retain the ultimate sovereign authority over the country.[1]

As the 17th Indian Division of the British IV Corps operating in Kabaw valley area planned for safe withdrawal to its headquarters at Tiddim, the 'Chin Levy' consisting of two classes of volunteers under the command of Norman Kelly, the Assistant Superintendent of the district was trying to provide effective logistical support. The 'A' class men were supposed to take an offensive role outside their own tract/village, where as the 'B' class was supposed to operate in their own locality. Each of the armed volunteers of the 1st group were paid Rs. 20 per month, whereas, those of the latter group were given Rs. 10 each per month.[2]

The 17th Division marched towards Tiddim when the road construction works were completed. A combine force including the Chin Levy defeated a strong force of the 33rd Japanese Division at 'Leisan Mual' (Basha Hills) on 25th May, 1943 in which many Japanese soldiers were killed. Despite these reverses, the Japanese 33rd Division continued to move towards Tiddim during May, June and July of the same year as a preparation for a counter-attack. In between, Col. Stevenson recruited volunteers known as 'Chinwags' to work at Falam whereas 'Chin Force' under the command of Major W.P. Peeble was set up to work at the Lumbang-Mualbem area.[3] Conversely, the Imperial Japanese forces also raised their own local levy force, i.e. 'Chin Defence Army' comprising local tribesmen. With that, the Japanese forces succeeded in capturing Falam, an important town on 7 November and Haka four days later. Since the British Army as well as the administrative personnel began to evacuate Chin Hills, many Burmese Government employees began to support the new Japanese regime. Obviously, the local population had to follow the directives of the Japanese forces. The villagers of Haka, Falam, Tiddim, Tonzang etc. had a tough time with the Japanese officers who extracted, labour, food and loyalty for the new regime.

Meanwhile, Subhas Chandra Bose, the Commander-in-Chief of the Indian National Army had established his Headquarters at

Rangoon in 1943. Earlier, Bose had arrived at Tokyo on May 16, 1943 immediately after he reached Sebang by a Japanese submarine. He met Prime Minister, Hideki Tojo on June 10 and again on June 14 soliciting support for India's Independence. Two days later on June 16 Tojo made a declaration to help the cause of Indian Independence.[4] By the end of June, Bose left Tokyo for Singapore accompanied by Rashbehari Bose, the elderly leader of Indian Independence League. On July 4, representatives of the League gave him a rousing welcome at the Cathay Theatre. The assembled crowd readily accepted Subhas as the new leader of the League.[5] The Indian National Army (INA) under the leadership of Mohan Singh had also been waiting since 1942 for the baton to be taken over by Subhas Chandra Bose. Thereafter, the Japanese military authority agreed to provide training and equipment for no more than 30,000 personnel organised in three divisions.[6] The first division with about 10,000 personnel and consisting of "Gandhi", "Nehru" and "Azad" regiments or brigades was put under the command of Mohammed Zaman Kiani. Some of the more active soldiers of three regiments formed No. 1 Guerrilla Regiment and was sent to the Malayan town of Taiping in September 1943 under the command of Shah Nawaz Khan for training in addition to 45 other handpicked young men who were trained in Tokyo's elite Military Academy.[7] In addition to the three divisions separate intelligence and field propaganda units, i.e. "Bahadur" groups had been organized for the three divisions. On October 21, 1943, Subhas proclaimed the formation of the Provisional Government of Azad Hind (Free India) in Singapor. By December 1943, four units of 250 men each had been attached for training to the Japanese divisions that would take part in the Kohima and Imphal campaign.[8] Just after the midnight in October 23-24, 1943 the Provisional Government declared war on Britain and the United States of America.

In March 1944, after an in-depth discussion among the top military brass and political leaders, the Japanese forces launched an operation code named 'U-Go' aiming at a major invasion of North East India. Three Divisions of Japanese 15th Army commanded by

General Renya Mutaguchi along with one INA Division advanced to North East India *via* Kabaw Valley and the Chin Hills. The combined Japanese-INA forces advanced through three important routes: (1) 33rd Division under General Yanagida was to proceed through Chin Hills-Churachandpur route against the British Indian 17th Division till Imphal, (2) 31st Division led by General Sato, stationed in and around Somra tract was to attack British garrison at Kohima and seized vital Railway and supply depot at Dimapur and then send forces to capture Imphal,[9] and (3) 15th Division under General Yamouchi had to cross Chindwin River at Homalin and Thaungdut and proceed *via* Tamu-Pallel route. All the three divisions were to encircle Imphal which General W. Slim, commander of the British Indian 15th Army used as the supply base for a future counter offensive.

On 7th March, 1944, General Mutaguchi had issued instruction for the offensive actions. The 17th Division commanded by General Cowan at Tiddim withdrew on 15th March, 1944. The retreating British forces were continuously attacked by the units of Japanese 33rd division all along the way. Two battalions of INA's "Guerrilla" brigade led by Shah Nawaz Khan reached Tiddim at the end of March to move along with Japanese forces.[10] According to Ian Lyall Grant 7 important battles were fought between the Japanese and the 17th Division led Allied forces along the Tiddim Road (3 in the Chin Hills and 4 at the Manipur Valley). At the battles at Tonzang, Singgel and Sakawng, the Japanese attempted to cut off the 17th Division line of retreat. The rugged mountain terrain coupled with the twists and turns plus the multiple winding up and down of the road provided ideal conditions for setting up military roadblocks.[11]

On 16-17 March, between Tonzang and Tuitum (Chin Hills), the Japanese forces set up roadblocks. Although, the roadblocks were cleared on the 18th, the Japanese soldiers managed to cross the Manipur River and marched towards north through the hills to seize control of the road.[12] By 5th April, all the Allied forces were completely withdrawn to Imphal, leaving the Chin Hills a free hand to theJapanese forces.

IB—Manipur

Bishenpur

As pointed out earlier, the fighting on the Tiddim Road involved repeated and determined attempts by the Japanese forces to break through to Imphal from the South-West direction. The British led Allied forces were equally determined to prevent this from happening. This led to ferocious fighting between the two sides for several months, between April and June 1944, until the British finally prevailed. Almost every village between Churachandpur and Bishenpur, particularly, Potshangbam, Ningthoukhong, Thinungei, Phubala and Moirang were most affected. All the villagers were asked by the local administration to vacate their houses at a short notice. Under the 'Denial policy' (Scorched Earth Policy) all the available grains, paddy and all forms of eatables along with houses were set on fire and an estimated amount of 1,00,000 *maunds* of paddy were burned down. Cattle and most of the household possessions of the local people were left behind. Many villagers took shelter in and around the Loktak lake and many even went up to Imphal where there were already heavy congestion.[13]

During the 1st half of May, there were several Japanese air attacks followed by heavy fighting at Ningthoukhong in which the British lost 12 tanks.[14] Major General Cowan sent the 48th Indian Infantry Brigade on a wide left hook into the Japanese 33rd Division's rear, while, the 63rd Brigade attacked from the front. Meanwhile, Major General Tanaka who had replaced Yanagida as Commander of the 33rd Japanese Division managed to capture the hills close to the 17th Division's HQ on 20th May. However, the 48th Indian Infantry Brigade who had already cut the road behind the Japanese on 18th May desperately fought through the Japanese forces to rejoin the helpless and cornered 63rd Brigade with heavy losses. Although the Japanese forces also lost much steam, but they managed to retain control of the area till around July. These areas were so badly affected that villagers could not return until it was too late for cultivation.[15] The INA's Bahadur Group under Shaukat Ali

Malik, a close confidant of Subhas along with the local volunteers were active in this sector. Malik fulfilled the confidence his leader had shown him by hoisting the Indian tri-colour at Moirang.[16]

Red Hill

As the occupation of Imphal was their main objective, General Yanagida's 214 Regiment took the lead and left their HQs (Ingourok) by May 16. Crossing Silchar track, Tairenpokpi, Nungnang, Khoirok River, Wainem and Irengbam villages the Regiment moved forward to concentrate at Lokpaching (Red Hill) and outskirts of Chingphu, which in fact was the HQs of 17th Division. Earlier some units of the Japanese force burnt down the suspension bridge across the Leimatak River to stop the incoming of Allied forces and supplies from Silchar. Units of 215th Regiment that were involved at Bishenpur battle came through the villages located at the fringes of the Loktak Lake avoiding confrontation with the Allies on the main road. The Japanese constructed 'Fox holes' and 'Gunner boxes' around the Red Hills. General Cowan countered the Japanese moves by forming a composite force representing infantry, tanks, sappers and artillery. The real confrontation took place between 25 and 30 May, during which fierce hand to hand, bayonet to bayonet fights took place. Although both suffered heavy losses, ultimately the Britishers prevailed and completely checked the Japanese from entering Imphal from the south.

Tamu-Shenam Saddle

After the Japanese troops crossed the Chindwin Rivers on 8 March, Lt. General Geoffry Scoones, Commander of the IV corps ordered that most of the Allied forces should withdraw towards Imphal as soon as possible. Thereafter the 20th Indian division under Major General Douglas Gracey which was at Tamu-Moreh area where a large supply dump was located withdrew to 'Shenam Saddle', 30 miles on the Tamu-Imphal Road after burning the supply dump as well as slaughtering 200 cattle which they had maintained for emergency purposes. General Yamamoto who led a newly formed group—a combination of some units of 15th and 33rd Japanese divisions, backed by tanks and heavy artillery moved forward to attack Imphal, but was confronted by the Allied forces at Shenam. On 4 April, 12 Japanese tanks were immobilized by the Allied anti-tank guns. From 8 to 22 April, there was heavy fighting for control of five peaks which commanded the main road. Initially, the Japanese captured a few of them, but were regained by the Allied. There were, however, heavy casualties on both sides.

Having failed to break through the roadblocks, Yamamoto sent some troops through the rough and indirect route to attack 'Pallel airfield' on 28 April. The INA's 1st Division under Md. Zaman Kiyani took part in this attack. The INA force which set up its Headquarters at Chamol was assisted by the 'Gandhi' and the 'Azad' Brigades commanded by Inayat Kiyaniand Guljara Singh respectively. Shah Nawaj Khan led Guerrilla Brigades which were in the Chin Hills were also instructed to join the front. In the encounter, there were 250 casualties and the group pulled back from Pallel.[17] During the confrontation, the inhabitants were evacuated by lorries from their villages and kept them at Imphal. Villages near Pallel and Tengnoupal not only suffered from Japanese demand of paddy and destruction of livestock but also that these villages couldn't do any cultivation.[18]

Nungshigum

The Japanese 15th Division after crossing Chindwin River encircled Imphal from the north. While its 60th Regiment captured a British supply dump located at Kanglatombi on the Imphal-Dimapur road,a battalion of the 51st Regiment seized the Nungshigum ridge which overlooked the airstrip at "Kangla" about 15 miles from Imphal. On 13 April, the 5th Indian Division backed by artillery, tanks and Air support resorted to counter-attacks. The Japanese thought that the slope was too steep for the tanks to climb up. However, as the "Lee tanks" climbed up, the Japanese forces used their anti-tank guns but with limited success. The Allied forces too suffered heavily; most of the officers were either killed or wounded but managed to retain control over the strategically located area. During this period, villages in the entire "Iril valley", i.e. Pourabi, Sekta, Chana, Pungdongbam, Sawombung etc., could not cultivate their land and agricultural activities could not be resumed properly until the expulsion of the Japanese forces.

Shangshak

One strong column of the Japanese 31st Division on its way to Kohima, was assisted by a few units of the 15th Division in over-running the whole area in an incredible speed. They confronted the British 50th parachute brigade, in the battle of Shangshak Hill between 22 and 26 March. The vastly outnumbered British forces held out for several days. Waves upon waves of Japanese forces attacked for a number of days, which crucially delayed the Japanese attack on Kohima. The hurriedly flown in 5th Indian Division came to its assistance to defend the place and ultimately the Britishers prevailed. Ukhrul was also recaptured by the Allied Forces after few weeks. The villagers near Litan and Shangshak suffered lost of livestocks and failure of agriculture.

A few units of the same Japanese force from Ukhrul captured Kangpokpi and subsequently controlled the Imphal-Dimapur Road from Mao to Kankpokpi by the 1st week of April. During this period, army personnel as well as supplies were airdropped. Infact, the Manipur plains were completely cut off from the rest of the country between March 29 and 23rd June. As a result of the disturbances, villages between Nungoi and Shaijang were unable to cultivate their fields throughout the year. Many other villages between Kangpokpi to Sekmai also could not carry on agricultural activities because of heavy fighting.

IC—Kohima

As stated earlier, the 31st Division of the Imperial Japanese army under the command of General Sato emerged around Kohima earlier than expected. One column was heading for Ukhrul with

Kohima as its chief objective, while the rest moved straight towards Naga Hills. The Japanese plan, as stated earlier, was to cut the main Imphal-Dimapur Road, north of Imphal and swarm towards Jessami. The whole force was to converge upon the British garrison at Kohima. The garrison was, however, warned by some Naga hill men and as a result defence positions were hastily constructed on a series of hillocks along a mile long ridge. At the centre of these defences were the Assistant District Commissioner's bungalow, his pretty garden and the Tennis Court, which subsequently became the centre of intense fights between the two forces.

The first shot in the Naga Hills was fired by the Assam Regiment and the Assam Armed Police, 30 miles east of Kohima at Karasom. Although these forces fallback from position to position and suffered from heavy casualties they succeeded in slowing down the movement of the 31st Division, thereby providing sufficient time to the Allied Forces for proper mobilization of their army. Kohima was under tremendous military preparation. Even the 500 convalescing soldiers admitted in the dispensary were armed while the non-combatants and hospital patients were shifted to a safer place. With every available man, including some from the administrative units the total strength of the garrison was increased to 1,000 personnel who had to fight not less than 15,000 Japanese men closing upon them. In the nearby Dimapur garrison, out of 45,000 persons on the list of the ration cardholders, only about 500 could handle rifles. The Commander of the garrison, Col. H.V. Richards called in every soldier although he could hardly get sufficient force. But General Slim ordered the 5th and 7th Indian Divisions to be airlifted from Arakan where the operation was halted. He also ordered 2nd Division from India to come for rescue works at Dimapur and Kohima.

Meanwhile, the Assam Rifles fighting bravely but sustaining heavy casualties were almost exhausted and on April 4, some 200 Assam Rifle personnel managed to fall back into Kohima's defence force. Major General Sato could have attacked an undefended Dimapur which was only 30 miles away but for reasons known to himself, he stuck to the idea of occupying Kohima only and therefore, waves of Japanese force attacked scantily manned Kohima. Meanwhile, Major General Stopford took over the affairs of the battle at Kohima and along with this the Allied position was stabilised. A force of the 5th Indian Division was flown in from Arakanand deployed to hold the 'Nichugard pass' almost adjacent to Dimapur because it was expected that it would be attacked after overrunning Kohima. The Kohima-Imphal Road was now controlled by the Japanese. However, it was to the fortune of Allied forces that the Royal British Airforce had an absolute air control over the region. During the daytime fighter aircrafts roared down almost to the jungle roof to augment the Allied firepower. They also dropped ammunition, medical supplies, water filled inner tubes and food to the hard pressed garrison and other Allied controlled points at Kohima. The 5th Division was also waiting for opportunities to move on to Kohima.

After some days, however, the position of the Japanese force had deteriorated due to their inability to either capture Kohima or get supplies from their base at Burma as the Allied Air Force had already cut off the supply lines. Sato, therefore, reversed his policies and sent the infantry force for attack only at night time; while, in the day time, the British positions were attacked by shells, mortars and machine gun. Although the British soldiers suffered tremendously in terms of casualties and exhaustion due to ceaseless fighting and sleeplessness, by April 6 they all concentrated at the garrison hill, their main position.

Despite a number of casualties, the Japanese force came closer to the office of the Deputy Commissioner. The battle of attrition finally took place between the two groups and there were hand-to-hand fight or lobbing of fused grenades at each other across the Tennis Court in front of the DC's main office. Casualties on both sides were very high and the Summer House hill was blood stained. For almost 10 days the Japanese seize of Kohima continued but on 15th April, 1944 a brigade of 2nd Division fought up the road to reinforce the army of the 5th Division at Kohima. Another stronger group of the 2nd Division supported by tanks, artillery and air support broke through the enemy line on 18th April to reach the defenders. Along with this, food and water supplies came to survivors of the British force. Two days later, on 20th April, some other men of 2nd Division came to their rescue to relieve the rest of the garrison.[19]

Although after 16 days the siege ended for all practical purposes, the Japanese still occupied some bunkers on a 7,000 yard forest whose sides were unscalable green cliffs. As long as this force was stationed there, the Imphal-Dimapur Road, the main supply line was still under their control. However, two Brigades of army, one from the 7th Division and the other from the Chindits had come south-east towards Jassami to block any possible Japanese reinforcement from the Chindwin and thus completed the process of encircling and isolating the Japanese from their supply lines. Till 30th April the Japanese control of the ridge was attacked. By 3rd May, artillery and tanks were brought from Dimapur for an all-out attack against the Japanese force. Although British attack was countered by cross fire from hidden hill tops, many Japanese died. Along with this, tanks began to crawl up and by May 13 the surviving enemy fell back.

As indicated earlier, in their push northwards from Ukhrul through the hills on the 27th March, the Japanese destroyed Karasom village and so also was the fate of Jessami a few miles further north. By the 18th April due to ceaseless fighting there was a complete disruption of normal life in Kohima and the surrounding villages. The Japanese patrol which went along the bridle paths from Kohima reached distant places like Sakhalu on the new Sema Road, Ghukia on the old Sema Road, Wokha on the Makokchung Road and Pedi on the Henima Road. The inhabitants of these places were absolutely terror struck and began looking for safer places. Kohima village which was occupied by the Japanese was completely destroyed by fire before the inhabitants could save their paddy or household goods. The place and its houses were torn and cratered by shells and bombs and honeycombed with trenches and bunkers. It was the centre of bitter fighting for weeks afterwards. Dead bodies of the war littered the place. The village wells had been to a large extent fouled or destroyed. Even some outlying medical dispensaries had either been destroyed or robbed by the army. The large village of Chedema was completely destroyed during the fighting and the same fate befell the villages of Aradura and Chandmari. The eastern half of Viswema village was blasted by the British guns and gutted by fire. Chizami was bombed by the Allied aircraft and in the process many houses were destroyed.[20]

Since the Japanese forces brought very little food with them, rice was requisitioned in very large quantities for their daily consumption as well as for their mules. They had specific instructions to treat the local people well and to pay for all supplies they collected, they distributed large quantities of Japanese currency and well forged Rs. 10 Indian currency notes among the villagers in return for food and labour. They also killed and ate enormous amount of chickens, pigs, cattles, mithuns and buffaloes. Although some Angami villagers succeeded in hiding their herds of cattle in the deep secluded villages of "Japvo range", the destruction of pigs was so complete that N.L. Bor in his report about the deteriorating sanitary conditions of the Naga hills villages due to the absence of pigs. Since the villagers fled to the jungles or to the field houses low in the valley, where they contacted malaria. The Japanese did not even spare the household goods. Cooking pots once used were smashed.[21] *Daos,* axes and hoes were collected and thrown away in the jungle or into the river.

In the eastern Naga Hills, the local people used to manufacture their own salt by using the local brine wells. The salt pans which were used in the manufacture were also destroyed. Even the Naga blankets and other clothes forcibly taken from the villagers were never returned to the owners. What was of crucial importance was the disturbance in the agriculture of the Naga Hills. The cultivation of the hill terraces was seriously interfered with and all the above mentioned villages got little or no crop. Although the Nagas made a great effort to do what they could, shortage of implements and the delayed planting of crops prevented the rice from setting seed.

Although both Imphal and Kohima were surrounded and put under siege for about two months by the INA-Japanese forces, their decision to travel light with limited supplies across long distances over difficult and treacherous terrain ultimately turned against them. Conversely, the Allied forces organized continuous air lift of supplies, armaments and security personnel throughout the siege period. In the numerous battles of attrition the Allied forces prevail due to superior air power. On the battlefields of Kohima and Imphal about 80,000 Japanese troops of 31st, 33rd and 15th division and 12,000 INA troops faced 1,50,000 British, British Indian, British West African and American troops.[22] By June when the siege of Imphal and Kohima were lifted, more than 30,000 Japanese perished either from bullets or hunger. Further, torrential rain in June-July compounded the problems of the retreating Japanese forces.

II
LOCAL PARTICIPATION

IIA—Manipur

Meiteis

Subsumed within the general trend of the war was the fascinating story of the responses of the local people to the war. Regarding the Meities participation to the war, three distinct trends are discernible from the available sources. Mr. Naki Ahmad Choudhury, a former soldier of the British Indian Army in an interview serialized in ten issues of '*Mingshel*', a local journal, discussed about the ordeal of the march of INA forces from Burma to Manipur. He talked about the difficulties faced by the INA-Japanese forces in getting food supplies and local help and also his experiences of how Col. S.A. Malik worked to get support from the members of the Nikhil Manipuri Mahasabha as well as the villagers of the Thanga. However, he hardly mentioned the fairly strong group of Meitei volunteers from around Bishenpur and Moirang who were working in the intelligence group under Col. Malik. M. Koireng Singh, Th. Angou Singh and a number of other writers, on the other hand, focused on the important role played by a group of Meities who were working in the Intelligence and Supply Department of the INA group. W. Mangol Singh representing the third stream highlighted, although in a cursory manner, the relatively unknown history of L. Guna Singh, a trader by profession and other Manipuris from Burma who operated in an around Pallel when the confrontation between the Allied and Japanese forces took place during May-June 1944.[23]

M. Koireng Singh wrote that the Indo-Japanese force along with 19 Manipuris based at Burma advanced by the Tiddim Road and entered Manipur. Three out of the above nineteen persons— Brahlop Sharma (Brahmapur), M. Ahanbi Singh (Moirang), and M. Chaoba Singh (Keirao) were arrested from Saikot and sent to Jail.[24] Mr. Naki Ahmad Choudhury, a former soldier of the British Indian Army also came along with the same force as a full-fledged member of INA group. When the Japanese force arrived at Moirang, the Allied army withdrew to Bishenpur and the inhabitants of the villages between Moirang and Bishenpur were given only one and half day time to vacate their houses. The Allied forces subsequently burned all the foods that the villagers could not take along with them. Immediately after the Japanese force arrived, they asked for Hijam Lrabot Singh although they were told that he was in Jail. The INA-Japanese force, however, got a lot of support from some of the politically conscious local leaders, like (i) M. Koireng Singh, (ii) I. Sanaba Singh, (iii) K. Kanglen Singh, and (iv) M. Mani Singh. Amu Singh in an interesting write-up highlighted the situation in which the supporters of the Japanese force collected rice and delivered to the Japanese camp at Phubala. He also pointed out the acute scarcity of some of the basic items like cigarette, sugar, rice etc., for the INA-Japanese group.

By the middle of April 1944, the Japanese force established full control over Moirang-Bishenpur area. According to

M. Koireng Singh, it was in such a situation that Col. Malik along with some local INA volunteers hoisted the Tricolour Flag on 14th April at Moirang Kangla and began to operate its activities from a nearby house as its headquarters. By the end of April, many members of the Praja Sanmelani and Nikhil Manipuri Mahasabha including (i) Th. Angou Singh, (ii) P. Tomal Singh, (iii) L. Bijoy Singh, (iv) S. Ibohal Singh, (v) I. Tombi Singh, (vi) M. Jatra Singh, (vii) W. Gyaneswar Singh, (viii) O. Keinya Devi, (ix) M. Amuba Singh, (x) M. Randhoni Devi, (xi) L. Lrabot Singh, and (xii) Kh. Jugeswar Singh reached Moirang and started working for the INA.[25] Although M. Koireng and Naki Choudhury wrote that the new recruits from Imphal and neighbouring areas were all members of the Mahasabha, there were many other active members of the Praja Sanmelani working as volunteers of the INA-Japanese group.

All these developments were informed to the local authority by Mr. Mangi Singh Thiyam, S.I. (F.I.B.) and other A.S.Is in their routine report to the Chief Intelligence Officer, Assam and also to the Political Agent. Suspicious activities about these persons were occasionally reported by the Investigation Bureau. Subsequently, the Political Agent of Manipur declared many of the active local leaders as traitors. Many other leaders of the Mahasabha were also blacklisted. Thereafter, the entire Branch Committees of the Mahasabha were wound up and most of the relevant papers of the organisation were also destroyed. By July-August 1944, the Indo-Japanese attack at Moirang and Bishenpur area had been checked by the Allied forces.

On the other side of the valley, near the Indo-Burma border, the INA-Japanese troops advanced by Imphal-Moreh road. M. Koireng Singh wrote that 13 Meiteis led by L. Guna Singh came along with the Japanese. L. Mukho Singh, a member of the "JIFS" gave the name of five important members of the group, i.e. (i) Thongam Amy (of Kindat), (ii) Saram Singh (Mandalay), (iii) Pato (Mandalay), (iv) Paching (Mandalay), and (v) Guno Singh (Mandalay).[26] L. Guna Singh and his party operated in an around

Pallel area. The group built up propaganda among the inhabitants of Somra track and Kabaw valley that the Japanese had come to give "Swaraj" to Manipur. The group was also instrumental in collecting supplies and information for the Japanese. The group, however, never came to Imphal. It is also generally believed that Guno Singh carried out his activities in the name of 'Manipur Party'. Even after the Independence of India he refused to be identified as a member of the INA group and hence he could not be accommodated in the official list of the freedom fighters prepared by the Freedom Fighters Cell of MPCCI, Manipur. Some other members of his group, however, agreed to be identified as members of the INA and hence were given freedom fighter awards. The Indo-Japanese attack at Pallel was checked by the Allied forces in the first week of May.

IIB—Kukis

In the hills, along the Indo-Myanmar border, quite a good number of people particularly the Kukis worked for the INA-Japanese forces during the early stage of its operation in Manipur. The S.I. and A.S.I. (F.I.B.) collected a large amount of information regarding 70 Kukis who belong to Kabow valley and nearby region for supporting the INA-Japanese forces but the Allied authority dropped many of the cases as most of them could not be authenticated. British officials, particularly E.T.D. Lambert and C. Gimson, were confident of the Kuki loyalty to the Allied group although there were reasonably sufficient evidences to prove Kuki's general support for the INA-Japanese forces.

It seems that the Kukis first contacted the Japanese agents in the area of the Chindwin bend, south of Homalin in the Somra track and the Kabow valley.[27] The Kukis used to visit these areas to buy rice. Later, some agents from this area particularly Hpo Htat, Hpo Heyenin, Taung Kin, Chan Gyun (all of Kweddaukon), San Ke (Hupet), Aungchan, Shwe Kun, Po Mwan (all of Naun Kham) and Pao Set (Thetwa) entered the country east of Ukhrul to contact the Kukis before the Japanese invasion. Tongkhothang, chief of Haokip clan and son of Pachei, one of leaders of the 1917

Kuki rebellion, was also believed to have crossed the Chindwin in November 1943 and contacted the Japanese to ask for 400 rifles to fight against the British. Although the Japanese refused to provide arms, an understanding was reached. The Japanese authority, in fact tried to gain influence among the various tribes by propaganda through the chiefs. The Kukis of eastern Ukhrul assisted the INA-Japanese force by harbouring and forwarding their agents. When the Japanese 31st Division came through the Somra tract, they were helped by the Kukis although many of them who accompanied the force were believed to be interested in looting. In the south and also in the north there were instances of Kukis assisting the Indo-Japanese army.

When the INA-Japanese forces came, they built up a lot of propaganda. The Japanese claimed that they came to give "Swaraj" (Independence) to India. They carried picture of Subhas Bose addressing or inspecting the INA army, displayed Congress colours on arm bands, carried Congress flags and also uttered 'Jai Hind' as a sign of greeting. In order to get sympathy and support from the local people, the Japanese army used to respond to any of the genuine socio-economic problems of the people. For instance, they said that there would not be "house tax" and "forced labour" under them and such propaganda certainly attracted the Kukis. The Japanese force also tried to appeal to the emotion of the Kukis by claiming that they descended from "Chongja" brother of 'Chongthu' from whom the Kukis claimed their descent. There was yet another form of propaganda. A widely known prophesy 'Nongpokthonghangani' (eastern gate will be opened) had been convincingly interpreted by the Japanese and claimed that they represented the eastern power. Such propaganda coupled with the rumour of Japanese bravery, an alleged setback of Indian freedom struggle, impending victory of Indo-Japanese forces, alleged retreat of Allied forces from Manipur, frequent ill-treatment of the Kukis by the Allied army etc., paved the way for the initial success of the Indo-Japanese forces among the local people, particularly the Kukis.

The INA-Japanese force was fairly popular in the early stage of the confrontation and even the 2000 strong Kuki volunteer force for the Allied group was subverted and by the middle of 1944 only about 400 pro Allied Kuki Volunteers remained. In November 1944, although the Allied authority identified as many 70 INA-Japanese active supporters from among the Kukis, after a careful scrutiny of the reports submitted by S.I. and A.S.Is. (F.I.B.), C. Gimson recommended only 8 cases for further investigation. The list of persons recommended by Gimson includes:

(i) Lamkhothang of Vayang Lankhoyam (He was supposed to be a deserter of Assam Regiment and identified by many people for his pro-Japanese propaganda),
(ii) Palet of Lamyang Tombi (He planted land mines on the road to Sita and as a result of that some allied Jeeps were lost),
(iii) Jamshei of Lamyang Tombi,
(iv) Pakang of Tonghlang (He joined Japanese V. force),
(v) Tongkhothang, Chief of Chassad,
(vi) Okhodam (He was Tongkhothang's 'Mantri'. He contacted the Japanese to resist the Britishers),
(vii) Kolvil of Saikot (He supplied rations to the Japanese), and
(viii) Seilut Kuki (He supported the Japanese in many ways).[28]

It may be interesting to note that the freedom fighters Cell of Manipur have so far identified 71 Kukis for working with the INA-Japanese forces.

IIC—Tangkhul Nagas

Some of the Tangkhul Nagas of Ukhrul also worked for the INA-Japanese army. Immediately after the occupation of Ukhrul on 21st March, 1944, the INA-Japanese force tried their best to get support from the Ukhrul people. They distributed INA badges, Indian National Flag and white armbands with Japanese words among the local people.[29] The local people were also told by the Indo-Japanese army that they came to free the people from the clutches of the British Government. Subsequently, the Tangkhuls formed a 'Cooperation Committee' consisting of Ngalangzar (3rd clerk of Ukhrul), Rambung (4th clerk of Ukhrul), Yarnao (teacher), Changyoh (petition writer), Paul (teacher), M.K. Shimray, Thisan and Kunga. The Committee further accommodated three local Kukis—Phatnikphang of Tolloi, Seilut (2nd clerk of Ukhrul) and Selkhoseh Kipgen (teacher). Mr. Ngalangzar, Phatnikphang, Seilut and Selkhoseh were made Chairman, Secretary, Assistant Secretary and Store Registrar in-charge respectively.[30]

The Committee was divided into three Departments—(i) Interview Department, (ii) Supply Department, and (iii) Labour Department. The Interview Department was responsible for the collection of information and nobody was allowed to see the Japanese army officers without its permission. Mikha, Thesan, Ningsei, Ngalangzar, Yangmasho (master), Konrei (master) and a few other important Tangkhuls and some Headman of the villages were in the Interview Department. The main function of the Supply Department was to impress paddy, rice, pigs and chicken from the villagers and supply them to the INA-Japanese army. Mr. Changyoh, Mr. Yarnao and Mr. Ngashamphang were in the Supply Department. To enable the Indo-Japanese army in getting sufficient supplies, the Chairman of the Committee gave the army authority the names of the villages, the number of houses and the list of supplies that they could collect from the villagers. The Labour Department impressed coolies and they arranged guides wherever necessary. Although such a detailed organisational structure was formulated, the Tangkhuls in general evaded helping the Indo-Japanese forces. In fact, many other Tangkhuls worked for the Allied establishment under the leadership of Bob Khathing. 'V' force and its informers arrested as many as 79 and killed 95 Japanese soldiers when severe confrontation between the Allied and the INA-Japanese forces took place. No wonder, a Japanese officer told a village headman immediately before their retreat:

> We came 5,000 strong but we have had 3,000 casualties. We are withdrawing to Mawlaik and will

> return in December. When we came, we trusted the Kukis and Nagas but they deceived us. Next time we come, we will have no mercy on the civilian population.

By August-September 1944, the INA-Japanese force began to retreat from Manipur and the Naga Hills. Along with them went many of the local supporters. Guna Singh and some Kukis including Lamkhothang, Palet, and Jamshei went along with the Japanese retreating army. Some of the Meitei supporters of the INA (about 19 persons including two women) who were declared as betrayers by the Political Agent also went along with the INA-Japanese group to Burma. Among them was K. Gopal Singh, who died near Kalymyo. When the group reached Burma, they were lodged at 11-Kondogalary Guest House. L. Irabot Singh, Kh. Jugeshwar Singh and I. Tombi Singh joined active service in INA whereas Smt. Keinya Devi and Smt. Randhoni Devi joined the Jhanshi Rani Regiment.

IID—Nagas of Naga Hills

So far as the responses of the Nagas of the Naga Hills are concerned, it may be stated that the common people were not happy as they were impressed by the Japanese as coolies to carry heavy loads for long distances.[31] The treatment of people at first was on the whole fair but there were also isolated cases of rape, maltreatment and even murder.[32] The coolies were tied up at night to prevent them from escaping. Since the Japanese were suspicious of possible Naga attack, they collected systematically all the hoes, axes and *daos* and threw them into the rivers and jungles. Some of the spears and guns were, however,

> "hidden by the Nagas and were used afterwards with good effect." When the opportunity arises the "Nagas discovered that the Japanese head was not proof against a well placed blow from a billet of wood and many were disposed of in this way."[33]

In contrast to this, the colonial policy of dealing with the hill tribes of North East India was very subtle and slow process of colonisation. The missionaries were also instrumental in laying a smooth foundation for the penetration of colonial administrative and economic forces. Ursula Graham Bower, a lady anthropologist who came to Northeast India to study the Zeme Nagas of North Cachar Hills toured the neighbouring areas extensively and canvassed support for the Allied forces. The V Force was also organised and many Nagas were recruited as its volunteers.[34] In their dislike for the collection of supplies and coolies, the Nagas went so far as to give information to the allied group.[35] In many cases, the inhabitants of the villages laid down ground signals, which indicated to the allied aircraft that the village was occupied by the Japanese troops. In several other cases, many Naga volunteers penetrated the Japanese line and brought back invaluable information.

The British authorities were indeed, thoroughly impressed by the Nagas responses to the war. Dr. N.L. Bor, the Director of Assam Relief Measures (ARM), noted that the Nagas reactions "in all respects (were) exemplary." He went on saying:

> The personal and material damage they suffered was much greater as the result of our military against the Japanese than any they suffered directly at the hands of the later. Everywhere, however, there was a complete understanding of the necessity for measures taken and in spite of their severe material losses there is quite a buoyant feeling that all was just in the days work.[36]

Col. H.E. Short, the Chief Medical Officer of ARM was of the same assessment that:

> There was a real pride [among the Nagas] in their loyalty to the British rule. This pride is fully justified because they did not merely passively endure... but when possible were active helpers against the

> Japanese in the form of pottering work, rescue of stragglers, bringing of important and reliable military information and even the giving of wrong information to the Japanese.[37]

It was precisely because of such attitudes that the Britishers were in full sympathy with the Nagas and he remarked:

> "All these facts make it a moral obligation on our part to give back all and more than they have lost provided their independence is not undermined by pampering."

III
POST-WAR SOCIO-POLITICAL CHANGES

The war period, thus, was a time of intense socio-economic and political cross-currents. The changes during the wartime provided material as well as ideological basis for strong political movements during 1946-1949 period. It was during such a time of tremendous change that the economic base of the nascent Manipuri and Naga middle class was strengthened through massive investments in transportation, trade, supply and construction works. Ideologically, the Manipuri and Naga middle class was exposed to the national and international political trends and therefore, was on the lookout for opportunities to struggle for broad socio-economic and political changes in their respective states. As far as the Manipuri and the Naga masses were concerned, the disturbances shook their traditional way of life. They began to feel the impacts of the market economy as it penetrated into the remote areas of the region. The people of Manipur and Naga hills, thus, became receptive to various political ideologies. The politics of Naga National Council, Kuki National Assembly, Manipur Communist Party, and above all the politics of Indian National Congress backed by strong organizational networks at the State as well as district level in both the two places are to be examined against such a backdrop.

As far as the political trend in Manipur Valley was concerned, it may be pointed out that a large section of Meitei middle class who worked with Mahasabha had been desperately trying to set up a unit of Indian National Congress and ultimately Manipur State Congress was formally established in October 1946. A few other leaders of Meitei middle class belonging to the Krishak Sabha went to Burma along with the retreating INA-Japanese force and returned by August 1946. Majority of the group along with H. Irabot Singh worked for a Left Wing peasant movement under the banner of Manipur Communist Party/DOC, CPI. From 1946 onward, the two political groups began to launch systematic campaign for political democratization and broad socio-economic change in the state.

Regarding the political situations in the hill areas, the observations of Mangi Singh Thiyam seems to reflect the then political scenario. He wrote:

> The Hills at last seem to awaken. They got up by the cries of Democracy and Independence all over the world and especially by the India Independent cries. It had its own interests to safeguard. They were very much worried during the last Gandhi-Jinnah talks and were greatly relieved that it ended into nothing. There was no room for the minorities in their thoughts. Though politically included within the orbit of India, at least, felt that historically they had never been subdued either by the great Hindu Kings or the Muslim Kings. Moreover, they were not cared for at all. It is only the British who took the Hills under the laws and led them up to the path of civilization. In appearance they still differ from the rest of India. By the influx of so many Indian troops of various class and by their habit of treating the hill people strangers all men and women in the Hills let alone those who know little education, they all feel their difference more.[38]

On the issue of political strategy of the Hill people, Mangi wrote:

> "they were going to send to H.E. the Governor of Assam ... (a petition) and they desired that the petition be forwarded to H.E. the Viceroy and then to His Majesty the, King. The suggestion was to establish hill administrative unit in Assam-Burma border by taking similar areas from N. Burma. It originated from the speech of Sir R. Reid, Ex-Governor of Assam about these Hills in London and its recent origin is from the Naga Hills. All bless this proposal."[39]

The report of Mangi Singh may be appreciated against the background of socio-economic assessment provided by N.L. Bore. Dr. Bore wrote that even the remotest of Manipur Hills (and adjoining areas) began to change their way of life due to presence of army and considerable inflow of money. Bor further wrote that with increased use of consumption goods like soaps, mugs etc., which were supplied by mobile canteen every week, the standard of living of the Hill people had grown tremendously. Thus, it is fairly reasonable to argue that a large section of educated and politically conscious group of Manipur Hills, along with other leaders of North East Indian Hill areas in collaboration with some of the colonial officers were toying with the idea of a separate administrative unit in the hilly Indo-Burma region.

Within such broad trend, there were varied ethnocentric political currents. The Mao Nagas under the leadership of A. Daiho and influenced by the politics of Naga National Council launched a struggle for the inclusion of Naga inhabited areas of Manipur into Naga Hills. The Mizo Union also made inroads into the Kuki areas of the Southern Hills of Manipur and began to demand the integration of Kuki inhabited areas into the Lushai Hills. In the western hills of Manipur, the Zeliangrong Nagas also continued their long drawn out struggle for the unification of the Zeliangrong inhabited areas of Manipur, Naga Hills and North Cachar Hills. Thus, although most of the traditional chiefs and the general masses continued to believe in the historico-political entity of Manipur, the educated elites of Manipur Hills began politics of ethnic consolidation and ethnic identity.

In the Naga Hills, Zapu Phizo, an Angami leader returned in June 1946 after his long wartime sojourn in Burma to preach his politics of Naga Independence. Although the NNC (Naga National Council) which he had founded initially demanded local autonomy of Naga Hills within the state of Assam, after India's Independence, they raised the demand to secede the Naga Hills from India. The movement still continues. It may be pointed out that during the war and even a decade after the event, the people of the region were linked up very closely with the people who inhabit the north-western Burmese Hills.

NOTES

1. Lian H. Sakhong (2003). *In Search of Chin Identity: A Study in Religion, Politics and Ethnic Identity in Burma*, Thailand: Nias Press, p. 195.
2. Pum Khan Pau (2014). "Situating Local Events in Geopolitical Struggle between the British and Japanese Empires: The Politics of Zo Participation during the Second World War", *The Journal of Imperial and Commonwealth History*, *42*(2): 674.
3. *Ibid.*, p. 676.
4. Sugata Bose (2011). *His Majesty's Opponent,* Delhi: Penguin Books, p. 243.
5. *Ibid.*, p. 244.
6. *Ibid.*, pp. 251-252.
7. *Ibid.*
8. *Ibid.*, pp. 266-67.
9. T.N. Dupuy (1963). *Asiatic Land Battles: Allied Victories in China and Burma*, Franklinn Watts, p. 22.
10. Sugata Bose, *Op.cit.*, p. 276.
11. Pum Khan Pau, *Op.cit.*, p. 2.
12. *Ibid.*
13. N. Lokendra Singh (1993). *Manipur and Second World War, Imphal: Manipur State Archives*, p. 10.
14. William Slim (1981). *From Defeat to Victory,* U.K.: Cassell and Company, p. 325.
15. N. Lokendra Singh, *op.cit.*, p. 11.

16. Sugata Bose, *op.cit.*, p. 275.
17. Sugata Bose, *op.cit.*, p. 277.
18. N. Lokendra Singh, *op.cit.*, p. 11.
19. T.N. Dupuy, *op.cit.*, p. 23.
20. N.L. Bore, A Report on the Measures of Rehabilitation and Reconstruction undertaken by the Government of India in Naga Hills and Manipur State in 1944 in order to repair the ravages caused by the Japanese Invasion of 1944.
21. *Ibid.*, p. 4.
22. Sugata Bose, *op.cit.*, pp. 275-276.
23. N. Lokendra, *op.cit.*, p. 14.
24. *Ibid.*
25. *Ibid.*, p. 16.
26. P. Ray S.I.P. C.I.D, I.B. (Burma) Interrogating Officers Interrogation Report of L. Mukho Singh, File No. XLI, Cabin 29, Japanese War (Secretariat Library, Manipur).
27. N. Lokendra, *op.cit.*, p. 18.
28. *Ibid.*, p. 20.
29. Letkhoseh Kipgen's report entitled, "Notes on Tangkhul Cooperation Committee", dated February 1945.
30. *Ibid.*
31. N.L. Bore, *op.cit.*
32. *Ibid.*, p. 4.
33. *Ibid.*
34. V Force began in April 1942 with the help of Assam Government. The V force was to be organised in six groups—Tripura, Lushai Hills, Chin Hills, Imphal, Kohima and Ledo.
35. N.L. Bore, *op.cit.*
36. *Ibid.*, p. 80.
37. *Ibid.*
38. Reports of S.I. (F.I.B) Forwarded by C. Gimson *vide* Memo No. 5464-5A/orgl to Central Intelligence Officer Assam, dated 25-11-1944.
39. *Ibid.*

4

Manipur in the Geo-Political Mapping of India's Winning Freedom

Y. Modhu Singh

Introduction

The internal division itself within the Congress into Moderates and Extremes in the wake of long drawn out freedom movement of India is a part of the process of India's winning freedom in 1947. The moderates who believed in the loyalty to British Crown, solemn pledges made by the British Government to the people of India, orderly progress and constitutional agitations and again who demanded wider employment of Indians in higher public offices, reduction in heavy land revenue payments, expansion and reform in the then existing Legislative Councils etc. did not pose any threat to the foundation of British colonial rule in India except concession of constitutional development in gradual manner and that too, after adequate pressures and inputs. It could not be an exaggeration that it was the INA which waged a war of national liberation with martyrdom under the Provisional Government of Azad Hind with Netaji at its head and Supreme Commander-in-Chief of the armed forces and brought about national freedom in

1947. The military engagement itself in the 'Battle of Imphal' and *satyagraha* in the rest of India under the leadership of Gandhiji were the 'two blades of the sword'[1] which were reciprocal to each other towards India's winning freedom.

Collecting Storms

Behavioural investigation of Netaji would reveal that patriotic zeal of Netaji was manifested in the form of a radical, revolutionary and militant. His radical feelings could not compromise with the sentiment of constitutional reforms adopted in slow pace by the British colonial rule in India and 'petition and representation' methods adopted by the Congress as a means for winning freedom. It was the intention of British colonial policy to isolate Netaji from Gandhiji and Congress and branded him as fascist. British media played a major role in this behalf.[2] Gandhiji accidentally became a pawn in the hands of the British when he refuted the proposal of Netaji to take up arms in war against the British when the latter met him in Sevagram in 1939.[3] Even though Gandhiji explained to Netaji about the "favourable situation" of India after the World War-II. Netaji could not accept it simply by saying "I do not like the kind of freedom to be begged for." It made the British to land on an advantageous position leading to irreversible isolation between the two patriots.

Undaunted by the refusal of Gandhiji to his proposal for military option Netaji was fully determined to upfront the British imperialism. Anti-Compromise Conference at Ramgarh in March 1940 and demolition of Holwell Monument etc. only provided a better opportunity resulting his daring escape from India to reach Berlin *via* Kabul (April 4, 1941).

When Netaji met Hitler (May 29,1942) ideological clash took place between Netaji and Hitler over issue of freedom of India.[4] Racial prejudice of Hitler culminating into non-cooperation to the cause of armed struggle against British regime in India could not hinder the burning flame of Netaji for the liberation of Indian masses from further enslavement of Indian nationhood. Situations in SEA provided another better opportunity. At that time 3 million Indians in East and SEA were prepared for liberation of 380 million people of India.[5]

The Nazi campaign in Europe and heavy pressure on France and the Dutch brought about a power vacuum in SEA. The Japanese attack on Pearl Harbour (December 7, 1941) and subsequent overrun of the entire SEA was the best opportunity for the historic destiny of India's freedom struggle. The fall of Singapore in the hands of the Imperial Japanese Army on February 16, 1942 led to the foundation of the INA[6] which was eventually swollen into five strong combat and non-combat divisions (including two divisions under training). Thus, the course of war in Europe had a collateral impact on the Indo-Japanese offensive preparation, more pertinently, establishment of INA, formation of the Provisional Government of Azad Hind and its offensive war in Manipur later.

Formation of the Provisional Government of Free India about which Netaji had already made a clear vision in his Kurseong Address in 1940[7] became a reality when he made the historic proclamation on 21st October, 1943 at Singapore. Main objectives of the provisional government were to wage war of liberation and set India free from British imperialism and establishment of government at the free will of the people of India. NEI, particularly Manipur which is a part of SEA came into the centre stage of the first combat ground by geo-political reasons and Imphal became strategically important location.

Operation 'U' Go

Netaji had a belief that the invading army of the INA would be welcomed as liberators of India on her soil. Preparation and operation of the 'Battle of Imphal' had already been planned. Three divisions of the Imperial Japanese Army and one division of the INA were to be engaged. The operation was under the command of Lt. General Mutaguchi. Formation of the three Imperial Japanese Army Divisions were 33rd Division (under Lt. General Yanagida), 15th Division (under Lt. General Yamauchi) and 31st Division (under

Lt. General Sato) and their Head Quarters were located at Kalimyo, Thaungdut and Homalin-Tomanthi—all in northern Burma lying nearly in vertical position facing westward respectively 17th British Division (under Lt. General Cowan) located at Tiddim, 20th Division (under Lt. General Grasey) at Kabaw Valley and 23rd Division (under Lt. General Roberts) at Imphal. Each of the three Nippon Divisions came forward with a regiment of the INA and they were engaged in Arakan, Manipur and Nagaland. Field Marshal Slim of British Army planned how to face the Japanese offensive. Accordingly he withdrew the British columns from the frontiers and concentrated in the Imphal Valley and fought the decisive battle over there. A Division of the British Army (Division No. 5) was airlifted from Arrakan to Imphal.

Moreover, fighting a decisive battle in Imphal Valley could be more advantageous for them due to superior air power by all-weather air fields at Pallel and Koirengei (both in Manipur Valley). Therefore, continued possession of Imphal by the British as 'fortification' against the Indo-Japanese offensive or, its capture by the Indo-Japanese forces to act as 'springboard' had become strategically so decisive to determine the course of war in future. Coincidentally, Netaji had a clear perception that liberation war from without would invoke intensified civilian uprising against British rule within. By December 1943 four units of Bahadur Groups having 250 men each were ready to take part in the Arakan and Imphal Campaign. They were intelligence and field propaganda units almost prepared to penetrate behind enemy lines, subvert the loyalty of British Indian troops on the battle fields and educate the Indian prisoners before they joined the INA.[8]

As planned the 31st Japanese Division swept with speed to overrun Ukhrul, capture Kohima and blockade Imphal-Dimapur Road there. But it was resisted by the British at Shangshat near Ukhrul on March 19, 1944 in which a British Company (C Company) entirely lost at the cost of 153 Japanese sepoys and 7 officers. It was the first ever fierce battle fought between the British and the Japanese forces on the soil of Manipur. Could Lt.

General Sato thrust deeper into Dimapur where supply reserves were garrisoned it could have inflicted the British grievously and Japanese ration could have been a solution. Besides, Netaji reckoned that once the British were forced back from Imphal, the plains of Assam and Bengal will be opened to the INA forces with triumphant entry in Calcutta by autumn (1944).[9] We have a reliable source that trusted lieutenants of Z.A. Phizo in Nagaland and Gopinath Bordoloi in Assam were prepared to extend co-operation to the liberation army. The 15th Division was to move and send an advance guard *via* Ukhrul to cut Imphal-Kohima Road at Kanglatongbi and attack Imphal from the north in conjugation with an assault from the south by the 33rd Division. A detached column of its division known as 'Yamamoto Forces' was to drive the 20th British Division from Tamu, attack Pallel (to capture the Air Base) and Imphal from the south-east. Thus except for Bishenupur-Silchar track Imphal was cut off. Virtually Imphal was under seize by the Indo-Japanese soldiers. However, the British used the advantages of air superiority; transport squadrons were pressed to provide continuous air supply; prepared counter-offensive to break the Indo-Japanese grips on the hills surrounding the Imphal Plains. The seize was thus short-lived.

Battle Grounds in Manipur

Manipur bore the brunt of war when two powerful bombs were dropped over Imphal in the month of May 1942 by Japan as their first air raid. Many innocent people including women and children were killed. All the prisoners from Imphal Jail escaped; treasury and banks were looted; business at Khwairamban Bazar, Imphal paralysed; prices of essential commodities shot up; salt fetched at Rs. 5 per seer/kg and kerosene Rs. 150 per tin; educational institutions closed for six months; most of the people left their homes and hearths and took shelters in far-flung villages; Imphal became a deserted ghost city; even the State Darbar, the highest administrative seat had to be shifted to the house of Shri Khomdram Angangjao at Kwakeithel and other important offices were shifted to different places. Thus, the people of Manipur were apprehensive of an impending war of massive scale. And Imphal became the forward base built up by the Allied Forces. Subhas Brigade of INA and Division 33 of the Japanese Imperial Army switched rapid offensive from Kalimyo; blockaded the 17th British Division at Tonzang; followed the retreating 17th Division of the British Army; thrust deep into the southern hill ranges of Manipur after crossing the Indian (Manipur) border on 18th March, 1944 and occupied vast tracks of territory. In the meantime some 32 Manipuris (Meiteis) who earned their livelihood in Burma joined the INA under the leadership of L. Guno Singh of Khurai, Imphal in the battle front as advance party. 13 out of 32 Manipuris reached Pallel and tried to secure support of the local people. A large number of erstwhile 'V' Force also joined the movement and participated in the war front. The rest 19 Manipuris marched down Khuga Tampak (valley), now in Churachandpur District. Out of them four members, namely M. Ahanjao Singh of Moirang, B. Balhop Sharma, M. Chaoba Singh and S. Yaima Singh were arrested from Saikot and taken them to Calcutta to be released after the war.[10]

In the hills of Manipur one Paikhomang Kuki of Shakok village (now in Sadar Hills District) contacted the Japanese and liaised between Taokhothang, Chief of Chassad, the biggest Kuki Chief in Burma and NE India and Indo-Japanese officials. Later, as mark of friendship a traditional feast of *satin-salung* (liver and heart of animal) was arranged in which 135 Kuki chiefs and 30 others took part. The feast was attended by the hill leaders from Kuki tribes and Indo-Japanese officials. The Kukis took irreversible vows by biting *hampi-ha* (tiger tooth), a traditional practice of the Kukis to help and cooperate each other in their common cause and thereby stood against the British. Emissaries were sent to other Kuki chiefs residing in different parts of Burma, Assam and Manipur. And similar feasts were also arranged in the same line. Thus, many Kukis enrolled themselves as porters, informers, messengers, civil suppliers, even fighters etc. At Tuikhiang Camp in Chin Hills at the behest of Indo-Japanese forces formed Chin Defence Army (CDA) with an avowed objective to expel the British from India. A large number of hill people were enlisted in the campaign too.[11]

People of Manipur in the valley got alerted when a hand bill was brought secretly by an officer of the INA from the INA Advance Base Camp at Molai near Indo-Burma border and passed on to one Lungam Lungdim, Kuki by tribe residing in Mompi village near Sugnu who again handed it over to Dr. Gulapchand Singh, the then medical officer posted at Sugnu and Dr. Gulapchand brought the bill over to Thochom Anhou Singh of Singjamei (Imphal) on 7th March, 1944 who happened to be the Chairman of Praja Sanmelani, an active political organisation in Manipur. The hand bill appealed to the people of India to join and enlist support to the INA. Shri Th. Angou Singh in his return reply said that some people would definitely join the INA within a month or so.[12] Sooner Shri Angou Singh along with twelve other members of the Sanmelani, namely P. Tomal Singh, S. Ibohal Singh, I. Tombi Singh, L. Bijoy Singh, L. Kanhai Singh, M. Jatra Singh, W. Gyaneshwor Singh, M. Amuba Singh, L. Irabot Singh, Kh. Jugeshwar Singh, Smt. O. Keinya Devi and Smt. M. Randhoni Devi sneaked into Moirang and worked together with local people of Moirang in the war efforts. Village chawkidars had alerted local people of Moirang and its neighbouring villages about the imminence of the war. The 17th British Division could not resist the fast advancing Indo-Japanese forces and as such, they were compelled to retreat leaving completely behind all the southern hill ranges of Manipur (now Churachandpur and Pherzawl Districts) upto Potsangbam (near Bishnupur). Manipuris celebrated Cheiraoba (New Year) Festival on 14th April, 1944. In the morning, it was reported secretly that some Indo-Japanese forces had reached Tronglaobi, a village 5 km away to the south of Moirang (where this national seminar is being held). Local leaders, namely Shri M. Koireng Singh, Shri K. Kanglen Singh, Shri L. Sanaba Singh and Shri M. Mani Singh went to Tronglaobi and had discussion with them. In the evening at 5.00 p.m. a column of Bahadur Group (Intelligence Wing of the INA) with Col. Shaukat Ali Malik at its head accompanying Japanese soldiers led by Capt. Ito arrived at Moirang at the invitation of local people led by Shri M. Koireng Singh (who later became Chief Minister of Manipur). Col. S.A. Malik planted the Tri-colour Flag with Springing Tiger super-imposed at the middle of the flag in a ceremonial manner at the historic Moirang Kangla (an ancient citadel where coronation of successive kings of Moirang was held). Moirang was privileged as the sacred soil of India liberated for the first time by the INA from the British colonial rule. About 50 local people attended the ceremony. Col. S.A. Malik addressed the gathering and Shri M. Koireng Singh translated the address in Manipuri. The translation stated *inter alia* ...

> "The Provisional Government of Azad Hind had declared war on Engand and America with a commitment to complete the creation of Greater East Asia and bring welfare to the people of India by defeating the Anglo-American forces. The Indian National Army with the unstinted support of the Japanese Government has now crossed the Indo-Burmese border and in the course of the struggle for the liberation of the people of India from the British colonial yoke we have now reached Moirang. Our commitment is the March to Delhi and unfurl the Tri-Colour Flag at Lal-Killa. Many had died on our way to reach here (Moirang) and many would die on our way to Delhi. However, expulsion of the enemy from the sacred soil of India is a compulsion for us. We shall fight and the people of Manipur would provide supplies to us. Nothing about us shall be passed on to the enemy and everything about the enemy should be passed on to us. This is a way that people ought to do as a part of contribution to our single-minded mission—expulsion of the imperialist forces from India ..."[13]

The message was well received by the jubilant crowd and felt thrilled that they were the first liberated people of India though many of their family members evacuated Moirang and took shelters at the island hills of Loktak Lake, namely Thanga, Ithing, Sendra, Mamang Ching, Omba Ching, Khongjai-ngamba Ching etc. Very shortly an Advance Headquarters was located at Moirang in the residential building of Shri Hemam Nilamani Singh. It ran a war time office for about three months perhaps to conduct forward military operations and administer the liberated areas.

Netaji created civil affairs group called Azad Hind Dal. On March 16, 1944, A.C. Chatterjee was appointed Chief Administrator of the liberated territories to take charge of administration within India. The initial team of about 70 administrators had already left Rangoon for the border on March 8, 1944. There was clear instruction on the task of administration in liberated territories such as, to restore of essential utility services, provide reliefs to the refugees, maintain law and order, reassure safety and security etc. Once military operation ceased a provisional provincial administration would be established under Provisional Government of Azad Hind until in future, a permanent government of free India could be organised.[14]

The war tensed the local people and their involvement in the war efforts were active. M. Koireng Singh and K. Kanglen Singh led in the mobilisation of voluntary donation of rice, dry fishes and grains from local populace for the Indo-Japanese forces who stayed at Moirang and its adjoining villages. They donated 80 maunds of rice and 40 maunds of dry fishes at the first instance and they were piled up at the outhouse of K. Kanglen Singh to be distributed elsewhere. A large amount of food grains was transported by headloads, bullock carts and Kangkots (sledges) driven by buffaloes to the villages where columns of Indo-Japanese forces stationed.[15] Thus, the people of Moirang provided food to the liberating soldiers numbering about ten thousand for long three months. There were reports that Japanese soldiers fighting in different parts of Manipur were reduced to skeletons due to starvation but those who fought in and around Moirang were a difference. Some 800 *foubots* from the family granary of H. Nilamani Singh were voluntarily exhausted just to feed the soldiers. Also he handed over Rs. 21,000 (which fetched very high value in the market at that time) to Col. S.A. Malik which was of great help in the conduct of war. In return Nilamani was honoured by Malik with a title 'Sethji'.[16]

The British knew that local people had extended support to the Indo-Japanese soldiers and treated them as liberators by providing food and shelters and did espionage works for the liberation army. Accordingly, the British undertook 'Scorch Earth Policy' and burnt down all the residential houses in Moirang numbering about 1,000 except seven or eight which belonged to Shri Phairembam Tonjao Singh, Shri Philem Achouba Singh, Shri Maibram Chaoba Singh, Shri Mairembam Angangyaima Singh, Shri Laishangbam Birmangol Singh, Shri Hemam Nilamani Singh, Shri Konjengbam Iboton Singh etc. The first two houses were used as 'hospital'[17]and the last one as mentioned above as the advanced INA head Quarters.

Battles and pitched battles were fought in different parts of Manipur and mention may be made among them were at Torbung, Thoya (Moirang), Kwasiphai, Toubul, Maibram-Lotpa Ching (Red Hill), Kanglatongbi, Kameng, Palel, Shangsak (Ukhrul), Kohima etc. Local people bore the brunt of war; innumerable people died and wounded, lost properties and livestock etc. Oral accounts still are handed down in Manipur about the loss of lives and properties in the war. Intensity of the war in Manipur is testified in the two letters from General I. Fujiwara, a leading officer of the Imperial Japanese Army engaged in the war. In his account he mentioned a number of field hospitals, thousands admitted as patients/bullet injuries, eight burial grounds at Laimanai, Wood Hills (relating to Toubul Battle), Ukhrul, Moreh, A.B. Mission (along Kangpokpi-Kohima Road), Kokadan (located to south-west of Bishnupur), Moirang and Kanglatongbi and over 2391 bodies of the Japanese army were buried in these war zones. In that account Fujiwara also mentioned four burial grounds of the Japanese Army to the south, east and west of Kohima at Kegubema, Tuhema, Singanheimei and a location 2 km south-west of Kohima where altogether 1950 dead bodies were buried. At one instance 1500 Japanese soldiers died while fighting 'pitched battles for 40 days' to capture Kohima. In his estimate "seventy thousand Japanese soldiers, thousands of INA fell ...Probably tens of thousands of Indian soldiers on the side of British Army also died in the battle." By analysing the two letters[18] we can conclude that fiercest battles were fought in different parts of Manipur and locations surrounding Kohima. Eye witnesses accounts of people of Moirang exuberate that trees and bamboos were reduced to trunks due to cross-fires and bomb splinters; grounds were dug out with innumerable bomb holes due to intense bombing in tonnes; mine bomb explosions, killed many civilians; aerial raids during night by British bombers claimed hundreds in and around Moirang alone.

At the cost of untold sufferings amongst the civilian populace and deaths and wounds of military personnel of both camps Indo-Japanese forces could liberate territories consisting of 1,500 sq. miles stretching from southern Manipur (now Churachandpur and Pherzawl districts) upto Potshangbam in Bishnupur District.[19] Men and officers in the advanced INA Headquarters and Hikari Kikan office (located very nearby) were busy at night with local leaders led by M. Koireng Singh and H. Nilamani Singh who used to come from their respective shelters in hill islands of Loktak Lake. The said Advance Headquarters is still standing to testify the vividness of war bearing the torn marks of machine gun fires and bomb splinters.

With the set in of monsoon accompanying torrential rains the Indo-Japanese forces suffered reverses. When retreat orders came from Rangoon they were to retreat and all the Manipuris who were involved in the war efforts had to retreat to Burma along with the retreating INA soldiers. Moirang and its adjoining areas were declared as 'enemy zone' and 'shoot-at-sight' orders was passed on five active leaders of Moirang, namely, M. Koireng Singh, H. Nilamani Singh, K. Gopal Singh, K. Kanglen Singh and M. Sanaba Singh.[20] K. Kanglen Singh took refuge in the thick weeds and *phoomdis* of *Keibul Lamjao* while the rest four left Moirang for Rangoon on 16th July, 1944.

Netaji ordered suspension of operation on 21st August, 1944. After monsoon the 14th British Division took offensive in Burma and the INA were on the defensive and that too at the cost of heavy casualty. Rangoon was re-occupied by the British and Indian troops numbering about 17,000 strong contingent were captured as 'prisoners'. Those 'prisoners of war' who put up tough fight as soldiers of an organised army (INA) and waged a legitimate war for the national liberation of India were forced to be treated as felons, mercenaries, traitors and deserters and subjugated to the Indian Army Act and were brought to be court-martialled. They were denied the status of Prisoner of Wars (POWs).

Impact of the War on India's Winning Freedom

The historic Red Fort Trial began its proceedings on 5th November, 1945. The best argument of the Chief Defense Counsel, Bhulabhai Desai with classic examples from British history was not honoured by the British due to colonial interest. It sparked the revolt in Royal Indian Navy in Bombay and later spread to Karachi, Delhi, Madras and Calcutta. The police swung into action and firing killed 217 and wounded more than 2000. Over a thousand men of the Royal Indian Air Force camped at Bombay demonstrated in sympathy of the navy. The mutineers equally retaliated when the police and military opened fire at Bombay and Karachi. Names of Shah Nawaz Khan, P.K. Sehgal and G.S. Dhillon, leading officers of the INA became the household words in India.

Colonel P.K. Sehgal in his article "Victory in Defeat" strongly reflected a reaction to the British regime:

> "The British troops were mostly young (Indian) conscripts whose sympathy with the cause of the INA soon became apparent.... The first surprise the British received was when one of the Gurkha soldiers sought an interview with his commanding officer to get a discharge from his regiment because he wanted to join the INA ...... as witnesses for the prosecution and

> defence told the court the whole history of the INA it had an electric effect in the country.[21] Field Marshall Auchinleck, the Commander-in-Chief of the Indian Army who remitted the sentence of transportation passed on the three INA officers 'for waging war against the king was overweighed by the consideration of prudence than of clemency.'[22]

Auchinleck wrote in a minute,

> "I have no doubt at all that to have confirmed the imprisonment solely on the charge of waging war against the King would have probably precipitated a violent outbreak throughout the country, and created active and widespread dissatisfaction in the army, especially among the Indian officers and more highly educated rank and file. To have taken this risk would have seriously to jeopardise our object."

In other words, the British realised that they would no longer receive the blind loyalty from the native troops. The transfer of power had to be accelerated.

An English writer, Alafair Lamb observed,

> "... the agitation against their trial when the war was over, together with 1946 mutiny in the Indian Navy seemed to suggest that the British could not rely much longer on the Indian forces to keep India under British control."[23]

The British Prime Minister, Clement Atlee alluded on March 15, 1946:

> "... to the spread of national idea, not least perhaps among those soldiers who have done such wonderful service in the war as being responsible for his subsequent decision to quit India on August 15, 1947."[24]

Conclusion

By geographical compulsions and patriotic temperament of the people of Manipur she became a theatre of liberation war, her soil wetted with the blood of martyrs and unsung heroes, countless innocent people, men, women and children died, flag of freedom hoisted ceremonially on her liberated soil. However, I am afraid even today very few could believe that the INA had liberated a part of the sacred soil of India, precisely, Manipur from the British colonial rule and established their authority over there (at Moirang). History has vividly testified that freedom was granted to India in 1947 due to the resultant effects of the Liberation War on the soil of Manipur and Naga Hills. However, it seems that the people of Indian mainstream were overwhelmed with the story of defeat of the INA in the hands of the British Army. The two war cemeteries at Imphal and a third one at Kohima and ceremonial memorial services on different battle grounds of Manipur speak the same tone. Indian leaders, scholars and people at large, read of Garbaldi, Mazini and Bismark and their contribution to the process of Italian and German unification. Nonetheless, contribution of the people of Manipur and venture of Netaji and the INA for losing the fetters of bondage of 380 million Indian people from the clutch of British colonial subjugation leading to the ultimate national freedom is sunken deep into an inappropriate chapter of Modern Indian History in spite of the fact that the Red Fort Trial accelerated the pace of the dawn of India's freedom. People of India random adjudge the value of 'Two Blades of a Sword.' An imbalanced tilt is always seen in disfavour of the people of NE India, Netaji and the INA even though the deeds were unparalleled, unique and heroic. Shall the nation accept (that) it is a deserving tribute!

NOTES

1. M. Manindra Singh (Ed.) (1993). *Souvenir*, Golden Jubilee Celebration of Azad Hind Government, Imphal, p. 49ff.
2. Sugata Bose (2013). *His Majesty's Opponent*, Gurgaon, p. 274.
3. S.K. Bose (Ed.) (1973). *A Beacon Across Asia*, New Delhi, p. 98.

4. *Ibid.*, 138.
5. Kusum Nair (1946). *INA*, Bombay, p. 47.
6. *Ibid.*, p. 5 ff.
7. S.K. Bose (Ed.) (1981). *Crossroads*, Calcutta, p. 322 ff.
8. Sugata Bose (2013). *His Majesty's Opponent*, Gurgaon, p. 248.
9. *Ibid.*, p. 273.
10. M. Manindra Singh (Ed.) (1993). *Souvenir*, Golden Jubilee Celebration of Azad Hind Government, Imphal, p. 44.
11. M. Jugindro Singh (December 11-12, 2018). *Was Not He Right,* a National Seminar organised by Asiatic Society, Kolkata on the occasion of 75th Anniversary of INA and Provisional Government of Azad Hind, Kolkata, pp. 2-3.
12. M. Manindra Singh (Ed.) (1972). *Souvenir*, 75th Birth Day Celebration of Netaji Subhas Bose, Imphal, p. 46 ff. *See* M. Manindra Singh, *The Synthesizing Role of the INA Martyrs' Memorial, Moirang and The Indo-Japanese Peace Cenotaph, Lotpaching (Red Hill)*, pp. 26-30.
13. *See* M. Koireng Singh (1985). *Contribution of the Manipuris in the INA Movement*, a National Seminar paper on Netaji and INA, Moirang, 1985, p. 45. Also *See* M. Manindra Singh (Ed.) (1972). *Souvenir*, 75th Birth Day Celebration of Netaji Subhas Bose, Imphal, p. 43ff.
14. Sugata Bose (2013). *His Majesty's Opponent*, Gurgaon, p. 271.
15. An interview with K. Achouba Singh, a local porter (during the war), Moirang, dated 29.03.200.
16. Hemam Nilamani Foundation (2017). *A Biography of Hemam Nilamani Singh, Freedom Fighter*, Moirang.
17. An interview with M. Nilakomol Singh, a neighbour of Ph. Tonjao Singh, Moirang, dated 04.05.2009.
18. Letter from I. Fujiwara, Fujiwara Asia Research Institute, Tokyo to T. Bijoy Singh, Secretary, Japanese Delegation Reception Committee, Moirang, Manipur, India, dated 25.02. 1975. *See* also letter from I. Fujiwara to Shri H. Nilamani Singh, Moirang dated 06.03.1973.
19. Kusum Nair (1946). *INA*, Bombay, p. 47.
20. *See* M. Koireng Singh (185). *Contribution of the Manipuris in the INA Movement*, a National Seminar paper on Netaji and INA, Moirang.
21. *See* P.K. Sahgal (1985). *INA, Victory in Defeat*, a National Seminar paper on Netaji and INA, Moirang.

22. N.G. Jog (1969). *In Freedom's Quest*, Poona, p. 281. *See* Y. Modhu Singh (1945). *The Red Fort Trial*, Published in Souvenir, Platinum Jubilee Celebration of Provisional Government of Azad Hind, Imphal, 2018.
23. Daya Mukherji (Ed.) (1997). *Subhas Chandra Bose: Accelerator of India's Independence*, New Delhi, p. 88.
24. N.G. Jog (1969). *In Freedom's Quest*, Poona, p. 284.

5

Indian National Army/Azad Hind Fauj (INA) in Imphal Campaign

Shukhdeba Sharma Hanjabam

Imphal Campaign: Delhi Chalo *versus* Defence of Burma

The strategic aims of the Japanese and Netaji were quite different. Japan saw the Imphal Campaign as a pre-emptive strike to reconquer Burma, and Netaji conceptualised its role as a catalyst for a civilian uprising against British rule.[1] Field Marshall Count Terauchi, Commander of the Southern Army, emphasizes propaganda as the primary purpose of Japan's co-operation with the INA.[2] The Imphal Campaign for the INA was an all-out struggle for Indian liberation.[3] Netaji's desire to take Chittagong first, then push on into Bengal, was shared during the discussion with Army Chief of Staff Sugiyama in Tokyo,[4] Netaji felt Japan and INA should have immediately attacked Chittagong to help the anti-British revolution in Bengal, which would spread rapidly all over India.[5] In this context, the Imphal Campaign was conceptualized; thus, we witnessed differences in strategies between the Netaji and Japanese authorities.

The Provisional Government resolved to declare war against Anglo-American allies at the second cabinet meeting held at midnight on 22/23 October, 1943. On the evening of 23 October, Netaji announced the Cabinet's decision at a public rally in Singapore. Netaji, recalling his statement that "the first drop of bloodshed on Indian soil must be that of a soldier of the INA" during his discussion with Field Marshall Count Terauchi, Commander of the Southern Army, in August 1943, started preparing the INA for its first assignment in the Imphal Campaign. The Imphal Campaign commenced on 8 March, 1944.[6]

On 7 January, 1944, Netaji transferred the essential departments of the Provisional Government to Rangoon, and on 25 January, 1944, the Supreme Command of the Azad Hind Fauj was also shifted to Rangoon.[7] Headquarters was located at a bungalow of Zeyewadi Sugar Factory Office No. 09. Netaji was settled west of the Shwe Dagon Pagoda in a house left vacant when its occupant, a retired Indian Medical Officer, evacuated to India. Rani of the Jhansi Regiment occupied a two-story bungalow in a large compound at Thingangyone. Zeyawadi is a place near Toungoo, about 150 miles north of Rangoon.[8]

Advance parties of troops had arrived and were located in parts of the barrack at Mingaladon airfield, about sixteen miles from Rangoon. Some of the contingents, such as the Bahadur Group and the Intelligence Branch, were located in different parts of Rangoon city. The Quartermaster-General's Branch was put under Lt. Col. Timaya. A large Ordinance Base was established in Rangoon, where all the Army required equipments were collected and stored and then distributed to the different units and formations as needed. The General Staff Branch was also organized and put in charge of Lt. Col. Habibur Rahman. It collects all information and intelligence from contacts established in the front and India. A large Base Hospital was established in Myang, about eight miles from Rangoon.[9] The Advance Headquarters of the Provisional Government, Azad Hind Fauj and Azad Hind Dal, was established at Maymyo on 7th May, 1944, as the Imphal campaign progressed.[10]

Netaji stated in the radio speech that the INA fought on eight sectors along a frontier stretching 800 miles, from Arakan in the south through Hukong and Chin Hills right up to Kohima and the plains of Imphal in the north.[11] The Imphal Campaign was initially actively engaged by a small team of Bahadur and Intelligence groups in Arakan, Bishnupur, and Kohima. The team was supported by the INA 01 Division comprising (i) Subhas Brigade, (ii) Gandhi Brigade, and (iii) Azad Brigade. Nehru Brigade—part of the No. 1 Division, could not participate in the Imphal Campaign. The Rani of Jhansi Regiment was also not directly involved in the Imphal campaign. However, it is worth mentioning that the Rani Jhansi Regiment, particularly the nursing section, tremendously helps the soldiers in challenging health scenarios, particularly at their base hospitals at Monywa, Maymyo, and Mandalay.[12]

Major General M.Z Kiani commanded the Division with its Headquarters at Chamol, Manipur. The Regiment Headquarters of the Subhas Brigade was at Myitha Haka (Nauchawang)—presently in Chin State, and the Regimental Headquarters of the Gandhi Brigade was at Khanjol, Manipur. The Regimental Headquarters of the Azad Brigade was at Narun—north of Moreh, Manipur.[13]

> 18th March, 1944 was the proudest day for INA as it was on this memorable day that INA crossed over India. Netaji announced the historic event to the world through a press conference on 21st March, 1944.[14]

Bahadur and Intelligence Groups

The Bahadur and Intelligence groups of 8-10 soldiers attached to the Japanese forces were already deployed at the battlefront before the deployment of the Subhas, Gandhi, and Azad Brigades. The groups successfully engaged on the battlefront and helped collect information, interrogate captured POWs, and do propaganda work among the British Indian Army. These groups were distributed under various sectors[15] as:

(i) Arakan Sector was commanded by Shaheed Colonel Misra and Major Mehar Das,

(ii) Bishnupur Sector was commanded by Colonel S.A. Malik, and

(iii) Kohima Sector was commanded by Shaheed Major Maghar Singh and Shaheed Major Ajmere Singh.

Arakan Sector

On 9th February, 1944, the INA fired the first shot in Arakan. That was the proudest day for Netaji Bose.[16] In a Special Order of the Day, issued by Netaji[17] on 9th February, 1944[18] the battle of Arakan was mentioned. Lt. Col. Misra commanded the Bahadur Group, and Major Mehar Das was the second in Command. The Special Order of the Day reads as

> "The eyes of the whole world are focused on the Arakan front, where events of far-reaching consequences are taking place today. The glorious and brilliant actions of the brave units of the Azad Hind Fauj, working in close concert with the forces of the Imperial Nippon Army, have helped to foil all attempts by the Anglo-American forces to start a counter-offensive in this sector."
>
> "I am sure that the brave deeds of our comrades on the Arakan front will be a great inspiration to all officers and men of the Azad Hind Fauj, wherever they may be stationed at the present moment."

Subhas Brigade

Netaji, after many discussions, convinced General Kawabe, Japanese Commander-in-Chief in Burma, on 7th January, 1944, and General Katakura, Chief of the General Staff, Commander-in-Chief in Burma, for an independent role of INA in the Imphal Campaign. A new guerrilla regiment (Subhas Regiment) was raised in September at Taiping, consisting of the best soldiers from the three regiments of the No. 1 Division. Lt. Col. Shah Nawaz Khan was appointed as its Commander.[19]

After their training, the Subhas Brigade (No. 1 Regiment of 01 Division) moved to Rangoon from Taiping by rail, road, and water routes from 9th November, 1943 to 24th November, 1943. The regiment has 3200[20] soldiers. The main body of the regiment arrived in Rangoon in early January 1944. The regiment was put up in military barracks at Mingladone. During the movement from Taiping to Rangoon, Sepoy Jit Singh—A Gharwali died of an air attack by the British forces. He was the first martyr/Saheed of the Regiment.[21] On 27th February, 1944, Lt. Col. Shah Nawaz Khan received the order, and by 4th March, 1944, the respective battalions moved to the front from Rangoon. Netaji, during his speech on 3rd March, 1944, before the troops departed to the front, stated,

> "You are the strength of my arms, the force with which I shall be able to protect rights, and everything depends on what you achieve on the battlefront."

Haka-Falam Sector, Chin Hill

The independent assignment allotted to the Subhas Brigade was reported to test the battle worthy of the INA. The sector assigned to the Brigade was the most challenging sector to hold, mainly because of the terrain and not so much from the enemy position. Haka-Falam is a mountainous area. Falam is situated at 6000 feet and Haka at 7000 feet.[22] It was reported that a significant part of the regiment had little to do with fighting. The soldiers were engaged in carrying rations and building roads. The Commander reported to Netaji, "it is very pained to report to Your Excellency that the very high spirit and enthusiasm of my soldiers are gradually changing into disappointments." The Commander reported that of the ten companies of the 2 and 3 Battalions, seven companies were engaged in broadening road and carrying rations.[23]

The task allotted to the Subhas Brigade (No. 1 Regiment of 01 Division) commanded by Lt. Col. Shah Nawaz Khan was:

(i) to prevent the Lushai Brigade and Aijal Brigade of the British and allied forces from advancing on Kalewa and thereby threatening the main supply, and (ii) to carry out offensive operations on the Haka-Falam fronts in the direction of Lungleh. Japanese authorities assured that, once the Japanese forces started the main offensive, they would be given an opportunity to lead the advance into India.[24]

Commander Shah Nawaz Khan established his regimental Headquarters at Myitha Haka (Nauchawang) on 24th February, 1944 and took over the charge of the defence of Falam on the next day and of Haka on 3rd April from the Japanese. They have successfully patrolled the areas around Falam, and in March, the third Battalion was called upon from Kalewa to take part in action against Tiddim. In May, a part of the 2nd Battalion raided the British patrol base at Klang, about 25 miles west of Haka.[25] The successes of the Subhas brigade in the Haka and Falam in the Chin areas and the Kaladan Valley, supplemented by the Bahadur group in the Arakan sector, resulted in the retreat of the British and allied forces. On 11th April, 1944, the British withdrew towards Bishnupur.[26] The advancing Japanese 33 division and INA forces led by Col. S.A. Malik along the Tiddim sector hoisted the national tri-colour flag at Moirang on 14th April, 1944. They established the INA Provisional Headquarters at Moirang.

INA Hq, 1944 at Moirang

INA HQ (under renovation)

Flag Hoisting at Moirang

On 14th April, 1944, INA troops led by Col. S.A. Malik and Captain Ito of the Japanese 33 Mountain Gun regiment arrived at Moirang. They hoisted the national tri-colour flag of INA at the historic Moirang Kangla.[27]

Place of Flag Hoisting on 14th April, 1944, Moirang

INA established its Headquarters at Moirang for three months (14 April, 1944 to 15 July, 1944) till the retreat at the residence of Shri Hemam Nilamani.

The People of Manipur extended full support to the INA Provisional Government with information, rations, cash, kinds, and other items required by the Headquarters.

Kohima Sector

Subhas Brigade was ordered to move to the Kohima sector on 12th May, 1944 to support the Japanese 31 Division, which was on the verge of retreating as they could no longer sustain themselves.[28] The Bahadur and Intellectual groups commanded by Shaheed Major Maghar Singh and Shaheed Major Ajmere Singh were already fighting in the front along with the Japanese Division.[29] Col. Shah Nawaz Khan started marching for Kohima on 14th May, 1944. The order reads,

> "That the main body of the Brigade would proceed to Kohima and would be preferred, on that fall of Imphal, to advance rapidly and cross the Brahmaputra into the heart of Bengal."

However, the responsibility of the Subhas Brigade was still to hold and defend the Haka-Falam front. So, 150 soldiers at Haka and 300 at Falam continue to defend the position. The unit travelled through Myitha Haka-Tamu-Humine-Ukhrul-Kharasom, and Kohima.[30] With their continuous reinforcement, the British forces attacked more vigorously and recaptured Kohima.

The Japanese Division started retreating by the night of 30th May, 1944[31] and by 4th June, 1944, Commander Shah Nawaz Khan met Commander General Sato, which ordered him to withdraw from Kohima to Ukhrul.[32] The Japanese 31 Division was falling back from Kohima to reinforce the Japanese 15 Division when the INA regiment reached Ukhrul.[33] Similarly, the Shah Nawaz Khan Regiment reached south of Kohima by early June. When they arrived, the regiment had to retrace its tortuous steps back through the mountain trails. The only condition for the men was that they had seen Assam and stood on Indian soil.[34] The INA and Japanese forces have been retreating since then towards Burma.

Gandhi Brigade: *Tamu-Pallel Sector*

Gandhi Brigade, consisting of 2800[35] men were commanded by Col. I.Z Kiani. The Brigade reached the front in April 1944 and was assigned an independent sector west of the Tamu-Pallel road to carry out guerrilla activities on the Tamu front and the airfield at Palel. The Brigade hurriedly reached the battlefront without their heavy military equipment from Kalewa due to the miscommunication that Imphal was falling anytime. However, the Brigade is facing a powerful enemy supported by artillery and air support, with one Division holding this front with one Brigade to the east of the road (strongest around Leimatol Hill), one Brigade to the west of the road (strongest around Yapu bridge) and one Brigade (around Palel Airfield).[36]

The biggest strike of the Gandhi Brigade was the attack on Palel airfield. Commander Major Pritam Singh, along with around 300, attacked on 2nd May, 1944[37] with only light automatics and rifles and carrying only one day ration. When they could no longer hold the airfield, they destroyed the enemy planes parked in the airfield. But after the heavy engagement, the Gandhi Brigade suffered heavy casualties and lost approximately 250 men.[38] Besides the attack on the airfield, the defence of the Regimental Headquarters at Khanjol was one of the greatest operations by the Gandhi Brigade. The British and Allied forces, particularly the Scottish soldiers of the Sea Forth Highlanders, attacked with air and artillery support. With the general withdrawal, 17 officers out of 94 and 250 jawans out of 300 soldiers of the Gandhi Brigade managed to reach Mandalay, all being in shattered health.[39]

Azad Brigade: *Tamu Palel Sector*

Azad Brigade of 01 Division, consisting of 2800[40] men were commanded by Col. Gulzara Singh. The task of the Azad Brigade was to carry out an intensive guerrilla activity against the British forces around Palel. The area of operations allotted to them was east of the Tamu Pallel road. The Brigade Headquarters was at Mintha. However, they could not be engaged in the large-scale offensive as they withdrew from the Order of the Divisional Commander. The Azad Brigade withdrew to Kalewa *via* the main Kalewa-Tamu road at the same time as the Gandhi Brigade.[41]

Netaji Subhas Chandra Bose in North East India

There are many instances where Netaji's presence was at Imphal and Kohima, where the greatest world war was fought. However, we need further research to ascertain the references and the claims. Some of the situations or references are listed:

> On 16th April, 1944, Netaji wrote to Brahmachari Kailasam of Ramakrishna Mission in Singapore "before crossing the frontier" that things were going "very well at the fronts". Netaji concluded the letter by stating, "We will be meeting them in free India." Sujata Bose noted that once he did so, he was unsure when he would be able to communicate with Kailasam again. Besides, the INA's soldiers, personnel belonging to the Reconstruction Department from Singapore and Rangoon, had gone forward.[42] Around this time, Col. S.A. Malik hoisted the Tri-colour flag at Moirang on 14th April, 1944 and established the advanced INA Headquarters at Moirang.

Moreh, Tengnoupal District, Manipur

In an article, "Netaji's last visit to India," published in the "*Sun*" Magazine of May[43]1989, it was reported that Netaji stayed a night at Moreh in 1944. The statement was given by Seva Singh Undi, who hailed from the southern Shan State of Burma and has remained at Moreh since 1973. He said he met Netaji for the first time in October 1944 when Netaji came to lecture at Maymyo near Mandalay to about 300 young INA recruits. Seva Singh Undi was a new recruit who joined the INA in September 1943 and acted as an interpreter for both Japanese and INA at Moreh. He further stated that Netaji came to Moreh to encourage the freedom fighters stationed on the frontline. General Mohan Singh, General Dhillon, Sheel Badra Yajee, MP, M. Koireng Singh, President of INA Martyrs Memorial Committee, and other freedom fighters came to Moreh in 1968 to locate the place where Netaji stayed but remained unsuccessful. Again, in 1972, another Central team led by Sheel Badra Yajee visited Moreh but failed to find the place.

The article further reported that Seva Singh Undi visited Dalip Singh Kapoor at his residence in October 1987 and narrated his association with Netaji. Undi was later introduced to General Dhillon, Sheel Bhadra Yajee, and Captain Yadav at INA Headquarters in January 1988 and decided to erect the Netaji statue at Moreh. They also fixed the unveiling ceremony for 21st October, 1989. But the activities remain inactive.

Saikot Village, Churachandpur District, Manipur

Kawlvelthang, then Chief of Saikot village, Churachandpur District of Manipur in the Indo-Myanmar Border, touching the Chin State of Myanmar, claimed that Netaji Subhas Chandra Bose came to Khuga Valley in Churachandpur District, Manipur. Professor Laldena, in the article "Indo-Japanese Soldiers in the Khuga Valley of Churachandpur, April to August 1944," stated that it might not be possible for Netaji to visit Churachandpur when they were on the retreat.[44] There have been no further significant claims after the article by Professor Laldena.

Ukhrul District, Manipur

Y.A. Shishak, an 84-year-old INA veteran from Ukhrul, proudly claimed that he has the INA's Tiger Springing Flag, which was "hoisted for the first time in liberated India by Netaji".[45]

Phek District, Nagaland

A book titled "Discovery of Netaji Subhas Chandra Bose: *Delhi Chalo Last Camp in Nagaland*" written by Vekho Swuro, published by Netaji Memorial Development Society, Nagaland, Kohima, claims that Netaji not only visited the state but stayed there for over two months (April-May) in 1944.[46] However, Historical records show otherwise, and many[47] from Nagaland also questioned the authenticity of the report. INA-related sources written by INA veterans and others show that only a small team of Bahadur and Intelligence group took an active part in the Kohima sector, along with the Japanese 31 Division. The Subhas Brigade, led by Shah Nawaz Khan, could not be involved in the Kohima sector as the Japanese Division, Bahadur, and Intelligence groups were retreating when they reached Ukhrul and Kohima.

Way Forward

The battle fought by INA in the Imphal Campaign is now completing 80 years. They remain unsung heroes and are not yet adequately appreciated and acknowledged. The INA heroes who fought in these battles and the battle sites are yet to be documented and investigated appropriately. The INA Martyrs and Museum Complex at Moirang is the only INA-related site that stands today. But the condition of the complex and the museum needs improvement in terms of Infrastructure and materials. Taking over the advanced INA headquarters by the Government of Manipur in 2021 was another new development related to INA. But developing the Heritage building seems to have been done mainly from the tourism perspective. It is suggested that an expert team redevelop the heritage building (INA HQ) so that it could reflect the stories of those days.

The British and Allied Forces and the Japanese have built memorial sites and even museums in Manipur. Unfortunately, there is no memorial site for INA soldiers where INA veterans, families, friends, students, and youth could offer prayers to these brave soldiers and recall their sacrifice for their motherland. The celebration of 75 years of Independence will be incomplete without acknowledging the contribution of the INA, who fought for Indian Independence in the Imphal Campaign.

Dedication

The paper is dedicated to Late Dr. Aheibam Koireng Singh (1977-2022), a close associate and my mentor-*cum*-brother. We hope to continue his legacy of addressing historical and contemporary issues through academic engagements.

NOTES

1. Bose, Sugata (2011). *His Majesty's Opponent: Subhas Chandra Bose and India's Struggle Against Empire*, Havard University Press, London, p. 266.
2. Lebra Joycee Chapman (1971, 2008). *The INA and Japan*, Institute of Southeast Asian Studies, Singapore, pp. 122 & 139.
3. *Ibid.*, p. 139.
4. *Ibid.*, p. 115.
5. *Ibid.*, p. 143.
6. Bose, Sugata (2011). *His Majesty's Opponent: Subhas Chandra Bose and India's Struggle Against Empire*, Havard University Press, London, p. 271.
7. Ghosh, K.K. (1969). *The Indian National Army, Second Front of the Indian Independence Movement*, Meenakshi Prakashan, Meerut, p. 170.
8. Fay Peter Ward (1995). *The Forgotten Army: India's Armed Struggle for Independence 1942-1945*, The University of Michigan Press; Reprint edition.
9. Chatterji, A.C. (1947). *India's Struggle for Freedom*, Chuckerverty, Chatterjee & Co. Ltd., Calcutta, pp. 163-65.
10. *Ibid.*, pp. 191-92.
11. Maw, B.A. (1968). *Breaking Through in Burma: Memoirs of a Revolution, 1939-1946*, Yale University Press, New Haven, p. 352.
12. Chatterji, A.C. *op. cit.*, p. 233.
13. Bose, Sugata (2011). *His Majesty's Opponent: Subhas Chandra Bose and India's Struggle Against Empire*, Havard University Press, London, p. 277.

14. Ayer, S.A. (1972 reprint 2019). *Story of INA*, National Book Trust, New Delhi, p. 57.
15. Khan, Shah Nawaz (1946). *My Memories of INA & Its Netaji*, Rajkamal Publications, New Delhi, pp. 78-79.
16. Maw, B.A. (1968). *Breaking Through in Burma: Memoirs of a Revolution, 1939-1946*, Yale University Press, New Haven, p. 352.
17. Plata, K.R. (1946). *My Adventure with the INA*, Lion Press, Lahore. pp. 122-23.
18. Bhardwaj, R.C. (1994). *Netaji and the INA*, Lok Sabha Secretariat, New Delhi, p. 106.
19. Ghosh, K.K. (1969). *The Indian National Army, Second Front of the Indian Independence Movement*, Meenakshi Prakashan, Meerut, p. 152.
20. Gaini Kesar Singh (1947). *Indian Independence Movement in East Asia, Singh Brothers*, Amarpali, Lahore, p. 115.
21. Khan, Shah Nawaz, *op. cit.*, p. 70.
22. *Ibid.*, pp. 88-89.
23. Ghosh, K.K., *op. cit.*, pp. 184-85.
24. Khan, Shah Nawaz, *op. cit.*, p. 86.
25. Ghosh, K.K., *op. cit.*, p. 176.
26. Singh, Laiphrakpam Nishikanta (2021). *Three Months of Provisional INA Government in Manipur and Contributions of Local Population*, Intellectual Forum of North East, Imphal, p. 144.
27. *Ibid.*, pp. 144-45.
28. *Ibid.*, p. 149.
29. Chatterji, A.C., *op. cit.*, p. 180.
30. Khan, Shah Nawaz, *op. cit.*, p. 100.
31. Singh, Laiphrakpam Nishikanta, *op. cit.*, p. 150.
32. *Ibid.*, p. 101.
33. Ghosh, K.K., *op. cit.*, p. 185.
34. Lebra Joycee Chapman (1971, 2008). *The INA and Japan*, Institute of Southeast Asian Studies, Singapore, p. 177.
35. Gaini Kesar Singh *op. cit.*, p. 115.
36. Khan, Shah Nawaz, *op. cit.*, pp. 112-13.
37. Bose Sugata, *op. cit.*, p. 276.
38. Khan, Shah Nawaz, *op. cit.*, pp. 115-16.
39. Singh, Rajeshwor Yumnam (2021). *INA's Honour at the Battle of Imphal and Its catalyzing Impetus to India's Independence*, Intellectual Forum of North East, Imphal, p. 210.
40. Gaini Kesar Singh, *op. cit.*, p. 115.

41. Khan, Shah Nawaz, *op. cit.*, p. 122.
42. Bose Sugata, *op. cit.*, pp. 274-75.
43. Kongbam Meghachandra (1989). "Netaji's last visit to India", *Weekly Sun, Magazine*, 13 May.
44. Lal, Dena (2014). *Indo-Japanese Soldiers in the Khuga Valley of Churachandpur*, April to August 1944, Hueiyen Lanpao (English edn.), 28 March.
45. Jayakrishnan (2018). *This forgotten war hero of Subhas Chandra Bose's INA lives to tell the tale*, / TNN / 26 January 2018, https://timesofindia.indiatimes.com/city/hyderabad/this-forgotten-war-hero-of-Subhas-chandra-boses-ina-lives-to-tell-the-tale/articleshow/62653376.cms
46. Nishit Dholabhai (2004). *Nagaland claims place in Netaji story*—Book claims INA chief was based in Phek during Battle of Kohima, December, 09. https://www.telegraphindia.com/north-east/nagaland-claims-place-in-netaji-story-book-claims-ina-chief-was-based-in-phek-during-battle-of-kohima/cid/697155
47. *Open Letter to Governor on Netaji and Naga Hills* (WWII) https://www.nagalandpost.com/index.php/open-letter-to-governor-on-netaji-and-naga-hills-wwii/

6

Footprints of Our Noble Sons in the World Turning Event

A Remembrance

Priyadarshni Maisnam G.

Introduction

Popularly called Netaji, Subhas Chandra Bose, stands aloft among the many freedom fighters that India has produced. His contribution and character is unique. He provided the leadership when it was most needed. He gave a definite direction, the internal input, which invigorated the freedom struggle movement and intimidated the British Administration. Netaji was of the firm belief that the British could only be thrown out by force.[1] He had no constitutional means and peaceful methods for the attainment of freedom. He disagreed with Gandhiji's method of struggling for freedom. He thought that India under Gandhiji's Principle will not attain freedom and never achieve at all. He could not rely on Gandhiji on this. While working as an active protagonist of the Congress, he along with Nehru had formed the Forward Block.

Relating to this matter, Bhattacharya[2] has stated that in 1921, Subhas Chandra Bose returned to India from England after resigning from a promising career. On resigning from the Indian Civil Service, he dedicated himself for the cause of India's freedom with his heart and soul, under the leadership and guidance of Chittaranjan Das. The politics of C.R. Das was the mature expression of that political idealism still nebulous in young Bose's mind. C.R. Das' dedication to *Swaraj* or self-governance was unambiguous and categoral. No wonder Subhas felt he had found his leader and decided to undergo his political training with him.[3]

Rise of the revolutionary struggle for freedom started by Gandhiji in 1920, developed the middle class group who were led first by C.R. Das and later on by Subhas Bose. After the incident of Chauri Chaura (5th February, 1922), the socio-political condition was completely changed particularly in Bengal because some of the earliest settlers in Calcutta had amassed wealth and property during the John Company's days and dominated the Calcutta Society for nearly a century because of their financial power.[4] Since his entry into politics, his personality made him so popular and, of course, had taken the role of leader who inspired the well to do tycoons, edging their way slowly to the Congress platforms in order to ensure their earthly possession which had been acquired by being loyal to the British.

Regarding his anti-imperialist struggle and *Sansyavada*, Netaji engaged in a non-existent war with the British Government for the attainment of our political freedom.[5] Subhas categorily rejected all the constitutional measures initiated by Gandhiji and introduced two paths for easily attaining goal: "uncompromising military and compromise". He further suggested to face a major imperialist nation like Britain is not an easy task. So, he wanted the supply of necessary resources depends on our ability to keep up the enthusiasm of the people and maintain the spirit of opposition towards the government.

Moreover, Ghose and Dhar[6] have maintained:

> Subhas' outburst against Gandhi's and Aurobindo during the Calcutta Youth Congress Conference in 1928 is often presented in defence of the contention

> that he could never take Sanyas. The essence of his criticism was indeed in line outlook towards life, but presenting them without any reference to the context grossly distorts this incident. It was a time when Chittaranjan Das' death had left a huge vacuum in the political scope of Bengal and the Gandhian wing led by Gandhi himself dominated Bengal Congress.

As an instance, Subhas opposed Gandhiji's resolution on Dominion Status at Calcutta Congress in 1928. Along with that, he also pointed that the Round Table Conference was a misnomer. He gave reasons to it, "a handful of non-descript Indian nominated by the alien Government would be representing to do with the bidding of the British politicians." This had irritated Gandhiji and Nehru. Subhas' never fell in line of sycophants of the British. He believed in his deeds and words. He vehemently rejected the Delhi Pact better known in history as the Gandhiji-Irwin Pact (March 1931) and he out-rightly declared as a painful document and called to "Strike when the iron is hot".[7]

The long rule of India under the British, ultimately made India weaker and that developed inferiority complex which continued till India got freedom. It is obviously true that India witnessed stiff hardship till she achieved Independence. Subhas had foreseen the future. The social, economic and political forces working in unision within India were never possible. It rather contradicts with the British till her legitimate aspirations were fulfilled. Thus to defeat the British was to win freedom for India. In the course of the freedom struggle of India, the role played by Subhas was significant. His quality was unique as is described by his biographer, N.G. Jog:

> "Bose became the man of the hour ... if, by some miracle he had returned to India, he would have carried everything before him as Napoleon did after his escape from Elba."[8]

This is the truth of which Mahatma and Nehru and the Congress were afraid.

Several factors were responsible for winning our freedom from the British clutches. Though, the Indian National Congress Party acted as the centrifugal force, there were many parties like Indian League, Muslim League, Communist Party, the Liberal Federation, Swarajya Party, Forward Bloc, India Independence League under Rash Behari Bose and individuals whose name never appeared in history, who had struggled hard for Indian Independence. Indeed, perhaps the violent ways of Subhas had also contributed a lot for the same. His charismatic leadership had influenced thousands of people which led the birth of Azad Hind Fauz (INA)—one major force fighting for India against the British. Before the Madras Congress Session in 1927 Subhas supported Nehru for an ultimate objective to gain Purna Swaraj or complete independence for India.[9]

Subhas made an escape from India, on January 16-17, 1941 he slipped out of his home at Elgin Road, Calcutta in disguise in the midst a few dozen CID personnel posted onward, reached Delhi in the evening of 18 January, 1941 boarded the train for Peshawar[10] through Afghanistan and reached Germany on April 3, 1941. He was no stranger to Germany for he had spent time and time again in Europe during 1934-1937 though mostly in Germany, he went to Italy where he met Mussolini several times and to Austria, also. How much Subhas Chandra Bose loved India can easily be seen from his actions to the cause of India that can be confirmed by Govind Talwalkar's article "Among the Nazis".

> "He was shocked by the cases of maltreatment of Indian students in Germany and Goering's attack on Gandhiji. Subhas even wrote to Dr. A. Franz Theirfelder, Secretary General of the Indian Institute in Munich condemning the attitude of Nazis and demanding an apology from Hitler for his speech and Goering's attack on Gandhiji."[11]

It is to be noted that during his earlier visits and stays in Germany, he could not meet Hitler personally despite his several attempts but on 27th May, 1942, was able to meet the top brass of

Germany. Furthermore, Subhas had asked Hitler to clarify passages in Mein Kampf (a book which gave a very inaccurate account of his own life and set out his beliefs)[12] which were insulting to India Hitler explained that they were mainly aimed at discouraging the pacifist tendencies in Germany which might have been further influenced by the Indian movement.[13] In fact, Hitler had discouraged the non-violent path followed by Indian freedom fighters for two reasons.[14] Firstly, the weapon Ahimsa went against Nazism and, secondly, he admired the British imperial policy, because Hitler, had helped to copy the same after conquering Russia.

Ultimately, Subhas Chandra Bose reached Japan, Hikadi Tojo, the then Prime Minister welcomed and promised him to support in his mission.[15] When the Japanese conquered the Malay Peninsula; a large number of Indian soldiers felt prisoners into their hands. Under an agreement with the Japanese Government, Bose, now called Netaji (Leader) organized them into an Azad Hind Fauz or Indian National Army.[16] It will be interesting to know in details how the INA worked under Subhas Bose as maintained by Harvani:[17]

> "Bose became the Supreme Commander of the INA, but did not take a military rank. He gave up the civilian class he had worn in Europe and usually military uniform. After the crisis of late 1942, the number in the INA had fallen to about 12,000. Another 10,000 or so were recruited from amongst the prisoners by what, the British called 'the demagogic oratory of S.C. Bose, and during 1943-1945 about 18,000 different figures have been given for the total, most seem to be in the 40,000 range. Bose wanted three divisions and at least 50,000 men. The Japanese sanctioned the first three divisions. Without heavy artillery or air power, and confined mainly to small arms these men were prepared for guerilla warfare. Senior officers of the INA were recruiting and training the civilians who helped to man the other two divisions which were eventually sanctioned. There were training centres in Malaya and

> Burma. The forces of the INA were given spiritual or more accurately political training. British intelligence believed that this political emphasis was given to the detriment of ordinary military training."

He inaugurated the Government of Free India at Singapore at Cathay Cinema amidst splendour and society. On October 21, 1943, which is red letter day not only in the life of Subhas but also in the history of India's Independence Movement, the Provincial Government formed was immediately recognized by the World's nine countries including the three World Powers—Japan, Germany and Italy. At midnight on October 23, the Government declared war on Britain to effect liberation from their dominion. Earlier, the Indian National Army which had been formed by Rash Behari Bose and Captain Mohon Singh and others, was reorganized and revitalized after he took over the leadership (4 July, 1943).

The INA Headquarters was shifted to Rangoon in January 1944.[18] Subhas Chandra Bose motivated the Indian National Army with famous call "Give me blood and I shall give you freedom". The INA reached the Arankan Front on 4 February, 1944 and marched towards their Motherland with the clarion call of "Chalo Delhi" on their lips (*ibid.*).[19] The Azad Hind Fauz crossed the Burma border on 18 March and for the first time, stood on the soil of India.[20] Another significant area initiated by him was the involvement of Indian women in actual military action. Back in 1928, Subhas had been instrumental in raising under the leadership of "Colonel" Latika Ghosh a Congress Woman's Volunteer Corps that had marched on the streets of Calcutta in full uniform.[21] When in 1943 he raised the expatriate INA in South East Asia, he decided to add a women's regiment, which he called the Rani of Jhansi Regiment, named after Rani Lakshmibai, the legendary leader of the Revolt of 1857.[22] Thus, it was started with the 20 women[23] maintained by Col. Dr. Lakshmi Swaminadhan Sahgal[24] the Commander. In fact, she was the organizer and captain of the Regiment.[25] Under Bose's able leadership and strategy the INA marched victoriously to Indian borders and hoisted its tri-colour flag at Moirang, where a monument stands now in his name to honour his supreme sacrifice for the country. Thus the Japanese army and the INA attempted to march to Delhi through Burma, Manipur, the Naga Hills and Assam, where they got stuck with distraught of their ambition when forced into great battlefields of Imphal, Kohima, Bishnupur, Kakching, Pallel, Moreh, Tamu etc. in which thousands got killed while many other perished through hunger and diseases in the jungles, villages and roadsides.[26] In this connection, Joykumar[27] is in the opinion, "During the historic venture of the INA coincided with the transitional political environment the people of Manipur had contributed their services along with some historical personalities as a representative of the state to the best of their capacity by extending their hands for the success of the noble cause."

It is imperative to elaborate how Manipur became a Warfield during Second World War. It was the first ever fierce battle fought between the British and the Japanese forces on the soil of Manipur.[28] On 10 and 16 May, 1942 Imphal, the capital city of Manipur had already been bombed by the Japanese as their first raid.[29] Thousands of Indian refugees were fleeing from Burma through Manipur. And, Imphal became the forward base of the new forces built up by the Allied Forces.[30] The Fourteenth Army under the Command of Lieutenant General William Shim, subordinated by the Indian IV Corps. Commanded Lieutenant General Geoffrey.[31] The intelligentsia including the Nikhil Manipuri Mahasabha—a political organisation had been waiting for the impending changes in the emerging political and military scenario of the world. As had been said by Netaji, "The enemy of the British is the friend of India". Germany, Italy and Japan though they were branded as fascist, all the leaders and workers of the Mahasabha regarded them as friends contended by Koireng.[32]

Moreover, the Nikhil Manipuri Mahasabha had identical ideas and objectives with the Indian National Congress who welcomed the appeal made by Netaji. Thirteen members of the Sanmelan, who were in fact from Imphal and Nambol, namely[33] (1) Th. Angou Singh, (2) P. Tomal Singh, (3) S. Ibohal Singh,

(4) I. Tombi Singh, (5) L. Bijoy Singh, (6) L. Kanhai Singh, (7) M. Jatra Singh, (8) W. Gyaneswar Singh, (9) M. Amuba Singh, (10) L. Irabot Singh, (11) Kh. Jugeswar Singh, (12) Smt. O. Keinya Devi, and (13) Smt. K. Randhoni Devi reached Moirang secretly. They joined together with the members of Moirang and worked out their plans which can be seen by their actions. Naki Ahmed Choudhary, a resident of Keikhu, who also an erstwhile member of Nikhil Manipur Mahasabha, did campaigning for INA movement. He could convince some people including H. Nilamani Singh from Moirang.[34]

The INA along with the Japanese forces based in Burma, commanded by the Formidable Lieutenant General Renya Mutaguchi[35] reached Manipur on 18th March, 1944 by crossing the hill tracts of Indo-Burma border[36] the 15th Japanese Division with one INA regiment marched towards Tamu and Ukhrul in two ways. Henceforth, captured and liberated Sangshak, Ukhrul (24 March), Moreh (31 March) and Paletwa (Pallel) and Tengnoupal (20 April)[37], another group of division, however, further advanced towards Imphal-Dimapur road but they could not come down to the valley[38] and for that matter the British forces could also fortified valley to a great extent. Now, the combined forces of INA and 33rd Japanese Infantry under Lieutenant General Motoso Yanagida[39] Division advanced upto Kohima and Imphal towards Tiddim Road by capturing the 17th Division British Defence Base at Khuga Valley, Yaiyok (Zezo), Thingkaiphai, Churachandpur.[40] This was known as the operation U-Go which planned to isolate and capture Imphal, Kohima and proceed on to Brahmaputra Valley to cut off the whole Allied forces supplies route towards Northern Burma.

In this connection, it is relevant to mention that some 32 (thirty-two) Meetei who earned their livelihood in Burma joined the movement under the leadership of Shri L. Guno Singh of Khurai (Manipur)[41] and operated in the battle-front as an advance party. 13 out of the 32 Meeteis reached Pallel and tried to secure the secrets of enemy and also sought the support of local people. One of them was arrested at Sugnu.[42] The rest 19 (nineteen) marches down to Khuga Tampak now in Churachandpur District. Out of them, four members, namely M. Ahanjao Singh of Moirang, B. Bhallop Sharma, M. Chaoba Singh and S. Yaima Singh were arrested from Saikot and taken them to Calcutta to be released after the war.[43]

A large number of Manipuri tribals who were the erstwhile members of the British "V" Force also joined the movement and participated in the war front. When the call came from Netaji Subhas Chandra Bose, the Kukis also joined him and laid down their lives for the liberation of India[44] from alien rule as may be evidenced from the fact that there were the large number of Kukis in the whole of North East India who were in receipt of Tamra Patra, in recognition of their sacrifice as Freedom Fighters.[45] Henceforth, first one Kuki, named Lulngam Lhungdim even brought the message of Netaji from Chamol (INA Advance Base Camp) and handed it over to Dr. Gulapchand Singh, the then Medical officer posted at Sugnu, which re-handed over to Shri Thokchom Angou Singh of Singjamei, Imphal.[46] Secondly, Paikhomang Kuki of Shakok (now Sadar Hills) played a very important role in convincing Tongkhothang Chief of Chassad, the biggest Kuki chiefdom in Manipur, Assam, Nagaland and Burma.[47] Regarding this, Modhu has maintained that the chief performed the Kuki customery rites, Satin-Salung[48] and hampi-ha[49] in which 135 Kuki chiefs and 30 others attended.[50] They resolved to stand together fight collectively. Thus many Kukis enrolled themselves as porters, informers, messengers, civil suppliers, even fighters etc.[51] Then the British force began to retreat and took defensive measures at Phougwakchao—Ithai, Tronglaobi and Okshangkhong but it was of no avail.[52] Consequently they were forced to retreat from its surrounding areas to Phuballa, Ningthoukhong and then to Bishenpur[53]—Thus, Koireng[54] in his view—

> the withdrawal of the 17th British Division was completed on April 13, 1944. Before the retreat of the British from Tronglaobi which was their strong defence base till April 13, 1944. In the early morning of April 14, the leaders of the Indo-Japanese advance

> party had discussions with (1) M. Koireng Singh, (2) L. Sanaba Singh, (3) K. Kanglen Singh and (4) M. Mani Singh and others, all of Moirang at Tronglaobi Village. After taking stock of the situation, at about 5 p.m. on the same day, i.e. April 14, 1944 at about 5 pm by Col. Saukat Ali Malik, the Commander of the Bahadur (Intelligence) Group, hoisted the Tri-colour Flag with springing Tiger as emblem at the historic Moirang Kangla[55] where the INA Martyrs' Memorial Complex is, at present taking shape as a mark of liberation from the British yoke.

About 50 (fifty) locals including H. Nilamani attended the ceremony.[56] It was unfortunate that the Germany's defeat in the war in April and her surrender on 3rd May, 1945 as well as the dropping of atom bombs in Hiroshima (6th August, 1945) and Nagasaki (9th August, 1945), compelled Japan to surrender to the Allied forces in the middle of August 14, 1945, the INA at Rangoon also surrendered. The members from Manipur were also arrested by the Rangoon occupying Allied Forces from their hiding places through a tip for Manipuris and put in Rangoon Central Jail. It will be relevant to know that Manipuris who took part in the INA at Rangoon were in Guest Houses at Kandogulay, Rangoon. (1) L. Irabot Singh, (2) Kh. Jugeshwar Singh and (3) I. Tombi Singh joined the active services of the INA and the amazing was (1) Smt. O. Keinya Devi and (2) Smt. M. Randhoni Devi joined Jhansi Rani Regiment. The other members were attached to the Intelligence group of the INA.[57]

The INA surrenderees were refused POWs status by the British authorities and instead treated as deserters and traitors.[58] The INA engaged in the Imphal Front were brought to India earlier and some of the secret agents were caught and summarily shot.[59] Obviously, four from Moirang (Manipur), namely M. Koireng Singh, H. Nilamani Singh, K. Gopal Singh and L. Sanaba Singh were declared 'traitors' for their involvement in espionage works for the INA who established an Advance Headquarters at Moirang for a period from

April 14 to May 16, 1944. 'Shoot at-sight' orders was passed by the British on the four activists of Moirang.[60] However, despite set-backs Subhas did not lose hope, his aspirations to achieve independence was living. On the 25th April, 1945, a few days before the Japanese evacuated Rangoon, he flew out of the capital leaving behind a message in which he exhorted the Government and people of Burma for their help and hospitality, and stated, *inter alia*:

> "I am leaving Burma with a very heavy heart. We have lost only the first round. There are many more rounds to fight.... I have always said that the darkest hour precedes the dawn. We are now passing through the darkest hour; there the dawn is not far off; India shall be free."[61]

Whatever said and done, we assure that his total mobilization of the Indians in South East Asia for the cause of the country's liberation from British Rule, his achievement as President of the Indian Independence League and as Prime Minister and his foundation of the Indian National Army, its organisation in the foreign land, its programme for complete independence—all speak of his highest degree of capability during the Second World War. The great mission was executed in a grand manner and successes of the INA brought about a great damage to British interests in South East Asia.[62] Moreover, Rajaram[63] contended that "the Indian Armed Forces began to see themselves as defenders of India rather than of the British Empire. This, more than anything else, led to India's freedom." In this connection, it is pertinent to observe the contention of Chhabra:[64]

> "The public enthusiasm shown at the time of the INA trials the demonstrations of the Calcutta students on 19 November, 1945, who despite the police firings and lathi charge, could not be prevented from marching to the Dalhousie Square; the violent Mutiny of 3000 naval ratings on 19 February, the spread of this trouble to Karachi, Madras, Calcutta and Delhi and

> sympathetic hartals in the cities; all this showed that the fire of disaffection had spread from students to labourers, peasants, shopkeepers and now even to the common soldier without whose help the British could not stay on even for a day."

By War's end, Britain was ready to let India go.[65] Furthermore, Rajaram[66] justifiably maintained:

> "This is also the reason why the British Empire disappeared from the face of the earth within an astonishingly short space of twenty years. Indian soldiers, who were the main prop of the Empire, were no longer willing to fight for the British. What influences the British decision was mutiny on 18th February, 1946 of the Indian Navy following the INA trials in 1946. While the British wanted to try Subhas Bose's INA as traitor, Indian soldiers saw them as nationalists and patriots. This scared the British. They decided to get out in a hurry."

Moreover, Sharma[67] has contended that Netaji might have lost the war but won his countrymen's hearts. His heart rending 'Jay Hind' the INA logo has become the accepted form of greeting in the Indian Army, the political gentry and even the rural populace in post-1947 India.[68]

Knowing the historical facts, Rajaram[69] emphatically asserted and reaffirmed on the subject matter that great historian R.C. Majumdar wrote, "Subhas Bose with his INA campaigns probably contributed more to Indian Independence than Gandhiji, Nehru and their movements." Moreover, the result of Subhas Bose's activities was the rise of the nationalist spirit in the Indian Armed Forces. As a matter of fact the Quit India Movement launched in 1942 were not the last uprising against the British Rule in India, it was rather a part of the ongoing politics in India in which Subhas had played a pivotal role. Nothing can take away this credit from him at any point of time. Let us remember that Nations and

Governments need statesmen and men of substance not of charm and woolly idealism. Subhas Chandra Bose was one such radical personality of substance, faith and dynamism in our freedom struggle.

Conclusion

Thus, INA movement under the leadership of Subhas Chandra Bose was a collective effort against the mighty power. Many people, even from Manipur irrespective of their community fought heroically though it could not be shown as victor directly. Therefore, as a mark of respect and acknowledgement to their sacrificial and sincere contribution, people remember them by offering their homage to these Noble Sons.

NOTES

1. Priyadarshni M. Gangte's Paper "Netaji And National Freedom Movement", *The Sangai Express*—2nd-6th September, 2006 and *Imphal Free Press*, 20th-26th September, 2006.
2. Sishmita Bhattacharya (Ed.) (2011). *Purabi Roy's the Search for Netaji New Findings*, Purple Peacock Book and Arts Private Limited, Kolkata, 2011, p. 29.
3. *Ibid.*
4. B.K. Ahluwalia and Shashi Ahluwalia (1983). *Netaji and Indian Independence,* Harnam Publications, Delhi, p. 23.
5. Sisir K. Bose (Ed.)(1970). *Subhas Chandra Bose: Fundamental Questions of Indian Revolution*, p. 1.
6. Chandrachur Ghose and Anuj Dhar (2019). *Conundrum*, Vitasta Publishing Pvt. Ltd., p. 668.
7. J.B. Bhattacharjee (1977). *Cachar under the British Rule in North East India*, Radiant Publishers, New Delhi, p. 286.
8. Sisir K. Bose (1975). *Netaji And India's Freedom*, Netaji Research Bureau, Calcutta, p. VI.
9. Bipan Chandra (1972). *Amales Tripathi and Barun De: Freedom Struggle*, National Book Trust, Delhi, p. 150. B.K. Ahluwalia and Shashi Ahluwalia, *op. cit.*, p. 150.
10. Lok Sabha's Commorative on Netaji's on His 115th Birth Anniversary. Lok Sabha Secretaiat, 23rd January, 2012.
11. B.K. Ahluwalia, *op. cit.* p. 81.

12. Donald Lindsay (1978). *European History 1870-1960*, Oxford University Press, p. 192.
13. B.K. Ahluwalia, *op. cit.*
14. *Ibid.*
15. Lok Sabha, *op.cit.*
16. R.C. Mazumdar, H.C. Raychoudhury and K. Datta (1946). *An Advanced History of India*, Macmillan India Press, p. 978.
17. Ansari Harvani (1996). *Gandhi to Gandhi*, Gyan Publishing House, New Delhi, p. 200.
18. Lok Sabha, *op. cit.*
19. *Ibid.*
20. *Ibid.*
21. Sekhar Bandyopadhyay [2009, 2010 (Rep)]. *From Plassey to Partition, A History of Modern India*, Orient Blackswan Pvt. Ltd., New Delhi, p. 396.
22. *Ibid.*
23. *Souvenir: Golden Jubilee Celebration of the Azad Hind Government*, Edited and published by Mairembam Manindra Singh (1993), p. 36.
24. Col. Dr. Lakshmi Swaminadhan Sahgal's Paper "Reminiscences of My Days in the INA" presented on the occasion of 93rd Birth Anniversary of Netaji Subhas Chandra Bose held at Moirang, Manipur on 23rd January, 1990.
25. Mira Seth (2001). *Women and Development—The Indian Experience*, Sage Publication, Thousand Oaks, London, p. 46.
26. Manindra Singh Mairembam, "The Synthesizing Role of the INA. Martyrs' Memorial: Moirang; and the Indo-Japanese Peace Cenotaph: Lotpaching (Red Hills) in H. Dwijasekhar Sharma (Ed.) (2009). *New Insights Into The Glorious Heritage of Manipur*, Vol. 2, Akansha Publishing House, New Delhi, p. 492.
27. H.C. Shobha (Ed.) (2020). *Souvenir, 108th Birth Anniversary Celebration of Hemam Nilamani Singh*, Moirang, p. 59.
28. *Ibid.*, p. 21.
29. *Souvenir, op.cit.,* p. 43.
30. *Ibid.*
31. Thanghaulien Gangte (2008). *Inheritance, Churachandpur*, Manipur, p.15.
32. *Souvenir, op. cit.*
33. *Ibid.*, p. 45.
34. H.C. Sobha, *op.cit.*, p. 39.
35. *Souvenir, op. cit.*

36. *Ibid.*, p. 68.
37. Madan Mohon (Ed) (1978). *Life and Times of Subhas Chandra Bose*, Vikas Publishing House Pvt. Ltd., New Delhi, p. 299.
38. *Souvenir, op. cit.,* p. 44.
39. H.T. Gangte, *op.cit.*
40. *Souvenir, op.cit.,* p. 68.
41. *Ibid.*
42. *Ibid.*
43. H.C. Shobha, *op.cit.,* pp. 21-22.
44. *Proceedings of the Indian History Congress, 71st Session Malda, 2010-11*, Arun Bandopadhyay, Secretary IHC, Department of History, University of Kolkata, p. 643.
45. *Freedom Fighters of Manipur, Congress Centenary Year 1985*, Freedom Fighters Cell, MPCCI, Imphal, Manipur.
46. *Ibid.*
47. H.C. Shobha, *op.cit.,* p. 22.
48. Satin-Salung means liver and heart of animal.
49. Hampi-ha means tiger teeth. Both are related to Kuki customary rite in which oaths are taken.
50. H.C. Shobha, *op. cit.*
51. *Ibid.*
52. *Souvenir, op. cit.*
53. *Ibid.*
54. *Ibid.*, pp. 45-46.
55. It is the spot where the coronation of the kings of Moirang—from the first King, Phang Phang Ponglen Hanba down to the last King, Moirangthem Ramananda Singh took place. Guide Book on Martyrs' Memorial, Moirang Manipur—A Centre of Pilgrimage for the People of India, Department of Art and Culture, Government of India, Department of Art and Culture, Government of Manipur, 2009 (Rep.), p. 6.
56. H.C. Shobha, *op.cit.,* p. 23.
57. *Souvenir, op.cit..* p. 47.
58. Dr. Y. Modhu's paper "The Red Fort Trial 1945 presented in the Seminar on the occasion of Platinum Jubilee of Azad Hind Government organized by All India Forward Block, Manipur State Committee on 21st October, 2019 at Manipur Press Club, Majorkhul, Imphal.
59. *Ibid.*
60. *Ibid.*

61. Quoted in Testament of Subhas Bose. Being a complete and authentic record of Netaji's Broadcast speeches, Press Statements etc. compiled and edited by Arun, Delhi Publications, 1946, p. 247.
62. S.R. Bakshi (1991). *Subhas Chandra Bose*, Anmol Publications, p. 317.
63. N.S. Rajaram, *History Causes and Consequence, Ch.II, Distortion in Indian History*. Accessed on 08/08/2017.
64. G.S. Chhabra (2004). *Advanced study in the History of Modern India,* Vol. III (1920-1947). Lotus Press, New Delhi, p. 209.
65. Richard Attenborough (1982). *The Words of Gandhi*, Harper Collins Publishers, New York, p. 105.
66. Rajaram, *op. cit.*
67. Sharma, *op.cit.*, p. 493.
68. *Ibid.*
69. Rajaram, *op. cit.*

7

World War II, INA and Manipuri Literature

A Synoptic Survey

Kakchingtabam Ruhinikumar Sharma

World War II is one of the greatest catastrophic events of twentieth century which impacted the lives of millions of people across the world. In World War II, over sixty million men and women were killed and many more were maimed which is much more than the people killed in World War I. As the British colonial government unilaterally declared India a party to the War it was responded with widespread condemnation across all sections of Indians except the Communist Party of India. Even Mohandas K. Gandhi despite his strong reservations against British colonial rule who sided with the British on many occasions was determined to oppose the moves of the British India Government to make India a party to the war against the Axis forces represented by Italy, Germany and Japan. Indian National Congress' response was the famous "Quit India Resolution" of 8th August,1942 and the response to the 'Bharat Chhodo' call was met with large scale violence all over India with public enthusiasm hitherto not witnessed in India's struggle for freedom.

A Recapitulation

Subhas Chandra Bose (1897-1945) was one of the fearless leaders of the nationalist movement in India. He was twice elected the president of the Indian National Congress in 1938 and 1939. In his election for the second time as the President of the Indian National Congress, he was opposed by Mahatma Gandhi. He resigned from the Congress presidentship and started a new party known as the Forward Bloc. The remaining account of Subhas' imprisonment, release and escape from house detention, subsequent release and onward journey and heroics indulged in for India's liberation and freedom, establishment of Azad Hind Fauz (INA) has been left out of the purview of this chapter to avoid repetitiveness. Yet a few lines outlining the importance of Azad Hind Fauz (INA) in the history of India's struggle for freedom is given hereunder to situate the narrative within a broader perspective.

Importance of the Azad Hind Fauz (INA) in India's Struggle for Freedom

INA occupies an important place in the history of India's struggle for freedom. The formation of the Indian National Army and the brave fight put up by the INA men opened the eyes of the British Government to the danger of reasons why the British Government continued to maintain their hold on India and that was ultimately one of the reasons why the British Government decided to grant Independence to India. The members of the INA did not die or suffer in vain. They have a place of honour in the history of India's struggle for freedom. The Provisional Government set up by Netaji Subhas Chandra Bose and the Indian National Army organized by him brought the Indian question out of narrow domestic sphere of the British Empire into the field of international politics. The recognition of the provisional Government of free India by Japan, Germany and Italy and other countries gave a new status to India. The world opinion was affected by the exploits of Netaji Subhas Chandra Bose and Indian National Army. The Indian National Army also proved that Indian soldiers were also willing to sacrifice his life for the sake of the country. The officers of INA set up a brilliant record of communal harmony and Commandership.

Hugh Toye gives his estimate of INA in these words, "There can thus be little doubt that the Indian National Army, not in its unhappy career on the battlefield, but in its thunderous disintegration, hastened the end of British rule in India. The agitation which surrounded the trials turned the issue of Independence for India into an instant burning question once more." (Hugh Toye, *The Springing Tiger*, Sixth Jaico Impression, 1978: 175).

World War II and Manipuri Literature

At the very outset the present writer would like to make a clarification regarding the use of the term 'Manipuri Literature'. Here 'Manipuri Literature' is meant to denote the literary works in any genre and is not only confined to the works produced in Meiteilon or Manipuri but also covered works in other languages that deal with themes or issues concerning Manipur. Hence, the term is used in its wider sense and in a larger context. In this case, Manipuri literature too has not lagged in capturing the World War, especially because Imphal, and for that matter the entire state was in the grip of war for more than a year. Since there was large scale internal displacement of people as a result of the face to face fighting between the combating forces supplemented by intermittent air raids, Manipur, particularly Imphal Valley wore a deserted look. Homestead lands belonging to different *leikais* (localities) were overnight turned into army camps. On 10th May, 1942, Imphal witnessed bombardment by the Japanese forces for the first time. From the onwards Imphal became a centre of Japanese invasion and British resistance. Because of the repeated air raids people in large numbers left their homes followed in quick succession to interior areas of the land for safety of their lives.

Normalcy gradually returned in Imphal around 1946 after the withdrawal of Japanese forces and Azad Hind Fauz soldiers as their joint campaign ended in disaster. This was the time people returned to their respective original homes vacated by the Allied forces. Gradually normal activities started opening up in a slow and gradual manner. Economic and educational activities started picking up. The then existing theatre halls in and around Imphal, which had to remain non-functional during the war gradually started staging plays. Proscenium theatre in Manipur already enjoyed a large following. Manipur Dramatic Union (MDU) for instance staged a hugely popular play titled Naba-Mallika penned by Khwairakpam Chaoba (Chaoba Singh 1895-1950) of the famed Chaoba, Kamal Anganghal triumvirate of Manipuri literature.

As mentioned earlier when peace gradually returned in Manipur, a few litterateur of the land started picking up their pen recording and recollecting events of the contemporary Manipur. Mention may be made of Rajkumar Shitaljit Singh, Rajkumar Sanahal Singh, Khwairakpam Chaoba Singh, Keisham Kunjabihari Singh, G.C. Tongbra and a few others followed suit in later years.

Rajkumar Shitaljit Singh (1913-2008), a well-known teacher of Ram Lal Paul High Schhol, Imphal was the first native who sketched a biographical account of Subhas Chandra Bose titled *Netaji Subhas Chandra Bose amasung Azad Hind Fauz* (Netaji Subhas Chandra Bose and Azad Hind Fauz) and it was published in 1946. This small book running into 52 pages divided into three chapters provide a well written account of the life and activities of Subhas Chandra Bose in a chronological order. It was probably the second biographical account of a great Indian nationalist after Bal Gangadhar Tilak by the legendary leader Hijam Irabot Singh. Though short, but in a lucid manner Shri Shitaljit profiled the career and character of Subhas and described him as one of the greatest patriot India had ever produced in her history. In a convincing manner the writer depicts the humane side of Netaji, as Subhas was affectionately called by Indians including Gandhi in his concerns for the wounded soldiers of INA in Burma. This book with much success helped a lot in showing Subhas Chandra Bose in a positive light among the youth of the time. The present writer is fortunate enough to possess a copy of this rare book handed over by an elder long time back. To be frank, Netaji was the most popular icon in our school days in comparison with other national leaders who wielded more political power and authority than him. In fact, he was our lionised hero of the past.

Rajkumar Sanahal Singh (1918-1990) in his 'History of Manipur' published in 1947 gave a short but convincing account of the war and efforts made by Bodhchandra Singh, the Maharaja of Manipur to keep morale of his subjects high during those tumultuous days. It was because of the Maharaja's consistent effort that people of Manipur mostly remained loyal to the Allied forces rather than the liberation forces of Azad Hind. The book carries a statement of Subhas Chandra Bose where the leader acknowledged reverses made by his forces: "In Imphal and Burma we have lost the first round in our fight" (n.d., *Hindustan Standard*). However, Field Marshal Slims, Commander of Allied Forces assessment of the situation clearly shows how the Allies were struggling to hold on their positions at Imphal against the determined combined forces of INA and the Japanese. To quote Slims, "The remarkable fighting withdrawal of the 17th Indian Division back to Imphal and the tenacious defence of Kohima by a small scratch garrison in the early days actually converted the two "miscalculations" into contributory causes enemy's complete defeat" (*The Times of India*, February 9, 1946). The antipathy of the Maharaja of Manipur was more visible against the Japanese than the INA personnel. In this connection the *Hindustan Standard* carries a statement of the King on 3rd April, 1944, where it was explicitly stated that, "I and my people will fight the Japs to the last if he ever attempts to get here. My place is here by the side of my people." He further made his position clear, thus, "In the hour of danger I must stand by my people." May be the top leadership of INA was not in a position to correctly assess the mood of the Manipuris and the exact nature of British control over the Kingdom.

The trials and tribulations of the war and sufferings endured by the people is well depicted in the writings of Hijam Guno Singh (1926-2010), a versatile writer. His three novels *Khudol* (1964),

Aroiba Paodam (1966) and *Bir Tikendrajit Road* (1983), though written from different settings are somehow connected with the events of Second World War. These novels portray lived experiences of different characters, the tale of love, devotion, sacrifice and sometimes treachery. However, in *Aroiba Paodam* along with the romantic tales of the protagonists running in full steam, yet there is another aspect of love—love for the motherland, yearning for freedom, freedom of the motherland from the bondage of continued enslavement. Motherland is the place where umbilical cord of the natives are buried and mingled with her soil inseparably. Thus the father of the female protagonist took the extreme step of leaving her grown up daughters and sons to the care of her eldest daughter went to the jungles unannounced to fight for the liberation of motherland from foreign rule. The creative élan of the writer compels us to read the novel till its end with the eagerness to know what comes next. *Mother and Motherland are Greater than Heaven* is the *mantra* that metamorphoses Shajouba, father of the female protagonist Jamuna to chart for the untraded path of freedom by joining Azad Hind Fauz.

Manipur and World War II: (In verse), With a Glimpse of the World in two volumes (1980, 1981) is almost an epic poem in English language by Sanasam Gourhari Singh (1911-1988) who needs no introduction. Suffice enough to mention, Sanasam Gourhari Singh was a teacher, administrator above all an accomplished writer. This man had the ins and outs of twentieth century Manipur history. This monumental two volume account runs into around ten thousand stanzas may described as a classic of Second World War literature produced from Manipur so far. Space does not permit us to go into the details of what Gourhari had penned in this book. Almost the second volume focused on detailing the various battlefields that took place in Manipur and her neighbours and its outcome. Though the writer was closely associated with the King of Manipur in various capacities during the war the writer could not but refrain from calling Subhas Chandra Bose as Netaji. It might be of interest to note that 162 stanza of four line running into 648 lines have been devoted in describing the life and activities of Subhas Chandra Bose. Some specimens are given hereunder to illustrate the point further.

> With panoramic view of the world history
> Shining bright in his mind's clear eye
> Subhas Bose lived defying pains of pillory
> For sacred cause of India's freedom high. (3235)
>
> Had he any hope of getting India's freedom
> Without action from abroad as a basis
> He wouldn't have India during a crisis
> But it was only British promise's boredom. (3323)
>
> He said he was not by any Axis men deceived
> Losing prestige of India he'd not have lived
> He went to Japan as she fought India's enemy
> His choice was for India's good, not ignominy. (3325)
>
> He said, "When you go back to India, dear
> Tell people I've been fighting without fear
> To the last for mother India's liberation
> They should fight now in continuation. (3372)
>
> "I'm sure India will be free before long
> Now nobody can keep India in bondage",
> It was Netaji's last statement at the stage
> It was in keeping with his oath strong. (3373)

Shri Sanasam Gourhari's *Manipur and World War II* is a highly readable account of World War II in verse from Manipuri perspective. Though written in verse form, it is almost a historical account of the War and associated battles taking place in Manipur and its adjoining areas.

Awonba Samaj (1995), by Thiyam Indrakumar Singh, a voluminous novel of 406 pages almost looks like a social history of Manipur during 1939-1948 rather than a creative work of fiction. The novel depicts the existential crises faced by common man in their day-to-day life during the uncertain days of Second World War. Without much pondering in actual terms, it reflects on the political economy of the land conditioned by the ravages of war and resultant displacement of the people and their yearning to build a new society based on social equality. (Thiyam Indrakumar Singh, *Awonba Samaj*, Imphal, 1995).

A person who is more known for political statesmanship but who unexpectedly forayed into writing was late Yumnam Yaima Singh (1922-2017), a social and political activist of more than five decades of active public life. After retirement from public life due to advancing age, Yumnam Yaima devoted his spare time in writing; authored and published *Nungshinana Hingminnaba (2004), Punshigi Khongchatta (2005), A Piece of Tenth Lok Sabha (English, 2005), Sita Ram (2011), and Manipuri Language bu Nipalsuba Schedule da Chalhankhiba.* Of these books the first two are worthy of mention. *Nungshinanana Hingminnaba* (Living in Harmony), a novel published in the year 2004 is a vivid portrayal of war years and the accompanied changes brought about by the war. How the complexes of the war hardened the lives of common man giving way to simple and unsuspecting lives of the common people for a more materialistically craving life with full of suspiciousness inherent in it. Like the earlier work of Indrakumar, the author craves the eagerness for a harmonious existence among humankind for a better society. *Punshigi Khonchatta* (Journey of Life) published in 2005 the author endeavour to tell the story of his life and time contextualising it with the changes that took place in Manipur. Born in 1922 in a village called Oinam, south of Imphal valley, the writer witnessed and experienced the *Japan Lan,* as Second Word War was locally known from close quarters. Being exposed to social and political currents of the time and his association with Nikhil Manipuri Mahasabha Yaima Singh was gradually drawn towards the activities of INA under the influence of one Wangkhem Gyaneswar Singh of Nambol, a man well-versed in Bengali and was closely following the activities of Subhas and his INA by reading *Anandabazar Patrika*, a popular Bengali language newspaper. At Gyaneswar's preaching

Yaima was gradually drawn towards Netaji and his movement. Accordingly, a local branch of INA was established with the objective of extending men and material support when the forces of INA entered Manipur. Processions were conducted with slogan like *Delhi youna changsillu* (chalo Delhi) and *Netaji ki jai* (victory to Netaji) etc. with distribution of airdropped pamphlets under the caption 'Give me blood, I will give you Freedom' an appeal made by Subhas Chandra Bose calling upon his countrymen to fight for the freedom of India. The maltreatment of persons possessing copies of the pamphlet by British sepoys is well recoded in Yaima's account. As war fever gets stronger they could not work in open and functioning of the Nambol branch abruptly ended, the author remained and worked underground as was constantly searched by the British Military police for his involvement in the activities of INA. On the other hand, Gyaneswar and his spouse left for Burma to join INA. If intensive probes are made, we might come across many more such stories of unknown faces and unheard voices of their involvement and association with the INA.

Of all the World War II literatures on Manipur produced so far by Manipuri writers, the most interesting and detailed one is the memoir of Khuraijam Nimaicharan Singh (b. 1937), writer, lyricist and translator. *Manipurda Prithibigi Anisuba Lanjao amasung Eina Angang Oiringei* in Manipuri distributed in 28 short chapters running into 140 pages was published in 1997. The enlarged English translation of this book titled *The 2nd World War in Manipur and My Childhood* consisting 30 chapters was published in 2017 with the addition of some photographs and well-illustrated maps. As the title itself suggests, the book in both versions are a short autobiographical account-cum-memoir of the childhood days of Khuraijam Nimaicharan Singh along with his vivid experience of the Second World War period, as well as some of the important battles fought in Manipur, retold in brief. The author rightly visualise what happened at Imphal just after experiencing bombing for the first time in 1942. In the words of the author:

> "After the first bombing the then Imphal town was no better than a place without a ruler or government. ...Those were the days when one could not procure things even though he had money to buy his needs because all market places were deserted without any seller and buyer. So the situation compelled the poor to go to the affluent people for their help either in terms of food crops or anything they needed for their bare subsistence. In those critical days, it was a common understanding to render help to one another with whatever they could afford to give in order that the situation may be eased to some extent. Other necessary things or materials were also exchanged among them in the form of barter economy" (2017: 17-18).

> "In such a time, there were also mean fellows, mostly neighbours who used to stealing things from those houses, which were left unguarded by those householders. This type of theft and stealing habit of some people was also rampant in the deserted localities in Imphal during the period" (*Ibid.*: 18).

In subsequent chapters the author went further to describe how a beautiful place called Manipur—"The Little Paradise on Earth" was turned into one of the most decisive battlefields of Second World War and how it changed his life along with that of Manipur. But as the title of this chapter suggests we do not have much liberty to stray here and there. So let me confine to the chapters concerned with INA. Two chapters of the book, viz. The Japanese and the INA in the final march into Manipur, War plan of the Japanese and the INA outlined the Japanese-INA plan to enter into Manipur and mode of operation to be carried out against the Allied forces.

In the words of the author,

> "...after a number of meetings and discussions between the Azad Hind Fauz and the Japanese government, it was unanimously resolved to co-operate with each other

in the Imphal campaign, a big invasion through jungles and mountains until the British forces were driven out from Imphal, the last British stronghold. With this objective, they were then approaching towards Imphal from the north-eastern and southern borders of Manipur. According to the plans of their attack, it was that the 15th Japanese Divisions was assigned to attack up to north-western side of Manipur in order that the Imphal-Dimapur Road be cut and blocked at Kohima. These forces were penetrating endlessly from the Ukhrul side on the north with their arms and ammunitions. Another 31st Division had fought with the British army and succeeded to cut Dimapur road the main life-line at many points. After a lot of intermittent fighting on their way, the Japanese army at the cost of their lives could thus press southward up to Kanglatongbi where a grim battle was raged with the occupying force of the Anglo-American army. It was said that there was a big loss of lives on both sides, but no further advance towards Imphal could be achieved by the Japanese. For the execution of the abovementioned plans, the names of Japanese generals and commanders like Yamauchi, Sato and Mutaguchi may not be left out. It was under their bravery, skills and experience that an action known as operation U could be carried out from the north-eastern and south-eastern regions bordering Burma and Manipur. Among the Division Nos. 15, 31 and 33 which were under the command of General Mutaguchi, the INA was also accounted as a good counterpart to them. After a number of fightings in Burma since 1942 the Japanese 33 division was already posted in the Kabaw Valley as their base camp. In their further plans, the seize of Imphal-Tarau and Tiddim Roads were their objective so as to cut-off the said roads from British vehicles thereby facilitating only Japanese supply on these roads. In this way, the 33 division with the INA were pressing hard towards Imphal plain from the southern side. It was a grim period of the time, when rains of monsoon season were heavily pouring all day and night, and in the unwelcome circumstances, they had to suffer a lot, not only from the British bullets but also from want of food, medical aids, adequate arms and ammunitions, and above all these, there were also the sicks and the wounded ones. Another force, under general Yamauchi, was also proceeding down from Tamu to Moreh and then to places near Pallel, a place of only 30 miles from Imphal proper. It was with these Japanese forces that the British had to face a grim, severe fightings at Maibam Lokpaching, known as the red hills to the Japanese; and the Britishers. In this fighting with the marauding Japanese the British had innumerable sacrifices at the cost of their lives and thus the further advance of the Japanese was successfully obstructed and repulsed their move. The man who planned all these for the Japanese army was General Mutaguchi. ...Energetic, skilled as he was, he had a strong ambition of this Imphal campaign with his firm belief that Imphal would soon be fallen into his hands before the monsoon. He even went upto the extent of making a peculiar example of Imphal as a big lake where a big fish was hiding; and the big fish (the British) would soon be caught and surrounded by his Japanese force" (*Ibid.*: 150).

However, "The Japanese were utterly disappointed when the chaos came on their way. The wearied armies had to run helter-skelter in the unknown jungles of Manipur when no food and arms could reach them from their far away camps. Their ammunitions were running short, besides, the number of the sick and

> the wounded were also increasing. They had none to care for them but to think of their own lives. To add to these, the heavy showers of the monsoon too was a grave menace to them. To imagine the plight of those helpless soldiers, one will surely feel the miserable fate they had been subjected to. Above all these, news of the Atom bombing by the Americans on Japanese capital cities of Hiroshima and Nagasaki could no more be endured in their hearts. It was the greatest of all the blows they had ever suffered, and now they had nothing but to give up all hopes of their existence." (*ibid.*)

Since the author had seen the activities of the British led Allied forces from close quarters it is quite natural that Nimaicharan does not have much experience to tell the tale of other side of the struggle and endurance experienced by the Japanese and INA soldiers. Despite these limitations the writer is quite successful in portraying how Manipur experienced the War.

This survey will remain incomplete if we leave out the contribution of Kshetri Bira Singh (b. 1948), one of the most accomplished novelists of all the contemporary writers of Manipur. Apart from novel, the writer also dabbles in other genres. His two recently published works are worthy of mention. *Ningthigi Ningthem* (1996) is the most voluminous and detailed work of historical fiction relating to Second World War and Manipur. It gives dare devilish account of a Meitei youth called Ningthem who was assigned various duties by the British Government. What is of interest in the novel is the craftsmanship of the writer in recreating the actions of the Allied forces in successfully carrying out a number of overt and covert operations against the Japanese forces against the backdrop in which the Japanese are gaining success after success in Southeast Asia against the former. Places like Nambol, Bishenpur, Moirang, Kakching, Pallel, Kanglatongbi, Senam where actual encounters had taken place in Manipur are well covered in this book. Though the focus of the book is more on Manipur, Naga

Hills and Burma, the author connects it well with Delhi, Kolkata, London and Formosa as centres of war management and diplomacy are given due importance. However, a drawback of the work is its almost near absence on the heroic exploits and sufferings endured by INA soldiers and volunteers in Manipur. Had the author given a little more space on Subhas Chandra Bose and INA the quality of the book would have enhanced considerably?

In *Kakchinggi Warida* (1518-1945), a treatise on historical and cultural accounts of Kakching published in 2020, the author contributed two precious chapters on Kakching entitled '2nd World War at Kakching, and 'INA (Azad Hind Fauz) at Kakching'. The first Japanese air raid at Kakching took place in the early November 1943 causing large scale displacement of local populace. Residential areas were under occupation of the Allied forces thereby affecting normal economic activities which could not be resumed in the immediate future. An interesting account provided by the writer is confrontation between the locals and some soldiers of the 11 African Divisions. According to this account some soldiers belonging to the Division frequented villages and made attempts to tarnish the modesty of local womenfolk. Enraged by the shameful and condemnable excesses committed by the soldiers and as a retaliatory action 11 soldiers were made to pay their lives. As a consequence movement of locals were severely inconvenienced, however, withdrawal of the said force eased the situation to a great extent (Bira, 2020: 165). For their involvement in murdering the Allied soldiers many locals continue to face ordeals. Nongmaithem Shakngou and Kshetrimayum Kundra Singh faced litigation for three years in connection with the incident (*Ibid*., p. 174). In the other chapter of the book the author tried to reconstruct efforts made by INA soldiers to win over British Indian soldiers in and around Shenam and surrounding areas albeit unsuccessfully. A large number of INA personnel lost lives because of the offensive carried out by the Gurkha soldiers of the Allies. As a last resort, a joint offensive carried out by the Japanese and INA forces with majority of the later made a serious assault on the Pallel Airfield of the Allied forces stationed at Kakching inflicted heavy damage by using magnetic mine-bomb thereby destroying a large number of aeroplanes. The devastating offensive was carried out on the midnight of 3-4 July, 1944 and afterwards the INA and Japanese soldiers made a complete withdrawal towards Burma from Kakching (*Ibid.*, p. 178). The author express his desire to establish a memorial in honour of the gallant INA soldiers who laid down their lives for the sacred cause they believed unto the last.

In Lieu of a Conclusion

For an individual, as well as for a nation, cultural memory is a complex and stratified entity strictly connected not only to the history and the experience of either the individual or the nation, but also to the way in which that very history and experience are read in time, individually and collectively. Each time, the past acquires new meanings and the same fact, even though it stays the same, is nevertheless shaped through remembrance; inevitably, it is juxtaposed to new backgrounds, to new biographies and to new recollections. We must, therefore, acknowledge that it is impossible to offer a final and absolute vision of the past, especially if the event to be recalled affects at once both the private and the public sphere of a heterogeneous community, as in the case of the memories of the two World Wars [*Memories and Representations of War*, Elena Lamberti and Vita Fortunati (ed. 2009: 1)].

There are many authors who documented the War in Manipur included E. Sonamani Singh's serialised autobiography in *Sahitya* and Kh. Nimaicharan Singh's *Memoir of War Scenes* greatly enriched our understanding of trials and tribulations of the people of those harrowing days. Kshetri Bira's *Ningthigi Ningthem* portrays beautifully a poignant tale of human suffering and endurances. Thus, the Second World War stories continue to remain inseparable from the minds of people across the region. An apology at the end is offered; owing to the constraint of time, the writer of this piece is not in a position to include literary works translated into Manipuri like *Yaruingam* by Birendra Kumar Bhattacharya and *The Wind Cannot Read* by Richard Mason.

REFERENCES

Elena Lamberti and Vita Fortunati (Eds.) (2009). *Memories and Representations of War*, Amsterdam, New York.

Hijam Guno Singh (1964). *Khudol,* Imphal.

________, (1983). *Bir Tikendrajit Road,* Imphal.

________, (1966). *Aroiba Paodam,* Imphal.

Hugh Toye (1978), *The Springing Tiger,* Jaico, Delhi.

Khuraijam Nimaicharan Singh (1997). *Manipurda Prithibigi Anisuba Lanjao amasung Eina Angang Oiringei,* Imphal.

Khuraijam Nimaicharan Singh (2017). *The 2nd World War in Manipur and My Childhood,* Imphal.

Kshetri Bira Singh (1996). *Ningthigi Ningthem,* Kakching.

________, (2020). *Kakchinggi Warida (1518-1945),* Kakching.

Rajkumar Sanahal Singh (1947). *History of Manipur,* Imphal.

Rajkumar Shitaljit Singh (1946). *Netaji Subhas Chandra Bose amasung Azad Hind Fauz,* Imphal.

Sanasam Gourhari Singh (1980, 1981). *Manipur and World War II: With a Glimpse of the World* in two volumes, Imphal.

Thiyam Indrakumar Singh (1995). *Awonba Samaj,* Imphal.

Thokchom Prafullo Singh (1996). *Kavi Khwairakpam Chaoba Singh amasung Mahakki Sahitya,* Imphal.

Yumnam Yaima (2004). *Nungshinana Hingminnaba,* Imphal.

________, (2005). *Punshigi Khongchatta,* Imphal.

8

The Second World War, INA, Colonial State Building and Local Participation in Manipur

Sylvia Yambem

Manipur and the Second World War

Manipur in the Northeastern frontier of Britain's Raj occupied a strategic position in the Second World War. Imphal lying 50 miles from Burma in the eastern frontier's impenetrable hills had seemed so far removed from any possible battlefront of the war, though with the entry of Japan in 1941, the war, it is said, approached Imphal without stealth and all too rapidly (Evans and Brett-James, 2016). The repercussions of war were felt as early as January-February 1942, and soon following the Imperial Japanese Army's conquest of Burma in March 1942, hundreds of refugees began to arrive at Imphal (Administration Report of the Manipur State, 1943-44). To these were added the Japanese air raids, beginning 10th and 16th May, 1942 that altogether killed 71 people and wounded 80 including 50 refugees. The air raids of which there were about 17 during 1942-1944 devastated the everyday life of the people as well as caused utter chaos and lawlessness.[1] While in the first air raid the areas of the Assam Rifles were targeted, in the latter the Residency and the bazar areas were hit.[2] Moreover within a few hours of the air raid almost every house in Imphal was abandoned with its inhabitants fleeing to the villages. The air raids created an atmosphere of chaos and disorderliness—the civil administration ceased to function, the Police did not show up for duty, when the jail's main gate was bombed on 16th May all the convicts escaped and in the centre of Imphal the only civilians remaining were a few pilferers and looters, the main bazar was gutted and the Women's bazar remain closed (*Ibid.*). The Manipur state durbar was even temporarily shifted to the residence of Khomdram Angangjao Singh at Kwakeithel (Singh, 2016).

The Indo-Japanese invasion comprising the Indian National Army of Manipur occurred in 1943. Two events, it is said, motivated and inspired the Japanese Imphal offensive:

> Wingate's Chindit[3] first expedition changed Japanese thinking. We thought that the north Burma jungles were a defence against British advance into Burma. We now realized that they could be traversed by both sides. We had no intention of advancing into India, just occupy Imphal and Kohima to further the defence of Burma. But Subhas Chandra Bose and Mutaguchi wanted to invade India after occupying Imphal. There was a serious anti-British movement in India, so it was hoped that the INA would operate in Bengal to assist the rising (Katoch, 2019: 9-10).[4]

Following the Chindit expedition, on September 1943 the 15th Army was ordered to prepare for the invasion of Manipur and the capture of Imphal. Lieutenant General Mutaguchi Renya, assisted by the 15, 31, 33 Divisions and the I Division of Indian National Army (INA), planned Operation "U-Go". In late January 1944, General Kawabe issued the final order to the 15th Army. Accordingly, the Japanese Divisions crossed Chindwin at Homalin and Thaungdut on 16th March. Within a week they reached

Ukhrul and through the 4 routes of Tiddim Road in the South, the Tamu-Pallel road in the South-East, and in the East the Chamu-Shangshak and the Somra tract-Kamjong route, the Japanese were expected to enter Imphal by 27th March. On 26th curfew was imposed in the Imphal valley. By 29th the siege of Imphal had begun and the Japanese 15th Division cut the road to Dimapur. The fall of Imphal was announced on 30th March, 1944 from Tokyo, (Administration Report of the Manipur State 1943-44).

The War directly affected Manipur and its inhabitants, who not only lost their lives but whose homes, livelihood, livestock were killed, captured and even intentionally destroyed. The natives became refugees in their own land (Devi, 2018). Not only were the inhabitants of Imphal forced to flee to the *lois* (villages) or hide in trenches following the Japanese air raids, but the arrival of the Allied Forces which led to the occupation of around 20,000 houses entailed that even in the midst of the war the native home owners had to look for shelter elsewhere! Moreover, schemes like the Denial Policy and Scorched Earth to deny food sources to the Indo-Japanese forces led to the burning of paddy, *kots* (granary) and killing of livestock. The War particularly the wartime exigencies such as the development of infrastructure-communication networks, contracts, supplies and distribution of goods, and the heavy inflow of capital also structurally transformed the Manipur society and economy.[5] However, the most astonishing development of the war was the local response and participation of the people to the *Japan Laan*, by which the Second World War was popularly known in Manipur. It would be naturally assumed that given the huge devastations caused by the Indo-Japanese invasion of Manipur, its inhabitants would support the war efforts of the British and the Allied-American forces whose primary objective was to repel the Japanese forces. However, this was as seen was usually not the case.

Exploring Local Response and Participation in the War

The period of the Second World War and the movement of the Indo-Japanese forces into Manipur saw the aggressive mobilization of the society. Both the Allied forces and the Indo-Japanese engaged in extensive propaganda to secure support for their respective causes, for instance, while the Japanese circulated the flags of the INA, Japanese badge, and even pamphlets signed by Subhas Chandra Bose declaring "troops of the Indian Army to throw up their hands and join the Indian National Army as soon as they come in contact with the Japanese soldiers" and even proclaiming that Subhas Chandra Bose, the Supreme Commander of the Indian National Army, will himself be coming to Manipur to get rid of the British yoke over the people,[6] the British actively supported by the Royal Family and through its various programmes like the Savings Scheme Certificates or even Tunisia Day celebration, and besides other activities and initiatives also tried to elicit local support to their war efforts. Both parties equally evoked emotions and sentiments to identify themselves with the natives, as well as freely used threats and surveillance to coerce support. However, while the most ardent local support to the British war efforts came from the Royal Family and the State's administrative machinery, local response and participation to the war was divided. This was because *firstly* people's support to the war was motivated and determined by their personal lived experience under the colonial state, *secondly* the colonial state's divisive governance also alienated some sections of the society, like the politically conscious middle class *Meiteis* and the *Kuki* hill tribes.

Historiography on local participation reveals distinct camps or groups each professing their loyalties to the contesting parties; *firstly* at the highest echelon of the society was the Royal Family who supported the cause of the British Empire's war efforts and the State's administrative system was transformed to meet the exigencies of the war, *secondly*, the politically conscious Manipuri middle class who identified with the Indian national movement supported Subhas Chandra Bose's INA-Japanese forces, and *lastly*, the common valley-hill inhabitants who also equally professed their loyalties to the British or the Japanese-INA forces.[7] Here it is important to emphasize that the loyalties of the middle class

Meiteis were inclined towards the INA, which they identified with the Congress (Indian National Congress). British archival records also labelled the politically conscious Meiteis whether belonging to political organizations like the Nikhil Manipuri Mahasabha or the Praja Sanmelani as "Congress men", and attempts were also made by the Assam Provincial Committee in 1939 to send their workers into Manipur. M. Koireng Singh (2018) one of the local Moirang supporter of the INA-Japanese movement observes that the local leaders naturally supported the INA-Japanese forces.[8] For the Kukis Indo-Japanese support was driven by their local grievances (Guite, 2010). The native's whether Meiteis, Kukis, Nagas and others, support for the Japanese were also motivated by their intensive propaganda on shared ethnicity between the north-eastern Mongoloid Indians and the Japanese (Mukherji, 2009, Devi, 2018).[9]

Mapping response and participation of the local people in the Second World War, however, is highly contentious. The contestations emerge largely because this is a relatively undocumented history, belonging primarily to the voices of the marginalized common people, suppressed by colonial writings and ignored by mainstream Indian literature. Fortunately, however, new emerging writings on the north-eastern region have begun to explore the impact and role of the north-east in the history of the Second World War, the contribution of the people as well as the consequences of the war on state building in Manipur and the people including the gendered dimensions of war (Dena, Lal, 1974, 2014, Singh, 1993, Singh, 1998, Mukherji, 2009, Guite, 2010, Pau, 2014, Devi, 2018, Katoch, 2019, Yambem, 2019, and Naorem, 2020).

The Royal Family and State Administration

Maharaja Bodhachandra Singh and the State administration gave full support and cooperation to the war efforts. For administrative convenience during the war the Maharaja declared the region as an operational area and even surrendered his authorities to the

General Officer Commanding-in-Chief (GOC), IV Corps of the Allied Forces. To meet the war exigencies the GOC was empowered to maintain and administer Martial Law as long as necessary, to appoint officers to administer it under his discretion, as well as to terminate the state of Martial Law when considered no longer necessary. The Manipur state administration was thus directly handed over to the GOC of the Allied Forces. Other wartime administrative measures initiated include the "Grow More Food" campaign carried out with active support of the state servants along with the Military Local Purchase Officers that succeeded in purchasing food for the military allied forces stationed in Imphal. It is reported that from October 1942-Sepetmber 1943 around 78,014 maunds of vegetables, 3,17,744 maunds of potatoes, 10,991 maunds of fruits, 11,435 maunds of charcoal along with 1,31,940 eggs, 82,322 ducks and chickens were purchased under the scheme (Manipur Administration Report 1943-44). War-bonds and Defence Savings Certificates were also devised as savings mechanism and means to combat inflation. Besides humanitarian initiatives such as the opening of camps to accommodate the thousands of refugees fleeing Burma was started as early as January-February1942 by Maharaja Bodhachandra and the Maharani. The Administration Report (1943-44) mentions that the Maharaja and the Maharani fed hundreds of these refugees coming from Burma. Manipur was swarmed by thousands of refugees whether Indian coolies, dock labourers, household servants, women and children, Anglo-Indians or Anglo-Burmeses, British families and even Italians and Swedes who were in-transit to Dimapur.[10]

Other notable members of the Manipur State Durbar (MSD or Durbar) and government officials who canvassed for public support include R.K. Bhaskor Singh and L. Ibungohal Singh who in public meetings boosted public morale and support for the Allied forces, or even S. Nodiachand Singh and C. Niladhwaja also supported Allied forces. The success of the Grow More Food campaign was possible with the cooperation of the MSD members, who were allocated their respective jurisdiction for popularizing the state sponsored programme. The National War Front Committee that was inaugurated on 23rd January, 1944 at the Palace Durbar Hall had as its Chairman the Maharaja and the State War-Fund Committee members as primary members. The Front was an initiative of E.F. Lydall, the President of the Manipur State Durbar which constituted the highest decision making body in the state.

The support given by the Royal Family and the State administration was, therefore, *in toto*, whole-hearted. It was also as expected, because the Manipur state established following the Anglo-Manipuri War of 1891 had vested political authority in the hands of the minor King Churachand Singh who had been nominated by the Queen Empress from the collateral line of the monarchy. King Churachand also established his loyalty to the British Empire "by placing both his services and the resources of his state at the disposal of the King Emperor" to the cause of the First World War. In return the Raja was made a C.B.E. in 1917 and was awarded the hereditary title of Maharaja and the K.C.S.I. star in 1934. Likewise at the outbreak of the Second World War, Maharaja Churachand Singh besides once again placing the resources of the state at the disposal of the King Emperor in 1939 also gifted an amount of Rs. 85,000 from the state funds to His Majesty's Government for the purchase of an aircraft (*Ibid.*). His son, Maharaja Bodhachandra Singh, thus naturally carried forward this loyalty to the British Empire. Hence along with the members of Durbar and the State administration, the state administrative machinery were geared towards the mobilization and canvassing of mass public support to the war efforts of the British Empire.

The Manipuri Middle Class Participation in the War

Popular participation in the war varied between the support for the British and the Indo-Japanese force. Even in the valley, some sections of the politically conscious Meiteis did not support the British. Rather they constituted one of the main sources of local support for the INA forces in Manipur. The role of the Meiteis in the war and their support to the INA-Japanese can be seen in the writings of M. Koireng Singh, oral testimonies as well as from the archival records. Koireng Singh (2018: 45) notes that a message for support appealing to the Indian National Congress and the people of Manipur in general seeking unreserved support to the Indo-Japanese forces was brought from Chamol (INA Advance Base Camp) by a Kuki named Lungdam (or Lunggam) and was directly handed over to Dr. Gulapchand Singh, who was the Medical Officer posted at Sugnu. This same message was then passed over to Shri Thokcom Angou Singh of Singjamei (a Praja Sanmelani member). The Meiteis according to Koireng Singh earnestly supported the Indo-Japanese invasion from its very early stage. 32 Meiteis under L. Guno Singh of Khurai constituted an advance party for the invading forces. He further mentions that 13 of them reached Pallel and even attempted to procure the enemy's secrets. M. Ahanjao Singh, B. Balhob Sharma, M. Chaoba Singh and S. Yaima Singh were arrested and lodged in Calcutta at the Egle-kacha staging camp until the end of the war. Other prominent names of the INA supporters included 13 members of the Nikhil Manipuri Mahasabha: Th. Angou Singh, P. Tomal Singh, S. Ibohal Singh, L. Tombi Singh, L. Bijoy Singh, L. Kanhai Singh, M. Jatra Singh, W. Gyaneshwar Singh, M. Amuba Singh, L. Irabot Singh, Kh. Jugeshwar Singh, and including two women members O. Keinya Devi and K. Randhoni Devi who in order to assist the INA-Japanese forces, covertly travelled to Moirang. Moirang was central to the Indo-Japanese military strategy; areas like Maibam Ching Lotpa, Ningthoukhong, Bishnupur and other places in Bishnupur-Moirang experienced the direct onslaught of the war, and the Indo-Japanese continued to occupy the area till July 1944. Moirang was also central to the INA's narrative as it was here at Moirang in 1944 that the Indian flag was first unfurled in India. Koireng Singh recounts the event leading to the unfurling of the flag:

> In the early morning of April 14, the leaders of the Indo-Japanese advance party had discussions with Sarva Shri (1) M. Koireng Singh, (2) L. Sanaba Singh,

> (3) K. Kanglen Singh and (4) M. Mani Singh and others all of Moirang at Tronglaobi village. After taking stock of the situation, at about 5pm on the same day Col. Soukat Ali Malik, Commander of the Bahadur (Intelligence) Group planted the Tricolour flag with the Springing Tiger as emblem at the historic Moirang Kangla where the historic INA Martyrs Memorial Complex is, at present, taking shape (2018: 45).

Many Japanese officers and soldiers including Captain Ito of 33rd Mountain Gun Regiment also attended this event according to Koireng Singh (*Ibid.*). The translated version of Col. Soukat Ali Malik's speech, is given below:

> "....The Provisional Government of Azad Hind had declared war on England and America with a commitment to complete with the creation of a Greater East Asia and to bring welfare to the people of India by defeating the Anglo-American Forces. The Indian National Army with unstinted support of the Japanese Government has now crossed the Indo-Burmese border and in the course of its struggle for the liberation of the people of India from the British yoke we have now reached Moirang, the ancient citadel of Manipur. Our commitment is the march to Delhi and unfurling the Tri Colour Flag there at LAL KILLA. Many had died on our way to reach here (Moirang) and many would die on our way to Delhi. However, expulsion of the enemy from the sacred soil of India is a compulsion for us. We shall fight; and people of Manipur would provide supplies to us. Nothing about us shall be passed on to the enemy; everything about the enemy should be passed on to us... (*Ibid.*)"

This message Koireng Singh adds was well-received by the jubilant crowd, who he writes "fell thrilled that they were the first liberated people of India though many of their family members evacuated Moirang and took shelter at Thanga, Sendra and Mamang Ching. They voluntarily donated provisions to the advance Indo-Japanese forces. The voluntary campaign was led by Shri Khumam Kanglen Singh of Moirang" (*Ibid.*).The British had declared the areas surrounding the INA Headquarters, which belonged to H. Nilamani Singh, according to Koireng Singh as "enemy zone". The Political Agent also declared K. Gopal Singh, L. Sanaba Singh, H. Nilamani and Koireng Singh as traitors.

Colonial surveillance records also corroborate the support extended by the local Manipuris to the Indo-Japanese forces. Extensive surveillance was maintained over the movements of the people. Reports such asthe S.I. F.I.B. tour diary mentions Kiyam Gopal Singh as the leader of the Manipuri Jap-helper in Moirang, Mairembam Koirengmacha for supplying to the Japs rations, Thangarakpam Ibohal Singh for supplying rations and sheltering the Japs in his house, Sanaba Singh had contacts with Naki Ahmad Choudhury, Kanglen Singh choukidar provided boats to the Japs at Sendra. Another Report states Raj Kumar (not a complete name), a local inhabitant and Col. Malik of the INA also maintained some sort of relationship. The Report reads as:

> "Raj Kumar was arrested at Imphal by Br. His wife approached Col. Malik for monetary assistance for her expenses and for getting her husband released. She was given Rs. 100 for her expenses. Besides some more money was given to her for getting her husband released. 4 days after Raj Kumar returned from Imphal and went to S.A. Malik. He reported about—1. Return of Indian Tps to rear from Imphal. 2. Reinft. of American & Br tps to replace Indians. 3. His interrogation & release by Police."[11]

A Report from the Central Intelligence Office, Assam to the Political Agent, Manipur also mentions contact between Col. S.A. Malik and his officers and the Congress minded Manipuris of Moirang Khunou. It says that the Jif (Japanese Indian Force) who was interrogated revealed Kuna Singh and Jnaneswar Singh as local agents responsible for collecting information for Malik.[12] Archival records also provide detailed information on individual inhabitants like Tomal Singh of Chinga Makha, Kanha Singh of Chinga Makha, Angou Singh of Chinga Makha, Bejoi Singh of Saga Lambal, Jatra Singh of Bishnupur, Giamashor of Nambol, Munal Singh of Kakwa and Amu Singh of Nambol who were voluntarily helping and supporting the INA-Japanese with food, essential supplies, men power etc.[13] Other reports also mentions R.K Yaiskul Sana who was found possessing a pass with the stamp of the Japs,[14] and detailed movements and actions of Congress-men like Thokchom Angouba Singh of Thokchom Leikai, Singjamei, a Congress-man who was now a pro-Jap suspect who had gone to Moirang,[15] Congress-men of Mayang Imphal like Souraisam Bidyaswar Singh, Thangjam Birchandra Singh, Ningthoujam Tomchou Singh, Sagonsem Krishna Singh, Maisnam Mera Singh[16] and Thangarakpam Ibotol Singh of Moirang now living at Thanga who acted as a conduit between Bidyaswar Singh and the Japs.[17] 25 Congressmen, it is reported were also paid Rs.100-Rs.200 each for providing military information from Bishanpur, Imphal and other posts.[18] Even information on women participation and support for the INA-Japanese forces is also mentioned in the Tour Diary of S.I. F.I.B. Manipur, which says: 2 Manipuri women also went with Kiyam Gopal and others to the Japs. One of the women it states is Tongoubi[19] who was also the leader of Manipuri Women Agitation (referring to the second Nupi Lan of 1939).

The Hill Tribes in the War

The Kukis according to Guite (2010) actively supported the Japanese in the *Japan gal* (Japanese war), even before the Japanese invasion of the north-eastern frontier. Citing colonial archival records Guite writes "The Kukis were one of the first groups to contact the Indo-Japanese forces in the Chindwin valley in 1943. A Central Intelligence Officer (Assam), E.T.D. Lambert, in his report to Gimson and others, has noted that the Kukis first contacted the Japanese in and around the area in the Chindwin bend, south of Homalin, in the Somra Tract and Kabaw Valley, in 1943. He said that, Tongkhothang, Chief of Haokip clan and son of Pache, one of the leaders of 1917 rebellion, was believed to have crossed Chindwin River in November, 1943 to contact the Japanese and have asked for 400 rifles to fight against the British. It was one Paokhomang Kuki of Shakok who had first contacted the Japanese during the same time and was "largely instrumental in getting Tongkhothang, the Haokip Chief, to visit the Japanese in Burma round about the same time" (2010: 292). Moreover, as mentioned earlier, it was a Kuki who carried Subhas Chandra Bose's message appealing for support to the Manipuris. Archival sources also list the names of the Kuki Japanese helpers from Burma: from Makot-Paboi Kuki and Thangkhopao Kuki, from Kultuk-Tangkhongam Kuki, from Kaikai—Thangkhokai Kuki and from Lakhan Khuman-Haojakhup Kuki late Section Commander of L.C.

A.S.I.K. Ringshi of Chassad's report also mentions "Tongkhothang the headman of Chassad who became the Raja of Haokip collected soldiers to help Jap Troops and Japs V Forces and all Kukis were very happy because all Kuki of Chassad and Chamu area are found good friendship (the Japs)."[20] The same report further states that at least three meetings were arranged at Nungso, Maokot and Chassad villages. Inorder to support the Japanese the villagers collected rice, also guided the Japs Troops, and besides seeking information on those men who were helping the British they also threatened and intimidated those working for the English. A.S.I. K. Ringshi also writes that the following men, namely Paokhomang of Shakok village, Yangkholet of Shakok village, Onkhoram of Chassad village, Khoignam of Chassad village and other Kuki and Japs officer had come to Bungpakhanao looking for N. Chishung Group Major of V Force and Inchanshi Headman of Bungpa. However, since these men were not present "they told to the villagers of Bungpa that your village is helping the British so villagers must be killed. Therefore, our villagers gave them

Rs. 300 to Kukis to save our life, so must villagers are difficult to help British government."[21]

Professing their loyalty towards the Japanese, the hill tribes also began to desert the V-Force and the Assam Rifles. The British had established the V-Force as a form of stay behind organization in case the Japanese crossed the Indo-Burma frontier.[22] The British maintained detailed information on the names of those who had deserted the V-Force like the case of Pao Khomang Haokip of Phange village Ukhrul who in 1942 had joined the V Force and had even risen to the status of Section Comd was arrested for desertion.[23] Pao Khomang Haokip the report stated played an active role in not only guiding the Japanese forces, but also arranging Kuki guides and had even forced the villagers to hand over their rifles and guns which had been issued by the V Force.[24] Other names recorded include Lamkhothang and Vumkhothang Haokip of the 4th Assam Rifles and Mangkhohen Kuki of 3rd Assam Rifles who had also deserted to the Indo-Japanese forces (The Freedom Fighters of Manipur cited in Guite, 2010). Lakothang Kuki of Vajang village had also deserted the 1st A. Regiment and had become the Captain for the Japs. The note also mentions that those who have been reported to join the Japs "are said to have been pressed by Lamkhothang."[25] The Japanese Nishi-Kikan (the Japanese-INA intelligence organization) stationed at Homilin also had about 20 Kukis under Captain Izumiya (*Ibid.*).

Some sections of the Nagas also supported the Indo-Japanese forces. British reports mention Kaikhu Angami-Naga from Khonoma Naga Hills who was working as agent of the enemy[26] while S.I. F.I.B Lungleh's report also records "one Sheilhut, the 2nd clerk of the SDO, Ukhrul had joined the enemy side." To assist the Indo-Japanese the Tangkhul Nagas had established a Co-operation Committee[27] having the three departments of Interview, Supply and Labour whose objective was to provide the Indo-Japanese forces with food, to arrange guides as well as supply essential items (Kipgen cited in Singh 1993: 20-21). The Japanese also equally mobilized for support amongst the villages in Ukhrul, and at one such event while speaking in the house of the Ukhrul village headman the Japanese team comprising 1 Japanese Lt, 3 other Japs of unknown rank, 5 Sukte Kukis along with Lenthong Sukte the chief of Khosak village, Tiddim Sub-Division, 2 Gurkhas and Sarengla a Tangkhul girl, emphasized on the discriminatory policies of the British, saying "if it were the Neapon Government Thangkhuls would have been one of the most advanced tribe in Manipur hills." The role of Sarengla, however, was ambiguous because another report mentions that the Nungsung headman of Kangpat village and the Yangkhoshei headman of Meitei had reported to the Japs officer that "Sarengla who can speak English and knows nurse. She must be arrested otherwise she may help the British so she was arrested."[28]

A Fragmented Colonial State Building

The native princely state of Manipur became a subordinate state of the British colonial empire in India in 1891. From 1891 to 1947 colonial rule in Manipur saw numerous stages and phases; from the period of regency to direct rule by the King. Despite the changing labels of governance, colonial state building followed the colonial ideology of governance through its extractive economic policies and divisions of "us-them" between the native inhabitants.[29] Events like the Nupi Lan and the Kuki rebellion (which are too lengthy to be narrated here in full) were a consequence of this ideology of colonial governance, that was both extractive and divisive in nature.[30] It is in this background that the Second World War came into Manipur. Consequently, the attitude, response and participation of the people also reflected this fragmented state-society relationship.

M. Koireng Singh's experience of the Second World War and people's participation supports the argument that the local people particularly the so called Mahasabha or Praja Sanmelani members and the politically conscious Manipuri's identified the Indo-Japanese invasion of India with the Indian national movement whether Congress, Gandhi or Subhas Chandra Bose. Manipur being a princely state of British India, however, did not have a Provincial Congress Committee, but nevertheless developments in Manipur including its emergence as a subordinate native state in 1891 following the Anglo-Manipur war had garnered a lot of international and national news coverage, this surely would not have escaped the attention of the Indian freedom leaders. Moreover, attempts had been made by the Assam Provincial Congress Committee to send its workers into Manipur at the time of the heightened socio-political development in 1939, particularly the emergence of political organizations like the NMM or the Praja Sanmelani and most importantly the outbreak of the second Nupi Lan.[31] It is with this expectation of support that Subhas Chandra Bose had sent his message or letter of appeal to the people of Manipur for the Indo-Japanese forces. Colonial records also mention the support of these so called "Congress men" referring to the NMM/Praja Sanmelani leaders who supported the Indo-Japanese forces.

Similarly, it is with this expectation of freedom or liberation from both the feudal and colonial forces, that the politically conscious Meiteis supported the Indo-Japanese. The Japanese, also aware of the prevailing socio-political developments in Manipur, had even inquired on the whereabouts of Hijam Irabot Singh. Rumours had also circulated that Japanese certificates signed by Irabot had been distributed to the people, suggesting Irabot's support for the Indo-Japanese in the Second World War. The British too kept surveillance on Irabot Singh. A memo dated 29 July, 1944 to Gimson, the Political Agent mentioned that Irabot was in jail.

Local personal experience also guided the Kukis support for the Japanese. There were about 6000 Kukis who actively participated in the Second World War and who most significantly supported the Indo-Japanese war efforts.[32] However, in their support for the Indo-Japanese, Guite (2010) notes, and I quote here "their core concern was in the liberation of the Kuki territory from the colonial yoke. It was also a desperate 'way out' from an intolerable condition of existence created by the wicked colonial officials, their irresponsible troops, the harsh process of new laws, forced labour, porting system, various odd taxes, extortions, tortures and all other forms of exploitations. It was a political action based on the actually existing consciousness of the people illuminated by seamless level of local discontentment." Thus the Kukis support was determined by their own experience, though conditioned by the policies of the British colonial state. Likewise the Zo, according to Pau (2014) though possessing a history of anti-British feeling nevertheless largely supported the British war efforts. Few Zos only conditionally supported the Japanese, in order to save their families after the British withdrawal from the so-called new Masters, the "To thak". Otherwise it was the Chin Levies who played an important role in creating havoc to the Japanese forces, and ensuring British victory whether in the battle of Bhasa Hill or their withdrawal from Imphal in 1944 or at Ngalzang. The Zos were also motivated by their experience as well as the need to safeguard their future interests especially under the changing dynamics of governance presented in the period post-Second World War.

Conclusion

The Second World War deeply affected Manipur. The war transformed Manipur, not only in terms of the devastations associated with war, but also in the context of the changing social-cultural-economical-political developments. Local participation in the Second World War in Manipur was determined by people's personal experience and interests, which was equally shaped by the larger framework of British colonialism. People's pre-war lives and political-social experiences had repercussions in the developments during the war. Most importantly the Second World War and the nature of local participation that occurred within the larger framework of a divisive colonial administrative system had wider implications to the development of a fragmented state-society relationship in post-colonial state building in Manipur.

NOTES

1. Between two years of the war from May 1942 to 1944, Imphal experienced 17 air raids: beginning from May 10th to 16th, 1942,

that killed 71 people and 80 wounded, including 50 refugees, then in 1943 there were 3 air raids respectively on April 20th and 21st which killed 90 killed and wounded 49 and on November 9th which killed 3 and wounded another 3. As the intensity of the war increased in 1944 there were 12 air raids in 1944—on March 16th and 17th which killed 1 and wounded 16, on April 3rd, 10th, 15th, 17th, 22nd and 26th which killed 1person and on May 1st, 6th, 10th and 11th which killed 4 and wounded 6. An annual memorial is organized on 20th April at Khurai Chingangbam Mandap to remember the victims. The 20th April bombing marked the largest loss of lives in one single day in the history of Manipur during the war. See, Kaotoch, Hemant Singh (2019). *The Battlefields of Imphal: The Second World War and North East India.* Oxon: Routledge, pp. 14-15.

2. The air raids killed 70 civilians and wounded around another 80 civilians. Within a few hours of the air raid almost every house in Imphal was abandoned with its inhabitants fleeing to villages. In the second air raid 25 bomb craters were counted in the Residency garden. See, *Administration Report of the Manipur State for the Year 1943-1944.* 1945. E.F. Lydall. Imphal: State Printing Press. Evans, Sir Geoffrey and Anthony Brett-James (Reprint Edition 2016), *Imphal: A Flower on Lofty Heights*, Sunmarg Publishers and Distributors: New Delhi, p. 31.
3. British Brigadier Orde Wingate's column—comprising 3000 men-penetrated one foot deep into Burma from Imphal. The Chindit expedition called Operation Longcloth was launched in February 1943 from Imphal which served as the base and Wingate's headquarters. See, Evans and Brett-James, *op. cit.*, Katoch *op. cit.*
4. Katoch citing the remarks of a Japanese soldier from the book *Forgotten Voices of Burma, op. cit.*
5. Singh, Lokendra N. (1993). *Manipur During World War II (1941-45): Socio-Economic Change and Local Responses.* Manipur State Archives, Directorate of Arts & Culture. Government of Manipur: Manipur, Singh, Lokendra N. 1998. *The Unquiet Valley: Society, Politics and Economy of Manipur, 1891-1950.* New Delhi: Mittal Publications. Naorem, Deepak (2020). "Japanese invasion, war preparation, relief, rehabilitation, compensation and 'state-making' in an imperial frontier (1939-1955)", *Asian Ethnicity, 21*(1): 96-121.
6. Information from the Report of ASI Chinghui dated 19.10.44. Manipur Secretariat Library, File No. XLI, Cabin No. 29 "Japanese War".

7. For detailed information see Singh 1993, 1998 *op cit.,* Dena, Lal. 1974. 'INA Movement in Manipur: Myth or Reality', Proceedings of Indian History Congress (35th Session), 1974, pp. 365-69. Dena, Lal. 2014. Indo-Japanese soldiers in the Khuga valley of Churachandpur April to August 1944. 28, March 2014. Hueiyen Lanpao. Pau,P. Khan. 2014. Situating Local Events in Geo-Political Struggles between the British and Japanese Empires: The Politics of Zo Participation during the Second World War, *The Journal of Imperial and Commonwealth History, 42*: 4, 667-692, Guite, Jangkhomang. 2010. Representing Local Participation in INA–Japanese Imphal Campaign: The Case of the Kukis in Manipur, 1943-45, *Indian Historical Review, 37*(2): 291-309, Naorem, Deepak *op. cit.,* Katoch, Singh, op cit., Singh, Koireng, M. (2018). Contribution of the Manipuris in the INA Movement. *Souvenir*, Golden Jubilee of the Azad Hind Government, pp. 43-48. Mukherji, Priyadarsi. 2009. *Netaji Subhas Chandra Bose: Contemporary Anecdotes, Reminiscences and Wartime Reportage.* Har Anand Publishers: New Delhi. Devi, Gitarani. Leishangthem. 2018. *How Women Remember War: Unearthing memories of the Second World War in Manipur.* New Delhi: Zubaan. Yambem, Sylvia. 2019. The INA and political development in Manipur, presented at the "INA and North East India" national seminar organized by Maulana Abul Kalam Azad Institute of Asian Studies (MAKAIAS), Kolkata at the INA Martyrs' Complex, Moirang, Manipur on 3rd and 4th August 2019.
8. Singh, 2018, *op. cit.*
9. Archival records also attest to the Japanese propaganda of shared ethnicity. Japanese War, *op. cit.*
10. These refugees were also taken care of by Padre Jones and Molyneux in the camps. See, Evans and Brett-James, *op. cit.*
11. Extract from No.1 F.I.C. Interrogation Report No. F/2789. Japanese War, *op. cit.*
12. Copy to Letter No. 40/J.C./44(7). Dated 10.8.44 from I.B.-A.D (F)- To C.I.O. Assam, Japanese War, *op. cit.*
13. List of Manipuris who helped the Japs. Japanese War, *op.cit.*
14. Copy of Report from M.S. 2 (Agent No.2) D/14.8.44. Japanese War *op. cit.*
15. Memo addressed to the Political Agent, Manipur from S.I. F.I.B Manipur dated 20.6.44. Japanese War, *op. cit.*
16. Report of S.I. F.I.B., Manipur dated 3.7.44 forwarded to the Political Agent, Manipur, Japanese War, *op. cit.*

17. *Ibid.*
18. Extract from No. 1, F.I.C. Interrogation Report, Japanese War, *op. cit.*
19. The Report also mentions that Tongoubi is most likely to be the wife of Gyaneswar Singh. Japanese War, *op. cit.*
20. Extract copy of report D/19.8.44 received from A.S.I.K. Ringshi of Chassad, Japanese War, *op. cit.*
21. *Ibid.*
22. According to Evans and Brett-James the V-Force was fashioned along the lines of the Spanish guerrillas during the Peninsular War, whose main functions were to provide information, supply columns and dumps and harass the enemy of rear areas. There also exists some ambiguity on the origin of its name, though it had been speculated that the name V-Force had something to do with the Prime Minister's V sign. See, Evans and Brett-James, *op.cit.*, p. 83.
23. Interrogation Report, 16th August, 1944. *Japanese War, op.cit.*
24. Copy to No. 3 "V" Ops Area Letter No. GM/206/I/7 of 18/8/44. *Japanese War, op. cit.*
25. Report submitted to A.S.I. Sita on 4.10.44. *Japanese War, op. cit.*
26. Extract from the Report dated 27.5.44 of A.S.I. Tamenglong, *Japanese War, op. cit.*
27. The Committee comprised Ngalangzar (the 3rd clerk of Ukhrul), Rambung (the 4th clerk of Ukhrul), Yarnao and Paul (teachers), Changyoh (the petition writer) and others. Its Chairman was Ngalangzar, Phatnikphang: Secretary, Seilut: Assistant Secretary, and as Store Register: Selkhoseh Singh, 1993, *op. cit.*
28. Extract copy of Report D/19.8.44 received from A.S.I. K. Ringshi of Chassad, *Japanese War, op. cit.*
29. Colonial official writings emphasized upon the difference between the Hindu Meiteis of the valley and the hill tribes. See, Dun, E.W. (1992). *Gazetteer of Manipur (1886)*, Delhi. Mackenzie, Alexander. (2007). *History of the Relations of the Government with the Hill Tribes of North-East Frontier of Bengal*, Calcutta: Home Department Press, 1884, New Delhi. Reid, Robert Sir (1983). *History of the Frontier Areas Bordering on Assam: From 1883-1941*. Eastern Publishing House, New Delhi, p. 68.
30. Yambem, Sanamani (1976). "Nupi Lan: Manipur Women's Agitation 1939," *Economic Political Weekly*, February 21, 1976. Dena, Lal (2016). *History of Modern Manipur (1762-1949)*, Jain Book Shop Publication, Imphal. Parratt, Saroj N. Arambam and Parratt,

John. (2001). "The Second 'Women's War' and the Emergence of Democratic Government in Manipur", *Modern Asian Studies, 35*(4): 905-19, Bhadra, Gautam (1975). "The Kuki (?) Uprising (1917–1919): Its Causes and Nature", *Man in India, 55*(1): 10-56. Guite, *op cit.*

31. Earlier known as the Nikhil Hindu Manipur Mahasabha, the dropping of the word Hindu transformed the NMM into a political organization, even leading the Maharaja to withdraw his patronage and to forbid the state government servants from becoming members. For further information on the political developments of this period, See Dena, Lal (2016), *op. cit.*
32. According to the JAC Memo of the Kuki INA Pensioners there were 24 Kukis INA killed by Allied forces, another 15 who had been arrested in Rangoon and other places in Burma and later deported to the Calcutta jail, 586 persons arrested and imprisoned in India by the Allied forces and a large number of about 5,377 who though not arrested went underground. See, Guite 2010.

9

Manipur Pauna Independence League and Second World War*

Wairokpam Mangol Singh

The activities of Manipur Party were done mostly by Shri Laishram Guna Singh. His educational qualification was Bachelors of Arts (BA), Bachelors of Law (BL). He was an employee in the Milling Department of Burma Corporation Limited (BCL). In December 1941, he quit his job and migrated to Mandalay. The following day after the dropping of Mandalay for two times he migrated to take refuge at Sagaing. In that place, those Japanese soldiers who arrived there were fed by them. Those soldiers by holding his 'sikha' (long left over hair at the top on the back of the (shaven) head of a devout male Hindu) said him in an interrogative gesture, 'Gandhika?'. He responded by saying Gandhika Gandhika. That means he belonged to Bharat (India) of Gandhi. Guna Singh and Babudhan Sharma escorted and transfer those soldiers up to Yethaong Station. After sometime he again returned to Mandalay and formed the Manipuri Paona Independence League. Uthonten Sharma, head of the village was its President. The said league was very much related with Indian Independence League (IIL).

*Translated by Aheibam Koireng Singh & Shukhdeba Sharma Hanjabam.

By September 17, 1942, after Japan completed capturing all the parts of Burma (present day Myanmar) a Japanese officer and Burmese Police officer came to 'Tamidoji Pounaju' where Guna Singh resided, a place where a big 'Bamon' (Brahmin) village of princess daughter of Mandalay king was situated. They went back after expressing their desire to talk with the head (Ayaluji) of this village, and also asked the people to wait in the afternoon. 'Thourani Janma' falls on that appointed day, 18 September, 1942 due to which there could be reservations and differences of opinion. The head of the village, Brajala requested everyone to meet the Japanese officer as it was an initiative from Guna Singh, the most prominent personality of the village. He went after saying so.

As stated, a Japanese officer along with a police inspector of Burma came at 12.00 hours. The head of the village, Brajala Sharma, Churamani Sharma, Bayen Sharma and Murkha Sharma also came. All of them talked with the officers who came. After talking for some time, all five of the Manipuris along with the two officers who came went to Mandalay to meet their superior officer who was in-charge of Upper Burma. After reaching the place, they found the officer in the innermost room. The said officer was the most superior one in Upper Burma. The officer stood up and saluted at seeing them. They also returned the salute. He requested them to sit at the chairs surrounding his working table. However, they remained standing. When the officer asked them why they didn't sit, they replied, "You are the most high ranking officer of Upper Burma, so we wanted to show our respect by remaining standing". The officer replied, "That may happen during British period, but the Japanese didn't follow such practice." He then said, "Everyone who came here are all my elders, all are masters, I am superior to my soldiers only during wartime, I am a junior and follower to your all. After some time, they all sat down. Fuji, a Japanese officer who was well conversant with the Burmese language sat at the rights side of the officer. Fuji then asked whether there was any among them who had been to Manipur. In it, Madhu Sharma confirmatory replied in the affirmative. When asked whether he was well familiar with Manipur, he replied, he didn't.

At that juncture, the superior officer asked whether there was anyone among them who came from Manipur. In it, Brajala Sharma replied, "Guna Singh came from Manipur, there is no one in Burma who is well familiar as him." Then the officer asked Brajala to exchange his seat with Guna Sharma for a while. That way the said officer sat closely near with Guna Singh. He then brought out a map of Manipur and they discussed and interacted with each other about the things he intended to know and clarify. Shri Guna then said, for us also, a party by the name, 'Manipur Paona Independence League (MPIL) was formed quite early in advance with the objective of liberating India with Manipur in particular. On hearing it, he very happily said, "we also wanted to give you independence by driving away the British. Now let us work together. We are very much satisfied in hearing your words, we, Japanese, will now help your party, please let me know if you need us, we also will let you know, if we need you." After that the officer drop them back by his car. That time, Guna Singh was very much involved and took charge of many activities of the MPIL and worked in close association with Indian Independence League (IIL) and intelligence agencies.

The party then started preparing for going to war which were to be assisted by Japan. Guna Singh had to become a leader of the 'Manipur Party as 'Hikari Kikan'(Japanese liaison office responsible for Japanese relations with the Indian National Army) Japanese officer had expressed his desire of doing so. Japan, Manipur Army and Indian National Army (INA) also known as Ajad Hind Fauz would together be going for war. The period during the year 1942 not only saw the ferocity of the Japanese war strategies and attacks, it also witnessed a great political earthquake known as 1942 August Agitation. The movement that started peacefully turned violent. More than 10,000 civilians died due to injury by police's bullet and 60,000 were arrested.

Formation of INA

On 15 February, 1942, Singapore had fallen in the hands of invading Japanese army resulting to the capture of more than 70,000 allied armies. One Japanese Officer declared in his speech at Farrer Park in Singapore that a military force will be formed by the Indian soldiers from among those captured to fight the British. It resulted to the formation of Indian National Army by Captain Mohan Singh and some Indian officers captured by the Japanese formed the Indian National Army (INA). The first INA was collapsed and the head of the Indian Independence League (IIL) took Captain Mohan Singh into custody in September 1942. Already there had been organisation by the name IIL. In 1940 July 2, Subhas Chandra Bose came to Japan from Germany. He formed a provisional Government of Free India on 21 October, 1943 and he revived. Netaji went underground on 26 January, 1941. After sometimes, he reached Germany. The said government took oath stating that it was consented by 2,23,000 Indians in North Asia. INA had different wings—Headquarters, Hindustan Field Force, Sher Dil, Guerrilla Group, Special Service Group, Intelligence Group and Reinforcement Group. The INA had more than 23,000 soldiers.

War Preparation for Manipur

Shri Chandramani Sharma and Shri Brajala Sharma who were in company with Shri Guna Singh all the time also had to go for war. All three of them went to 'Maymyo' (town in Central Burma, also called PyinOoLwin) and talked with Shri Gopal Singh of IIL, Captain Nepali Sharma of INA, Lieutenant Naka Murasan who was in charge of Memiyo Headquarters and some Japanese officers about the war they were going. He rigorously started taking charge of the work in relation to the office of Hikari Kikan of Japan. On the second day of his reaching Memiyo, the British plane airdropped the bomb at about 9.10 pm. Shri Brajala Sharma went back the following day. Shri Guna Singh, after working for about four-five days discussing about the hill routes by taking out the map, war strategy and the appropriate time of entering to Manipur was transported to Mandalay by Lieutenant Naka Murasan in his jeep. After reaching Mandalay, Shri Chandramani Sharma was also sent back home by giving Rs. 100.

Shri Guna Singh and Shri Chandramani Sharma, in May 1943 went to Rangoon Headquarters to discuss about the war. They reached Rangoon at about 10 pm with great difficulty by travelling very riskily in train for five days. Because of the fire that enflamed by the airdropped bomb, the night was all bright. In the morning of the following morning, they got up early and met Lieutenant Fuji at the office of Hikari Kikan situated in Golden Valley of Burma.

The said officer told Guna Singh that he would arrange for his food and lodging. But, it was declined by Guna Singh stating that he wanted to stay at Meitei village as he had to meet the Meiteis settling in Rangoon. The officer then positively commented and gave him Rs. 200 so that he could use it for other things. He went to Waimi Meitei village of Rangoon and met the masses and expounded to them that it was the bounded duty of every Meiteis to drive out the British who had enslaved them. Every Meiteis who lived far away from Manipur wanted to spearhead the venture to safeguard the prestige of Manipur. All of them look red-faced due to their emotive urge to take revenge against the British. Many elders including Shri Thanin Singh and Lairenlakpam Irabot said, "It is fortunate and propitious for Manipur that you came out with a spirit of sacrifice to serve your motherland at such a ripe time to wage war so as to drive out the British by the inclusive forces of people from all racial backgrounds of India. May god bless the mission."

Shri Guna Singh, by staying at Basti Waimi Village went everyday at Hikari Kikan office for discussing various strategies of war. At the completion of about ten days or so, Shri Guna Singh was frequently let known by the Japanese officers about the dropping of bombs by the Japanese at the islands of Pacific (*Prasant*) Ocean and at various places of India and also discussed by taking out the map. When the turn for discussing on Manipur came, he always strongly insisted for not dropping the bomb in any other areas except the places occupied by Assam Rifles, P.A. Bungalow and the Military. He also asserted to leave the shrine of Shri Govinda which was worshipped by Manipuris with strong reverence untouched while dropping bomb. He tried to save the people of Manipur as much as he could. He told the Japanese officers that Manipur Valley was a densely populated area with houses built mostly of bamboo, woods and thatch. If one house got caught fire, it would burn the whole village. Rice granaries and other edible items were also stored inside the house, he further told. Hearing his words, the Japanese officers assured him to not frighten.

Shri Guna at once told to Lieutenant Fuji while talking with him at Rangoon office of HikariKikas that, "We wanted to restore the lost independence of Manipur by befriending with you (Japan) for our emancipation from slavery and bondage by defeating the British. And atrocities were committed to the women of Manipur by cruelly inflicting them with bayonet wounds during the women's war. The women of Manipur spend the entire night restlessly with great difficulty. Paona and many other patriots were martyred in the war of independence. Bir Tikendrajit and Thangal were hanged to death. We started to take up this act to revenge for all such acts."

Hearing these words, Lieutenant Fuji stood up and by holding his hands happily stated, "That yearning for serving the nation by keeping aside the self-interest is what we actually wanted."

The war by Japan and INA against the British in India would be from two fronts—one from Manipur and the other from Arkan side which was to be preceded first from the Manipur side. It was because of this reason that the participation of Manipur League was inevitable. The Lieutenant further made it known to Shri Gune Singh. From that time onwards, the Japanese gave Shri Gune was given Rs. 100 each for a week as allowance. Rs. 200 was also given to Shri Gourahari to spend for his expenses. Japanese Press also had Bengali language and Bengali script. Guna Singh also had to like in Meiteilon (Meitei Language) to distribute as pamphlet. So, the next day the pamphlet written in Meiteilon was made known to the Japanese. It was at first to be discussed at the office and subsequently to look after the works of the Bengali compositor by going to the Press. In that way, two different pamphlets were printed. After about half a month, Shri Guna Singh was told to travel to Singapore by air and meet Subhas Chandra Bose there. At this Shri Guna enquired about when Subhas Chandra Bose would be coming to Rangoon. Guna Singh got the reply that Subhas Chandra Bose would be coming after a week. So, it was decided to meet Netaji when he came to Rangoon.

Mr. Fuji then asked Shri Guna Singh to give in writing the names of some politician who were interested in Manipur politics together with the activities they already have done for the freedom of Manipur and also the names of educated people in Manipur. In it, he mentioned the names of those whom he thought were well qualified. Among them were—Irabot Singh, Shri Elangbam Tompok Singh, Dr. Leiren Singh, Nongmeikappam Gopal Singh, Muhori, Koijam Amubi and Mohendro Singh stating that they gave up the respective post occupied by them and endeavoured for the welfare of the people. At this, the Japanese officers further enquired on what activities these politicians were doing, how they gave up their respective post. He replied mentioning that Shri Irabot gave up his membership for Sardar Panchayat (Manipur), Shri Tompok gave up his post of Clerk, Dr. Leiren deserted the palace and started publishing 'Yakairol' (tr., Dawn) for the benefit of the people. He also lucidly narrated about the Women's War which simultaneously erupted due to the discontent of the British misrule.

Among those who were educationally well qualified, he mentioned the names of—Shri Arambam Ibohal Singh [BA, Bachelors of Teaching (BT)], Shri Sougaijam Sanajaoba Singh [BA], Shri Kalachand Singh Shastri, Shri Krishnamohon Singh [Master of Arts (MA), BL], Shri Dwijamani Sharma [MA], Pandit Lalita Madhav Sharma [Bidya Ratna], Shri Shivanand Sharma and Pandit Atombapu [Bidya Ratna]. He explained elaborately about them.

Mr. Fuzi strongly insisted Shri Guna Singh to go to Singapore by plane and meet Netaji as the war march to India would begin from the route in Manipur. At such a midst, an Officer of Upper

Burma Molaik Field Headquarters repeatedly called up for completely one month at the Rangoon headquarters to send Shri Guna as they have faced many hardships in executing the work. Accordingly, Shri Guna Singh was happily well prepared to go to Molaik. One Japanese officer, one INA officer, and some INA soldiers escorted and transported Shri Guna Singh to reach Molaik on July end of 1940.

In their journey to Molaik, Shri Guna Singh and his companion Shri Gourahari Sharma entered Mandalay and met the President of Manipuri Paona International League, Uthonten and also with many of their friends and after letting them known that they have to go for war proceeded towards Molaik. At that time, transport connectivity was very difficult. They reached Molaik by ferrying at Motor Boat. At reaching that place, they were received by three officers—Captain Yamadea, Nagasisan and Sudusan.

They found one Senior Manipuri, whose name was Laimayum Murkha as employee in the office. At seeing Shri Guna Singh, he happily expressed that work would be able to express further. That took rest on the day of reaching there. On the morning of the following day, the locals of Meitei villages in Kendat came in large number and met Shri Guna Singh.

They told that "the Meiteis residing in Meitei villages of Kendat village were very much oppressed by AwaTaji. Japanese took whatever they wanted from the Meitei village and the Awas were kept protected. If the Japanese wanted a cow, they took it indiscriminately from the Meiteis and they also had to compellingly give it out of fear. However, Shri Guna made them to return by saying that he would come after about five-six days.

After that, they have thorough discussion on strategies and issues of war. Shri Guna Singh issued pass to Meiteis of Kendat and were drawn to Manipuri party for taking part in the war. The instruction written in the pass was, "Nothing shall be done to the person who is the bearer of the pass without informing the office of Shri Guna Singh, even if punishment has to be given as per the law, the said office shall be given prior information. After that the

Meiteis there were given the monthly ration amount respectively of Rs. 500, Rs. 100 and Rs. 150. Even a household of Lone widow was given the amount of Rs. 50.

Then after about half a month, Shri Guna Singh, as invited by the people of Kendat, went there which was three miles away from Molaikat. As desired and requested by the people, he went to meet the Taji of Kendat. The said Taji oppressed the Meiteis very much. Shri Guna Singh asked him whether he know who he was. At this Taji replied (in Burmese)—"*Bujichunotabirekhemya Manipuraachowabe*" meaning (courteously) know you have assumed charge of Manipur Government." Shri Guna Singh further asked—Why are you heinously supressing the lone Meitei village at your village." At that Haji replied, "It was not by me but by Japanese." Shri Guna Singh then told Haji, "If you did next time, remember the Meitei sword. Wasn't your Awa King earlier built Palace at the hillside of Shebo owing to fear of Meitei sword shifted to Iwang crossing over Irrawaddy, then to Amarpura and finally to Mandalay." Taji replied, "Hotobla Naukma Malukpu" meaning—"Yes, will not do anymore."

The use of Manipuri as forced labourer by the Japanese was also banned. Meiteis were sent to areas occupied by the British and used as spies. They also were made to dispense INA pamphlet at British army deployed areas.

One day a Japanese spy officer along with Taji came and asked to give her cow to a woman named, Keina-Amubi. In it, she show the pass that was distributed to her. Even after that, they insisted to give them her cow. The said woman came and approached Shri Guna Singh on that matter. Shri Guna Singh, when he went back, he found Captain Yamadasan, the officer in charge gone to Rangoon Headquarters. He met Nagasisan, the temporary in charge in place of him. Both of them talked about the matter raised by the woman at the top floor of the office building. The officer told Shri Guna Singh that according to the law of Japan, there's no provision which allowed to take things and belongings without the willing consent of the owner, however, it was done as they wanted it to feed the soldier. The officer further told, "Like you people, there were some among us Japanese who were completely vegetarians before 50 years ago, but because of the premonition that the British as they did it to the Japanese in most parts of the world, the Japanese also would try to be subdued, they also started to eat non-vegetarian food. It is quite surprising that after we reached Japan, we also started to eat snake, dog, almost everything indiscriminately. Those who eat non-vegetarian food can work for longer hours than who are vegetarians. If they themselves are not willing, we Japanese will not take anything from them. Tell this to your people without disclosing my name. The supply officer after taking the cow will also have to provide my share, they will not be eating it."

In that way, slaughtering of cows belonging to Meiteis was banned by issuing a pass. At hearing that the Hindus have also insisted to issue pass for them too saying, "because of we are Hindus, we don't want the cows be slaughtered. Passes were issued for them too thereby saving the cows of the Meitei and the Hindu from being slaughtered. If the source of religion was to seek truth and purity, then there shouldn't have any difference between religions.

Afterwards, the supply officer was tricking in trying to take the cow. When Guna Singh met the supply officer, he said –

> "We came to give Swaraj to your people, we would be fighting war with the British so you people should heartily give the cow as it is meant to feed the cow who are facing hardships and difficulties deep inside the hills."
>
> In hearing that Shri Guna responded, "Swaraj means having the capability to protect the culture and religion of the native land. Hindus worshipped cow as god. If you demand to give cow to slaughter and it, then it is not the swaraj we wanted."

That way slaughtering of cows owned by Hindus and Meiteis was completely banned. After that he return to Molaik and started engaging in many war related activities. In the evening, the British aeroplane used to come and airdropped bomb directing to their office and also fired machine guns. They, after having meal in the early morning, had to go to the hills and work in the early morning. Maps brought out by Japan had all the information exhaustively in detail. It contained all the villages and connectivity. Food productivity of the place to be landed was first assessed and evaluated because there would be problem of marching for war due to land connectivity. Because of it, the ration for ten-fifteen days had to be carried by each person. It was so discussed that they would have their food from the places they reached and the costs of which would be met later after the end of the war. The Japanese officers asked Shri Guna Singh and Shri Murkha under what political arrangement they wanted Manipur to put. At that they replied, Manipur was a princely state but of late we have been under the rule of British colonialism otherwise Manipur have never been under any colonial subjugation. So Manipur would be an independent sovereign state as existed before." Their stated stand was also agreed by the Japanese.

There were five parties in the office—(1) Manipur Party; (2) Uteji Party (Burma); (3) Amar Singh Party (India); (4) Khan Party (India); and (5) INA Party led by Lieutenant Bhim Singh and Lieutenant Shyam Singh. Other parties were taken responsibility by their respective party leader. In the case of Manipur Party, responsibility was borne by Shri Guna Singh and Shri Murkha Singh.

Tomba Singh and Babu Singh from among the Meiteis and Takun who was a head of Awa spy were sent to establish relations with the people of the hills. That way they got Holkoyam Kuki who was a minor child of 12/13 years of and another of 30 years of age from Holkom Basti to help them in their mission. Afterwards Yolpao Kuki, Lamkhothang Kuki and Lamjangam Kuki also joined in. The Meiteis in Burma from Kalemyong, Mandalay, etc. also came together at Kendat and were ready prepared to go for war. Those Meiteis gathered there were given training by Mr. Mayurasan. In March 1944 the recruits of Manipur were distributed under the Japanese officer—Mister Miyurasan and Naga Nisan. Along with 13 Meiteis they climbed up the Chin Hills and proceeded to Churachandpur. Their names were:

1. Shri Balhav Singh, Bamon Leikai;
2. Shri Mairembam Ahaljao, Moirang;
3. Shri Salam Yaima Singh, Soibam Leikai;
4. Shri Takhellambam Chandra Singh, Khurai;
5. Shri Mutum Chaoba Singh, Keirao;
6. Shri Laishram Ningthemjao, Kendat;
7. Shri Tomba Singh, Kendat;
8. Shri Kshetrimayum Babu Singh, Tera Keithel;
9. Shri Oinam Maipak Singh, Charangpat;
10. Shri Ningthoujam Gulap Singh, Heirok;
11. Shri Laishram Tomu Singh, Kendat;
12. Shri Tombi Singh, Kendat; and
13. Shri Mangi Singh, Kendat.

Already six persons have been sent in that direction. They were:

1. Shri Nongthombam Amu Singh, Huikap;
2. Shri Chanam Amu Singh, Thoubal Wangkhem;
3. Shri Sanajao, Thoubal;
4. Shri Kongkham Angou Singh, Wabagai;
5. Shri Sapam Angou Singh, Kabow Wakching; and
6. Shri Thounaojam Tomba Singh, Moirang.

Led by Shri Guna Singh and Shri Murkha, the remaining Meiteis along with leaders from the hills climbed Changpal, Libung, and Khongkang Basti situated at the southern boundary and proceeded towards the hill ranges of Sircom and Aungpasu for the war.

The name of those who took part in it were:

1. Shri Laishram Guna Singh, Lairikyengbam Leikai;
2. Shri Laikhuram Murkha Singh, Thangmeiband;
3. Shri Loukrakpam Murkha Singh, Keirao;
4. Shri Aribam Atombabu Sharma, Thangmeiband;

5. Shri Amu Singh, Thangmeiband;
6. Shri Nongthombam Amu Singh, Kendat;
7. Laishram Yugendra Singh, Kendat;
8. Shri Batou Sharma, Mandalay;
9. Shri Sitasen Sharma, Mandalay;
10. Shri Bamao Sharma, Mandalay;
11. Shri Sagolsem Khomdon Singh, Kendat;
12. Shri Iboton Singh, Kakching; and
13. Shri Maibam Thagoi Singh, Kendat.

From among those leaders, Shri Laikhuram Murkha Singh was migrated from Thangmeiband and settled to Kendat from where he came for war.

When the said party came for war at Changpol, the British army fled out of fear without even putting down the '*Aloo Bhaja*', (Potato Fry) from the flame. Japanese army chased and killed many of them. Shri Lamkhothang Kuki and Onkhothang brought in many Kukis from the rival V Force to the Manipur Party. Because of the bringing in of many Kuki Chiefs, Shri Guna Singh and his companion Yamadasan appointed him as the Captain of the V Force of Manipur Party. That way more and more hills men were brought in. Shri Lamkhothang Kuki hailed from Tengnoupal sub-division of Wayang Village.

That time, it was very much inevitably in need to send persons to Manipur to make aware of the emerging activities. When the manpower to carry out such activity was found to be very difficult, Shri Lamjangam Kuki along with his wife, Hoyakim, with great difficulty and hardships reached Manipur through Sugnu route. Letter and documents of the party were also given and let known of the reasons to Potsangbam Tomal Singh, Shri Laishram Kanhai Singh, Shri Thokchom Angou Singh because of which they gave maximum cooperation to Japan and INA. Lamjamang Kuki was once again sent to Sugnu and he brought the head of Sukom from Sugnu. Dr. Gulapchao Singh provided medicine and also gave maximum cooperation in the war for freedom of Manipur. Lamjangam Kuki was the head of the spy of Manipur party. He was also from the Wayang Village of Tengnoupal.

The party while camping at Sircom hill ranges were summoned by sending V Force and most of them turned up and also brought ration from their respective locality.

Afterwards the British army in Tukmu fell into the hands of Japan and those commodities abandoned were later used by the Japanese. The Chief of Sihao, Limkhuisei quit from his job of Section Commander of British V Force and joined the Manipur Party. As an officer, he was very hard working and did his duties speedily up to reaching Angprasu. After reaching Angprasu, Thongkhusat also after leaving the British force also joined the Manipur Party and assumed charge as leader of the V Force. Captain Yamadasan treated him very favourably hoping that they would soon be reaching Imphal. Following it so many village chiefs and leaders joined in. By the time they reached Chamon camp, they became the respective heads of V Force and counterbalanced the strength of enemy force.

After raising the camp at Angprasu, the Manipur Party received help from most of the village chief of the hills. Following it, camps were also raised at Chamon, Wangku, Khongjon, Monjang, and finally at Yaiphou. At one night, INA and some V Force led by Japanese officer, Yamadasan went for war at Chandel and had an exchange of fire. When Yamadasan burned their garrison, most of the villagers ran away. They captured one civilian. One day, a civilian who came for fishing at Chakpi was caught by the Manipur Party V Force and released him after detaining for six days with the instruction to spy on the British and inform them.

At a camp in Yaphou, there were also some 1000 INA soldiers under the command of a Subedar Major and Captain Devi Singh. There was an incident of bomb dropping at that place after about half a month. Simultaneously, the British fired multiple heavy artilleries round from Pallel and landed quite often very near to them at Chakpi River. At the same time, machine guns were also fired from the top of western hills along with airdropping bombs.

Officer Yamadasan suggested to withdraw from there towards Khonjon side leaving some Japanese and INA soldiers there to guard the place, so they accordingly withdrew at Khongjon. In that incident, Shri Guna lost his war diaries and other many important documents. Among the casualties, some V Force and INA soldiers were injured, and some death casualties among the INA soldiers. Also one Halukhusei from among the V Force also died. They then erected camp at Wangku and stayed there with great hardship.

The Large Footstep at Bongli

At the south, the 77th Indian Infantry had already crossed Nigthi and Irrawaddy river of Burma in February 1943 and cut and dismantled tracks in many parts at 'Katha' (town in Sagaing region, Burma, on the west side of the Irrawaddy River) at the railway route of 'Myitkyina' (means 'near the big river', capital city of Kachin state in Burma situated in the west bank of Ayeyarwaddy river). The rations for their soldiers were all airdropped from the plane. In January 11, 1944, troops of 15 Indian Corps captured and took over 'Maungdaw' (A town in Rakhine state, Western Burma). The British greatly hurdled and inconvenienced the Japanese in ferrying their goods by airdropping bombs in most of their routes. In the west some 500 miles ahead, Chinese-American army of General Stilwell came down to 'Hukaung Valley' (located in Tanaing township, Mythkyina District, Kachin state, Myanmar) which was situated at the root of Ningthi River. He took rapid advances towards the south. On May 17, the Chinese Army from towards the east crossed Salwin River and proceeded up to Myitkyina Airport. In Katha, the 3 Indian Division posed danger to the four important places of Japan. They were:

1. Myitkyina and Mandalay Railway route;
2. Land route at the Western bank of Ningthi river from 'Homalin' (a town in north-western Burma, in Hkamti District of Sagaing region which lies on the Chindwin river) to 'Ingdao';

3. The route reaching 'Bhamo' (a city in Kachin state, Northern Myanmar situated on the bank of Ayeyarawady River) which passes through Shan state in the west; and
4. Water routes of Ayeyarawady reaching Bhamo.

So, with the eminent danger in most of the supply lines of Japan, the ration for the soldiers in Manipur have almost dried up. The deteriorating condition in Burma coupled with the insufficient ration due to seizure of all available routes compelled them to retreat. Captain Nagao San told to Shri Guna Singh, "You all should retreat to Burma and wait for the war and again go for war after one or two year because America is approaching nearer to Japan in the Pacific ocean. We had to first protect our capital city. Then afterwards we will go for war to India."

On 6 May, 1945, the Allied Forces completely took over Burma. The activities of Manipur party were also completely stopped.

NOTE

Excerpts of Wairakpam Mangol Singh's authoured book, *Prithivigi Anisuba Lanjao Amasung Manipur Party*, 1984 (2nd Ed.).

Theme II
INA AND MANIPUR

10

A Flower on Lofty Heights (*Takane No Hana*) and INA in Manipur

Rajkumar Ranjan Singh

A Flower on Lofty Heights, preciously called '*Takane No Hana*' (in Japanese), is the place discovered by the Japanese during the Second World War in 1944. The place is popularly known as Imphal, the capital city of Manipur, once an independent kingdom having its own culture and civilization for more than 2000 years. Imphal was a significant theatre of World War II, and the war took a U-turn from this place. Imphal is also the place where the world-famous Polo game was born out of its native sport of Sagol Kangjei. Until today, Kangla, the capital complex of the then kingdom, stands as an exotic symbol for describing a 'Flower on Lofty Heights' and deserves to be conserved as a World Heritage site. One Prof. Robin Wilson from the United Kingdom, visited Manipur University in the early 90s and described Imphal as (abbreviated) International Medium for Peace, Humanity, Art, and Literature.

Imphal was one of the targets of the British army and the Japanese army during the Second World War, and it was also the entry point of Netaji Subhas Chandra Bose's Azad Hind Fauj for the liberation of India. The occupation of Burma (now Myanmar) in 1942 by the Japanese army brought the Second World War to North-east India. On March 8, 1944, the Japanese, under the command of Lieutenant-General Mutaguchi, launched its 15th and 33rd Army Division in Imphal to destroy the British 4 corps based in Manipur. The Japanese feared that the British could use Imphal as a vast military base to recapture Burma, which was already under their control under the Greater East Asia Co-prosperity Sphere. On the other hand, the Britishers used Imphal as the strategic defence post against Japanese intrusion into British India. Consequently, Imphal became a significant theatre of war during the Second World War.

INA Indian soldiers, though part of the Japanese campaign, were not mere mercenaries but committed patriots who laid down their lives for the motherland. Considering the diverse social composition, they are also portrayed as a brilliant example of communal harmony and comradeship. INA also sent out a strong message to the foreign rulers that they could no longer rely on the Indian troops serving them; there were internal tremors and nationalistic insubordination within the British Indian army.

Subhas Chandra Bose, the Prime Minister of the Provisional Government, was the Head of the State and also the Supreme Commander of the Indian National Army. The first division of the INA, with some ten thousand soldiers, was put under the command of Colonel Zaman Kiani. It was divided into three regiments/brigades, which Bose named after Gandhi, Nehru, and Azad in an honest effort to make the cause of Freedom common to all nationalists.

The INA selected the best soldiers from among the three regiments. It formed the No.1 Guerrilla Regiment under the command of Shah Nawaz Khan, the first action-oriented outfit fighting for the liberation of India. Six different routes intersected at Imphal Plain, and the Japanese attempted to break into and run through. These roads were the Kohima-Imphal road and the path down the Iril River Valley from the north, the Ukhrul road from the north-east, the Tamu-Pallel from the south-east, the rugged

Tiddim highway from the south, and the Silchar-Bishenpur track from the west.

The Allied and Japanese forces were fighting to gain control over the land of 'Flower on Lofty Heights' (Imphal). "What do we find when we get there? You'll find a little paradise on Earth"—E.M. Somerville. The Indian National Army, in collaboration with the Japanese for the liberation of India, had hoisted the National Tri-Colour Flag for the first time on the soil of the Country in 1944 and also established the Provisional Government of Independent India at Moirang, Manipur. The establishment of the Provisional Government at Moirang by INA internationalized the issue of Colonial British India in a big way. Subsequent recognition of Netaji's Provisional Government of Independent India by other foreign countries was like an ultimatum to the Colonizer. It is rightly comprehended today that the INA's endeavours also hastened the process of India's Freedom.

We, Manipuris, are very proud to be a part of the freedom struggle directly linked with the INA campaign. At Moirang, Manipur, the Indian National Army's tri-colour flag was first hoisted on April 14, 1944, on the Indian mainland (the Andaman event was far away from the mainland, though it preceded Moirang). The first INA office on the Indian Soil was set up at Moirang, some 35 km from Imphal; the revered office still stands protected. This is where INA operated the First Provincial Government of the Independent India (as declared by INA). And from this location, the slogan Delhi Challo was further echoed and reverberated. More than 7000 INA soldiers waged the Imphal Battle. People are still narrating the heroic stories of the INA campaigns locally known as Japan Lan (Japan War).

11

Three Months of Provisional INA Government in Manipur and Contributions of Local Population

Laiphrakpam Nishikanta Singh

Pre-War Situation of Manipur

On Sunday 10th May, 1942, Imphal was bombed by Japanese aircraft and Manipur became involved in World War II. The second bombing was on Saturday the 16th of May, 1942. In 1942, the Japanese Army had driven the British, Indian, and Chinese troops out of Burma. British and Indian troops had occupied Imphal. However, the Japanese dropped the idea of further advance due to difficult terrain and supply considerations. The Japanese Commander in Burma, Lieutenant General Shojiro Iida, felt that it would be unwise to continue the advance, right into India even after the rains. Thus further advance was paused. Let us examine the situation in Manipur post-aerial bombing

There were chaos and a pandemonium nearing anarchy. The panic-stricken population started fleeing from the capital to remote areas. Even, the State Durbar (Assembly) shifted to Kwakeithel. All these resulted in an uncontrolled price rise. Essential items were brought from Silchar mostly on foot. Besides, 2 lakh refugees fled due to the Japanese occupation of Burma. The Allies, especially the British began concentrating troops in Imphal, basically to use it as a forward base for the battles in Burma, to give a battle against the Japanese onslaught, or even use it as a launching pad for a counteroffensive. Thus, the depopulation of Imphal was liked by the British. General Slim also eventually quartered in Imphal.

Being a princely state, no political activities were allowed in Manipur. Even the Congress party was not allowed to function and Gandhiji was prevented from entering Manipur. Nikhil Hindu Manipuri Mahasabha was the only proactive political party functioning at that time.

The Arrival of the Indian National Army and Activities of Nikhil Manipuri Mahasabha

Netaji sought the assistance of the people of Manipur. He sent a message asking the people of Manipur to help the INA and Japanese Army who had crossed into Manipur. This message from INA camp at Chamol was brought by a person named Lungdim and handed over to Dr. Gulapchan Singh, who was the then medical officer at Sugnu. It was then given to Thokchom Angou Singh of Singjamei, Imphal of Nikhil Hindu Manipuri Mahasabha. They had similar ideas for independence and welcomed the appeal of Netaji.

Accordingly, two members of the Mahasabha, Laishram Jogeshor Singh, and Hawaibam Ranbir Singh went to Jiribam and organized a meeting in the house of Meitram Kanglenjao. A resolution was passed for receiving the INA and Japanese as liberators on the condition that Manipur is declared independent from the British and be recognized as a liberated part of the Indian subcontinent. Accordingly, one member, K. Kunjabihari Singh was tasked to establish secret contact with Japanese monks in the Mahabali forest, right in the heart of Imphal. Eventually, some leaders of Mahasabha and the Praja Sammelani (a newly floated party led by Irabot) joined INA on their arrival in Manipur. These included Thokchom Angou Singh, Potsangbam Tomal Singh,

Liashram Kanhai Singh, Longjam Bijoy Singh, Kiyam Gopal Singh, Mairembam Koireng Singh, Hemam Nilamani Singh, Laiphrakpam Sanamba Singh, and Laishram Guna Singh. Most of them led a unique lifestyle wearing khadi dresses etc.

In mid-1942, L. Jogeshor Singh was arrested for transmitting information about Kumbhirgram airport to the Japanese. Meanwhile, the State Police began rounding up the members of the Nikhil Hindu Manipuri Mahasabha. Many fled to Burma and joined the INA. Eventually, all those Manipuris who fled to Burma accompanied the INA back to Manipur. The local INA members and sympathizers were under surveillance by the military. Many were arrested and lodged in the Langthabal Military jail which virtually turned into an interrogation centre. The inmates were brutally tortured. Maisnam Gopal Singh of Lamshang and Angou Singh of Lamlong (Khurai) were inhumanely tortured and released when they were about to die and died soon after their release.

The Aim, Planning, and Preparations for Attack on Imphal

When Japan joined the war, there was no plan to extend it to Indian soil. But seeing the momentum of success and inability of the Allies to check the Japanese onslaught and also based on the intelligence reports that the British forces in Manipur and Chittagong were unprepared, Japan started considering the capture of these two towns. It was appreciated that the capture of Imphal would rob the British of a suitable base for a counteroffensive in Burma, which was already with Japan. It resulted in the aerial attack on Imphal on 10th May, 1942, as already brought out above. But this was not followed up because of Japanese inhibitions of stretching too far especially the logistic system.

Meanwhile, the Allies exploited the Japanese indecisiveness. They prepared and strengthened operation and logistic capability to hold Imphal and also support the operations in Burma. During 1942-43, the Allies improved the lines of communication to Assam. Many logistically important airstrips were laid in Manipur and its neighbouring areas. Imphal-Kohima-Dimapur road was substantially improved, the rudimentary Silchar-Imphal road was also repaired and a road from Imphal to Tiddim was also constructed. The United States Army, with Indian labourers, also constructed several airbases in Assam for flying supplies to China. This air route, which crossed several mountain ranges, was known as the Hump. The Americans also began constructing the Ledo road, to connect Assam with China.

In July 1943, Netaji Subhas Chandra Bose arrived in Singapore. Netaji passionately insisted on the capture of Imphal or Chittagong or both, at the earliest, when the Allied forces were least expecting it. Netaji appreciated capture of these could trigger an Indian revolution. He planned that once Imphal is liberated, he would install on the Indian soil an effective Provisional Government of Azad Hind. This would bring more Indians to join the anti-British revolt. On 21st October, 1943, the Provisional Government of the Azad Hind was formed under Netaji Subhas Chandra Bose. On 23rd October, Netaji declared war on Britain and the USA.

The above insistence of Netaji, along with the fact that the Allies could anytime be launching a counteroffensive into Burma, prompted the Japanese Military Strategist to decide on a pre-emptive offensive on India both trigger an Indian revolution and also blunt a British counteroffensive. Further Japanese 15th Army Commander, Lt. General Mutaguchi, felt that the capture of Imphal could be exploited by advancing to the Brahmaputra River Valley which will cut the Allied supply lines to their front in northern Burma and China.

Netaji also discussed the nuances of cooperation between the Japanese and the INA forces with General Kawabe, Commander-in-Chief of the Burma Area Army. He insisted that both should enjoy equal status in all respects. They also agreed that the territories liberated on the Indian soil must be handed over to Major-General A.C. Chatterjee, Governor-designate of the liberated areas.

Unfortunately, the Japanese High Command at Tokyo took a too long time to make a final decision. This delay gave more time to the British forces to prepare. The Japanese decision taken on

12th August, 1943, was revealed to Netaji only on 26th August. Further, the order for the offensive on Imphal was issued only on 10th January, 1944 from Tokyo. The commencement of the operations was further delayed due to late in the arrival of the 15 Japanese Division from Siam. Ultimately on 10th February General Kawabe issued the final orders to the 15th Army commanded by Lt. General Mutaguchi with a rider that the campaign be completed within a month because thereafter monsoon was to commence.

Meanwhile, the Allies were also preparing for going on the offensive themselves in early 1944. The Indian 15 Corps was advancing in the coastal Arakan Province, while the British 4 Corps had deployed two Indian infantry divisions almost to the Chindwin River at Tamu and Tiddim. These two divisions were widely separated and vulnerable to being isolated.

The Imphal offensive, Operation 'U -Go', as it was called, was to be launched in March 1944. It was an infantry-based operation but Moltke's theory of operational art was applied. The basic concept of operation was two division-size forces advance from Eastern and Southern axes while one divisional size force goes further north and cuts the British main artery of Imphal-Dimapur line of communication at Kohima and exploit up to Dimapur railhead. This main attack was to be preceded by a diversionary attack in the Arakan, codenamed 'Ha-Go', in the first week of February. This was to draw in the Allied reserves from Assam and also create the impression that the Japanese intended to attack Bengal through Chittagong. Allocation force and task are as given below:

1. 33rd Infantry Division under Lt. General Yanagida to attack Imphal from the South.
2. 15th Infantry Division under Lieutenant-General Yamauchi attack Imphal from the North.
3. Yamamoto Force, formed from units detached from the 33rd and 15th Divisions under Major-General Yamamoto, supported by tanks and heavy artillery, attack Imphal from the East.

4. A separate subsidiary operation, the 31st Infantry Division under Lieutenant-General Sato to isolate Imphal by capturing Kohima, exploit to the Allied supply base at Dimapur railhead.

Japanese generals had some reservations about the battle-worthiness of the INA forces. But they finally agreed to the participation of INA in these operations as Netaji insisted that the battles of Imphal and Kohima would represent the crucial battles for the liberation of India and therefore that, not only the INA should spearhead the attack, but the first drop of bloodshed should be that of an INA soldier. Altogether some 8,800 INA combatants took part in the offensive. The INA formations which participated are given below:

1. 1st INA Division (Gandhi Brigade) under Maj. General Md. Zaman Kiyani along Tamu-Pallel axis.
2. 2nd INA Division (Subhas Brigade) under Maj. General Shah Nawaz Khan along Ukhrul.
3. Special Task Force (Intelligence Group) commanded by Colonel S.A. Malik along Tiddim-Moirang.
4. The Azad Brigade commanded by Colonel Gulzara Singh, at Tamu-Pallel sector.

British Forces

The14th Army under Lieutenant General Slim was overall responsible for the Burma campaign. 4 Corps commanded by Lieutenant General Geoffry Scoones was at Imphal. Disposition of formations are given below:

1. 20th Indian Infantry Division under Major-General Gracey was at Tamu.
2. 17th Indian Infantry Division under Major-General 'Punch' Cowan was at Tiddim, the division had two brigades only.
3. 23rd Indian Infantry Division under Major-General Roberts in reserve was in and around Imphal.

4. 50th Indian Parachute Brigade under Brigadier Maxwell Hope-Thompson was north of Imphal, undergoing jungle training.
5. 254th Indian Tank Brigade under Brigadier R.L. Scoones was in and around Imphal.

Initial Battles

The Indo-Japanese troops crossed the River Chindwin on 8 March. But Scoones gave his forward division orders to withdraw to Imphal only on 13 March. The 15th Japanese Division of Lt. General Yamauchi moved towards Tamu and Ukhrul in two columns and captured Ukhrul. They advanced towards the Imphal-Dimapur road for their onward attack on Imphal from the north-west. 20th Indian Division at Tamu fell back to Pallel without difficulty because two battalions of Yamamoto Force were delayed in northern Burma. The 1st INA Division under Major General M.Z. Kiyani also joined the Imphal campaign and fought with the Yammoto force at the Pallel sector. Simultaneously, the 31st Japanese Division commanded by Lt. General Sato advanced to Kohima through Homalin and Jessami. Meanwhile, Major General Shah Nawaz Khan's 2nd INA Division reached Ukhrul.

Lt. General Yanagida's 33rd Division moved from the south along Tiddim Road. The Indo-Japanese columns advanced very fast with heavy guns and tanks. 17th British Division could not resist. On the Japanese left flank, the INA's Subhas Brigade, led by Shah Nawaz Khan, reached the edge of the Chin Hills below Tiddim and Fort White at the end of March. From this position, the 2nd Battalion of INA sent troops to relieve Japanese forces at Falam and Hakha, from where they sent out patrols and laid ambushes for the Chin guerrillas operating under the British and took some prisoners. During the early part of the offensive, the Bahadur Group was successful in inducing British Indian soldiers to desert. A force under Khan's Adjutant, Mahboob "Boobie" Ahmed, attacked and captured the hilltop fortress of Klang Klang. The 3rd Battalion of INA meanwhile moved to the Fort White-Tongzang area. The Allied forces retreated vacating the entire area right up to Potshangbam due to the pressure of the advancing Indo-Japanese columns. On 11 April, 1944, the British withdrew to Phubala and Ningthoukhong as the 17th British Division occupied defences at general area Bishnupur.

On 13 April, when the British vacated from their positions at Moirang to Potsangbam, there was jubilation among the local people of Moirang as they knew that INA forces will be arriving soon. Some leaders including M. Koireng Singh spent a sleepless night on the 13 April, hiding under the Moirang Lamkhai Bridge and watching out eagerly the British 17th Division retreating from Tronglaobi. The following day, the Indo-Japanese forces reached Tronglaobi and occupied the British camp. L. Sanaba Singh, M. Koireng Singh, and K. Kangken Singh went to Tronglaobi and welcomed the INA forces and invited them for the formal flag-hoisting on the mainland Indian soil on the 14th April, 1944 at Moirang Kangla (the ancient seat of power).

Liberation and Tri-Colour Hoisting

On 14th April, 1944, on the auspicious 'Chairoaba' day (local year ending ceremony), INA troops led by Colonel S.A. Mallick, along with Captain Ito of the Japanese 33rd Mountain Gun Regiment arrived at Moirang. In a brief ceremony, the national tri-colour flag of INA with the 'Springing Tiger' as emblem was hoisted in the evening, on the same day at the historic Moirang Kangla. This is the first time that the tri-colour was ceremonially hoisted on the mainland of India. More than half of the present Manipur, measuring nearly 10,000 square kilometres of India, for the first time, became a liberated area. This liberated area consisted of up to Pallel in the south-east: Kameng, Sekmai, Kangpokpi, and Kanglatongbi in the north-east; Torbung and Moirang in the south-west; Bishnupur and Irengbam/Lokpaching (Red Hill) in the heart of the valley. Only a small portion of the Imphal Valley and Tamenglong could not be liberated. This vast area was under the control of the INA for nearly 3 months, till the INA withdrew on

15th July, 1944. After the flag hoisting ceremony, the local people presented the arms and ammunitions, abandoned by the British which has been collected by them, to the INA force commander. This was a very proud and happy moment for INA, its Supreme Commander Netaji Subhas Chandra Bose, and the people of Manipur.

Colonel Mallick addressed the gathering on the occasion. The gist of Colonel Mallick's address is: The Provisional Government of Azad Hind had declared war on England and America with a commitment to complete the creation of Greater East Asia and bring welfare to the people of India by defeating Anglo-American forces. The Indian National Army with the support of the Japanese Government has now entered into the sacred soil of India's mainland. In the course of its struggle for the liberation of the people of India from British slavery, we have now reached Moirang, the ancient citadel of the Manipur kingdom. Our commitment is to march to Delhi and unfurl the Tri-Colour flag there at Lal Killa. Many had died on our way to reach here and many would die on our way to Delhi. However, the expulsion of the enemy from the sacred soil of India is a must for us. We shall fight. We appeal to the brave and patriotic people of Manipur to support and provide supplies. Nothing about us should be told to the enemy; everything about the enemy must be informed to us. This is how people can contribute to our single-minded mission of expelling the Imperialist forces from India. Freedom of India is very near; near at hand; we shall win. There would be progress and prosperity for the people of India after it. So give us your helping hands in our collective efforts of freeing India from slavery.

Finally, Colonel S.A. Malik's Bahadur Group (Special Task Force-Intelligence) of the INA, fighting with the 214 Japanese Regiment of the 33rd Division, established its Headquarters at Moirang on 14th April, 1944. Thus, Moirang was the seat of the Provisional Government of Azad Hind Fauz from where it administered all these liberated areas of Manipur which was nearly 10,000 sq. km for all these three months. The people of Manipur extended full support and cooperation to the INA, supplying ration, donations, and other materials.

Many Manipuris joined the INA and post-Independence, approximately 200 such persons of Manipur were awarded freedom fighter pension by the Government. 17 important INA freedom-fighters of Manipur, including two women, are Mairembam Koireng Singh, Hemam Nilamani Singh, Kiyam Gopal Singh, Laiphrakpam Sanaba Singh, Potsangbam Tomal Singh, Thokchom Angou Singh, Sarungbam Ibohal Singh, Imphal, Mutum Amuba Singh, Laishram Irabot Singh, Khumbongmayum Jugeshor Singh, Laishram Kanhai Singh, L. Bijoy Singh, I. Tombi Singh, W. Gyaneshwar Singh, Moirangthem Jatra Singh, M. Randhoni Devi and O. Keina Devi. The last two joined the Jhansi Rani Regiment. The other members were attached to the intelligence group of the INA. They not only help in gathering intelligence but organizing the much-needed supply and casualty evacuation. They organized a human chain supply system for Indo-Japanese forces fighting at Potsangbam and Bishenpur. Elsewhere the locals arranged rice and other provisions.

So Near Yet So Far: Stalemate

The Allies took up defences in the foothills surrounding Imphal valley. By the beginning of April, the momentum of the Indo-Japanese forces was high, attacking Imphal from three directions. Imphal and adjacent areas became a battleground. The attack from the South, aimed at capturing Bishenpur, succeeded in cutting off the old Cachar Road. Considering the precarious situation, the British had earlier strengthen the 17th Division in Bishenpur and surrounding areas with 23rd Division and also part of the 20th Division. A column of Indo-Japanese forces advanced through the hills to the west of Bishenpur. Due to lack of supply, they halted at Maibam Lokpa Ching or The Red Hill, a hillock located on the outskirts of Imphal, North of Bishnupur, barely 10 km from the airport on the Tiddim Road only 10 miles. They succeeded in cutting off the British but suffered heavy casualties due to British artillery fire. The main Indo-Japanese advance along Tiddim-Imphal road was halted in Potsangbam, 2 miles south of Bishenpur, as troops of the 17th Indian Division had recouped and rejoined the battle. Meanwhile Yanagida, the Japanese division commander was relieved of command at the end of the month as he was too cautious. The battles in and around the Bishnupur-Moirang sector and old Cachar road were one of the fierest and continued from March till their retreat in July 1944.

In the East, the opening of the only metalled Imphal-Tamu road was vital for the attacking forces to allow tanks and heavy artillery to reach for the main battle of Imphal. On 4 April, Yamamoto Force attacked 20th Division at Shenam saddle, a few miles north of the saddle was Palel airfield, one of the only two all-weather airfields in the plain. From 8 to 22 April, there was heavy fighting for five peaks that dominated the road. The Japanese breakthrough was lost to the Allies' counter-attacks. Casualties were heavy on both sides. Having failed to cut off the enemy, Yamamoto sent a major raiding force North to raid Palel airfield. The INA's Gandhi Brigade or 2nd Guerrilla Regiment, of two battalions led by Inayat Kiyani, took part in this attack. On 28 April, they attacked Palel. They tried to induce some Indian defenders to surrender, but the defenders rallied after initial hesitation. Another INA group carried out demolitions around Palel but withdrew after they could not link with Japanese units. The Gandhi Brigade was short of rations, having brought forward only one day's supplies, and lost 250 soldiers mainly due to artillery fire after they pulled back from Palel.

In the North, the Japanese 15th Division cut off Imphal. They captured the British supply dump at Kanglatongbi which had been emptied. They also captured Nungshigum Ridge which overlooked the Koirengai airstrip at Imphal. This was a major threat to the 4 Corps. On 13 April, the 5th Indian Division counter-attacked, supported by massive air support, massed artillery, and the M3 Lee tanks of B Squadron of the 3rd Carabiniers. The attackers also lost heavily, every officer of the Carabiniers and the attacking infantry, i.e. 1st Bn., the 17th Dogra Regiment were killed or wounded.

Thus, Imphal was invested by the Indo-Japanese from three sides, cutting off all the three lines of communication and a fall of Imphal was expected any time. It was not generally known in India that around that time Netaji had coined the immortal slogan of 'Jai Hind' and 'Delhi Chalo' due to British propaganda, disinformation, and censorship. In a broadcast over the Azad Hind Radio on 6th July 1944, Netaji addressed: "Father of our Nation! In this holy war of India's liberation, we ask for your blessings and good wishes."

Stalemate

In May, there was a stalemate, all attacks by the Indo-Japanese forces had ceased. Allies' counter-attacks were successfully blocked by the Indo-Japanese forces. But the Allies had complete air superiority as the Japanese air force was diverted to operations in the Pacific. The last major effort by the Japanese Army Air Force had been over the Arakan in February and March.

Unfortunately, that year there was an early monsoon. By mid-May, the Indo-Japanese forces were in great difficulty due to a shortage of ammunition, rations, medicine, and other essential supply. Malaria was rampant. The Indo-Japanese forces also lacked air support. On the other hand, the British were reasonably comfortable with their logistics. They received fresh reinforcements. With complete air superiority, powerful tanks, and heavy artillery they blunted any offensive action by the Indo-Japanese forces. The Japanese 31st Division which had so valiantly fought at Kohima could no longer sustain. They started retreating by the night of 30th May. Shah Nawaz Khan's No. 2 INA Division which was rushed from Arakans to Ukhrul Sector could not influence much. Khan met Sato near Sangsak and was advised to fall back. Even while retreating, they were harassed by the enemy throughout. The bloodiest battle of this sector was fought at Sangsak.

In the Pallel too, the Yamamoto force lost most of its forces in the Tengnoupal area and could not take full advantage of the surprise attack upon Pallel airfield by Major General M.Z. Kiyani's No. 1, INA Division. They could not proceed beyond Pallel.

The Final Attempt

The Indo-Japanese forces made a last attempt in June 1944 as they were still not prepared to call off the campaign, even in the light of all those reverses. Major General Tanaka took over the 33rd Japanese Division from Lt. General Yanagida in June 1944. He immediately started preparing for a fresh attack on Imphal by using all available resources and issued a Special Order on the 2nd June, 1944 in the name of the Japanese Emperor. Monsoon had already set in, thus weather-wise it was not suitable for operations. The Japanese HQ at Tokpa Khul realized that the Imphal campaign had failed due to the underestimation of the fighting strength and defences of the enemy. In the Bishenpur sector, the strength of the 214th Regiment which started with 4,000 men was reduced to only 460 of which only half were battle-worthy on the eve of their final withdrawal in July 1944.

Many died not merely in battle action, but due to malnutrition, starvation, and disease like malaria, dysentery. Eye-witness local population of Manipur told stories famished Indo-Japanese soldiers surviving on edible jungle roots, more like the dead than alive, during those critical days. And many wounded and captured soldiers preferred to commit Hara-Kiri, rather than falling into enemy hands. Ultimately the Japanese army realized that despite braving all these difficulties, the five-month-long Manipur campaign was lost. In the face of the imminent heavy casualty, monsoon, and the impossible chance for any further operation with the depleted strength, General Mutaguchi, Commander of the 15th Japanese Army gave orders on the 20th July, 1944 to all the fighting troops operating in Manipur to retreat.

Thus ended the five-month-old campaign. For the Japanese 'Imphal' remained the forbidden fruit. It proved elusive exactly like the Japanese proverbial saying 'A flower on the Lofty Heights' which means "Something which, though very tempting, is after all beyond one's reach."

Unique Place of 'Imphal' in the Freedom Struggle

Thus Imphal has a unique place in the Indian Freedom Struggle because the Manipur Campaign turned out to be a decisive factor in the fight for Indian independence. Many INA officers and soldiers belonging to various linguistic groups at home and abroad who were Hindus, Muslims, Sikhs, Christians etc. were killed and their blood flowed together and intermingled to ultimately become one, i.e. an Indian, at that a proactive Indian, rather than a passive one. This was the lesson most distinctively taught by the great Netaji Subhas Chandra Bose. He made all passive Indians truly patriots who would lay down life for the nation. Irrespective of which region they hailed, or which language they spoke or which religious faith they practice or which strata of society they belong to, he insisted they were all not only fellow Indians but members of the same family, fighting for a cause—the greatest cause of 'freedom of one and all.

From April to July 1944, Moirang and the surrounding areas of the INA Headquarters were declared as 'enemy zone' by the British. K. Gopal Singh, L. Sanaba Singh, H. Nilamani Singh, and M Koireng Singh of Moirang were declared as traitors by the British Political Agent in Manipur. Order of shoot-at-sight was given. Further, all 17 members of the Mahasabha were black-listed. Scorched earth policy was extended to all villages from Torbung to Ningthoukhong area for the first time in Manipur in the last part of March 1944. Areas from Moirang to Ningthoukhong were heavily bombed by the British, many civilians were killed and injured; almost all the trees and bamboos were uprooted. In Moirang, more than 1,000 houses were set ablaze.

Many patients died and got injured in the bombing. Shri H. Nilamani Singh, one of the INA members suffered a minor injury in his hand. On their way to Rangoon, during the retreat, his only son of late K. Tomba Singh died at Enjung Camp on 17th August, 1944. His last rites were performed with full military honour on the bank of Myantha.

After the surrender of Japan to the Allied forces in the middle of August 1945, the INA at Rangoon had to surrender. The INA members from Manipur in Rangoon were also arrested and put in Rangoon Central Jail. They were brought to Calcutta and released after detention and interrogation. They were received by the INA Reception Committee and stayed at Calcutta. They returned to Manipur on 6th May, 1946. They were asked to report once a week to Imphal Police Station.

Thus ended the effort to liberate India. But this awakening by INA led to mutiny and other forms of insubordinations amongst the British Indian forces. This scared the British and they realized they cannot subdue and hold on to India, as, after World War II their military power was in no position to suppress the proactive Indians. Hence, the effort by INA hastened up the departure of the British from India.

12

INA Headquarters, Moirang, 1944

Hemam Nilamani Singh

The people of India never reconciled themselves to British Imperialism. The Indian people rose up in defiance and struggled from the very beginning. By adopting various forms of peaceful and armed struggle India achieved her Independence.

It is a worth mentioning that in 1942 the "Quit India" movement was launched throughout India under the leadership of Mahatma Gandhi on one side and on the other hand, four Divisions of the Indian National Army (INA) under the Supreme Commander, Netaji Subhas Chandra Bose began to march towards Delhi with the slogan of "Chalo Delhi" by declaring war against the British Government from South East Asia for the cause of Indian freedom within a short period of six months.

After the dropping of bombs at Imphal in May 1942 and in the beginning of 1944, Manipur became a war field during the Second World War. The INA along with the Japanese forces reached Manipur on 18th March, 1944 by crossing the hill tracks of Indo-Burma border. When they advanced up to Manipur, the British forces could not stay in the hill areas except the valley areas. The combined forces of the INA and the Japanese soldiers advanced up to Kohima and Imphal. Another Front of the combined forces advanced towards Tiddim Road by capturing the British Defence Base of Yaiyok (zezo), Thingaiphai and Churachandpur. Then, the British forces began to retreat and took defensive measure at Phougwak-Chao-Ikhai, Tronglaobi and Okshongbung but of no avail. Consequently, they were forced to retreat from Moirang and its surrounding areas to Phublla, Ningthoukhong and then to Bishnupur. When the INA and Japanese forces captured the British Defence Base at Tronglaobi, Sarva Sri L. Sanaba Singh, M. Koireng Singh and with some people went to Tronglaobi and met Col. S.A. Malik in the morning of 14th April, 1944. In the evening of the same day, they came to Moirang and Col. S.A. Malik, leader of the Intelligence group of the INA planted the Indian Tri-colour Flag on the 14th April, 1944 and about 5 pm at Moirang Kangla, (Manipur) the sacred soil of India for the first time as a liberated area. Col. Malik and Captain Ito of Japanese forces delivered speech regarding the objectives of the INA. Then, they declared Moirang as their advance Headquarters and the same was established at the residence of H. Nilamani Singh. Col. Malik was working at Moirang Headquarters for about two and half months. He lived together with H. Thambaljao Singh, father of H. Nilamani Singh. At the same time Captain Harik Singh and Dipchand Singh of the INA were also working at the Headquarters. Naqi Ahamad Choudhuri and Dr. Chakrabarti came at the Headquarters occasionally to discuss the strategy and tactics of war and to collect information. Bachan Singh and Harnam Singh were working at Sendra Hill. They disguised themselves by wearing Manipuri dresses in order to get much information. Lt. Ando and some other Hikarikikan group of Japanese soldiers were also staying at the residence of H. Lukhoimacha Singh and neighbouring houses nearby the INA Headquarters.

Many young and old leaders of Moirang met Col. Malik and promised to supply food and other materials of the INA and Japanese forces. Col. Malik entrusted them to collect information of war. Shri H. Nilamani Singh had given all the paddy he had to the INA without cost. In order to get the advantage of war, Indian currency was also needed. Accordingly, H. Nilamani Singh arranged Rs. 21,000 and handed over to Col. Malik in exchange of Japanese currency. At this, Col. Malik satisfied and gave him the title of 'Sethji'. The people of Moirang felt great pleasure just at the thought that Moirang was under the control of the INA as the liberated area.

Then the combined forces tried to capture the British Defence Base at Bishnupur. That is why, a fierce battle was fought between the combined forces and the British. The INA and the Japanese forces coming from the side of Tongjei Maril (old Cachar road) also tried to give hindrance to the British supply line from Imphal to Bishnupur by a blockade at Lokpa Ching (Red Hill). But, the British Defence Base could not be captured. During the period, K. Gopal Singh, L. Sanaba Singh, H. Nilamani Singh and M. Koireng Singh were working in the intelligence group. Other leaders from Imphal and Nambol, namely Th. Angou Singh, P. Tomal Singh, L. Bijoy Singh, L. Kanhai Singh, I. Tombi Singh, Sh. Ibohal Singh, I. Jatra Singh, M. Amu Singh and his wife Randhoni Devi, Gyaneshwor Singh and his wife Keinya Devi came to Moirang and joined the intelligence group. The people of valley as well as of the hill areas of Manipur supported the INA and the Japanese forces.

In course of the war, the British army again marched towards Moirang by crossing Manipur River and Kumbi from Sugnoo side. When they advanced up to Moirang Khunou, the combined forces of the INA and the Japanese soldiers tried to resist the British. Consequently, a hard battle was fought between them. At the battle, the strongly re-enforced British forces used incendiary bombs and other weapons to re-capture Moirang. As a result, almost the dwelling houses of Moirang caught fire and turned into ashes except ten houses approximately. Captain Ito and many soldiers of the combined forces lost their lives in the battle and wet Moirang with the blood of Martyrs. Afterwards the combined forces attacked against the British and defeated them. Thus, Moirang was again under the control of the INA and Japanese forces.

Then the INA and the Japanese forces had been facing a lot of difficulties due to rainy season, deteriorated condition of roads, scarcity of food etc. Consequently, they were forced to retreat towards Burma. And all the Manipuris who joined the INA and worked as helpers were also declared traitors by the British Government. On 20th July, 1944, they were leaving for Rangoon. In the course of their journey, the Manipuris, namely K. Gopal Singh, L. Sanaba Singh, H. Nilamani Singh, M. Koireng Singh etc. faced many problems owing to frequent bombings by the British in day time, and almost the journey was in the night time without sleeping. When they reached Saikot Village, M. Amu Singh, his wife Randhoni, Gyaneshwor Singh, his wife Keinya Devi also accompanied with them in the journey. On 31st July, 1944, they reached the Sikha Camp. On 2-8-1944 while they were crossing a suspension bridge, the British plane exercised bombing upon them. Immediately they rushed into the dense jungle for taking shelter. On the way, K. Gopal Singh was seriously ill. He was brought by a *palanquin* made of bamboo and arrived at Pintha on 9-8-1944. There they meet Dr. Chakrabarti who once work at Moirang, gave medical treatment for the recovery of Shri Singh. On 15-8-1944, they reached the INA camp of Enjung village. After two days, K. Gopal Singh unfortunately expired on 17-08-1944 and created by the side of Chinwin River with great military honour. On 25-8-1944 they started for Rangoon for Enjung village. On 2nd September, 1944, they arrived Ubank Camp, Seigang on 8-9-1944, Mandalay on 10-9-1944, Pegu station on 15-9-1944. Lastly they reached the Headquarters at Rangoon on 16-9-1944. They along with Col. Malik met Netaji and H Nilamani Singh offered to Netaji a sum of Rs. 3000 which was entrusted by his father, H. Thambaljao Singh for the INA fund. By an order of Netaji, Manipuri groups had undergone training at Rangoon for the expedition of Imphal which was strategically important place to liberate India.

On hearing the news of Germany's defeat in the war as well as the dropping of atom bombs in Hiroshima and Nagasakhi, the Axis power had to surrender in the hands of the British. At this time, some Manipuri groups were staying at Kandogaley of Rangoon for many months. On 8-9-1945 Shri H. Nilamani Singh was arrested by the British army and put in the Pabedan custody for many days. Then he was imprisoned for seven months at Rangoon Central Jail. When the INA Leaders—Shah Nawaz Khan, Sahgal, Dillion etc. were released after the Red Fort trail, Shri H. Nilamani was also released from Rangoon Central Jail. The Manipuri group was brought to Calcutta by ship batch by batch. Shri H. Nilamani Singh, M. Koireng Singh arrived Imphal on 6th May, 1946.

In commemoration of the historic event of the INA and the Japanese soldier who martyred in the freedom struggle of the INA Matyrs' Memorial Complex at Moirang in the magnificent style is going since the Foundation Stone of the INA memorial Hall was laid by Shri U.N. Dhebar, the then President of the AICC on November 25, 1955. The visit of the 9th Finance Commission at the Complex and subsequently a provision of Rs. 10 crore being earmarked for completion and renovation of the complex, preservation of the erstwhile INA Headquarters at Moirang during the World War II and beautification of Moirang—all recognise and conform the historical importance of Moirang. A provision for Rs. 11 lakh made by the Advisory Committee of the INA Martyrs' Memorial Complex for the preservation of the INA Headquarters at Moirang is a significant step, positive and forward to cater the wishes of the intelligentsia, freedom fighters and may walks of life that the headquarters is being converted shortly into a national monument by opening a research institute of Netaji and the INA for the younger generations to come.

The hardships co-shared by the INA, the Japanese forces and the people of Moirang as well as of Manipur in the line of executing the historic responsibility of liberation from the British responsibility for liberation from the British Imperialism cannot be underestimated. Can the ruins that suffered in the process be compensated?

Jai Hind

13

Azad Hind Fauz and the Advanced INA Headquarters, Moirang

Mairembam Prithviraj Singh and *Khelena Gurumayum*

We all know that while the freedom of India was attained through an extended, composite, and multi-pronged struggle, the INA movement led by Netaji Subhas Chandra Bose was a key component that eventually compelled the British to leave India.

Even in death, the courage of Netaji inspired all the Indians to resist and challenge the authority of the British. The original Advanced Headquarters of the INA still exists in splendour at Moirang Konjengbam Leikai and has finally become a tourist site of international significance, which it always deserved to be. From this place, the INA and Japanese forces mobilised to attack the British position of the 17th British Column at Bishnupur in an attempt to capture Imphal, the capital of Manipur, which was crucial for the 'Delhi Chalo' mission. Once Imphal is liberated, Netaji could install an effective 'Provisional Government of Free India' on Indian soil, which should offer an opportunity for more and more Indians to organise an anti-British revolt.

Netaji Subhas Chandra Bose was convinced that freedom is not to be begged for but to be won. To achieve this end, he escaped from his house arrest in disguise and reached Berlin on 3rd April, 1941. Except for indirect support, the meeting with Adolf Hitler wasn't fruitful, so Netaji considered shifting all his plans towards South East Asia. Subhas Chandra Bose organised the Indian Legion in Germany with 8000 British Indian soldiers who became POWs in Egypt. The slogans "*Give me blood, I will get you freedom*" and "*Challo Delhi*" were raised from Azad Hind Radio, Germany, on 9th August, 1942.

Singapore fell into the hands of the Japanese Imperial Army on 15th February, 1942. The sixty thousand troops of Allied Forces (comprising 32,000 Indian Armies, 15,000 British Armies, and 13,000 Australian Armies) led by a British officer, Colonel Hunt, had to beg for unconditional surrender at the Ferrar Park Stadium, Singapore on 17th February.

Major General Fujiwara of the Japanese Imperial Army classified thirty-two thousand Indian prisoners of war and established the Indian National Army (INA). He appointed Captain Mohon Singh as General Officer in Commanding (GOC) of the new formation. This was a strategic movement of Japanese forces in the warfare sense of Emperor Hirohito, which was "Asia for Asians only". From Germany, Netaji then undertook a perilous underwater journey for 90 (ninety) days to reach Sumatra and arrived at Tokyo by air *via* Penang and Manila on 6th May, 1943. He met the Japanese Prime Minister Tojo twice and, with his energetic enthusiasm, secured the unstinted support of the Japanese Government for the movement to free India at any cost. Subhas Chandra Bose arrived in Singapore on 2nd July, 1943. He took charge as the Supreme Commander of the INA and the Indian Independence League (IIL) formed by Rash Behari Bose. Then he reorganized the "Azad Hind Fauj" and declared the formation of 'Provisional Government of Azad Hind' at Cathey Cinema Hall, Singapore, on 21st October, 1943. On 23rd October, 1943, the Azad Hind Government declared war against Britain and the USA.

In March 1944, the three Japanese forces of the 33rd, 31st, and 15th divisions, along with the INA Subhas Brigade, crossed big rivers, mountainous ranges, and dense jungles and started to invade Manipur Valley. The 31st Japanese Division, along with a regiment of INA, captured Kohima, with the exception of Tennis Court, Dimapur Road. Thus, the only lifeline of Manipur was blocked for about one month, and all essential commodities for Allied forces at Imphal had to be supplied by air. The 15th Japanese Division of Lt. General Yamaguchi marched towards Tamu and Ukhrul in two ways, and Ukhrul was captured. They further advanced towards Imphal Dimapur road to cut Imphal-Kohima road at Kanglatombi. Then, the 1st INA Division, under the command of Major General M.Z. Kiani also joined the Imphal campaign and fought along with the Yamamoto force in the Pallel sector.

Simultaneously, the 31st Japanese Division (MATSURI), commanded by Lt. General Sato, advanced to Kohima through Homalin (North Burma) and Ukhrul. Meanwhile, Major General Shah Nawaz Khan's 2nd INA Division could reach Ukhrul to help Sato. By 7th March, 1944, the 33rd Japanese force of Lt. General Yanagida (YUMI), with one INA regiment, marched towards Tiddim Road. The Front of the combined forces of the 33rd Japanese Division and Bahadur Intelligence Group of INA moved towards Tiddim Road by attacking the British Defence Base of 17th British Column of Yaiyok (Zezo) at Thingaiphai, Churachandpur. The British were forced to retreat and took defensive measures at Phougak-chao-ikhai, Tronglaobi and Okshongbung.

The attack on Moirang commenced with canon fire by the Indo-Japanese forces from southern hills range called Khoingoujeng Hill towards Moirang on the evening of 13th April, 1944, and a fierce encounter took place between the British and Japanese soldiers at Phougak-chao-ikhai and Tronglaobi. A large column of British forces had to retreat towards Laiga Stream and Chengei (Moirang). Most people of Moirang had already evacuated and taken refuge at the chain islands of Thanga, Ithing, Sendra, Omba, Mamang Ching, Khongjaingamba, and Keibul hillocks within the Loktak lake. Moirang town had become a battlefield. The local youth led by Shri Mairembam Koireng Singh volunteered for the precautionary measures for the safety of the people of Moirang.

Lieutenant Endo led the infantry attack from Torbung, Terakhongshangbi, and Tronglaobi and another attack was led by Captain Ito of Japanese forces from Kumbi, Thoya. The British had to retreat towards Phubala by abandoning all arms, cannons, and artillery at Okshongbung. All these were keenly observed over a whole sleepless night by some local youth, including M. Koireng Singh while hiding under the Moirang Lamkhai bridge. The area of Moirang was totally cleared and swept away of all enemies up to Potshangbam by the Japanese and INA forces by the night of 13th April, 1944. The retreating British forces took advantage of the darkness of night and secured a firm position to camp for the defensive line at the hillocks of Bishnupur.

Eventually, Kumam Kanglen Singh of Moirang had the chance to meet the INA military officials Colonel Shaukat Hayat Ali Malik and Naki Ahmad Choudhuri (a Manipuri Muslim born in Keikhu Muslim village) at Tronglaobi. The INA officials asked for a meeting with Mairembam Koireng Singh, the local leader of Moirang and an active member of Nikhil Manipuri Mahasabha. So, the four persons, namely Mairembam Koireng Singh, Kumam Kanglen Singh, Meinam Mani Singh, and Laiphrakpam Sanaba, met with the INA officers in the morning at Tronglaobi. The INA officers persuaded the local leaders to affix an appropriate place for hoisting the tri-colour flag at Moirang. Under the guidance of M. Koireng Singh, Col. Shaukat Hayat Ali Malik, Commander of the Bahadur Intelligence Group of the INA, hoisted the Tri-colour Flag with the springing tiger as an emblem at the historic Moirang Kangla on the evening of 14th April, 1944, in the presence of around forty locals, Captain Ito of the 33rd Mountain Gun Regiment of Japan, Naki Ahmad Chouduri and many Japanese and INA soldiers, to mark the unique liberation of Moirang from the clutches of the British colonial rule. The Moirang Kangla was chosen by Shri M. Koireng Singh and his team because the Kangla is a sacred place and the seat of power where coronations of the ancient kings were held. This day, 14th April, 1944, shall be remembered in the history of the freedom struggle of India as the Day of the Revolutionary Declaration of Freedom of the United India.

The flag unfurled at Moirang, Manipur, symbolized the united aspirations of the united people of India from Imphal to Peshawar and Kashmir to Kanyakumari. This is the uniqueness and significance of the liberation of Moirang. Hemam Thambaljao Singh, the father of Hemam Nilamani Singh, provided his residential house with tin roofing at Moirang Konjengbam Leikai to set up the Headquarters for the Indo-Japanese forces. It was thus the first and only Advanced Headquarters of the INA on the liberated soil of India. Col. Shaukat Ali Malik and his officers worked at this Headquarters for three months. It was from this place where the INA and Japanese forces mobilised to attack the British position of the 17th British Column at Bishnupur in its attempt to capture Imphal, the capital of Manipur.

Hemam Nilamani Singh, Mairembam Koireng Singh, and Kumam Kanglen Singh, apart from providing whatever was available in their possession, led the mobilisation of voluntary donations of rice, dry fish, and other grains from the local people for the ration of Indo-Japanese forces who stayed at INA Headquarters, Moirang, and its adjoining areas like Phubala, Sunusiphai etc. They provided the food grains and other edible items by head-carrying, buffalo sleighs, horses, bullock carts, or whatever means available.

Fifty to sixty persons were involved in the delivery of the food materials. In the first instant, three tons of rice, along with another one and a half tons of grains, vegetables, dry fish etc., were provided. Providing rations for thousands of the Indo-Japanese forces for a period of three months during a situation of war was no mean task; it reveals the involvement, encouragement, and participation of the public of Moirang and Manipur in the Freedom Movement of India. Thirteen other members of the Nikhil Manipuri Mahasabha, namely (1) Th. Angou, (2) P. Tomal, (3) S. Ibohal, (4) I. Tombi, (5) L. Bijoy, (6) Kanhai, (7) M. Jatra, (8) W. Gyaneshwor, (9) M. Amuba, (10) L. Irabat, (11) Kh. Jugeshwor, (12) O. Keinya Devi, and (13) M. Randhoni Devi also secretly came to Moirang to join the INA and support the arriving Indo-Japanese forces. Apart from providing rations, the locals also provided Col. Shaukat Ali with much-needed information and intelligence about the enemy camps on a daily basis.

From the INA HQ at Moirang, the INA and Japanese forces mobilised to attack the British position, i.e. the 17th British Column at Bishnupur but could not proceed as it was well manned, equipped, and supplied; moreover, they occupied a better position. On the other side, America intensified its attack on Japan and compelled it to reserve all its air force and resources to defend the motherland. Thus, the Indo-Japanese forces on their expedition to Imphal were left high and dry without any supplies or air support.

The heavy monsoons which had arrived a month early made transportation and mobilisation almost next to impossible; many of the Indo-Japanese forces also died of malnutrition and diseases like malaria due to the shortage of medicine and supplies.

Still, the combined forces of the 1/214 regiment, 1/215 regiment, and the disintegrated part of the 33rd Division converged at Maibam Lotpaching (Red Hill) and prepared to attack Imphal. They constructed "Pimples", "Foxhole", and "Gunner Boxes" around the entire region of Red Hill. Then, they blocked the supply lines to the 17th Column of British at Bishnupur. Meanwhile, Field Marshall Slim of the British Army found the right time to utilize the whole reserves of the Allied Force. All the while, he had been increasing the reinforcement day-by-day by airlifting *via* the Koirengei Airfield and formed a Composite Force called 'Woodforce' to sweep away the stiff resistance offered by the Indo-Japanese Forces at Maibam Lotpaching (Red Hill). Woodforce was a combination of a group of the 17th Column at Bishnupur and a large number of fighters from the Imphal side with heavy artilleries—the powerful Bofor field guns and Lee Tanks. On the other side, the Indo-Japanese forces had very limited stock except for their stiff courage. Despite the shortage of bullets, arms, and ammunition, they kept fighting with their hands and bayonets with war cries and still proceeded forward. The Allied Forces could not control this onslaught of courageous Indo-Japanese fighters.

Finally, Royal Air Force planes had to be used to gun down and bomb the Indo-Japanese side to wipe out the route completely. This was the bloodiest battle called the 'Battle of Imphal,' which lasted from 24th May to 30th May, 1944. The casualty of the Indo-Japanese regiment was so incredibly high that at least 2000 men were killed from the aerial bombing at this battle.

Ultimately, the Japanese army realized the eventuality of defeat due to the imminent heavy casualty, monsoon, and the impossible chance of another fresh operation with the depleted army strength. Then, General Mutaguchi, the Commander of the whole Operation, ordered all his fighting troops operating in Manipur to retreat towards Rangoon on or before 25th July, 1944.

Consequently, the surrounding areas of the Headquarters of Moirang were declared an "enemy zone" by the British. The 17 members of Mahasabha who had joined the INA were listed as traitors, and a "shoot at sight" order was issued against them by the British Political Agent in Manipur. The four members from Moirang, namely K. Gopal Singh, L. Sanaba Singh, H. Nilamani Singh, and M. Koireng Singh, had to leave Moirang from their hide-outs on the night of 20th July, 1944 and proceed with a perilous journey on foot to re-join with the INA at Rangoon. The aged K. Gopal Singh, who was also the father-in-law of M. Koireng Singh, expired due to illness before reaching Rangoon. The British retook Rangoon in May 1945, and the three freedom fighters from Moirang were eventually captured by the British and imprisoned at Rangoon Central Jail. On 18th August, 1945, official Japanese radio made the controversial announcement of the death of Netaji Subhas Chandra from third-degree burns after his overloaded plane crashed in a Japanese-occupied air base at Taihoku, Formosa (now Taiwan).

In his biography, Netaji rightly said, "In the mortal world, everything perishes and will perish, but ideas, ideals, and dreams do not. One individual may die for an idea—but the idea will, after his death, incarnate itself in a thousand lives. That is how the wheels of evolution move on, and the ideas, the dreams of one generation are bequeathed to the next."

The courage of Netaji Subhas Chandra Bose inspired all the Indians after his death. His followers as POWs became the heroes of the Nation. When the Red Fort trial started, the British Government felt the heat of the rising sentiment of the whole country. In January 1946, a massive strike was imposed by officers and pilots of the Royal Indian Air Force (RIAF). By February, the ships of the Royal Indian Navy (RIN) also joined the mutiny. Civilians in Mumbai joined the strikes as well. This was a clear sign of mass rebellion against the British Government, resulting in the final independence dialogue.

Owing to the prevailing situation, all POWs of INA had to be released. The three persons of Moirang, namely M. Koireng Singh, H. Nillamani Singh, and L. Sanaba Singh were also released from their imprisonment at Rangoon.

The Sacred Moirang Kangla, where the first flag declaring the liberation of India was hoisted on 14th April, 1944, is a constant reminder of the courage and ideals of Netaji Subhas Chandra Bose and the Indo-Japanese forces and will remain a hallowed place of pilgrimage for all Indians and Japanese, for ever. The INA Martyrs' Memorial Complex stands in pride here as a testimony to the courage and sacrifices of the Indo-Japanese forces. To this day, the valley of Manipur remains sanctified by the blood and tears of the brave soldiers of the INA and Japan, who had fought and given up their lives to bring freedom to the country.

Until 2020, the only Advanced Headquarters of the INA on Indian soil, located at Moirang Konjengbam Leikai, from where some of the most important movements in the Freedom Struggle of India took shape and transformed into action, did not receive due recognition, if not completely forgotten. For seventy long years, i.e. from 1944 to 2020, the original structure of the Advanced Headquarters of the INA, which belonged to the Late Shri Hemam Thambal Singh, had been protected and preserved by his sons and descendants without much of any support.

Hon'ble Chief Minister Shri N. Biren Singh, in 2020 took the initiative to protect the historic monument, that is the INA Headquarters and develop the compound into a befitting Complex to honour the sacrifices of our freedom fighters and to preserve the narrative of Manipur's contribution to India's Struggle for Freedom. The Government of Manipur then acquired 1.6193 acres from 31 residents to set up the Complex and allotted alternative land to the affected residents.

Now, the INA Headquarters compound has been developed into a beautiful complex with the INA Headquarters in its heart. A replica of the granite monument of the INA's memorial in Singapore before its demolition by the British Indian Army in 1945 has been erected at the compound with the motto of the INA, i.e. ITEFAQ (Unity), ITMAD (Faith) and KURBANI (Sacrifice) inscribed.

In fulfilment of the BJP Government's commitment to the freedom fighters of the Nation, the INA Headquarters Complex was remotely inaugurated and dedicated to the public by the Hon'ble Prime Minister of India, Shri Narendra Modi, on 4th January, 2022. A 165-foot-tall tri-colour flag, which is the tallest in North-East India, was newly erected in the Complex and was unfurled by Union Home Minister Shri Amit Shah on 6th January, 2023 in a grand function.

The Advanced INA Headquarters, Moirang, is a tourist destination for all freedom-loving citizens worldwide. May it for ever remind all the Indians of the courage and sacrifices of the Indo-Japanese forces and their supporters and inspire everybody towards a selfless and strong sovereign Nation. *Jai Hind*!

14

Contribution of the Manipuris in the INA Movement

Mairembam Koireng Singh

The sensational escape of Netaji Subhas Chandra Bose from India on January 16, 1941 with a firm determination of organising an army of liberation outside the country and his arrival in Germany on April 3, 1941 *via* Kabul and Soviet Russia were historical events. On the other hand, on December 7, 1941 Japan captured Pearl Harbour, overran Malaya, Singapore and Burma in quick secession; Andaman and Nicober Island fell under Japanese hand. Thus, Japan could establish her power over the Pacific and the Indian Ocean. Even Calcutta and Madras got the brunt of war. On May 10 and 16, 1942 Imphal, the capital of Manipur was bombard by the Japanese as their first air-raid. Many innocent people including women and children were killed. All the prisoners from Imphal Jail escaped. Treasury and banks looted and subsequently closed. All non-Manipur merchants left Khwairab and Bazar, the only business centre dealing with others from outside Manipur. As a result, Manipur was isolated completely from others part of the world in respect of business. The most essential commodities like salt and kerosene were to be carried by head load from Silchar to

Cachar road. The cost of salt and kerosene unimaginably reached Rs. 5 per seer and Rs. 150 per item respectively. Nearly 2 Lakh of Indian refugees were fleeing from Burma through Manipur. And, Imphal became the forward base of new forces built by the Allied forces.

The State Darbar, the highest administrative seat had to be shifted to the house of Shri Khomdram Angangjao Singh (retired engineer) at Kwakeithel and other important offices were shifted to different places. All the educational institutions were closed for six months. Imphal became a deserted city. Most of the citizens vacated their houses and took shelter in different far-flung villages. The vacated houses were occupied by the army personnel. It results the activities of the Nikhil Manipuri Mahasabha, the only political organisation in Manipur, to take a subdued tone. The intelligentsia of Manipur had been waiting for impeding changes in the emerging political and military scenarios of the world. As had been said by Netaji, "The enemy of the British is the friend of India" Germany, Italy and Japan though they were branded as fascists, all the leaders and workers of the Mahasabha regarded them as friends.

After three month's journey in two successive submarines of Germany and Japan, Netaji reached Tokyo on May 6, 1943. He could reached an agreement with the Government of Japan through his political acumen; he reorganise Azad Hind Fauz with the formation of the Provisional Government of Azad Hind. Brigades after the name of Gandhi, Subhas, Nehru and Azad, in addition a women regiment after the name of Jhansi Rani were raised; training centres for the new recruits and Balsena. The proclamation of Provisional Government of Azad Hind was declared on October 21, 1943 the Azad Hind Government declared war on Britain and America. Netaji in his speech expressed his profound satisfaction at the declaration of war as the Head of Government of Azad Hind as well as Head of the liberation army. He gave the clarion call "*Chalo-Delhi*" and asked all the officers and jawans to march towards Delhi with the will "do-or-die" and liberate 300 million Indians from the British yoke.

In the month of March 1944, three Japanese Army Division along with Subhas Brigade entered the Indian Territory after crossing the rivers, different hill ranges and thick forest and attempted to thrust deep inside the territories of India. 31st Japanese Division along with a regiment of INA reached Kohima town, now the capital of Nagaland; fought a fierce battle and ultimately captured the town with the exception of importance place like Tennis Court. Dimapur road, the only life-line of Manipur was blocked for about a month. All essential commodities for the allied forces at Imphal had to be supplied by Air.

15th Japanese Division with one INA regiment marched towards Tamu and Ukhrul in two ways. Ukhrul was captured. They further advanced towards Imphal-Dimapur road. In the meantime, another group of the Division reached Pallel but they could not come down to the valley. 33rd Japanese Division along with one INA regiment marched towards Tiddim Road. In this connection, it will be relevant to mentioned that some 32 Meiteis who earned their livelihood in Burma joined the movement under the leadership of Shri L. Guno Singh of Khurai (Manipur) and operate in the battle front as an advance party. 13 of the 32 Meiteis reached Pallel and tried to secure the secret of the enemy and also sought the support of the local people. One of them was arrested in Sugnu. A large number of Manipuri tribals who were the erstwhile members of the British 'V' Force also joined the movement and participated in the battle front.

Another 19 members of the 32 Meiteis Advance Party marched towards Tiddim road reached Khuga valley, now in Churachandpur Distrct in the month of March 1944. Out of them, four members, namely (1) Shri M. Ahanjao Singh, (2) Shri B. Balhob Sharma, (3) Shri M. Chaoba Singh, and (4) Shri S. Yaima Singh were arrested and taken them from Manipur and kept at Egle-kacha staging camp in Calcutta till war was over.

Indo-Japanese Forces advanced very fast with heavy guns and tanks. 17th British Division could not resist the advancing forces; as such they were compelled to retreat leaving completely behind all the southern hill ranges, now Churachandpur District and villages up to Potshangbam into the hands of the advancing Japanese and INA column. Jubilation ran large among the local people of Moirang at the advance of the Japanese forces and the INA. Some leaders (including the writer) spent a sleepless night on the 13th April hiding themselves under the Lamkhai Bridge and watching eagerly about the progress of retreat of the British Columns (17th Division) towards Bishnupur. Thus, the withdrawal of the 17th British Division was completely on April 13, 1944. Before the retreat of the British from Tronglaobi village, some three miles away to the south of Moirang it was their strong defence base till April 13, 1944. Closed behind them the Japanese and INA forces occupied the vacated areas. In the early morning of April 14, the leaders of the Indo-Japanese advance party had discussion with Sarva Shri (1) M. Koireng Singh, (2) L. Sanabi Singh, (3) K. Kanglen Singh, (4) M. Mani Singh and others all of Moirang at Tronglaobi village. After taking stock of the situation at about 5 pm on the same day Col. Soukat Ali Malik, Commander of the Bahadur (Intelligence) Group planted the Tri-Colour Flag with Springing Tiger as emblem at the Historic Moirang Kangla where the INA Martyrs' Memorial Complex is, at present, taking shape. Many Japanese officers and soldiers were also assembled. All arms and ammunition abandoned by the British forces were collected by the local people and handed over to Col. Saukat Ali Malik. Captain Ito of 33rd Mountain Gun Regiment (of Japan) and Col. Malik addressed the gathering. Col. Malik's version was translated before gathering by the writer and gist of the version was:

> "... The provisional Government of Azad Hind Fauz declared war on England and America with a commitment to complete with the creation of Greater East Asia and bring welfare to the people of India by defeating Anglo-American forces. The Indian National Army with unstinted support of the Japanese Government has now crossed the Indo-Burmese border and in the course of its struggle for the liberation of

> the people of India from the British yoke we have now reached Moirang, the ancient citadel of Manipur. Our Commitment is to march to Delhi and unfurl Tricolour Flag there at Lal Killa. Many had died on our way to reach here (Moirang) and many would die on our way to Delhi. However, expulsion of the enemy from the sacred soil of India is a compulsion for us. We shall fight; and the people of Manipur would provide supplies to us. Nothing about us shall be passed on to the enemy; everything about the enemy should be passed on to us. This is a way that people ought to do as a part of contribution to our single—minded mission.—expulsion of the imperials forces from India. Freedom of India is very near, near at hand; we shall win it and we shall have progress and prosperity of the people of India after it. So give us your hands; our collective efforts should cause India free from slavery."

The message was well received by the jubilant crowd and felt that they were the first liberated people of India though many of their families evacuated Moirang and took shelter at Thanga, Sendra and Mamang Ching. They voluntarily donated provisions to the advance Indo-Japanese forces. The voluntary campaign led by Shri Kuman Kanglen Singh of Moirang.

A Special emissary brought a message from Netaji appealing to the leaders and workers of the Indian National Congress and to the people of Manipur in general to extend unreserved support to the Indo-Japanese forces who had crossed Indo-Burmese border and reached Manipur. The message was brought by Chamol (INA advance Base Camp) by one Kuki, named Lungdam had handed over to Dr. Gulapchand Singh, then the Medical Officer posted at Sugnu. It was again handed over to Shri Thokchom Angou Singh of Singjamei, Imphal.

Since Manipur was a princely state, the Congress was not allowed to be formed and functioned. Even Gandhiji was not allowed to enter Manipur. But the leaders and workers of Nikhil

Manipuri Mahasabha which has identical ideas and objectives with the Indian National Congress welcomed the appeal made by Netaji. Thirteen members of the Mahasabha, namely Sarva Shri (1) Th. Angou Singh, (2) P. Tomal Singh, (3) S. Ibohal Singh, (4) I. Tombi Singh, (5) L. Bijoy Singh, (6) L. Kanhai Singh, (7) M. Jatra Singh, (8) W. Gyaneshwar Singh, (9) M. Amubi Singh, (10) L. Iabot Singh, (11) Kh. Jugeshwar Singh, (12) Srimati O. Keinya Devi, and (13) Srimati M. Randhoni Devi reached Moiranf secretly. They joined with the members of Moirang and worked together with the people of Moirang. Large quantity of food was collected for the Indo-Japanese forces and carries out espionage activities. All the surrounding villages up Ningthoukhong was under the control of INA with its Headquarters at Moirang for three months till 15 July, 1944. The building of the Headquarters belonged to Shri H. Nilamani, Freedom fighter, which stands till today. The surrounding areas of the Headquarters was declared 'enemy zone' by the British. Sarva Shri (1) K. Gopal Singh, (2) L. Sanaba Singh, (3) H. Nilamani Singh, and (4) M. Koireng Singh of Moirang were declared as traitors by the British Political Agent in Manipur. Orders of shoot-at-sight were passed on them. Then all 17 members of the Mahasabha (13 members who came down from Imphal and 4 members from Moirang) were black listed. Scorched earth policy was extended to all villages from Tronglaobi (PhougwakchaoIkhai) to Ningthoukhong area for the first time in Manipur in the last part of March 1944. Moirang to Ningthoukhong were heavily bombed; many civilians were killed and injured; almost all the trees and bamboos were uprooted. In Moirang more than 1000 houses were set ablaze with the exception of five or six.

The fast advancement of Indo-Japanese Forces with heavy guns and tanks were resisted by the British at Bishnupur. Even hand-to-hand fighting took place in between Bishnupur and Ningthoukhong. Both the British and Indo-Japanese forces tried tooth and nail to overpower each other. The battle between the British and the Indo-Japanese forces in the area was one of the bloodiest in the Battle of Imphal. The object of the Indo-Japanese forces was to capture the strongly fortified British camp at Bishnupur. On failing to capture the British camp the Indo-Japanese forces bypasses the area; followed the western hill ranges, and put up a blockade to British supplies at Lokpaching (Red Hill) for 48 hours at the cost of heavy casualties on both sides. But, it was recaptured by the British forces after heavy fighting. The Indo-Japanese could not pass heavy guns and tanks through Bishnupur. Thus, the chance of attacking Imphal was remote. Had the Indo-Japanese forces succeeded in capturing the British camp in Bishnupur and Imphal in succession the course of Indian history might have changed?

Heavy rainfall started in the beginning of July. All the Indo-Japanese forces started retreating in the middle of July. After getting retreat order from the Rangoon Headquarters Col. Malik, Commander of the Bahadur Group was compelled to leave his Headquarters at Moirang in the middle of July 1944 along with those members of Manipur Party. Many army personnel on their way to Rangoon died due to starvation, dysentery and diarrhoea after a long journey on foot through Tiddim Road. The party reached Kalemyo, a border town of Burma. On their war to Kalemyo they suffered a lot. They took cover in the dense forest during the day and marched on foot during night. Their ration on way from Tiddim to Kalemyo was maize and only after Kalemyo, they could get rice. After Kalemyo they proceed farther towards Kalewa and from Kalewa to Ye-u (on their way to Rangoon). The civilians on their way from Kalewa to Ye-u were escorted by one Gurkha Lieutenant of Bahadur Group who died at Ye-u. It was one of the terminal railway stations nearest to the border. The trains were driven by fire wood and coaches were open. The trains had daily services but only during the night. At day time, engines of the trains were sidetracked behind the cover of thick jungles and coaches were kept scattered. At dusk, the engines and coaches were connected and took proper shape for service. The party reached Segaing. It happened to be a big Manipur village. The inhabitants of Seigaing spoke (and still speak) Manipuri in pidgin form. There was a wooden bridge constricted over the Irrawaddi River. Three of its wooden spans were blasted by the British. As such, the bridge was no more communicable. Therefore, the party from Manipur crossed the river by motor boat in small groups. Immediately after crossing the Irrawaddi they arrived at Mandalay and then Rangoon. Trains running between Mandalay and Rangoon were of good ones.

All the Manipuris whose energies by dire necessities and compulsions had been exhausted in venturing the retreat through wild-animals-infested jungles, dangerous hill ranges and rivers their suffering did not come to an end. Acute malaria had affected them and no one was spared. They were hospitalised for medical treatment at Miyang Hospital, about 10 km away from Rangoon. Formerly, it was a public hospital. Later it was converted into military hospital for the INA. British aircrafts altogether eleven in number exercised aerial bombing over the hospital. Many patients die and got injury in the inhuman act of bombing. Shri H. Nilamani, one of the members from Manipur suffered minor injury in his hand. On their way to Rangoon, Shri Kiyam Gopal Singh, the only son of late K. Tomba Singh, Khadrakpa of Moirang died at Enjung Camp on 17 August, 1944. His last rites were performed with full military honour on the bank of Myintha (Chingwin) River.

When the party reached Rangoon, Netaji introduced them in an assembly of the INA officers and jawans. All the members from Manipur put up in 11 (eleven) guest houses at Kandogulay, Rangoon. Sarva Shri (1) L. Irabot Singh, (2) Kh. Jugeshwar Singh, and (3) I. Tombi Singh joined the active service of INA; and (1) Srimati O. Keinya Devi and (2) Srimati Randhoni Devi joined Jhansi Rani Regiment. The other members were attached to the intelligence group of the INA. These preparations were being made for the second phase of attack.

After the surrender of Japan to the Allied forces in the middle of August 1945 the INA at Rangoon had to surrender. The members from Manipur were also arrested by the Rangoon occupying Forces from their hiding places trough a tip for Manipuris and put in Rangoon Central Jail. They were brought to Calcutta (India) by ship and released after detention and interrogation for about 48 hours. The party was received by the INA Reception Committee and stayed at Calcutta. The Manipur party was sent to Manipur by rail and road at government expenses and reached Manipur on May 6, 1946 with an instruction to report to the state government. They were asked to attend once a week to Imphal Police Station for three months. Thus, ended the contribution of the Manipuris in the INA movement.

Last but not the least, it will be injustice on our part if we fail to mention about those friends who participated in the INA movement and worked together in Manipur Front for three months and went underground. When the retreat orders came in the month of July 1944 some left Manipur for Rangoon and suffered imprisonment there. But, those friends who went underground suffered in the nearby hills for about a year or so were not included in the list of freedom fighters, not to speak of 'Sanman' pension and facilities under the present amended rules of freedom fighters. The rule says that the persons who went underground shall have to be identified by a co-worker freedom fighter who suffered five-year imprisonment and enjoyed 'Sanman' pension and facilities. There may be many freedom fighters participated under the leadership of Mahatma Gandhi who suffered five years or more imprisonment available. But, in the history of INA movement no one is proper to be imprisoned for five years because of period of INA movement was less than five years.

I am to appraise the Government of India that the participation of the Manipuris in this movement had been compelled to limit only to those persons who suffered imprisonment at least six months. Those who went underground suffered pain in the hills were excluded by the present amended rules.

I am sure the people of India will agree with me logically that a large number of people of Manipur were involved in the last war of Independence in Manipur interacting between the Indo-Japan forces positively and allied forces negatively. The liberation army dispossessed from the British rule almost all the hills of Manipur, came down to the valley; occupied Pallel in the south-east; Kameng, Sekmai, Kangpokpi and Kanglatombi in the north-east; Torbung and Moirang in the south-west; Bishnupur and Irengbam/ Lokpaching (Red Hill) in the heart of the valley. Only a small portion of the Manipur valley could not be liberated. Without co-operation and involvement of the local people how three Divisions of Nippon Army and One Brigade of INA who entered Manipur with ration could continue heavy fighting for three months against the mighty Allied forces?

Long Live the INA Spirit, Jai Hind.

15

INA's Involvement in the Battle of Imphal

Yaiphaba Meetei Kangjam

Manipur, situated between India and Burma, was the gateway to the Indian National Army's march to Delhi. The capture of its capital, Imphal, along with the hill town of Kohima to the north, was also the objective of the Japanese Operation U-Go. For the INA, capture of Imphal would open the way for their advance to the Brahmaputra valley, Bengal and finally to Delhi. Peter Ward Fay in his book *The Forgotten Army* brings out how important it was for the INA to reach Imphal:

> To Shah Nawaz [Khan] and his battalions climbing the Chin Hills, to Prem [Kumar Sehgal] pushing papers in Rangoon though he would much prefer a field command, to Lakshmi [Sehgal] wondering when she will receive word to collect her women and go forward once more with Netaji, to Netaji himself— what is happening in and about Imphal is of enormous importance. Bursting into India, after all, is what the Indian National Army is all about, its

> *raison d'eitre*, the excuse for its existence. It can only be done at the Burma-India border. No other place offers an approach.

For the Japanese army, capturing Imphal may have been a part of their grand strategy to defend Burma but for the INA it was much bigger than that. For Netaji and his army, setting foot at Imphal and standing at the doorstep of their motherland would have given them the impetus and motivation to push themselves harder towards Delhi. However, harsh realities of the battlefield and early monsoon rains shattered their dream of reaching the capital of India. Hardly had they reached Imphal when they were forced to turn back along with their Asian friends, the Japanese Army.

Preparing to Storm the Gates of India

The final order to destroy the British forces in the India-Burma frontier before the arrival of the rainy season was given by Japan's Burma Area Army to Lieutenant-General Mutaguchi Renya's Fifteenth Army on 19 January, 1944. Fifteenth Army came up with the plan for a two-prong offensive Operation Ha-Go and Operation U-Go. Of the two, the Japanese main focus was Operation U-Go which was intended to destroy the British forces in Imphal and secure the areas in its vicinity. Operation Ha-Go which was to be carried out a month earlier was directed in crushing the British in Arakan in Burma and keeping their forces involved in defending Bengal thereby making things easier for the Japanese in their bigger offensive for Imphal.

The Japanese Southern Army and the Burma Area Army had been toying with the plan to strike at eastern India as early as September 1942. Subhas Chandra Bose, since the day he assumed command of the INA in July 1943, had also been preparing his troops for their fight to liberate India by joining hands with the Japanese. By March 1944, the 1st Division of the INA, which comprised Subhas Brigade, Gandhi Brigade, Azad Brigade and Nehru Brigade, was prepared for the Imphal offensive. The Ranis of the Rani Jhansi Regiment, 1st Hind Field Force, the INA 2nd Division and other smaller groups were undergoing training at the rear. Men from the Bahadur and Intelligence special groups had already been sent to the front well before the offensive.

It was not easy for Bose to make the Japanese treat his men and himself as equal allies in all respects and not as puppets for the latter. Initially, the Japanese were planning to use the INA men for espionage, intelligence collection and for propaganda purpose only in their operations. Bose had to do some hard convincing with Tokyo and the Japanese commanders in Burma to get some independent roles for his army. Netaji, as Bose was fondly called by his troops and others, met Lieutenant-General Kawabe Masakazu, Commander-in-Chief of the Burma Area Army in early January 1944. They discussed the deployment of the INA in the upcoming offensives and the level of cooperation between the INA and the Japanese Army. The Japanese C-in-C agreed to Netaji's condition that the INA should not be broken down into any formation less than a battalion and all INA units should be commanded by INA officers only. It was also agreed that the INA should be given an independent sector at the front to fight and all liberated areas in Indian territory should be handed over to the INA for administration along with the captured items.

Besides discussing and agreeing on other matters by both sides in the meeting, Netaji took the opportunity to clearly express his desires to Kawabe. He told the Japanese C-in-C that the INA should form the spearhead of the advance into India, and that the first drop of blood to be shed on Indian soil should be that of a member of the INA. It was also made clear that the only flag that would be approved to fly over Indian territory would be the Indian tricolour. Kawabe also assured Netaji to help the INA in Burma in all such matters as rations, medicines, evacuation of casualties etc. Having set up the framework under which the two armies would work together, Netaji worked harder to prepare his troops for the march to Delhi, but not before liberating Imphal.

INA in the Battle of Imphal

Mutaguchi's Fifteenth Army launched its Operation U-Go nearly a month after their Arakan Operation, Ha-Go, in the first week of March. Lieutenant-General Yanagida's 33rd Division pressed Major-General Cowan's 17th Indian Division from the south, aiming at Imphal along the road from Tiddim to Bishenpur. A week later, 33rd Division's Infantry Group, Yamamoto Force, came up the Kabaw Valley against Major-General Gracey's 20th Indian Division and tried to force their way into the Imphal plain across the hills to Palel. They were stopped at the group of hills called the Shenam Saddle. Major-General Yamauchi's 15th Division marched across the mountains north-east of Imphal and cut the main road between Imphal and Kohima. A third Japanese force, Lieutenant-General Sato's 31st Division went towards Kohima with the objective to block the reinforcements and supplies of the British IV Corps coming from the railhead at Dimapur to Imphal, completing the isolation of Imphal.

Mutaguchi planned to apply the most pressure on the British from the south-east of Imphal, up to the Tamu-Palel Road. He knew that the British had greatly improved the road. It was the shortest motorable route from the Chindwin to Imphal and also lead to another prime possession of the British—the all-weather airfield at Palel—a vital component in the defence of Imphal. It was for these reasons that Mutaguchi equipped the best fire power in the whole of Fifteenth Army to Yamamoto Force to face Gracey's 20th Division in the hills above Palel. It was in the fight on this sector that the INA's Gandhi Brigade (No. 2 Guerrilla Regiment) and Azad Brigade (No. 3 Guerrilla Regiment) showed active participation in the Battle of Imphal. These two brigades had a strength of 2,000 men each.

Gandhi Brigade and Headquarters of INA's 1st Division reached the Imphal front in mid-April 1944. The Divisional Commander, Colonel Mohammad Zaman Kiani, set up his headquarters at Chamol, a mountain village situated between Palel and Tamu. His cousin Lieutenant-Colonel Inayat Jan Kiani, Commander of

Gandhi Brigade, set up his base at the village of Khanjol. When the two Kianis met Major-General Yamamoto at Chamol on 17 April, they were told that Imphal would surely fall any day. Yamamoto asked the Commander of Gandhi Brigade to cover the left flank of his advance to Palel. This is exactly what the men of the INA had been waiting for—to get an independent role in the fight for Imphal. Earlier on 28 March, when M.Z. Kiani met Mutaguchi at Maymyo, he had been told to rush and join Yamamoto Force if he wished to be present at the fall of Imphal. In the haste and pressing anticipation of victory the Gandhi Brigade left all its heavy baggage, including machine guns, mortars and grenades at Kalewa. They had been told that each soldier would need just a rifle, fifty rounds of ammunition and a blanket. All other equipment and supplies would be acquired in Imphal, which was supposedly on the verge of collapse. This would later prove costly for the Gandhi Brigade in the battlefield.

Soon after establishing its base at Khanjol on 28 April, Gandhi Brigade was ordered to join the Japanese on attacking the Palel airfield. The date set for the attack was 1 May. The Japanese planned a thrust from the east of the airfield while the INA was to attack from the south at the same time with one battalion. When this order came, the men of the Gandhi Brigade had not eaten properly for three days. Many of them had fallen sick. There was no time to get the heavy equipment which they left at Kalewa. However, the men were in high spirits and they were determined to put up a good show.

A task force of 300 men selected from the whole brigade was formed and placed under the command of Major Pritam Singh for the attack. This force set out for their objective during the night of 30 April. After two exhausting night marches Pritam Singh managed to reach the southern flank of Palel. The men were under the impression that when they came face to face with Indian troops, their former comrades would not fire on them. At about half past ten on the night of 2 May, the leading company of this force came in contact with a Gurkha platoon outpost about five miles away from the airfield. The Gurkhas had heard the INA men talking and coming towards them. They coolly waited for them and opened heavy and accurate fire from close range. The INA men were surprised and began to flee and scatter in panic. However, Pritam Singh was able to collect them and resume the attack on the outpost with more caution. On his next move, he initially tried his best to talk to the Gurkhas and win them over to his side, but the Gurkhas were in no mood to oblige him. Then he ordered to attack the post. The Gurkhas were well entrenched and they fought off seven following attacks targeted at their strongly defended position before the INA finally retired. There were several casualties on both sides, but the INA suffered a heavy blow. The INA lost two officers and several men; about 35 more surrendered or were captured. Two Gurkhas were killed.

Pritam Singh then withdrew to a rear position and sent out a patrol of Bahadur Group to scout around a new route for another attack on the airfield. His regimental commander, I.J. Kiani, also brought up reinforcements and prepared to renew the assault. But even before they could gather properly to launch the new attack, the British, who were highly alerted now, sent in infantry, called up guns and delivered air strikes at tree-top level. After two days of facing the British assaults, Kiani ordered a general withdrawal to Khanjol. These two hugely weakened forces reached their base on 4 May. Besides the surrendered or captured men, the INA had suffered more than 200 casualties in their attempt to attack the Palel airfield. Pritam Singh's Bahadur Group patrol had surrendered too.

While the above narrative, which is based on several sources, did not mention about Pritam Singh's men actually reaching the airfield, Shah Nawaz Khan, in his memoir, claims that a party of Pritam Singh's force managed to destroy some planes in the airfield:

> In the meantime, the other party had successfully infiltrated through and captured the aerodrome, but they found no trace of the Japanese there and since they were not enough to hold the aerodrome by themselves

> they withdrew after destroying all the aeroplanes concentrated there.

Keeping aside the question of whether the INA destroyed planes or not, Hugh Toye gives much weight to a rather more interesting aspect of the INA's attempt to attack the Palel airfield:

> The failure at Palel and the subsequent casualties to Kiani's force were perhaps the most significant events in INA history since the arrival of S.C. Bose in the Far East. Bose had hoped, and his hope had become an axiom of INA propaganda, that when a formed body of the INA confronted British-Indian troops in the field, propaganda and not fire-power would decide the day.... Now this cherished illusion was shattered; that they were regarded by their former comrades of the Indian Army as traitors was suddenly plain to all.

After the failed attempt for Palel, despite several attacks by the British-Indian forces, the Gandhi Brigade stayed in and around Khanjol and Mittong Khunou throughout May. During this time poor rations, sickness and battle casualties took a toll on I.J. Kiani's men and wore down their morale. When Kiani visited Divisional Headquarters on 26 May to ask for supplies, he also reported that 25 of his men had tried to kill themselves. While the major strength of the remainder of his brigade has been given the task of transporting rations, hardly three companies could be used for the defence of their positions. Meanwhile, this same group of men came under frequent attack by the well-fed and properly armed men of the British Sea forth Highlanders.

British military intelligence reported that the INA fought well but always withdrew at the critical moment. Lt. Col. I.J. Kiani, for the problems faced by him in the battlefield, mainly blamed the Japanese failure to supply and support him. Even though Bose had been earlier promised all possible help by Tojo and Kawabe, relations between the men of the INA and the Japanese Army fighting in the Imphal front were deteriorating with each passing day. Under battle conditions in the midst of monsoon jungle, with no supplies, tempers were short. Each side accused men from the other side of arrogance. Protocol regarding saluting was the immediate cause of numerous incidents. In such situations, the prejudice of the Japanese soldiers towards the INA men of being 'surrendered and disloyal' often came out clearly.

Hikari Kikan, the Japanese liaison department attached to the INA, responsible for providing ammunitions and other supplies to the INA, failed terribly in their job. But the Japanese had their own problems. When their plan to rely on *Chachirukyuyo* (Churchill rations) and British supply dumps after the fall of Imphal in mid-April failed, the Japanese themselves were now very short of ammunition and supplies. Under these circumstances the INA divisional commander and Hikari Kikan could not do much to extract supplies from the Japanese for the INA men who, thus, continued to suffer.

There was very limited patrol activity and fighting on both sides in June due to the rains. By 15 June, hunger, malaria and other diseases reduced the strength of the Gandhi Brigade to less than a thousand men. Desertions, too, were going out of control. Even the second-in-command of the brigade had deserted and soon after leaflet assigned by him were dropped upon the men of the INA, appealing them to join the Indian Army without any fear. Such leaflets and safe-conduct passes were able to influence the minds of the men who were already in a very bad situation. The INA also exercised similar tactics but on a smaller scale. An extract from one of INA leaflets says:

> Bahadur Hindustani Sipahio (Fearless Indian soldiers), the ruthless British have sent you to fight your Asian brothers. Do you wish to remain their slaves? An army of free India is here, here in Burma, preparing to march on Delhi. Come join us! Death, death to the English!

It is doubtful these leaflets accomplished much. On the contrary, men from the Gandhi Brigade were deserting in such numbers that 80 of them had to be disarmed and sent to the rear. According to Shah Nawaz, by 30 June, 116 men had been surrendered or captured. Even then, Bose in his headquarters had been quite happy with the progress of the campaign, though behind schedule, and did not know the actual picture of the disaster that had befallen his army on the front.

The strength of the Gandhi Brigade was only 750 strong at the beginning of July when they finally withdrew from the areas of Khanjol, Mittong Khunou and Mombi Track.

The Gandhi Brigade and the Azad Brigade (No. 3 Guerrilla Regiment) of the 1st Division of the INA shared an almost similar experience although the latter arrived onlyaround 26 May at the front. Yamamoto utilized Azad Brigade to cover his right flank and thus deployed them on the east of the Tamu-Palel Road. Lieutenant-Colonel Gulzara Singh, the Commander of Azad Brigade set up his headquarters at Narum village. Even on its first arrival in the battle area the brigade was sorely depleted by sickness. The situation of a battalion of the Azad Brigade was such that by the end of June, of approximately 600 men a little more than 300 were available for combat; 250 stayed sick in the rear areas, 12 had deserted; 3 had committed suicide; and 3 had been killed in action. Another battalion was involved in some clashes with British-Indian forces around the village of Bongli from the end of June until they were ordered to withdraw around mid-July.

At the end of May, Lieutenant Colonel Shah Nawaz Khan, who had been busy with his Subhas Brigade (No. 1 Guerrilla Regiment) in the Chin Hills in Burma, was ordered by the 1NA 1st Division Commander to join on the central front. He, thus, took his 2nd battalion and remnants of the 3rd Battalion to the Naga Hills with the aim to reinforce the Japanese at Kohima but he was too late to get involved in the fight there. Although Shah Nawaz and some of his men are believed to have undertaken reconnaissance activities beyond Ukhrul in the direction of Kohima, the main body of his force stayed in the area of Ukhrul.

Colonel M.Z. Kiani ordered a general withdrawal of his regiment from the Imphal front on 18 July. The conditions in which the men of the INA retreated towards Burma were terrible, to say the least. It was a long march to Burma enduring the torrential rains without any warm clothes, fighting the pangs of hunger, bouts of malaria and dysentery. Added to the miseries were the feelings of defeat and humiliation thrown at them by the Japanese men.

In the Bishenpur sector, Colonel Shaukat Ali Malik, Commander of the Bahadur Group, hoisted the INA's flag for the first time on the Indian mainland on 14 April, 1944 at Moirang Kangla. The INA also set up its operational headquarters at Moirang. The Provisional Government of Free India (Arzi Hukumat-e-Azad Hind) administered the 'liberated areas' of Manipur from here for the next three months until Japanese-INA forces withdrew to Burma in mid-July.

Huge Toye cites official figures given by the General Headquarters, New Delhi in 1945-46 to give an idea of INA casualties in the Imphal campaign:

> The INA [1st] Division had started out for Imphal 6,000 strong; only 2,600 returned, and of these about 2,000 had to be sent at once to hospital. During the campaign 715 men deserted, about 400 were killed in battle, about 800 surrendered, about 1,500 died of disease and starvation.

INA and People of Manipur

It would be wrong to say that the Japanese-INA forces received massive support from the people of Manipur during their Imphal Operation. The main communities in Manipur—Meiteis, Nagas and Kukis—helped them as well as the British, into different degrees and for diverse reasons. Nonetheless, it can be said with much certainty that in the battle of Imphal, none of these communities supported en masse either of the two fighting parties. Altogether about 200 Manipuris joined the INA or helped them actively.

The INA, even before reaching the India-Burma border, was helped by a group of 32 Meiteis who were working in Burma. 13 out of the 32 people came as advance party on the Tamu-Palel sector and worked to gather intelligence and local support in the Palel area. The remaining 19 came ahead of the Japanese-INA forces on the Tiddim Road and reached Khuga valley in March 1944. Four of them were arrested and sent to Calcutta until the war was over.

In the Tamu-Palel sector, by the end of June, when the INA's Gandhi Brigade ran out of supplies, the local people in that area came forward to help. According to Shah Nawaz Khan, the local Nagas implored Lieutenant Colonel Kiani not to retreat. He remembers their words then:

> You are the army of India's liberation. You must not go back. We are extremely short of food ourselves, but we will collect whatever we can for you. We will live or starve to death together.

They went back to their villages and came with whatever rations they could collect for the men of the INA.

In the Bishenpur sector, Colonel Malik's Bahadur Group was supported by the people of Moirang and neighbouring villages in many ways. Besides providing money, food and information about British positions, all arms and ammunitions abandoned by the British forces were collected by the local people and handed over to Colonel Malik. About 20 members of the Nikhil Manipuri Mahasabha and Praja Sammelani, possibly the only two political organisations in Manipur then, also supported the INA. The INA sympathizers in Manipur were shadowed by the military police and many of them were arrested and tortured at the Langthabal military jail. At least 2 of them died soon after they were released, owing to severe punishment while in prison.

Majority of the people from Manipur who joined the INA came from the Kuki tribe. While many of them were civilians, a few of them were soldiers of the Indian Army and (British) Burma Army before defecting to the Japanese-INA forces. By the time of the Second World War, the Kukis had so much hatred against the British authorities that many of them readily joined the Japanese-INA forces in the hope of liberating themselves, their land and their people from British colonial rule.

When the Japanese and the INA retreated in the middle of July 1944, a group of Manipuris went along with them to Burma, sharing the miseries of the atrocious journey. At least one Manipuri is said to have died on the way. Upon reaching Rangoon, the team from Manipur became members of the various wings of the INA. In August 1945, the INA members from Manipur were imprisoned in Rangoon jail by Allied forces until they were brought to Calcutta and released after 48 hours of detention and interrogation. They finally reached Manipur on 6 May, 1946. In one of his writings, M. Koireng Singh, laments about his other group of Manipuri INA comrades who did not join them to Burma and went underground. They suffered in the hills of Manipur for more than a year trying to evade arrest. They remain even today as 'unknown, unsung heroes' while their friends, including Koireng himself, who were identified by the then authority were honoured as 'freedom fighters' after the war.

Conclusion

Subhas Chandra Bose dreamed of hoisting the Indian Tricolour flag and holding the INA's victory parade at the Red Fort in Delhi after driving out the British from India. For this to happen, he had calculated that when the men of his army, the INA, reached the plains of Assam, majority of the Indian soldiers in the Indian Army would defect and join the INA. This, he further anticipated, would destroy the might of the Indian Army and the British administration thereby facilitating him to reach Delhi and end colonial rule in India. His dream of freeing India from the clutches of the British came to a crashing halt with the retreat of his INA forces along with the Japanese from the Imphal front. Shah Nawaz Khan hugely blamed the Japanese for the fate of the INA on the battlefield. He believed that the Japanese liaison officers had an apprehension that the INA would not accept Japanese domination in any way and that it would fight Nippon from becoming a new master of India after the overthrow of the British. He also asserted that had it been not for the Japanese betrayal of the INA, the outcome of the Imphal Operation might have been in favour of the INA. On hindsight, his opinion is based on more of wishful thinking. Even Iwaichi Fujiwara who had been a true wellwisher of the INA throughout was disappointed at some point. Here's what he thought about the INA after the Imphal campaign:

> As a revolutionary Army, its morale was high and it was quite well organised; but the standard of its tactics, training and leadership was low.... It lacked, in particular, offensive strength and tenacity.

In fact, the INA was not well equipped too. Even the elite Subhas Brigade had no wireless sets, no transport, no stretchers and no weapons heavier than light machine guns, besides not having other essential items to fight against the well-armed men of the British Fourteenth Army. M.Z. Kiani, years after war, explained to some extent why the INA men were lightly armed. According to him, the understanding was that the Japanese, who were well-armed, would neutralize the British defences of India, and then allow the INA 1st Division to pass through. This would have made way for the rest of the INA troops in the rear to enter and carry out their operations deeper into India.

Although Netaji S.C. Bose and his army lost in their fight against the mighty British Army in 1944-45, his dream to liberate India from the British was realised soon after. Many Indians believe that it was Bose's INA who forced the British to accelerate the granting of Independence of India. This is the greatest legacy for Netaji and his army, and very well deserved too. The huge response given by the people of India to the famous INA Red Fort trials and the subsequent mutinies in the Royal Indian Navy, the Royal Indian Air force and the Indian Army give clear testimony of the support the INA received then. However, unfortunately, post-Independence narratives of the Indian freedom struggle tend to sideline the contribution of Bose and his men.

Indian history and world history may have ignored Bose and the INA knowingly or unknowingly but Imphal, which was the hallowed ground for Netaji and his army, will never forget their sacrifices. The INA Memorial Complex at Moirang—the only such place in the world—still fondly preserves the sacred spot where Colonel S.A. Malik hoisted the INA flag. The complex is also home to a statue of Netaji, an INA War Museum, an auditorium, a library and a replica of the INA memorial destroyed by the British at Singapore in 1945. One can see the watchwords of the INA inscribed on the top part of the memorial—Ittefaq (Unity), Itmad (Faith) and Kurbani (Sacrifice). The museum houses war relics, maps, documents and photographs of the INA and Netaji. A separate section in the museum is dedicated to the local people who supported the INA.

Not far from the memorial complex, one can see the house which was converted as the Headquarters of the INA, 76 years ago, still standing intact with bullet holes from the war time. The villagers of the then battlefields have not forgotten the sufferings of the Japanese-INA forces till today. All these are poignant reminders of the INA's involvement in the Battle of Imphal. Manipur and its people will always remember the INA men and its great leader, Netaji Subhas Chandra Bose, and will continue to spread the word about their sacrifices in India's freedom struggle to the rest of India and the world.

REFERENCES

Allen, Louis (1984). *Burma: The Longest War 1941-45*. London: Phoenix Giant.

Bose, Sugata (2013). *His Majesty's Opponent*. Gurgaon: Penguin Books.

Dr. Sobita, Devi K. & Minashree Mairembam (2010). *A Tribute to the INA: Freedom Fighters of Manipur*. Imphal. Department of Art & Culture, Government of Manipur.

Fay, Peter Ward (1993). *The Forgotten Army*. Ann Arbor: University of Michigan Press.

Kangjam, Y. (2019). *Forgotten Voices of the Japan Laan: The Battle of Imphal and the Second World War in Manipur.* New Delhi: INTACH & Aryan Books International.

Katoch, Hemant Singh (2016). *The Battlefields of Imphal: The World War II and North East India.* Abingdon: Routledge.

Khan, Shah Nawaz (1946). *My Memories of I.N.A. and its Netaji.* Delhi: Rajkamal Publications.

Singh, Durlab (1946). *Formation and Growth of the Indian National Army.* Lahore: Hero Publications.

Singh, (Gen.) Mohan (2020). *Soldiers' Contribution to Indian Independence.* New Delhi: Army Educational Stores.

Singh, Manindra M. (1993). *Souvenir of the Golden Jubilee Celebration of the Azad Hind Government.*Moirang. Souvenir Sub-Committee.

Sundaram, Chandar S. (1985). *The Indian National Army: A Preliminary Study of its Formation and Campaigns.* Montreal. McGill University (M.A. Thesis).

Toye, Hugh (1991). *Subhas Chandra Bose: The Springing Tiger.* Mumbai: Jaico Publishing House.

16

Relevance of Manipur in INA Movement

Moirangthem Shanti Devi

Introduction

The first attack of the Azad Hind Fauz was started on the 14th February, 1944. The INA (Indian National Army) had at that time three divisions of thirty thousand men and twenty thousand women under training. The first division, which fought in Arakan and Imphal popularly known as Gandhi Regiment was commanded by Inayat Kiani. The Japanese were helping themselves because unless India was free from the hands of British, the area conquered by Japan in the East Asia could never be safe (Pandit, 1988: 242). Indian National Army did not go alone that they always go together with Japanese Forces. It is said that at no time would any of its Units of less than a Battalion strength be detached for action; the INA under its own commanders, subject to overall strategic command of the Japanese, would fight as an allied army of equal status with the Japanese army; the INA would be subject to its own military laws and codes framed by the provisional Government of free India the administration of liberated Indian territories would vest fully and absolutely with the provisional Government of Free India. The sole objective of the INA and of the Provisional

Government of free India was to liberate India and once their enemies were thrown out of the country than they would be able to establish a new government of free country then they would be able to establish a new government of free India. It is also mentioned that Netaji knew very well that the result of the battle of Imphal was not very important to Japan. He also knew that Japan was sure to be defeated in the war. Perhaps he gave his observation after getting the experience of their fighting in the Pacific, so he strongly emphasized to sole responsibility of INA for the liberation of India. He believed that if he was able to control Imphal, definitely there would be stirred up on anti-British revolt in Eastern India and wide spread sabotage of the British military installations and mean of communication would be able to continue effectively (*Ibid.*, 267).

Relevance of Manipur in INA Movement

The British forces were forced to retreat from Burma and consolidated their position in Imphal. The Japanese forces began to enter inside the territory of Manipur from three different directions. At this juncture, the British government carried on a series of psychological warfare to win over the mind of the people of Manipur by distributing leaflets from the plane. Their main concern was to stop the possible moral and physical support of the people of Manipur in favour of INA. At that time the political condition in Manipur was also in a very fluid situation. The idea of the growth of political consciousness was very strong and the demand for the establishment of a responsible government in Manipur was very high. In short the idea of anti-colonialism and anti-feudal feeling was very much in the mind of the people of Manipur. The INA also distributed pamphlets to the people of Manipur and seek the support from them. It is said that some of these pamphlets were brought by two tribal people from Sugnu, a remote place in the southern side of the valley of Manipur. The message of Netaji appealed to the people of Manipur specially the leaders and workers of the Indian National Congress to extend unstinted support to the Indo-Japanese forces. The leaders and workers of the Nikhil

Manipuri Mahasabha which had an identical ideas and objective with Indian National Congress welcomed the appeal of Netaji.

In March 1944, three army divisions of Japan along with the Subhas Brigade entered Indian Territory after crossing the Chindwin River (Dasgupta, 1997: 38). By 19th March, the powerful Japanese formation 31st Division was ferociously attacked the Indian Parachute Brigade and British battalion at Ukhrul. Desperate fighting ensured for two days at Shanshak, 8 miles south to Ukhrul; and on 30th March Shanshak also falled into the hands of INA and Japanese forces and eventually all the roads into Imphal were effectively blocked (Lal, n.d: 178). The strong forces of the Japanese and INA compelled the 17th British division retreated through Tiddim road and left completely the southern portion of hill areas of Manipur on 10th April, 1944. Thus withdrawal of British troops from Moirang to Potsangbam was completed on 13th April, 1944 (Koireng, n.d). "Thirty-two Meiteis who earned their livelihood in Burma joined the movement under the leadership of L. Guno Singh of Khurai, Imphal, Manipur and they took part in the war. Thirteen out of 32 Meiteis reached Pallel as advanced party and tried to secure the recruits of the enemy and also to seek the support of the local people. 19 out of them marched towards the Tiddim road and reached Manipur Valley and out of them 4 were arrested by the British army at Khuga Valley at Churachandpur, Manipur in the month of March 1944" (Koireng, 1987: 588) A large number of Manipuri Tribals who were the members of the erstwhile British V force also joined the movement and took part in the war.

In the morning of 14th April, 1944 the leaders of Indo-Japanese Advanced Group had a discussion with M. Koireng Singh and some local men at Tronglaobi village. On the same day Col. Saukat Ali Malik, Commander of the Bahadur (Intelligence) Group of INA planted the Tri-Colour flag with Springing Tiger embossed on it at the historic Moirang Kangla, Manipur. On the next day the leaders and workers of the Nikhil Manipuri Mahasabha welcomed the appeal made by Netaji. 13 members of the Mahasabha from

Imphal joined with the members of Moirang and worked together with the people of Moirang and collected large quantity of ration and carried out espionage activities. They all join the INA. All the surrounding villages up to Nighthoukhong on the north were liberated from the British yoke. All the southern parts of Manipur from Ningthoukhong onwards were liberated from the British rule and the Provisional Government of Free India controlled the area for three months till 15th July, 1944. The INA and Japanese forces were able to get proper and regular food and all other essential things from the people of Manipur. To see this condition, the Political Agent of Manipur ordered to kill some leaders like M. Koireng Singh, L. Sanaba Singh, K. Gopal Singh and H. Nilamani. The 13 members of the Nikhil Manipuri Mahasabha were blacklisted by the government. A number of Manipuris joined the INA and contributed to the last fight for freedom from the British yoke. During the INA and Japanese forces stay in different parts of Manipur, the local people supported them in many ways (MPCC, 1985).

Finally, the INA and Japanese forces retreated. Many factors were responsible for that. The heavy downpour of the monsoon in this region destroyed all major activities. There were shortages of supply from the Japanese Government. The shortage of ration created a lot of havoc to Japanese and INA forces. There were no air cover from the Japanese side and at the same time the Japanese were losing its ground in the Pacific War. Some Manipuris also went back along with them. A batch of six Manipuri left Moirang for Rangoon with Col. Malik. It was unfortunate that the Germany's defeat in the war in April and her surrender on 3rd May, 1945 as well as the dropping of atom bombs in Hiroshima (6th August, 1945) and Nagasaki (9th August, 1945), compelled Japan to surrender to the Allied forces in the middle of 14th August, 1945, the INA at Rangoon also surrendered. The members from Manipur were also arrested by the Rangoon occupying Allied Forces from their hiding places through a tip for Manipuris and put in Rangoon Central Jail.

Manipur and Japan during World War II

As mentioned in the above paragraph, Japan dropped bomb on Imphal twice in the month of May 1942 heralding the beginning of World War II in Manipur. At Imphal within a few hours of bombing, almost every house in Imphal was abandoned by 1,10,947 residents generally leaving a male member of the family for guarding their properties and fled for safety to outlying villages (Ranjit, 2011: 3). Meitei primitive innocence had a knock on the head when the Japanese Army that tasted victory in South East Asia met its Waterloo in Manipur. Japanlan had promised to create havoc when it arrived in Manipur on 10th May, 1942. After the Japanese surrendered to the Allies on 6th August, 1945, it ended abruptly on August 15, 1945 (Mohendra, 2017). It was a simple matter of Americans dropping two small atom bombs over Hiroshima and Nagasaki. The INA forces cross the Indian frontier on 19th March, 1944 from the Kennedy Peak. They fought extremely well in spite of serious handicap and lack of armaments and air support, Pallel and Tamu fell. The Tiddim front led by Col. Shaukat Ali Malik with the Hikari Kikan group was following the route to Churachandpur in Manipur. They captured Moirang and put it under the control of the Provisional Government of Azad Hind.

By the end of June 1944 both the Japanese and British forces fought a severe battle with very heavy casualties on both sides. The British concern was to break the ring round Kohima and achieve a link up with beleaguered Imphal. The Japanese efforts on the other hand were directed to capture Imphal and its supply dumps before being driven off from Kohima and road blocks that had been put up between that place and Imphal. The INA and Japanese troops based in Moirang were fighting very hard in and around Bishenpur with the British forces. The British could bring more troops as reinforcement by rail and road up to Kohima from Assam and keep them regular supply; their IV Corps fighting in the Imphal plain was being reinforced and maintained through virtually uninterrupted air operations. Airlifting the 5th and 7th Divisions from the Arakan, which had a decisive effect on the combat around Imphal, was a development that the Japanese had initially overlooked. Because of uneven contest, tie INA and Japanese forces fighting in Bishenpur and around Imphal but could not capture Imphal.

By that time, a very heavy downpour started in the north-eastern India and Chin hills. M.Z. Kiani wrote: "The supply problem in fact had become so grave that by the third week of June, the INA were hoping that Imphal would not fall but that we all withdraw in time to the line of the Chindwin River, where supplies could be brought up. The fear was that available supplies in Imphal would not meet the requirements of all the Japanese and INA forces as well as the trapped IV British Corps and that innumerable soldier would starve to death. With the fall of Imphal further British supplies would naturally have ceased while the Japanese would not have been able to bring in any while the monsoon lasted, and there were still at least three months of the rainy season to go" (Kiani, 1985: 39). The Japanese attack on Imphal without doubt came within ace's of success. But there were many important factors operating against them in the beginning of 1944 when they started large scale operations, first in Arakans and then in the state of Manipur. Finally, they were withdrawn from the state and retreated fully.

In the month of March 1944, three Japanese Army divisions along with Subhas Brigade entered the Indian Territory after crossing big rivers, difficult hill ranges and thick forests and attempted to thrust deep inside the territories of India. The 31st Japanese division along with a regiment of INA reached Kohima Town and fought a fierce battle and ultimately captured the town with the exception of important places like Tennis Court. Dimapur road the only life line of Manipur was blocked for about a month. The 15th Japanese division with one INA Regiment marched towards Tamu and Ukhrul in two ways. Ukhrul was captured. In the mean time another group of the division reached Pallel. The 33rd Japanese division with one INA Regiment marched towards Tiddim Road. The Indo-Japanese force advanced very fast. Col. Shaukat Malik setup headquarters in the liberated town of Moirang.

INA and Their Efforts in the Periphery of Manipur

On 29 April, Mohammad Kiani proposed that the combined forces of Japanese and the INA should attack simultaneously on the Pallel airfield from two sides—the Yamamoto men from the west and the INA group from the south. But the attack was failed with a great set back. This was a turning point in the tide of the war. Japanese thought that Imphal would be fallen in the middle of April 1944. Then it would give a new opportunity to consolidate their position. They were of the view that if they capture Imphal it would be great gain to them because there was every possibility to capture a large number of prisoners from the IV British Corps which was fighting in Imphal plains. The majority of the Sepoys in the corps was Indian. The captured Indian troops were expected to provide potential recruits for the expansion of the INA. But Imphal did not fall as expected, and Japanese Division fighting for it was not only stalemated but was finding their supply position becoming precarious as the days passed. Hopefully for them the fall of Imphal was expected to provide large stocks of weapons and supplies which the British had accumulated at their bases for operation against Burma. So to render help for the improvement of the battle situation, the rest of the INA Division was hurriedly brought forward and deployed on the Tamu-Pallel sector of the front. At this time the situation was no doubt critical for the Japanese, but the INA had to face unexpected difficulties for lack of adequate arrangement in conducting itself in a manner that was expected of it as a fighting formation.

The 3rd (Nehru) Regiment had to march for over 200 miles to reach its forward base. In addition to the physical difficulties of terrain, lack of supplies coupled with long marches, the INA had several other handicaps. It is difficult to admit but the fact was that the Japanese Commander up to that time was not quite sure as to how the INA would behave once it reached the frontline. It definitely showed a lack of trust and confidence on their part in that they deployed it at places were not much damage would be done if the INA, either for military or political reason got out of hand started infiltrating into India and fighting independently (Kiani, 1985: 31).

On 5th May as if an order the monsoon started in the Chin Hills surrounding areas restricting large scale operations. They also converted the Kabaw Valley, the main channel of communication to the rear, gradually into a veritable sea of mud, and the dry streams into raging torrents, making it impossible for any wheeled traffic move, and causing a complete stoppage of supplies from the beginning of June. Meanwhile, the third Regiment, under Lt. Col. Gulzara Singh, having marched from Yeu, the rail head, to Kalewa, moved up the Kabaw Valley of Mintha, a distance of about 250 miles and reached their in the third week of May. The Regimental Headquarters was established of Narum, some 15 miles north-west of Mintha. They were protecting the fight flank of Yamamoto force, carrying out the harassing raids on the British lines of communications in the direction of Wangjing on the Pallel-Imphal road and generally to fill the gap between the Yamamoto force and the 15th Japanese Division on the right (*Ibid.*: 38).

By that time the first Regiment under Shahnawaz was still in the Haka-Falam area skirmishing with the Chin Levies of the British Lushai Brigade operating from Aizol in the west and both the regimental commanders and Kiani were keen that these forces should rejoin the first division in Pallel front as quickly as possible. This was restricted by the Japanese as they wanted to use the regiment for relieving pressure on their troops in the area of Kohima and Ukhrul to where they had started moving it. But only Shahnawaz and some of his staff could go past Ukhrul, but had to return in considerable haste, as the siege of Kohima had ended and Japanese retread in this sector had begun (*Ibid.*: 39).

Socio-Economic and Political Impact

Every movement has got its own impact in every aspect of their society. May be positive or negative but it rendered a lot of contribution in the ongoing developmental process in the life of the people of the society. In the case of Manipur also the INA and World War II has produced a tremendous impact in the future life of the people of this country. Manipur was the one of the main battlefield of the World War II and it affected almost all the normal life of the State. The worst part was its economy position during the wartime. During this period, due to insecure position in the life of the people almost all the activities of agriculture was completely stopped and people had to survive on rations. This system was continued till the first half of 1945. The price of the rice increased tremendously. It is recorded that the price of rice reaches either to Rs. 50 or 60 per mound, which was indeed, beyond the capabilities of the war torn people of Manipur. Even during the time of the World War II the army people destroyed all the food grains, which were stored by the people. Apart from this the security people devastated the life stock in many villages. No chicken and pigs could be found. To see this condition the local authority of the Manipur requested to the Government of India for relief measures. Accordingly, about 24 depots in the hills and plains were open and along with it ration were supplied to many villages and about one and half lakh people were fed. Such type of relief measures was not sufficient enough to meet the required demand of the people.

The Government of India also decided to give relief measures to villagers whose household articles were either stolen or loss during the war. Relief measures were also taken up for the construction of damaged houses. As many as 5,503 houses in 409 villages were destroyed. The worst affected areas were Moirang (550 houses), Bishenpur (26 houses), East area (2,100 houses in 160 villages), Valley area (1,463 houses in 59 villages), Sadar area (1,636 houses in 163 villages), Mao area (137 houses in 8 village) and West area (209 houses in 19 villages).

In spite of all these economic problems the people in general was able to get a very experience about the misdeeds committed by the imperialist forces. Though the INA could not fulfil its military mission, its political mission was more than achieved. As mentioned earlier the growth of the idea of political consciousness was started very late. But the INA movement gets a new impetus to the growing political consciousness among the people of Manipur. The sense of patriotism among the people of this place was a great achievement of the movement of India National Army. Even the common people, after having this experience could understand the political trend in Manipur as well as in India. Then it also helped in the strengthening of the relationship between the leaders of Manipur with the other national leaders of India. On the other hand it also helped to growth of a sense of oneness among the people and idea of nationalism was gradually emerged among the people of Manipur. The establishment of Manipur State Congress Party in the year 1946 was an immediate impact of the movement of the Indian National Army. The plank of the party was to establish a responsible Government on the basis of democratic principles. So the establishment of this party was undoubtedly laid basic foundation for having a close relationship between the All India Congress and the Manipur State Congress. Like the All India Congress Committee, the Congress Party of Manipur also challenged the colonial and feudal administration of the state; even they began to change the tone of the slogan.

Apart from its significance in the state it also produced unity in the national struggle. When the brave warriors of the patriotic army were brought to India for trial before the British court, the whole of India was protested as one voice. The INA movement gave a very good impact in the ideology of the peoples of the Manipur particularly among the middle class section. It gave an opportunity to expose to the national and international trends and gave the opportunity to fight for new socio-economic and political changes in the state. The politics of the different parties like the Manipur State Congress, Krishak Sabha, Praja Sangha, Kuki National Assembly, NCC and the Mizo Union in the hills may be examined for the background of the movement of Indian National Army. The hill people also awakened and they began to cry of democracy and independence. Sometimes, the idea of self-determination was also reflected in their mind. Gradually, a large section of educated people particularly from the hill areas came out and they began to take important role in the hill politics. Gandhi wrote this remarkable achievement in following words,

> "Although the INA failed to achieve its immediate objectives, they have a lot to their credit of which they might well be proud. Greatest among these was together under one banner men of all religion and races of India and to infuse into them the spirit of solidarity and oneness, to the utter exclusion of all communal parochial sentiments. It is an example which we should all emulate."

Conclusion

It will be relevant to know that Manipuris who took part in the INA at Rangoon were in Guest Houses at Kandogulay, Rangoon. The other members were attached to the Intelligence group of the INA. However, Subhas did not lose hope, his aspirations to achieve independence was living. On the 25 April, 1945, a few days before the Japanese evacuated Rangoon, he flew out of the capital leaving behind a message in which the Government and people of Burma for their help and hospitality. Whatever said and done, we assure that his foundation of the Indian National Army, its organisation in the foreign land, its programme for complete independence—all speak of his highest degree of capability during the Second World War. The great mission was executed in a grand manner and successes of the INA brought about a great damage to British interests in South-East Asia (Priyadarshni, 2012). Perhaps Netaji gave his observation after getting the experience of their fighting in the Pacific, so he strongly emphasized to sole responsibility of INA for the liberation of India. He believed that if he was able to control Imphal, definitely there would be stirred up on anti-British revolt in Eastern India and widespread sabotage of the British military installations and mean of communication would be able to continue effectively. Knowing the historical fact of facts, Rajaram emphatically asserted and reaffirmed on the subject matter that great historian R.C. Majumdar wrote, "Subhas Bose with his INA campaigns probably contributed more than Gandhi, Nehru and their movements in Indian independence." Moreover, the result of Subhas Bose's activities was the rise of the nationalist spirit in the Indian Armed Forces. As a matter of fact the Quit India Movement launched in 1942 were not the last uprising against the British rule in India, it was rather a part of the ongoing politics in India.

REFERENCES

Dasgupta Atis (1997). *The Role of INA in the Battle Field of Arakan and Imphal,* West Bengal, Netaji Birth-Centenery, Vol. Department of Information & Cultural Affairs, Delhi, p. 38.

Kiani, M.Z. (1985). "India's Freedom and the great INA Movement", *The Oracle, VII*(1), January, p. 35.

Kirby, Maj. General (n.d). *S. Woodburn: The war against Japan, 3*: 446.

Koireng Singh, M. (n.d). 'Manipur's Contribution to the Freedom Struggle of the Country', *Freedom Fighters of Manipur,* MPCC (I), p. VI.

Koireng Singh M. (n.d). (1987). "Manipur's Contribution to the INA Movement", *Legis News, II*(3), Manipur Legislative Assembly, August 9, p. 588.

Lal Dena (n.d). *History of Modern Manipur 1826-1946*, p. 178.

Mohendra Singh, Irengbam (2017). "My Japanlan memoir after four score years", *The Sangai Express,* August 19.

MPCC (I) (1985). "Freedom Fighters of Manipur: Who's Who", *Congress Centenary Year 1985,* Freedom Fighter's Cell MPCC (I).

Pandit, N.H. (1988). *Netaji S.C. Bose from Kabul to the Battle of Imphal, Sterling Publishers,* Pvt. Ltd., New Delhi, p. 242.

Priyadarshni M. Gangte (2012). "Revisiting Netaji's Role in the Freedom Struggle of India, INA and Manipur Perspective", *The Sangai Express,* Imphal, March 11. p. 3.

Ranjit Singh, M. (2011). "Japanese bombing of Imphal", *The Sangai Express.* Imphal, May 18, p. 3.

Yangmaso A. Shishak (1944). *Second World War in Manipur,* p. 1.

17

INA's Honour at the Battle of Imphal and Its Catalysing Impetus to India's Independence

Yumnam Rajeshwor Singh

Introduction

The Indian National Army of which Netaji Subhas Chandra Bose took personal command, was made up from civilians and Indian Officers and other rank prisoners of war, chiefly from those taken during the invasion and occupation of Malaya. The Guerrilla regiment under the INA consists of four Brigades. They were:

1. Bose Brigade under Lt. Col. Shah Nawaz Khan;
2. Gandhi Brigade under Lt. Col. I.J. Kiani;
3. Azad Brigade under Major Gulzara Singh; and
4. Nehru Brigade under Lt. Col. Aziz Ahmad Khan.

The No. 2 Guerrilla Regiment (Gandhi Brigade) and the Divisional Headquarters moved to Burma early in March, and after a short rest at Rangoon they started moving to the Imphal front early in April. The route and condition under which they travelled were the same as those faced by the Subhas Brigade. The Division was commanded by Major General (then Colonel) M.Z. Kiani, who was undoubtedly one of the most brilliant and daring Commanders of the INA. The Gandhi Brigade was commanded by Colonel I.J. Kiani who was a cousin of Gen. M.Z. Kiani. Col. I.J. Kiani was well known for his perseverance and doggedness.

Prelude to the Battle of Imphal at Mittong Khunou

On arrival at Tamu, the Divisional Commander found out that Imphal had not fallen yet and that severe fighting was going on in the vicinity of Pallel. He contacted the Japanese commander on the Pallel front and in cooperation with him and with Major Fujiwara (of Singapore fame) who was now a Staff Officer in the Japanese General Headquarters, it was decided that the No. 1 Division would have an independent sector to the west of the main Tamu-Pallel road and from there carry out guerrilla activity against the British forces on the Tamu front and against the Allied aerodrome at Pallel.

The Divisional Head Quarters were established at Chamol and the Regimental Headquarters at Mittong Khunou. Mittong Khunou is located at the south-east of Pallel Airfield. Although the Japanese concentrated its main effort on the Shenam bastion itself, Yamamoto did send the 'Gandhi Brigade' or 2nd Infantry Regiment of the 1st Indian National Army Division to capture Pallel from the south, the only time that the INA was used in an independent role. Major Pritam Singh with a force of 300 men attack the Pallel airfield on 3rd May, 1944. This attack on the aerodrome came as rude shock to the British who decided to counter attack and drive back the Gandhi Brigade from Mittong Khunou. After the Pallel Aerodrome attack, the British patrol activity increased very considerably.

Seaforth Highlanders Attack Mittong Khunou

Post-Pallel airfield attack, the British Battalion strongly supported by heavy artillery, attacked the foremost company in the vicinity of Mittong Khunou. With propaganda weapons of loud-speakers and heavy artillery effectively to aid, the British launched a large-scale offensive. The loud speakers repeatedly disturbed the calmness of the jungle air by threatening the INA: "either surrender, or else get ready to face death in the hilly area of Imphal." The loud-speakers shouted:

> "Gandhi Guerrillas, beware. We are attacking with big topkhana and with the superiority of arms and ammunition. If you want safety, lay down your arms in half an hour's time. Now 20 minutes are left. Only 10 minutes are now between your life and death."

Addressing the commander, the loud-speaker shouted:

> "Listen well, Commander Kiani, we will completely blow up your weak defences. We pity you and your regiment."

The leading platoon of the forward company was commanded by a young Second Lieutenant Ajaib Singh who had been trained at the INA Officers' Training School in Singapore. The Scottish soldiers of the Sea Forth Highlanders knowing that they were up against the INA attacked fiercely. It was the first battle of the Gandhi Brigade against British troops, and at the very sight of them they became wild.

The British soldiers came almost upon the trenches occupied by INA men, but time and again, they were beaten back with heavy losses. After their first setback, the British fell back and after reorganizing their troops they attacked again, this time supported by artillery and air support, but the gallant platoon of the INA led by their brave commander, held firm and continued to beat back attack after attack. Eventually, being unable to make any headway against the INA soldiers, the British called a halt and withdrew to their defences. Rallying his men, and collecting ammunition from the British dead and wounded left behind by the attackers, Lt. Ajaib Singh advanced from his position and approached the nearest British defence post. Another gun battle started, this time with British on the defensive. Lt. Ajaib Singh had captured a large number of rifles and grenades in the first engagement and he used them. He fired 30 grenades using 303 rifles. Lt. Ajaib Singh's small force had suffered severe losses, but he had inflicted far greater losses on the British. In the day's engagement, the British suffered at least 50 casualties, killed and wounded, while the INA losses were 10 killed and a few wounded.

During that time heavy rain had set in and made the ration and ammunition supply a most difficult problem. Due to the lack of proper food and medicines, the health of the INA troops deteriorated rapidly and by the middle of June 1944, they had become so weak that they could hardly walk a few miles, but despite this they stuck to their posts and in the face of repeated British attacks never retreated. At about this time the tide of the battle had turned. The British had managed to substantially reinforce their beleaguered garrison in Imphal, and were now in a position to launch the main offensive. Maj. General Shah Nawaz Khan in his account of the battle wrote "Their first move was to capture the heights occupied by the men of "Gandhi Brigade" around Mithong Khunou. This time it was an attack launched by a whole British Brigade, 3,000 strong, supported by heavy artillery and aeroplanes. Our old rivals, the "Seaforth", again led the attack. By a clever encircling movement, they surrounded one of our companies commanded by Capt. Rao, and it looked as if they would annihilate our force The situation looked extremely grave.

All the commanding heights and strategic points were in enemy hands. Besides this the strength of the Gandhi Brigade was very much depleted owing to widespread illness and battle casualties. In this particular action there were 600 INA men opposing approximately 3,000 well-fed British soldiers having infinitely superior arms and equipment. Our men fought most heroically. Col. I.J. Kiani, the Brigade Commander, himself was in the area of the company that was encircled by the British. He realized that unless the strategic heights were recaptured by them his garrison would be annihilated. He, therefore, issued orders to his officers to take possession of those heights at any cost." The

British force had the advantage over the INA as their defenses were at the top of the hills. The Regimental Commander, Colonel I.J. Kiani had calculated that, if the INA captured the hill occupied by their enemy, it would save his whole regiment. To save the lives of 1,700, the Regimental Commander was ready to sacrifice, 300 of his men in this surprise attack. The weather was unusually bitter and the INA soldiers had no warm clothes to protect them from the biting cold.

The Valour of Lt. Mansukh Lall

Lt. Mansukh Lall was ordered to recapture one of the heights. He was commanding a platoon consisting of approximately 30 men. With this small force he counter-attacked without any artillery covering fire, and recaptured one of the strongest posts occupied by the British. While leading his small, and semi-starved force up the steep ridge, he was wounded 13 times, through exhaustion and loss of blood, he staggered and fell to the ground His men seeing their gallant commander fall hesitated and slowed down their pace. Lt. Mansukh Lall, like a tiger that is mortally wounded but is determined to make the last charge, roared to his men and exhorted them to continue their advance and not to worry about him. They were very near the summit, and making a last supreme effort, with 13 bullet wounds in his body, he rose to his feet and personally led the final assault on the height which was to decide the fate of Gandhi Brigade that day.

K.R. Palta wrote,

> "... Lt. Mansukh, who was in the front line, received serious bullet wounds in his chest, thigh, arm and right hand. He fell, but rose again and again he fell. Though he was completely exhausted, he rose once again to lead his men to victory. The revolutionary slogans, the heroic spirit and the determination of our soldiers stood them in good stead. Brave Mansukh captured the hill and waved his hand cheerfully to his Commander,

> who was watching the battle. The Gandhi Guerrillas were saved due, to the dare-devil spirit of Mansukh, the brave INA, lieutenant."

Lt. Ajaib Singh was immediately sent to relieve the seriously wounded Mansukh. The first thing Ajaib Singh did was to stop the enemy observation post functioning by killing the English major, who was in charge of the Outpost (OP). He also killed two British captains who were handling the OP. Now the British artillery was functioning blindly.

The British killed many of their own men by wrongly concentrating fire on their own lines. The attack, which started at 7.30 a.m. the previous day, was over with an INA victory at 4 a.m. the following day. Seventeen British officers were killed and many of their men were either killed or wounded. On the INA side, four officers were killed and 150 other ranks killed or wounded. The Gandhi Guerrillas started withdrawing on July 18, 1944. By the time they reached Mandalay, out of 94 officers, only 17 were still alive, and out of 3,000 other ranks, only about 250 Jawans had managed to survive, all being in shattered health. The rest perished either fighting for the noble cause or suffered from diseases, which they had developed on the battlefield.

Medals and Awards

Many officers and other ranks of the Gandhi Brigade were recommended for the Shatru Nash. And many officers and men received the highest medals of bravery, the Sardar-e-Jang and, the Sher-e-Hind. Those were:

1. Major Pritam Singh, Sardar-e-Jang,
2. Lt. Ajaib Singh, Sardar-e-Jang (Class II),
3. Lt. Taj Mohd., Sardar-e-Jang (Class II),
4. Sepoy Kehar Singh, Sher-e-Hind,
5. Lt. Mansukh, Sardar-e-Jang,
6. Captain Sadhu Singh, Vir-e-Hind,

7. Capt. Rama Ji Rao, Sardar-e-Jang, and
8. Lt. Lai Singh, Sardar-e-Jang.

The INA fought extremely well in spite of serious handicaps and lack of armament and air support. They had no plane, no lorries for transport. The soldiers themselves had to carry munitions and supplies. The Japanese Air Force gave little or no assistance. The supplies of rations were extremely irregular and several INA men died of starvation. "I do not know what is the idea behind this deliberate starvation of my men", writes Shah Nawaz on July 17th. When the retreat began Shah Nawaz again noted "Japanese have left us completely in the lurch. They are running away themselves and are not bothering about us."

Battle of Imphal: Catalyst to India's Independence

The INA was defeated in the Battle of Imphal in March-June 1944. On 15th August, 1945, with the Japanese surrender in the Second World War, the INA was left with no option but to surrender. Almost all of them surrendered after their retreat from the Indian Border. It became one of the most important and difficult post war problems for the British Empire to decide how to deal with 19,500 former INA officers and men who participate the Imphal Campaign. The disposal of the question might well decide the success or failure of the British control of post-war India. The trial was the most ominous event since the Sepoy Mutiny of 1857. Its outcome would produce enormous impact and have a decisive influence on Indian officers and men in the British Indian Army, the watchdog for the administration of the British Empire over India.

The British Government of India thought it would demonstrate the prestige and power of the British Empire by executing betrayed INA officers following a military trial and by attempting to teach the Indian people, particularly Indian officers and men of the British Indian Army, a lesson in order to establish an unshakable control of India. The British thought it could be done. The decision produced a consequence opposite to their wishes; the British miscalculated and blundered despite their unrivalled experience in the administration of Indians, and their implementation of policy. Gandhi, Nehru and other leaders of the Indian National Congress seized opportunity on the blunder of the British Empire. They took advantage of the trial whereby the British were determined to punish severely 20,000 INA officers and men, whose relatives and friends were also serving in the British Indian Army.

Congress leaders tried to win British Indian Army officers and men to the Congress side and to mobilize the Indian masses in an anti-British movement. The trial was a God-given opportunity that would tip the scales of the movement decisively. It was as if Congress had laid a snare and the British Government had been caught. On September 14, Congress held an executive Committee in Poona and adopted and declared the resolution that INA officers and men are heroes who fought for the Independence of India and they should be released at once. The mass movement had started by then. In December 1945, Col. Dhillon once said, "Don't worry. India will gain independence within a year. If they execute any one of us, no Englishman will leave India alive."

Netaji Subhas Chandra Bose's discretion had enabled the INA to take part in the Imphal Campaign and had brought the INA within reach of Independence. Though the military campaign had ended in a fiasco, the political war of anti-British and pro-Independence agitation as a result of INA brought to victory. With the progress of the first INA court martial, the Indian people's anti-British and pro-Independence agitation spread like a fire, gaining in intensity. India turned into a raging elephant. The court-martial, originally intended to consolidate British control over India, turned into a trial to pass judgments on the criminal act of British control over India for 200 years and to give it the *coup de grace*.

Transcending differences in religion, race, class, language, political affiliation, and military-civilian rivalry, 400 million Indians, with their wisdom, talents and energy, were united together in rebellion. It was an unprecedented spectacle in India's history. It was truly a great national war of the Indian people in which their destiny was at stake.

Violent mass protest movement erupted in Delhi, Calcutta, Lahore, Madras and other principal cities on 5th November when the trial re-open. On the same day, in Calcutta where Netaji Bose was born, 1,00,000 people staged a huge demonstration, carrying with them placards bearing slogans such as 'Save INA National Heroes', 'Suspend the INA trial and release the defendants Immediately', 'British Go Home from India at Once'. They clashed with police everywhere and bloody tragedies spread in the city. Also there were riots in Madras resulting in countless number of casualties.

Every newspaper including *The Hindustan Times* (supporting Congress), *The Dawn* (supporting the Muslim League) and *The Statesman* (supporting the government) gave extensive news coverage to the INA trial and carried editorials about it. The first court martial entered its final stage in late December. The prosecution tried desperately to establish the case of treason against the British Crown by the three defendants and of Murder and tortures by INA officers and men. The defence and the defendants counter-argued, "The INA war of liberation is similar to the American War of Independence which fought against British control and exploitation."

It was a justifiable act, acceptable amongst the military establishment of an independent nation, for the defendants to have executed men who violated wartime military discipline in the battlefield, according to the principle of the INA's 'military criminal codes'. The INA as an army of the independent government, took part in a joint operation with the Japanese Army. It was not a puppet army. It was unjustifiable and illegal to try in a British military court the regular officers of an independent government which has the right to fight. At the conclusion of the trial, Chief counsel Dr. Desai delivered an eight-hour speech over two days declaring that "a subjugated people have the right to fight".

On 3rd January, General Auchinleck suspended the life imprisonment sentence of the three of INA officers, General Shah Nawaz Khan, Lt. Colonel P.K. Sahgal and Colonel G.S Dhillon.

General Auchinleck was very conscious of the fact that even officers and men of the British Indian Army who were responsible for maintaining India's peace and security were becoming awakened to national Independence, and that they could not be relied upon any more. He was afraid of the British Indian Army turning from a watchdog of the British Empire to an arm of the Indian National Congress.

The British government had succumbed to the demands of the Indian masses and had chosen the path of giving up the power of administration. The British government realized the irreversible course of the situation and began secretly to formulate the second best alternative—an honorable withdrawal while maintaining and protecting British interest in India as far as possible. The military trial in the Red Fort, contrary to their original expectation and calculation, created the decisive factor for the British withdrawal from India.

The historical significance of the trial was clearly expressed in the article contributed by Nehru and published on 17th January, 1945 as quoted in its preface, "... The issue of the trial is neither the legality of the court nor eloquence. It is a power contest between the administrator who controls India and the will of the Indian people. Its outcome is a victory for the Indians.... Will the trial, held in the last week of the year 1945, terminate the chapter of British control following that of the Mughal dynasty? Yes, the trial presages the end of that chapter."

NOTE

This present write-up is an improved and combined version of the two articles which the author originally wrote for E-pao (the complete e-platform for Manipuris) with a disclaimer that the articles just simply being an academic exercise of historical analysis has nothing to do with India's bilateral relation with any foreign country. The two articles are—(1) 'Battle of Imphal—Catalyst to India's Independence' posted on 24 January, 2018; and (2) 'Mittong Khunou: The Battle Honour of INA' posted on April 13, 2019 written to coincide the occasion of 14th April (2019), the first flag hoisting day of INA at Moirang.

REFERENCES

Geoffrey Evans & Antony Brett James (1962). *Imphal*, Macmillan & Co. Ltd., London.

K.R. Palta (1946). *My Adventures with the INA*, Lion Press, Lahore.

Louis Allen (1984). *Burma The Longest War*, Phoenix Press, London.

Shah Nawaz Khan (1946). *INA and Its Netaji*, Raj Kamal Publications, Delhi.

18

World War II and Its Changing Scenario in Manipur

An Overview

Kongbrailatpam Sarojkumar Sharma

World War II narratives recounting chains of pitched battles between the Allied and the Axis Forces and many more unforgettable events triggered in Manipur have transformed the tiny north-east state of India into a paradise for war veterans, researchers, domestic and foreign tourists. In the wake of the immense research and exploration of hordes of World War II sites, flow of stakeholders and interest groups in the state has increased manifold. As such, Manipur, besides its spell-bound scenic beauty, rich cultural heritage and glory in sports, has now come under the spotlight by the entire world for the significant war episodes. In addition to enhance their relations with India, the Japanese and UK governments have also extended developmental programmes to Manipur. Besides history books and written records, glimpses and total recapitulation of World War II episodes in Manipur are in the minds of the elders of every family of the state. Moirang, a small town in Manipur's Bishnupur district about 45 km south-west of Imphal remained as the most significant place and a living testimony of the war affairs of the Japanese and Netaji Subhas Chandra Bose's Indian National Army (INA) troops of the Axis Force.

It was on April 14, 1944 the INA/'Azad Hind Fauz flag was unfurled for the first time at Moirang by Colonel Saukat Hayat Malik, commander of the Bahadur Group and designated the area as its headquarters under Netaji's supervision, giving a big surprise to the British. A large number of Manipuris joined the flag hoisting ceremony and the state subsequently became a part of history. To commemorate and dedicate the brave INA soldiers, the INA Martyrs' Memorial Complex was set up by the government at Moirang. The complex houses a library, a museum and an auditorium as indoor structures and a life-sized bronze statue of Netaji in uniform, a fountain and garden as outdoor components. It stands as one of the important and tourist complexes and historical spots of the nation. From Moirang, located on the banks of the picturesque Loktak Lake, commanders of Japanese troops and their ally INA chalked out war strategies and operated to fight against the Allied forces.

Thousands of soldiers of both the clashing forces, besides many civilians, were killed and injured in various pitched battles across Manipur. Many remnants of the trail of destruction left by the Great War are currently being recovered elsewhere in the state. Significantly the twin World War II clashes of Imphal and Kohima (capital of Nagaland) have been named as the greatest ever battle involving British forces by the National Army Museum, London. The twin victories over the Japanese were voted the winner during a contest organized by the museum. While the Allied force's strategic military formation was based in Imphal, the Japanese and INA soldiers designated their war camp at Moirang where many Manipuris, mostly Moirang denizens, joined INA and fought against the Allied Forces. As Indian soldiers joining the war on both sides—Japanese with INA troops and the British as British Indian army—the Battle of Imphal merits its significance.

The Imphal Peace Museum, inaugurated in June 2019 to commemorate the 75th anniversary of the Battle of Imphal, is a living memory of the World War II as well as a symbol to usher peace in the world to the next generation. Standing at the foothill of Maibam Lotpa Ching or the Red Hill at Nambol in Bishnupur district, the museum, among other many war artifacts, also features names Manipuris, who joined the INA. Red hill saw one of the fiercest battles between the Allied and the invading Japanese forces. The British and the Indian army cemeteries in Imphal too remained as silent war narrators. Manipuris, who witnessed the great war, narrate their harrowing experiences to their children and grandchildren in leisure times and the war chronicles are quite lively to the younger generations. Many elders termed World War II as 'Japan Lan' (Japan War). During family trips, the war witnesses pointed out the sites where fierce battles took place alongside National Highways, state highways and other places in the state to their juniors and wards.

The recovery of large quantity of war artifacts likes bombs of different types, bullets, wreckage aircraft remains, barrels of the rare Arisaka guns, radio compass of Dakota aircrafts, Allied Khaki shirts, personal artifacts, oxygen cylinders used by fighter pilots, war manuals, vehicle parts etc. too bring afresh the war days to the denizens.

Netaji's Popularity in Manipur

Large number of Manipuris, including former chief minister M. Koireng Singh popularly known as Moirang Koireng, Moirang locals and eminent personalities and many Kukis had joined the INA and fought against the Allied Force. Late Colonel (retd.) H. Bhubon Singh, who was a young student studying in Imphal in a few years ahead of the war, had said that he saw people hanging the photographs of Mahatma Gandhi and Netaji on their houses' wall. Singh, who served in the Indian army from 1953 to 1977, said that Manipuris played a pivotal role in the country's freedom struggle.

Manipur Art and Culture Department along with the Indian National Army (INA) Martyrs' Memorial Advisory Committee, Moirang jointly celebrate Netaji's birth anniversary at INA Memorial Complex every year on January 23. Paying floral tribute to Netaji's statue, patriotic song competition among school children, delivering lecture on his iconic freedom struggle and the local people's contribution to the war by INA veterans and scholars are some of the key features of the day.

President of India Ram Nath Kovind, who visited the Complex on November 22, 2017, wrote on the visitor's book of the museum, "I offer my humble tribute to the brave soldiers of the Indian National Army who made supreme sacrifices to liberate Mother India under exemplary leadership of Netaji Subhas Chandra Bose. This monument reminds us of the valour of the INA and makes us commit ourselves to the service of the Nation." President Kovind is the second President of India to visit the complex after President V.V. Giri, who visited there on 21st October, 1972.

Japanese Bombing at Khurai in Imphal

The Khurai area in Imphal East district is one of key World War II sites in Manipur as a Japanese fighter plane had on April 20, 1943 bombed the placid locality, killing over 100 people, including women and children. On the fateful day, the bomb landed and exploded in the middle of a Mandap (Community hall in front of Hindu temple) while a huge religious feasting was on, inflicting the heavy casualty on the Meitei Vaisnavites. Khurai residents have been observing the civilians' death anniversary at Khurai Chingangbam Leikai Mandap where floral tributes are paid to the departed souls.

On the 74th anniversary of the tragic incident held on April 25, 2017, Deputy Chief of the Japanese Embassy (Political) in India Shunichi Inuoe attended the occasion amid a tearful scene, and on behalf of the Japanese army, he tendered apology to the victims' families and relatives. He also shared the grief and pangs inflicted by the people particularly the victims' families. Sunichi expressed his desire to hold interaction programmes of Japanese and

Manipuri youth to strengthen relations and diplomatic bond. The local people warmly welcomed and whole heartedly appreciated his visit at the tribute function facilitated by Imphal Campaign Foundation World War II and Tourism Forum, Manipur. As a token of appreciation for his visit, apologies and homage paid to the World War II victims' souls the Japanese envoy was gifted a Manipuri traditional dress and a phanek (wrap around) for his wife. Khuraijam Nimaichoron, whose father K. Angou was one of the victims of the deadly explosion stated that they don't have any ill-feeling with the bombing, saying that "War is war and everything is fair in war. We warmly welcome you Sir. We want to have a good relation with your country."

According to eminent World War researcher and founder leader of World War II Imphal Campaign Foundation Yumnam Rajeshwar, the Japanese fighter planes that flew from Burma air base dropped numerous bombs at different parts of Imphal valley in April to destroy Allied' Force's key installations and unfortunately one of the bombs landed at the Khurai Mandab. The victims' families said that that it was one of the deadliest incidents inflicting the heaviest casualty in the state during World War II. A photograph which was taken immediately after the bombing was also displayed to depict the destructions that occurred that day. Also a member of Burma Campaign Society, London, Rajeshwar handed over a list of Khurai bombing victims to their families. Japanese Ambassador Kenji Hiramatsu, who along with his team, visited the Khurai bombing site and paid homage to the souls on May 21 (2017), expressed 'remorse' to those killed in the Japanese bombing and prayed for the victims.

Japan and UK keen to take up Developmental Programmes in Manipur

All is not lost in the war as mutual understanding, reconciliation and extending helping hands among the nations came to the fore. On the occasion of the Commemoration of Platinum Jubilee of the "Battle of Imphal" held in Imphal on June 22, 2019, Ambassador of Japan to India, Kenji Hiramatsu invited promising youth of the north-east to work in Japan under the Technical Intern Training Programme.

Mentioning that 24 youth, including 6 Manipuris, had enjoyed the first-hand experience in Japan (in 2019) under the Youth Exchange Programme, Kenji stated that the Japanese Government is committed to have a strong relationship with India. Echoing Kenji, British High Commissioner to India, Dominic Asquith said that the UK government would work closely with Manipur government to bring economic prosperity in the state. "India, Japan and UK will collectively work together to overcome the challenges of the 21st century. As UN members, the three countries have common purpose in preserving and strengthening the international system of co-operation," Dominic continued.

On May 21, 2017, Kenji, during a meeting with Chief Minister N. Biren Singh, conveyed his country's willingness to extend co-operation to the State in certain areas like tourism, road connectivity, cleaning of Loktak Lake, school education, sanitation and sewerage system in Scheduled Tribe areas etc. The two leaders also discussed mutual co-operation between Japan and Manipur in skill development and employment opportunities in Japan, especially in the fields of nursing and manufacturing sectors. During the meeting, Biren Singh expressed his desire to explore the possibilities of introducing Japanese language course in Manipur, upon which Kenji assured to look into the possibilities of providing language teachers and learning materials to the State.

The meeting also discussed various options to ease traffic congestion in Imphal city were also discussed.

Homage to World War II Heroes and Reconciliation

On June 27, 2014, a large number of foreign dignitaries paid rich tribute to the souls of World War II soldiers, on the closing ceremony of the 70th anniversary of "Battle of Imphal" in Imphal. Then Manipur Governor V.K. Duggal said "We are gathered here today to remember and pay our homage to those who died during the Manipur theatre of the Second World War."

Wars throughout history have rendered millions dead and many more injured, besides damaging the economy of both the victor and the vanquished. War should no longer have a place in the society now. "We should all take a vow to work towards this goal," the Governor said. Field Marshall Willam Slim's grandson Hugo Slim was among the many foreign dignitaries who joined the ceremony. William, who led the 14th Army in the Burma Campaign, had stayed at a bungalow at the historic Kangla Fort in Imphal city commonly known as "Slim Cottage". Hugo said that he could at least aware of the war scenario after reading the book "*Defeat into Victory*" written by his grandfather Willam Slim. "More people will come to see the beautiful state of Manipur", he added.

On the occasion of the 73rd Anniversary Commemoration of Battle of Imphal, held on May 20, 2017 at Classic Grande, Imphal. Ambassador of Japan to India, Kenji Hiramatsu said "We must reconciliate from the bitterness of World War II and strive for peace and prosperity." Kenji assured that the Japanese Government would provide financial support in the developmental projects taken up in Manipur and other North-eastern States of India. Chief Minister N. Biren Singh said that World War II is one of the greatest events of the world that changed the mankind's course of history. "We all witnessed the unfathomable destructions, human tragedies leaving behind irreparable relationships amidst the transformation in the demographic profiles of many nations," he added.

Theme III
STORIES OF SELECT INA VETERANS

19

The Idea of Netaji, Manipur and the INA

Moirangthem Asnikumar Singh

I was born and grew up 3 miles from the place where the Indian Flag was hoisted by Colonel Shaukat Malik of the INA on 14 April, 1944. My late grandfather being contemporaries of our state's own figures like Koireng Singh (friends with Koireng) and Hemam Nilamani Singh also did no harm to my love, admiration and quest for tales of the INA and its exploits. The Indian National Army, although formed in 1942 under Mohan Singh's leadership in Singapore with Indian POWs was revived under Netaji's leadership in 1943. I grew up idolising the great man, deeply engrossed in the tales surrounding his aura of greatness and of course, his vision for a strong independent India. My admiration went to the extent that i used to argue with my fellow peers in school about how Netaji was perhaps the greatest military commander independent India could have had but like his "disappearance", this too shall remain a mystery for ever. When the MTF (Manipur Thinkers Forum); a platform where young, innovative minds can come together to shape opinions for a better Manipur, a lifelong dream of mine, was ready to be launched, the only place I had in mind to start its journey was the INA hall in Moirang. On the 18th of August, 2019 the MTF commenced its journey from the INA hall in

Moirang. This was a simple but heartfelt tribute to Netaji and his ideas.

The Tales of INA in Manipur

Following is a short excerpt from narration of the historic events that took place in Moirang during the Second World War.

The Indo-Japanese forces advanced very fast with heavy guns and tanks. The 17th British Division could not resist the advancing forces as such they were compelled to retreat leaving completely behind all the southern hill ranges (now Churchandpur and Pherzawl District) and the villages up to Potshangbam under the hands of the advancing Japanese and INA column. The people of Moirang and surrounding villages were jubilant at the sight of Indo-Japanese forces. Thus, the withdrawal of the British 17th Division was completed on April 13, 1944.

On the 14th April which happen to be Manipuri New Year Day, i.e. Cheiraoba, some leaders of Moirang led by M. Koireng Singh, L. Sanaba Singh, K. Kanglen, Meinam Mani Singh and others went to Tronglaobi village, some 3 miles to the south of Moirang which happened to be British strong defence base before their retreat but now occupied by the Indo-Japanese forces. The leaders had discussion with the Indo Japanese forces. After taking stock of the situation, at about 5 p.m. on the day Col. Saukat Ali Malik, Commander of the Bahadur (Intelligence) Group planted the Tricolour Flag with sprigging Tiger as emblem of the historic Moirang Kangla where the INA Martyrs Memorial Complex is, at present, taking shape. Many Japanese officers and soldiers were also assembled. All the arms and ammunitions abandoned by British forces collected by local people were handed over to Col. Saukat Ali Malik. Captain Ito of 33rd Mountain Regiment and Col. Malik addressed the gathering. Col. Malik's version was translated by M. Koireng Singh and the gist of the version was "the Provisional Government of the Azad Hind had declared war on England and America with a commitment to complete with the creation of Greater East Asia and bring welfare of the people of India by defeating Anglo-American forces. The Indian National Army with unscented support of the Japanese Government has now crossed the Indo-Burmese border and in the course of the struggle for the liberation of the people of India from the British Yoke, we have now reached Moirang, the ancient citadel of Manipur. Our commitment is the march to Delhi and unfurl the Tri-colour Flag then at Lal Killa. Many had died on our way to reach near (Moirang) and many would die on our way to Delhi. However, the expulsion of the enemy from the sacred soil of India is a compulsion for us. We shall fight and the people of Manipur would provide supplies to us. Nothing about us shall be passed on to the enemy, everything about the enemy should be passed on to us. Freedom of India is very near and near at hand. We shall win it and we shall have progressed and prosperity of the people of India after it. So, give us your hand, our collective efforts should cause India free from slavery."

The assembled crowd welcomed the message and they felt elated that they were the first liberated people of India although many of their family members were evacuated from Moirang and took shelter on the eastern hillocks situated at Loktak Lake. Local people gladly donated rice, dry fish and vegetable to the Indo-Japanese forces. The 13 members of Nikhil Manipuri Mahasabha, namely Th. Angou Singh, P. Tomal Singh, S. Ibohal Singh, I. Tombi Singh, L. Bijoy Singh, L. Kanhai Singh, M. Jatra Singh, W. Gyaneshwor Singh, M. Amuba Singh, L. Irabot Singh, Kh. Jugeshwor Singh, Keinya Devi and M. Randhoni Devi reached Moirang secretly from Imphal and other places. They joined with the members of Moirang and worked together in carrying out espionage activities. All the surrounding villages up to Ningthoukhong was liberated from the British forces. The southern part of Manipur from Churchandpur and Pherzawl District to Ningthoukhong covering an area of 15,000 sq. km was under the control of the INA with its Headquarters at Moirang for 3 months till July 15, 1944. The building of the Head Quarter belonged to H. Nilamani Singh INA freedom fighter and now stands at Konjengbam Leikai. The surrounding areas of the Headquarters was declared enemy zone by the British. Manipuri freedom fighters like K. Gopal Singh, L. Sanaba Singh, M. Koireng Singh and H. Nilamani Singh of Moirang were declared as traitors by the British Political Agents and "Shoot at Sight" order was passed on them. All the 17 members of the Mahasabha (13 from Imphal and 4 from Moirang) were black listed. Scorched earth policy was extended from Torbung to Ningthoukhong. The area was heavily bombarded and many civilians were killed and injured. In Moirang alone, more than one thousand homes were set ablaze with an exception of five or six.

Figures like Hemam Nilamani Singh and M. Koireng Singh feature in the state's folklore even today. Both of them went to play crucial roles in shaping Manipur's graph after Independence, with their monumental social contributions in the state's development. The idea that INA meant contributing to the society lives on in the great work they did in their times as colossal political figures in the state post-Independence.

What excites me even today is the emotional anecdotes I heard from my late grandparents about how the members of Nikhil Manipuri Mahasabha; M. Koireng Singh (in Thanga Moirangthem), H. Nilamani Singh (Sendra Hill) and their loyal lieutenants lived in hiding for a few weeks in our clan's numerous households in Thanga before they made their escape to Burma. During that period, our clan's elders formed a close bond with these brave men, due to shared ideals, respect and admiration for the INA's struggle in the face of the might of the British authorities. In 1945, they were arrested and endured a 7 month long rigorous imprisonment in Rangoon Central Jail. After their release, they reached Imphal on the 8th of May, 1946. My grandfather would narrate me deeply intriguing tales about their valour, tales which have been passed on through generations in our clan and the tradition continues even today.

Women on the Forefront

The INA was a great liberating and inspirational force for the section of Indian youth who had become disillusioned with over reliance on ideals and lesser focus on actual action. This section was growing rapidly in the early 1940s. The idea of women being given space within the Indian armed forces can also be traced back to the INA's Rani of Jhansi Regiment, which even today remains a source of inspiration for young girls aspiring to join the armed forces someday.

Netaji—The Man, the Myth, the Legend

The aura of Netaji transcended borders in his heydays. During the early days of World War II, the Japanese Intelligence services noted from speaking to captured Indian soldiers that Bose was held in extremely high regard as a nationalist and was considered by Indian soldiers as the only person who could lead an army fighting for India's independence. Bose's objection to Gandhi's pacifism is well documented. This objection perhaps stemmed from the fact that Netaji, as long as there was blood flowing in his veins could not tolerate Indians being perceived as being weak by anyone.

Ignominy to the Idea of Netaji

The Congress with its all inclusive agenda; on paper was the perfect umbrella organisation to lead the freedom struggle but its flaws were many. The constant disagreements between radicals, moderates, various other interest groups within the INC in the lead up to independence is well known. The Muslim League and the Congress' love-hate relationship ultimately concluded with partition. Gandhi and Ambedkar's constant and intense disagreements over various issues regarding minorities is another example. In this context, the British authorities saw Indians as a disunited bunch who were indecisive at crucial moments. The irony is that this indecisiveness glows brightly in the INC even today.

The Congress Party stayed in power for almost 6 decades since Independence. What is a disgrace to Netaji's indomitable legacy is the fact that it has been tampered with; to hide the flaws/blunders of the INC and its leaders in both pre- and post-Independence years. Incidents like the debacle of 1962 could have been averted if realistic rather than idealistic policies were guiding Nehru and his commanders.

Talking about commanders, highly respected young INA commanders like Gurbaksh Singh Dhillon and his colleagues were convicted in the infamous Red Fort Trials but were later released on orders of the then Commander In Chief, Claude Auchinlek after considering the rousing public support for their release. Dhillon was given his due recognition after more than 4 decades in 1998, with the Padma Bhushan when the BJP was in power under Bajpayee Ji's leadership.

Love and Oblation for the Nation

The INA was not just an army of rebels but it was much more than we were led to believe. It was an idea, a movement; that, the love for the nation came above everything else. For the brave hearts of the INA, spilling their own blood for India was a small sacrifice, about which they did not have the slightest of second thoughts.

The fact that the Congress downplayed the heroics of the INA and its bravehearts for 6 decades is a travesty and an insult to Netaji's vision of a strong, resolute India. These are ideas today's youth ought to live by.

A Long overdue Course of Action: Reviving the Ideas of INA in Manipur

The state of Manipur despite the trials and tribulations it faced in the 20th century, unequivocally made contributions in Indian nationalism, with its association with INA. The unfortunate part is that due to some reason or another, the heroism and contributions of Manipur in the freedom struggle have not been highlighted.

The need of the hour is the establishment of a dedicated autonomous agency under the purview of Ministry of Tourism and Culture for redevelopment and management of INA associated landmarks in Manipur. The composition of such an agency could be of concerned stakeholders as well as Central and State government functionaries. The acquisition of the original INA Headquarter in

Moirang Konjengbam Leikai by the government and a subsequent complete redevelopment of the complex to a world class state is something whose time has come.

And perhaps, the most requisite action in the current circumstances is a complete rebuild and expansion of the INA complex in Moirang with modern state of the art technology and set up. The aforementioned suggestions are something which will ensure a long overdue revival of the ideas of INA and worldwide recognition of Manipur's contribution in Indian Nationalism. And more importantly, the revival of such ideas will be a source of inspiration and guidance to the youth of a state which is blessed with talents in abundance but never fulfilled its potential.

Reinvigorating the Ideas of Netaji

In this day and age where some sections have the audacity to think and feel it is acceptable to criticise the commemoration of the true heroes of our motherland like Patel, Bose, it becomes necessary that the heroic tales of INA and Netaji ought to be a part of school curriculum for children of all age groups. It is paramount that the young students of this nation recognise and understand the values and ideals of men who sacrificed their lives so that their children could live in a proud, resolute and self-reliant India.

For the youth of today, it is crucial that they recognise the distinction between true heroes and pretenders.

As someone who truly admires Netaji and what he stood for, it is also genuinely hurtful and appalling to see Bengal, the place where he spent his youth and made his mark, being turned into a place where democracy in every form is being ridiculed by a Chief Minister who is so out of touch with reality.

It is circumstances like these that reinforces the argument of the need to instil Netaji's patriotic values and ideas amongst the hearts and minds of young Indians who will mould the destiny of this nation in the 21st century.

It is never too late or too 'out of touch' to look up to our heroes of the past for inspiration, especially when those heroes are men like Netaji.

20

INA in the Story of an Incomplete Diary*

Mongsatabam Makhonmani

Introduction

Inherent in the history of Manipur, Indian National Army (INA), I heard of it during my high school days around the year 1972. In my childhood days as a young student I did not give much thought to it. All that I know was that a memorial was there in Moirang. Since, I did not venture out much during those days. I hardly knew much of it. As a child, Moirang, for me was very far. Year 1976-77, I started making friends in the college. With that, crossing homestead, I began visiting friends in their homes. Then one day some friends from college and some friends from locality, we together went for a picnic lunch at Sendra that must be my first journey to Moirang. Those days, a lot of people go out for picnics to Sendra. Atop the hill, one could see people cooking in the corners. A local elderly guide showed the tree which *Khamba* climbed and sat on to watch *Thoibi* as she was fishing, pulling up her fishing net.

The road to Sendra was very bad and small too. Barely enough for two vehicles to pass by one another. Not able to drive in further,

---

*Translated from Manipuri by Aheibam Anita and Aheibam Koireng Singh.

we returned back. A girl, who said her name was Ibeton was using a boat to go to her school. I could vividly recall her sailing on her way to school. By evening as we were returning way back home the sight of water chestnuts piled up for sale on the foothills was awesome. Boiled, raw, peeled, unpeeled... heaps and heaps of them. Like the women rice vendors in the market the women were sitting in rows and selling them. As I recall, I remember the women sold them by the tins and baskets for measure. For 10 Rupees it was quite a quantity. We ate and ate with blackened lips on our way back time. We all bought to take back home too.

On reaching Moirang, we went to see INA. That was the first time I heard of INA. On the edge of the path to a big house, we saw a statue of Subhas Chandra Bose Standing. About Netaji, we knew since childhood about, as we had learnt about him in our early school books. But how Moirang, INA and Netaji are related, we did not know directly. We just saw the INA Memorial Hall from outside we did not go in. Our request for entry was denied as it was late. No one was there, so we returned. That was the first day we set foot on INA Moirang.

My grandmother and grandfather had some close elderly friends of Moirang. I had heard stories of lots of their friends from the place. When she heard of me visiting Moirang and our picnic at Sendra she gave me money to get water chestnuts for her. I got lots of raw one for her. One popular person from Moirang who even became the Chief Minister, Moirang Koireng was someone very close to my grandmother and grandfather, I remember that as a child, 'Moirang Koireng' called my grandmother *'Iche'* (eldest sister) and my grandfather *'Taibungo'* (elder brother) respectfully. It was during his tenure as the Chief Minister of Manipur, there was a function to celebrate the Statehood Day at Pologround. At the function I was made to perform a solo Krishna Dance. I guess that must be due to their closeness. Our grandfather passed away in the year 1964-65. I could not recall much of the event as I was too young. Here in this instance I am mentioning all these to relate with this essay.

The Beginning of the Incident

Year 1894, around this time, the wick of bomb of a story known to me about INA has started to burn. My grandmother often used to narrate to me the story of their fleeing at the Second World War. As a child, unaware of the fear and woes of a war I used to enjoy listening to her stories. It was when I was completing college, when she again told the story I was able to listen carefully. When the bomb dropped my grandmother hid in the pit along with my father and some children from the locality. She narrated while fleeing away from Imphal, she ran towards Lamsang carrying my father on her back. One woman from Uripok who went to fetch water was also killed in the bombardment. All such blows stuck me and I wanted to start a search about the war. I went to the elders where incidents of the Second World War happened and started collecting stories. I went everywhere to meet people and listen to stories. This became my work for some time.

Among the stories—the bombing of Chingangbam Mandop, the Memorial Tomb at Nambol Maibam Lotpa Ching, the incident at Irengbam village, south of Nambol where starving Japanese soldiers pulled away cattle from the cowshed which they later killed and ate and the Japanese trench at Thoubal. These were some of the unforgettable stories of the Second World War, I had collected. These stories, I had planned to structure into a big collection in my mind, only that it is unwritten. There was a time when I was moving fast but being in youth my thoughts got digressed and like early spring clouds, they drifted in the wind like the fluffy wools of the red silk cotton tree floating in the wind and changed direction. Thus, there was a pause in my research work on the war.

Then, I came across the Indo-Japan Friendship association in Manipur, I went ahead with my forgotten thoughts of the War yet again to find out more. Thus, I became a life member of the Association. I joined the Association to study the Japanese language and culture and learnt a bit of the language. I knew things which I did not know earlier. Meeting the Japanese war veterans who visit Manipur every year, travelling with them to some of the places related to the war increased my involvement. INA, of which I didn't knew anything I now began to understand clearly. The time was winter, a chilling December morning at that. Our teacher who taught us Japanese language, Phurailatpam Nandakumar had kindly sent me a message. Some Japanese war veterans along with the descendants of fallen Japanese soldiers would be visiting the state to pay homage to the departed. They would be going to Nambol Maibam Lotpa Ching and Irengbam village to perform some rituals and also meet some people. I was requested to guide them. Since, I was much interested on the subject, my teacher's message enthused me and I became involved all the more.

We hired a big tourist bus and along with the war veterans went to Irengbam village first. We felt so could and wore thick warm clothes but the not so well built Japanese came wearing T–shirt, least bothered of the cold. Seeing me feel so cold one of the veteran handed me a small hot pack to keep in my armpit. Having kept that in my armpit I gradually felt warmer. In a short while my whole body was warm. I no longer feel the cold. No words at that, since they came from a highly advanced country. There's a reason why they go about with light clothing in the cold. Though small, the hot pack had power. While with them they let me use the pack but did not give that away, they took it back. There, in Irengbam village at Bishnupur district they prayed offering fruits and flowers in a temple they had built. That was the place where their soldiers died. One of the veterans asked for a particular house. He took out a map he had brought and looked up the lanes, fields and meadows. Pointing at one house he proposed we go there and so we went together. It seemed he knew the surrounding of the house. He looked about everywhere, at his request I called out to the people inside the house. Some people came out. Seeing them he shook his head to show they were not the one he was looking for. Then when politely inquired if that was all of the family, they said one more was there, he was old and weak and bed ridden and could not move around much and now lying in bed. On our request to bring him out, the family member supported him and brought him out.

They sat him down comfortably in the frontal verandah. Seeing the elders, that Japanese veteran looked closely and seems to remember something and pointing his finger he said this was the man.

I was just obliging Oja Phurailatpam Nandakumar of his request to help and was accompanying the war veterans but knew nothing about the relation between the elders and the Japanese. The veteran then said, during the Second World War when they were searching for food they killed his cattle and ate it. When asked to the Meitei elder if the incident was true and if he remembers it, the elders replied in affirmative. The veteran identified himself as the man who had pulled away the cattle from his shed and killed and ate it. The war veteran introduced himself as that soldier and said that if he was alive till date it was because of that incident. The elder from Irengbam village was Irengbam Tollamu. He said the story was told by his elder brother Irengbam Bheigya. Bheigya had died. A tall well built man they both looked alike. Because of their similar looks, the war veteran took Tollamu to be the person he had met long ago. Most of the Japanese soldiers who were with the veteran at that time had died at that place. He survived. They came to pay tribute of fruits and flowers, where the Japanese soldiers fell. Today the war veteran had come back searching for the owner of the cattle they killed and ate, to pay the price for the animal, we were totally taken by surprise. He asked the price for the cattle. Instead of giving or taking the price money, when a long forgotten incident of fifty years had all of a suddenly very vividly come up in front of our eyes... it seem a bond was growing and a knot of love tighten between them. The Japanese presented some gift as that they had brought with them to the family and the people gathered there. From there we headed to the memorial Tomb at the foothills of Maibam Lotpa Ching and made offerings. I wanted all that to finish up soon and drop them at the hotel and do my own work.

My work was nothing but to go back to Irengbam village and know the story further. I grew anxious in my curiosity for the story but could not do anything at that moment. The work was not complete. The Japanese were looking for an old bed ridden man who lived west of the Maibam Lotpa Hill and met him. I didn't know who the man was. I did not go back to ask his whereabouts because the sickness the elder was suffering from seemed to be something like tuberculosis. After meeting the elder we all headed towards Wangkhei, Thambal Khong. This time the person we met was not a Meitei. We went to a Meitei-Pangal house. This elder was someone whom they knew very well. They gave him a hearing aid. After some talks among themselves, they winded up for the day. I was restless. Once I dropped them at the lodge. I first hurriedly turned back to Irengbam village and met the cattle owner the Japanese met with to find out the true story. I found out more.

During the war, everyone in Irengbam village fled away, narrated one Irengbam Tollamu. Their family members ran away to Heikhrujam, Kabowakching, a village in the west of Irengbam. Having made all the family members run away, only his elder brother, Irengbam Bheiga stayed back to look after the household and the cattle. During those days Meitei homes used to keep few tins of caramelised sugarcane juice. During the war those tins were hidden by burying them in the holes dug up inside the house. The Japanese soldiers scattered themselves and stayed in the vacant house after the families had fled away. One day a Japanese soldier walked out of the bamboo grove and pulled a cattle away from their cowshed. Seeing that Beigya ran towards the Japanese soldier and the two had a fight. The Japanese soldier was overpowered and pinned down. Suddenly some more soldiers came out of the bamboo groves and caught him and tied him up and they killed the cattle in his compound, cut and ate it. Sad and helpless against the armed soldiers he stayed back. They ate the animal since they had no food. The incident was an unforgettable and a sad one and the man called Irengbam Bheigya remembered it lifelong and was one of the untold wartime incidents.

The story told by Irengbam Bheigya, his aged younger brother lovingly told me again... that day his face reflected contentment, for the Japanese soldiers, long after the war, had come so far to that place where their fellow solders gave up their lives, in their remembrance. They felt it wrong to kill and eat the cattle and satisfy their hunger and save some of their lives, this Irengbam village, they cherished and to come back after fifty years and meet again and asking the price of the animal they had eaten, all these was so satisfying. The departed elder who then was with the Gods must too be satisfied. All grudges neutralized and cleansed. Through not related, but still, he said it felt like as if they were brothers of some previous birth and related by blood. This story makes me do more thinking. The incident is a mall story of Irengbam village during the war.

Stories of Second World War in Imphal did not end with this one. There were some untold stories in some places of Manipur. My curiosity grew and my search for stories of war time incidents did not stop. I became more involved in the works of Indo-Japan Friendship Association. That was the time when the Association was very active. One important functionary was our Japanese language teacher Phurailatpam Nandakumar Sharma. In his tenure as the Secretary, a lot of works were carried out. Because of him I also could learn much that I always wanted. He was the one who greatly encouraged me. The thought of making a film about the incidents in Manipur during the war for posterity came to my mind. For this, discussing with him I worked further. Oja Nandakumar introduced me to Oja Makino of Manipur University. Oja Makino, then did many writings about the war. Oja Nandakumar gave the news of some other war veterans visiting in the next year. Also the news that Japanese war veterans has lined up to visit the state every year. Unfortunately the number of days of their stay in Manipur was very less and also very few places were permitted to visit. The time they would come is winter. There were efforts by Oja Nandakumar regarding Inner Line Permit to extend their time of stay a little more.

A Related Small Story

For a Ph.D. research work on folklore of Langathel, I often used to visit the renowned artist 'Langathel Thoinu' who was famous for folk songs and the Moirangsai style of singing. Ema Langathel Thoinu and me, we knew each other from earlier times. Visiting her often I met her husband 'Pabung' (Father) Yumnam Budhamani whenever I visited her house, often Pabung Budhamani, sitting in the corner of the frontal verendah used to write something in a note-book. I asked Ema if Pabung writes down all the lyrics of her song, I often saw Pabung writing I said. Ema was a little annoyed and replied 'not at all, I don't know what your pabung is writing'. When I asked Pabung what he was writing to my utter surprise, he said 'war dairy'. "War Dairy" I was shocked. In the household of a soft artist someone is writing of tough things like war. It was unimaginable for me. Being a person curious and interested about the war, these words drew my attention. I changed my seat. I took the 'mora' (sitting tool indigenously made) near Pabung and sat near him. I asked which parts of the war was his dairy about. Pabung's face was a smiling one by nature. The lowered face raised up and with a serious look said, "It's about the Second World War in Manipur. My diary is almost done but something is amiss so cannot call it complete." I further asked him if I might know what it was. Looking at the Tulsi plant in the courtyard, he said. An article in the local dairy stating that 'Netaji Subhas Chandra had come and hoisted the flag of INA at Moirang' is not allowing me to complete my diary. This truth can only be trusted if a friend I once had would say it, but I don't know his whereabouts and that is missing link. I could not take this matter lightly. I asked him who this friend was, and which story was it.

He did not look at me but was intensely gazing at the courtyard. You all won't know, I once has a friend, a Meitei Pangal. He knows the true story about the INA. Other than him, I could believe nobody about the INA flag-hoisting at Moirang. Not knowing if the person to speak on INA is still alive or dead, I still am keeping this part of my dairy incomplete. I have a lot of discontentment. Hearing this I asked him again, who the Meitei Pangal was. What his name was. He calmly replied, 'I call him Choudhury'. His full name is Nake Ahmed Choudhury.

I believe God is there. I suddenly recalled the Meitei-Pangal I met along with the Japanese war veterans. Turning his face towards me from the intense gaze at the Courtyard asked me. "How do you know him? I then told him everything about my meeting with the Japanese war veterans. Hearing this I saw a bright smile on his face. "Do you know his house, where did you meet him? Let's go" he said. I knew the house and we got ready and went. A Friend, Pabung and me, we three came to Nake Ahmed Choudhury's house at Wangkhei Yonglan Lane in Thambalkhong Khetrigao. A slight horizontally structured house, there, a small wooden table and a chair was placed in the verendah. The compound was not a big one. With me in the front we walked in and I called out Pabung Nake. A woman come out and made us sit in the verendah. Pabung Nake and me knew each other. I had often come to give him the hearing aid. That's how I knew. We never sat down and talked properly. I also did not bother to. That day I was much interested. Pabung Budha and him looked at each other intensely the way one does to people they knew earlier and I watched them without even blinking. Pabung Budha was the one to begin, "Choudhury Saheb.... remember me?" Like meeting long lost family members they hugged each other tightly, both sides of the neck touching the others. Like Muslim on the day of Eid hugging their friends touching each other necks, there in front of my eyes in Pabung Nakes's verandah these two aged old friends affectionately hugged each other. They must have felt the relationship between them when they met. I did not feel that since I did not knew them much. Pabung Budha spoke bluntly, he began, "Choudhury Saheb we met at Moirang one day, then Choudhury was caught after that 'where were you taken?'

Pabung Budha's question was one that took me by surprise. The one to answer, Pabung Nake held his ear tightly and in a low voice said, "I cannot hear what you are saying." Pabung went closer and repeated the same words. Pabung Nake turned his face away and said, "I don't know what you are talking about, No body caught me." Pabung Budha's face darkened and Pabung Nake turned his face away. Pabung Budha's blunt start with unpleasant things like arrest must have marred the re-union between the two long lost friends. Pabung Nake started avoiding the talk and diverted away. The words would not have mattered had it been between people who knew one another closely. I came in between them requesting not to get angry. "Pabung Budha kept remembering Pabung Nake very often", I said, "I was the one to tell him Pabung Nake is still alive and knew his house and thus brought him." I took out the biscuit and gave Pabung Nake called out to make tea. Pabung Budha further said this son of mine (me, Makhonmani myself) is also studying about the second War War in Manipur. I am also writing a diary of what happened in Manipur. My diary is complete, but for one thing if I did not hear it from you cannot be true and have kept it blank. For that I have kept my diary incomplete. I was very happy to hear that you are still alive. Choudhury must give the true answer otherwise the history of the Second World War in Manipur would go the incorrect way. Who hoisted the INA flag at Moirang? Didn't Choudhury hoist the flag? Did Netaji come to Manipur? Please give me the true answers clearly.

Pabung Nake Choudhury seems a bit weak. He seemed a bit stronger hearing the mention of the INA flag. He replied he was the one who did, but did not speak much further. Due to his physical weakness he did not give much time. He looked tired to be sitting for long. A woman brought out tea; we drank together and returned back. Once inside the vehicle, Pabung Budha said, "Ibungo, you go and talk to him again without me. I will entrust you something. He himself did accept it was him who hoisted the INA flag at Moirang. This was what I wanted to hear in his own words. I would now write this truth in my diary. One more thing I wanted to know that he had not answered. It is troubling me. You go and take the stories without me.

Which incident, what happened between these elders... without knowing that and being a part of the conversation... I was dumbstruck and did not know what to think. Once we reached home, me and Pabung talked in detail. Pabung Budha told me a story of a long ago, much before I was born. Had I known the story

I would have gone myself to Pabung Nake prior to their meeting, then the reunion between the two would have been a complete one. But beginning with the wrong things out of over excitement at the news of Pabung Nake being alive and the desire to see him spoilt things. I then went to Pabung Budha to find out what actually happened between them and listened to the story.

In earlier times, prior to the war, the two of them studied together at CC Higher Secondary, sitting on the same bench they were good friends. Both were good students. Both aimed to become pilots. Intermediate Arts (IA) of those days, now equivalent of twelfth standard these days, completing that, they both headed to Calcutta to become pilots together. Without any guidance, we had gone without knowing where to go. On reaching Calcutta, seeing the jets in flights at sharp tilts on their sides, Pabung Budhamani was very scared. When he told this to Pabung Nake. He became very angry and said he was a coward and was so unbecoming of a Meitei. Pabung Nake stayed back to 'study pilot'. Pabung Budhamani returned back to Imphal alone. After that the two never met. Back in Imphal when he had no work the government was making efforts to open an office of industries. He was selected for training and went for it. He returned back after finishing the training. In those days very few educated individuals like Sanasam Gourahari and Sinam Krishnamohan were the influential people in the government administration. They examined the certificate of the training. They also examined the matric (Class X) certificate too. As per the matric certificate records, his name was known as Yumnam Budhamani. The Sahebs, when they gave the certificate after their training, wrote Mister Budha. The names did not match. Because of this difference in the names and alias being not allowed his hard work at the training did not bear fruit. He could not get the job. Frustrated, the certificate proved useless, he has no reason for keeping it. He tore it there on the spot, narrated Pabung Budhamani.

Later, one day Pabung Budhamani met the sahib who selected him for the training; he asked Pabung if he got the job. Pabung told him that the names in the certificate did not match and so could not get the job. Knowing that he was a good student convinced him again. "We are leaving Manipur, we know you are good, We will give you a job forget the rank. But you have to give a test." Saying this he was made to sit in an examination for recruitment of Amins for Land Measurement. They wanted to select him but also they wanted to do it clean and then they took his test. Some of the questions were—Draw two similar looking pictures. Pabung Budhamani said around seven of them gave the test at Johnstone School, Imphal. Most of them drew pair of oxen, saluting soldiers and many different pictures and went happily after submitting their papers. He was left alone, unable to draw anything. The invigilator on duty asked him "Mister Budha you are not able to answer anything." At last, a theorem came up in his mind and he drew isosceles triangles and submitted. "You are appointed", there and then he was appointed for the job, narrated Pabung Budhamani. He prayed to Gonvinda and tried his luck and drew the two isosceles triangles. Early in those days he was the first to become an Amin. That must have been a record. During the war he as the Amin (Land Recorder) measured the land to construct the airfield for the British planes to land at Tulihal Airport Changangei. He made very accurate land measurement. He was appreciated for he could accurately calculate the length, breadth and area. Thus, at that time he was employed under the British with salary.

It was the time when the Second World War was growing stronger. News of Azad Hind Fauz raised by Netaji coming into Manipur spreaded. Pamphlets with the headlines 'Join INA' carrying message of Netaji were strewn about and news of its establishment in Manipur was also heard. During the war while going for construction of roads and bridges people picked up these pamphlets which would land them in trouble had the Britishers come to know of it. The brief summary of the –

> "Brother, father, son and sisters and friends of Bharat. I pay my respect to you all. Please do not help Britain, instead of doing that Please help Bharat and Japan who have come together. I myself have come as a soldier.

> I Subhas have devoted both my body and spirit for Bharat Mata. It is my firm belief that this war would free us. If defeated, I would, even if I die, would never again return back to the lap of Bharat Mata."

One day a letter was delivered to Pabung Budhamani's hand. It read "Mister Budha, you must go to Moirang to carry out the land survey for the construction of market. Come to Babupara, Imphal. There a jeep no... ...would be waiting for you. You should be sitting next to the driver at the front seat. Leave the main seat vacant. On your way to Moirang, a man would be waiting at Ningthoukhong. He would also board the jeep. He will sit at the vacant front seat. Together you all would be travelling till Moirang and do the survey.

Since the order could not be disobeyed, on the appointed day and time, for the survey at Moirang. I went to Babupara, Imphal and found the jeep and following their orders climbed in and started off. There at Ningthoukhong a non-Manipuri joined us. Without talking much we drove towards Moirang. Being wartime, there were anxiety and worry. With prayers in our hearts we went ahead. In those days, due to the bad road, it took a long time to reach Moirang. At last we reached. Body was exhausted. The non-Manipuri told us to freshen up and to look for something to eat and drink. Wanting to have a cup of tea, I started looking for a local tea and snacks stall. After the search finally a small shop was seen half open. I walked in an asked if they would have tea, the tea was made. While having the tea, suddenly not from a far distance someone seems to beckon at me with his hands from among the dense wild water-plant leaves. On looking out again, the man had come quite close and was calling out. It was him, my one time friend who stayed back in Calcutta to study pilot, a Meitei-Pangal by the name Nake Choudhury. He took me aside into the wilderness and showed me the INA uniforms piled up there. He had come to Manipur and was staying there. He had come as the INA 'Manipur Branch captain' and started requesting me to join INA. Led by that non-Manipuri who had come with them Nake was caught and taken away. Pabung Budha was told to go back to Imphal without doing the survey and made to return. In this way Pabung Nake Ahmed Choudhury was caught right infront of his own eyes, this dream like incident was kept untold to anyone. Pabung Budhamani started writing this war dairy.

Listening to this story from Pabung Budhamani himself, I forgot I was breathing; such wonderful story made me more curious, my anxiety grew. For the rest, I was told to go and meet so I went to Pabung Nake Ahmed's house like a peon to take down his message. Pabung Nake looked weak and dull. Seeing me he looked disinterested but without wasting time, I started asking what I wanted to know. The problem with him was that he did not permit me to record our conversation. Camera too was not allowed. Those days recorders were not as good and did not have a camera. But a hidden video camera was on.

As narrated by Pabung Budha, they both went to 'study pilot' together. Pabung Budhamani got scared and returned to Imphal. Both stories were just the same till then, Pabung Nake's story was more of woes. After Pabung Budhamani return to Imphal he faced a lot of suffering in Calcutta. His money finished off and he had no food to eat. Calcutta, those days was a land filled with Netaji's voice. The call for Azad Hind Fauj and Challo Delhi resonated everywhere. The INA movement was very strong. Out of hunger, in search for food, he went up to the ship docked at the river banks of Hoogly and doing the loading, unloading etc. carrying loads just to earn for food. At that point, all that he could think of was food. Everywhere in Calcutta posters of 'Join INA' were put up. To try his luck, he enrolled himself. He sailed to Rangoon in a ship. There he underwent a very rigorous training. Most of the training were done in a dense jungle.

The long narratives, in between I crossed and questioned him who were the ones to instruct during the training. To my question, Pabung Nake answered spontaneously "INA was made in alliance with Japan". It was based on Guerrilla warfare technique, a very rigourous one at that. Secret war strategies of Japanese warfare and technique were learnt. I further questioned him, "the founder of Azad Hind Fauz and the person to raise INA, Netaji Subhas Chandra Bose, did you meet him in Rangoon?" Pabung Nake replied he 'never' met Netaji but it was a wonder. During the training we were told a very important person would be visiting and we must listen to him. During the training, it was so exhausted he did not want to hear anymore and so quietly sat at the back. One leader of INA came, he spoke a lot, and too exhausted he was dozing and missed out on what was said. Later on came to learn that the speaker was Netaji Subhas Chandra Bose. It was never let known in advance that Netaji would be coming and addressing. He came once or twice and spoke. Every time he looked different and we never knew it was him. Only after he spoke and left were we told that it was Netaji. That was the *modus operandi* of those days. "Had I know that Netaji was coming I would have been sitting at the front and listening to Netaji." This was Pabung Nake's narrative.

"When asked who the person from Manipur was I raised my hand since I being native and was familiar with the terrain was therefore made the captain and with three Japanese soldiers and seven of the Azad Hind Fauz, a patrolling party team was ordered to leave for Manipur." The person who gave the order was Netaji, It was later talked about. With me as the Captain, I led the team on foot through Rangoon to Manipur crossing Singhat, Churachandpur, then further to Moirang in the month of March. The journey was a month long one. To proclaim the presence of INA in Manipur, a tri-colour flag was hoisted at Hemam Nilamani's residence. I myself hoisted the flag and established the advance Headquarters. With the Moirang Base Camp efforts were initiated to raise an army of INA. Then he met with many Meitei individuals and held talks and discussions. A strong campaign was on to win more people on their side. Many important Meiteis joined in.

Until now what can be discussed is that the headquarters of INA at Moirang was established under the leadership of a Meitei Pangal by the name Nake Ahmed Choudhury. Another thing is, on April 14, 1944 Commander Colonel Shaukat Ali Malik hoisted the INA flag at a public function at Moirang Kangla. I came across the information now this must have been the second time the flag was hoisted. I myself took up the task of finding out the truth of the Meitei Pangal Nake Ahmed Choudhury was the man to hoist the INA flag for the first time. To find out I tried to meet Pabung Heman Nilamani when I heard that he has a house at Sangaiporou. I found out his house got to meet him. This respected elder knew Nake Ahmed Choudhury very well. When Nake was about to put up the flag at the tulsi mound in my courtyard, I told him to please move away to the side a little as that was a sacred space. Nake put up the pole little away towards the side of the house. This, he narrated to me. Some other things I discussed with him were only about Manipur women who were recruited in INA, he gave me two names, Keinya and Mutum Randhoni. He did not tell me the surname and address of Keinya. The shootouts between the Japanese and the British Soldiers happened at morning and evening always. For aiding the Japanese, K. Gopal, L. Sanajaoba, Heman Nilamani, Mairenbam Koireng were declared revolutionaries and ordered to be shot at sight by the then Political Agent of Manipur. In the short meeting with Pabung Hemam Nilamani I was given some more names of members of the advance party of INA, Manipur. They were Heman Nilamani, Potshangbam Tomal of Heirangoithong, Laishram Kanhai of Keishamthong, Longjam Bijoy of Keishamthong, Moirangthem Jatra of Bishnupur, Thokchom Angou of Singjamei, Sarungbam Ibohal of Singjamei, and R.K. Maipaksana of Chingmathak.

These facts I just mentioned was the truth Pabung Budhamani was fervently seeking for while he was alive. In his diary these were the things he had left blank. He would not take anybody else's words, only what Nake Ahmed Choudhury would say be the truth, thethe that was his strongest belief. When Pabung Budhamani wanted to find out the answers to the questions, Pabung Nake did not give a proper response, I later on, learnt the reason for that.

As the writer, I met with the two elders separately and collected their stories, Pabung Yumnam Budhamani and Pabung Nake met at Moirang and while they were talking of INA, Pabung Nake was arrested, this was already mentioned earlier. The part that follows would be the ultimate climax. When I went alone without Pabung Budhamani, I found out that in him there was one huge grudge against Pabung Budhamani. That was the cause of a conflict and affected the relation between them. He felt Pabung Budhamani arranged his arrest. He further narrated, how that day of his arrest was an unforgettable one till the present moment. The military camp at Kakching Lamkhai was a big camp of the British Amry during the days of the Second World War. He was taken there and tortured tremendously. The British soldier took him to be dead and he was thrown away. Because of the severe physical beatings both his ears drums were totally damaged and since then he could hear no sound. This deafness and weak physical condition was the reward for leading the revolt of INA bringing the tri-colour flag and hoisting it for the first time. This the Japanese War veterans knew and felt. Whenever the Japanese war veterans come to Manipur they bring specially made hearing aids for him. As a life member of Indo-Myanmar Association, I used to deliver the hearing aids to him at his house. Thus Pabung Nake and me knew each other.

Conclusion

Earlier I did not know Pabung Nake's story in detail. Two halves of the story came together. I had understood. One half from Pabung Budhamani, another half by Pabung Nake, I combined the two and one whole was compiled. Pabung Budhamani always thought Pabung Nake to be a very important leader of INA. He considered Pabung Nake to be missing, whether dead or alive or any of his whereabouts. Co-incidentally when I happened to mention a man named Nake to be still alive, turned out to be Nake Ahmed Choudhury of whom Pabung Budhamani has deep regards. So in the year 1996 on June 29 at 8:30 am they met. This very record was noted down by Pabung Budhamani in his diary. Meeting after a long time they recalled their stories. Pabung Nake held a bitter grudge. He always thought Pabung Budhamani was the informer. A loving friend from his days of youth who once studied with him, one whom he always kept thinking of, only whose words about INA would be the sole truth, this one person has all the while misunderstood him. This made him heart broken. His sincere truth from the heart—I clarified to Pabung Nake. Pabung Nake, he accepted the clarification about his misunderstandings and gave some more names of INA members to find out if they are still alive. If they are alive, told me to organise a meeting and sitting down together with Budhamani, they will then tell the real story, Pabung Nake told me.

The names of Manipuris elders who joined INA in Pabung Nake's list was same as those given by respected elder Heman Nilamani. One day Pabung Nake called me at home to meet someone. It was also a Meitei Pangal named Kayamuddin Pukhrimayum. Kayamuddin Pukhrimayum, I had already met earlier as a renowned young writer. We three sat down at Pabung Nake's house. He told me and Oja Kayamuddin, 'I have told in details about INA to Kayamuddin and made him write it down some stories other than those I have told Ibungo (myself Makhonmani) I have told verbally. You both write my story, thus he entrusted the task. Oja Kayamuddin worked at Government settlement department. He was very busy. Equally busy, we both could not meet often. At times, on his way back from office we used to sit down together and began working on the story. And we decided to start like that.

Carrying out Pabung Nake's words to organise the meeting soon I started to work upon and found most of them dead. I remember, only one R.K. Maipaksana to be alive and met him. I report the news to Pabung Budhamani, he was very happy. To give the news I went to Pabung Nake's house, Pabung Nake had a sudden demise, dead and was buried, to my disbelief a big lock hung on the door of his house. Sorrows come one after another to me. Kayamuddin Pukhrimayum was travelling in a Jeep when it overturned; he too died in the accident. All that was built up crumbled down.

Pabung Budhamani and me, all our dream went in vain. Pabung and me didn't meet for some time. Later on, one more news reached me "Ema Langathel Thoinu's husband Yumnam Budhamani is now no more." He left this world in the year 2001. The war diary he had written... with no one to fill it up... was still left incomplete. All these are, today, left as a story. Except for some very near and dear one, I had never let out these stories.

The story I am telling is not the complete one yet. There is more. This... is the message from my heart. Seeing INA at Moirang I humbly remember the role performed by the departed souls who are now in the world of Gods. Ignorant as I was whatever I learnt of INA was all because of them. I value deeply. I still remember Pabung Nake's words till today.

> "To win the hearts of the people...! The revolt that people do not support... would be hard to succeed."

21

A Pilgrim from Moirang

M. Jugindro Singh

Turning point in one's life spurs from within and without. It is the point of retreat when one says "YES" to the uncertainty and surrendered holistically which could bring about a change in the whole career of one's life, belief and action to transform radically. Such great transformative and trajectory phase occurred in the life of Subhas Chandra Bose when he studied accidentally the life and works of Swami Vivekananda. In his own words, Subhas Bose admitted "I was barely fifteen when Vivekananda entered my life. Then there followed a revolution within and everything was turned upside down."[1] He realised that Vivekananda gave everything what his teachers, religious Gurus and scriptures could not provide for. He wrote in his autobiography, "An Indian Pilgrim". "... From this study I emerged with a vivid idea of the essence of his teaching "Atmano Moksharthan Jagadhitaya"—for your own salvation and for the service of humanity that was to be life's goal."[2] He witnessed the Almighty in the form of Mother India. Sister Nivedita corroborated the same view and unequivocally pointed out "The queen of his adoration was his motherland". He was deeply influenced by the sayings of Swami Vivekananda who said "The naked Indian, the illiterate Indian, the Brahman Indian, the Pariah

Indian is my brother." Therefore, despite of all the differences, he treated all Indians alike and equal.

INA and Hemam Nilamani Singh

Such moment came in the life of Shri Hemam Nilamani Singh too. The moment was short, brief but quiet decisive. In search of a person who knew Bengali, Hindi and English at Moirang, INA soldiers came down at his residence. It was a little after dusk in the first week of April 1944. In his own narration, he wrote "This soldier introduced himself that he was a Manipuri and resident of Imphal (Keikhu). His name was Naki Ahmad Choudhary. Naki Ahmad Chaudhary gave a short speech before the small gathering. His speech dwelt upon the objectives of INA and its organisation under the charismatic personalities of Subhas Chandra Bose. After the speech, he brought forward some small sized photographs along with pamphlets and leaflets in different scripts of India. These photographs were that of Netaji himself in uniform and that of the NA soldiers on parades in Singapore. "The tri-colour National Flag (Flag of INA) was also taken out of his haversacks."[3] Netaji said "In this struggle there is no going back and there can be no faltering, we must march onward and forward till victory is achieved and freedom won."[4] It is a crystal clear statement that he and his INA was for India and her Independence.

Naki Ahmad Chaudhury informally invited him to join INA. Shri H. Nilamani Singh was fully convinced the gravity of decision and as well the very situation. Till then, he was much more a family member and quiet homely a person, a faithful son, a fair brother, an adorable husband, a loving father, a trustworthy friend and a good Samaritan. He willingly reciprocated to the call of Netaji and INA—"Total Mobilizaion"—for unparallel supreme sacrifice. Bose continued... "For the present I can offer you nothing except hunger, thirst privation, force marches and deaths.... But if you follow me in life and in death—as I am confident you will—I shall lead you to victory and freedom."[5]

The decision made him to break from his comfort zone, but out to the hell and horrors of the war—the worst and the fiercest war—this world ever witnessed since the beginning of human civilization the battle where even the strongest and the bravest doubted to tread, the battle where the God of Death roamed at liberty, the battle where the bullets hardly killed but the hunger, thirst privation, starvation, tropical diseases, giant leeches etc. as the great leader prophesized. Netaji asked for everything and as such, he too gave everything accordingly—his residence where the Indo-Japanese forces requisitioned as Advanced Headquarter; the granaries to feed the hungry mouths of thousands of uncompromised and death defying INA heroes; his fortune to meet their war expenses; his mortal body to be sacrificed at the altar of Mother India—leaving behind his beloved family members to their fate. He was one of the very few Indians who responded to the clarion call of Netaji '*Karo sab nichhabar bano sab fakir*' (Sacrifice all and be penniless mendicants for the sake of Motherland). At the first instance, Shri H. Nilamani Singh was without home, without family but THE MAN OF NETAJI.

His Role in INA

In his own narration, Shri H. Nilamani Singh, wrote—

> "I formally joined the INA on this memorable day (14th April, 1944), the day when the flag of INA was unfurled at Moirang Kangla) and from that day onwards my residence was used as the Head Quarters of the INA for some time until their retreat. My father, (late) Hemam Thambaljao Singh, was also residing in the same house for about 3 (three) months with colonel S.A. Malik. I was assigned to collect intelligence report and arranged for supply of food to the INA."[6]

Never before he was in the war and none of his family members were in the army. Nor did he try his finger on trigger. Not to say, to face enemy in the battlefield, he did not, on record, killed even an insect. All about his idea and experience in the battlefield was just a fiction of mind. But, he wonderfully discharged his assignment to the full satisfaction of Col. Saukat Ali Malik. "On joining the INA, I used to contact many youth and influential persons of the locality. I was fully engaged in reconnaissance and gave information to Col. Malik. After a few days some Manipuri leaders like Shri Potshangbam Tomal Singh, Shri Sharungbam lbaohal Singh, Shri Thockchom Angom Singh and others came from Imphal to Moirang and met Col. Malik. They came at Moirang Khunou and took up reconnaissance work from outside Manipur area."[7] He kept on record and continued "... I managed to supply food and essential commodities to the INA and placed at their disposal all my paddy and rice in stock free of cost. Besides, the Japanese army of Hikari Kikan group was also allowed the food and essential supplies. A sum of Rs. 21,000 in Indian currency was also given in exchange for the Japanese notes (Currency) to facilitate the INA in meeting their needs in the locality. Pleased with this, Col. Malik conferred me the title of 'Sethji' and he used to address me as Sethji, thereafter."[8] To the poorly equipped army who were without money, food and friend in an inhospitable forbidden land, the help and assistance of Shri H. Nilamani Singh was a heaven sent opportunity.

Japan Lan at Moirang

To the account of eyewitness—the battle ensued with the firing of two canon bombs from Khoigoujeng camp to Moirang in the evening of April 12, 1944. Soon the battle spread wide over at Phougakchao-Ikhai, Tronglaobi and surrounding areas. While Captain lto of 33rd Mountain Gun Regiment of INA led the occupying forces from Kumbi side, he killed hundreds of Allied Forces at Thoya Battle situated at close vicinity to Moirang village and Lt. Ando started capturing Torbung, Terakhongshangbi andTronglaobi along the Tiddim Road. Having been pressed heavily from various directions, the 17th Division of British Forces started to relinquish and retreated towards Phuballa and then to Ningthoukhong for further fortification at Bishnupur. In the face of the advancing forces at an alarming pace, Anglo American Forces hurried to collect their tanks, canons, heavy armour etc. but they failed and left behind at Moirang Okshongbung half burnt. On their retreat, they burnt down one thousand strong houses of Moirang surviving only a few seven houses.

INA at Moirang

Shri Kumam Kanglen Singh, the self-style king of Moirang was the first who encountered the Indo-Japanese forces. It was the clear morning of April 13,1944. He went down to Tronglaobi and welcomed the Indo-Japanese forces. Exhibiting a friendly gesture, he politely offered flattened rice and a lump of molasses to take that they declined dubiously. Realizing their intention, Shri K. Kanglen Singh retorted "Lo, I amtaking it". Saying so, he started eating the flattened rice with the molasses. The situation had become tense and aggravated due to language problem. Timely intervention of Naki Ahmad Chaudhary, a Manipuri from Keikhu, an erstwhile member of Nikhil Hindu Manipuri Mahasobha who facilitated to interpret comfortably saved the situation. The tired soldiers heartily partook the offerings and happily agreed to be the proud guests in the house of Shri K. Kanglen Singh.

Allied Strategy

During his retreat from Rangoon, Gen Slim learnt the Japanese war tactics from one Chinese General who said that

> "The Japanese confident in their own prowess, frequently attacked on a small margin of safety.... and estimated a force would usually not have more than nine day's supplies available. If (one) could hold the Japanese for that time, prevent from them capturing supplies and then counter attack (One) would destroy them."[9]

Everything that fell into the hands of INA turned into war materials—food to keep their soul into the frame of their body and weapon to fire relentlessly against the British forces. When they were asked what they would eat in the battlefield and what weapon would they used in the war, they would say with a smile on their face jokingly that Churchill would send them by air. General Slim treasured the secrecy of the Japanese war tactics and employed with their skill and efficacy in the war. The adoption of "Scorch Earth Policy" by Slim in the war was one such attempt and master stroke policy not to provide any sort of refuge or shelter and not to fall anything in the form of war materials and food into the hands of Indo-Japanese forces. The importance of Imphal was illustrated by Churchill's signal to Mountbatten, the Supreme Commander of South East Asia Allied Operations: "Let nothing go from the battle that you need for victory. I will not accept denial of this from any quarter."[10] The Allied commanders were very crafty and master strategist. Their plan was to pull back all the available forces within the parameter of Imphal and to cause maximum casualties to the invaders on the epicentre of Imphal plain. The capital city was well defended by numerous strongly fortified and well-defended localities known as 'Keeps'. These localities were ably supported by a numbers of self-contained, self-supporting and well-organized 'Boxes' which were heavily equipped, well-armed and when offended, the offenders would be fatally attacked from several other boxes outflanked around from the adjoining areas. There were several other 'mobile' and hard hitting 'general reserves' of the corps, instrumental only for launching counter attacks.

General Slim had already anticipated that the onset of the monsoon would turned the table in favour of the Anglo-American forces. As expected, the monsoon set in and thus incapacitated the Indo-Japanese forces on every move. Shri H. Nilamani Singh wrote:

> "After three months of establishing its headquarters at Moirang, the INA had to withdraw its forces towards Burma due to certain difficulties with the approach of monsoon, like deteriorating road and communication

facilities, shortage of food, severe attack ofcertain diseases etc."[11]

Ningthoukhong-Bishnupur Battle

The fiercest battle was fought at Bishnupur-Ningthoukhong sector. It lasted for several weeks starting from the first week of May upto Mid-June 1944. In this battle, the three Indian Brigades were hotly engaged against the 33rd Division containing the Flowers of Imperial Japanese Army. There were several instances of offensive and counter offensive fights causing heavy casualties on both sides. Both sides used tanks, heavy armours and hand to hand fight using bayonets in which three Japanese tanks were knocked out and two others were overwhelmed. Eight lorries were totally destroyed and ten others were captured by Allied forces. The Japanese casualties were estimated to several thousands and losses of Allied forces were also terrific. To the very disadvantages of Indo-Japanese forces, rain started from June 4 and continued upto June 14, 1944. The incessant rain flooded the entire area and cawed hindrance to every movement. Once more the superiority of the air and the introduction of one troop of medium tank ultimately carried the day and turned the scale in favour of the Allied forces. Heavy shelling and pouring of bullets caused maximum damage to the Indo-Japanese Forces. Slim noted: "There can have been few' examples in history of a force as reduced, battered and exhausted as the Japanese 33rd Division delivering such furious assaults, not with the objective of extricating itself, but to achieve its original offensive intention." He went on: "Whatever one may think ofthe military wisdom of thus pursuing a hopeless object, there can be no question of the supreme courage and hardihood of the Japanese soldiers who made the attempts. I know of no army that could have equalled them."[12]

Of the five Victoria Cross Winners in the Battle Imphal, four winners were from 'Ningthoukhong-Bishnupur Battle'. They were—

1. Sergeant Hanson Victor Turner (Posthumously) of the West Yorkshire Regiment for his actions on 7 June, 1944, at Ningthoukhong on the Tiddim Road.
2. Rifleman Ganju Lama of the 7th Gurkha Rifles for his actions on 12 June, 1944, Ningthoukhong.
3. Subedar Netra Bahadur Thapa (Posthumously) of the 5th Royal Gurkha Rifle for his actions on 26 June, 1944, at the British position called mortar bluff off the Silchar-Bishenpur Track.
4. Naik Agansing Rai of the 5th Royal Gurkha Rifles for his action on 26 June, 1944, at the British positions called Water Piquet and Mortar Bluff on the Silchar-Bishenpur Track.[13]

It speaks of the intensity, volume and significance of the war.

Captain Ito was killed in an encounter with the enemy at Ngankhalawai. It is said that he sneaked into the British Army Camp and killed numbers of soldiers. In his desperate attempt to escape from their hands, he killed himself. His body lay for some days and ultimately was cremated with honour by the INA volunteers of Moirang.

Retreat to Rangoon

Shri H. Nilamani Singh without his INA veterans Shri K. Gopal Singh, Shri M. Koireng Singh and Shri L. Sanaba Singh left Moirang on July 20, 1944 for Rangoon. They were seen off by Shri K. Apamba Singh and Shri L. Choudar Singh upto Wangoo. From Wangoo they followed the uncommon serpentine track winding up to the lush greenery Khoingoujeng Hill and reached Ngampi Village where they encountered the Indo-Japanese Forces on retreat. They stayed one night with them at Ngampi and took the alternate route down the hills to reach Saikot. At that time, Saikot was a big camp and was treated as Command Headquarters of INA. Of his journey, Shri H. Nilamani Singh narrated "In the journey, we had to hideout on steep hill tracts without food for several days. On 31st July,1944, we fed on sprouts of plantain as nothing was available for our food. On 2nd August, 1944, there was a heavy firing of machine guns from aircraft when we were crossing a river on a suspension bridge near milestone 149 and we sought to cover in the nearby jungle. On 4.8.1944 there was a heavy bombing from four aircrafts (fighters) at Tiddim Khunjao where Shri K. Gopal Singh had fallen ill seriously and was taken on bamboo *palanquin* for onward journey. On the morning of 9-8-1944 we reached Kalemyo and halted at Pintha where we found one doctor Chakravarty who was posted their as medical officer at Moirang. Dr. Chakravarty gave treatment and medicine to the patient and we stayed there upto 14-8-1944. On 15-8-1944, we arrived INA camp at Enjung Village. Very unfortunately, Shri K. Gopal Singh passed away there in the evening of 17-8-1944. It was Sunday. The dead body of Shri K. Gopal Singh was cremated with full military honour by the INA and Japanese Army." Thus ended the glorious chapter of "Grand Man of Moirang" who was crowded always by "Young Turks" consisted of a group of promising and brilliant youth who always looked up for them to be one of the finest politicians, statesmen and social workers of the time. They were frequently haunted by the nightmare of being chased down by fighters with the rat-tat of machine guns and being mowed over by bullets. Their minds move fast to reach Rangoon but their legs felt to carry exhausted bodies to the ultimate destination. On hearing the sound of approaching fighters, their bodies would sprang into action with the last leg energy to rush into the jungles to save their lives. The retreat from Manipur to Rangoon was perhaps one of the most deadly retreat.

Shah Nawaz Khan wrote:

> "Torrential rain had washed away all backs. The men made fresh tracks which soon became almost a knee deep mass of mud, in which many of the men got struck and died there. At that time there was no transport of any type with us. Almost every man was suffering from dysentery and malaria. No one had any strength left in him to help anyone else. It was a question of every man for himself and the devil take

> the hindmost. In that retreat I saw men eating horses which had been dead, 4 days ago. There were hundreds of dead human bodies of Japanese and Indian soldiers lying on either sides of the road. These were the men who had died either through exhaustion, starvation or disease and some, who being unable to face this ordeal any longer had taken their own lives by committing suicide, which they preferred to fall prisoners in the hand of the British.

All the medicines were finished. The doctor had nothing with which he could treat his patients, and to make matters worse, in those jungles there were millions of huge flies which attacked men and beasts alike as soon as they had the slightest wound and within half an hour there were hundreds of maggots in their wounds and in most cases there was no other alternative for the men than say Jai Hind and shoot themselves.[14]

After about a week's stay at Enjung, Shri H. Nilamani Singh and his party left for Rangoon on August 25, 1944. In his narration, he stated:

> "We caught a train on 7-9-1944 and reached Sagaing on 8-9-1944. We crossed over Irawady River on 9-9-1944 and arrived at Mandalay on next day. For two days we halted at Mandalay and proceeded to Pegu Satre, in the morning of 15-9-1944, we reached the branch office of Indian Independence League at Rangoon inthe afternoon of 15-9-1944. The next day I called on Col. Malik in the Head Office of INA at Rangoon and with his help we all met Netaji. I handed over a sum of Rs. 3,000 (Rupees three thousand) to Netaji for contribution towards the war fund being donated by my father."[15]

The Second Front

Subhas Bose heartily welcomed the Manipuri team and owned the courtesy to introduce them to the INA officials and Jawans. Before them Netaji lavishly praised their bravery and untold sufferings. Subhas Bose said:

> "That army is beaten which considered itself to be beaten, so long as many does not consider itself to be beaten defeat in any particular area does not mean real defeat."[16]

He recalled the Indo-Japanese forces who were ill-equipped, half fed and ragged cloth encountered the better equipped, well fed, the stronger and numerically superior Anglo-American forces and defeated everywhere in every battle. But when all preparations for the final onslaught was to be unleashed and targeted, torrential rains set in and the war engine had to stop abruptly and to retreat reluctantly. He said:

> "As soon as all our preparations are complete; we shall launch a mighty offensive against our enemies once again with the superior fighting qualities, dauntless courage and unshakeable devotion to ... victory shall be surely be ours."[17]

He streamlined for the second front and asked them to prepare and joined the "Imphal Front".

> "The forceful message of Netaji imbibed into the hearts of the gatherings. All men and women were equally determined for a second assault—a war that would untie the colonial grip in India."[18]

Accordingly, Kh. Jugshwor Singh, Shri M. Jata Singh, Shri L. Irabot Singh enrolled themselves in INA cadres. Smt. Mutum Randhoni Devi and Smt. Oinam Keinya Devi enlisted in Jhansi Rani Regiment, other Manipuris had to work in the intelligence wing. With the help of INA officers, Shri H. Nilamani Singh and Shri M. Koireng Singh strengthened 'INA Moirang Training Centre' at Rangoon and started to work enrolment, recruitment, training and enlistment. Havingbeen fully trained and prepared, they waited for the Second Round Conflagration with more commitment than before. But the will of Providence was otherwise. Shri Hemam Nilamani Singh wrote:

> "In May, 1945, the British Army recaptured Rangoon and we three (Shri M. Koireng Singh, Shri L. Sanaba Singh and myself) put up at Shan village by constructing a small house and took up tailoring business. On 8-9-1945, I was arrested by the British Army and detained in lock up at Pabedan (Police Station). I was imprisoned thereafter in the Rangoon Central Jail for more than 7 (seven) months."[19]

Then came the famous Red Fort Trial. The three INA officers, Colonel Prem Sahgal, Colonel Gurbaksh Singh Dhillon and Major General Shah Nawaz Khan were charged with "Waging war against the King-Emperor" as well as murder and abetment of murder. Proceedings of court martial was taken against them for other various charges—the treason, torture, conspiracy, murder and abetment of murder during the war. But they were considered to the real patriots of India who fought for liberation of India from British dominion. Subhas Chandra Bose was widely acclaimed as the "George Washington of India" and Photos of the three INA Officers with Netaji were taken on iconic status throughout the country. Unprecedentedly, the whole nation was electrified and aflame with patriotic zeal and fervour.

"With the release of the three officials—Shah Nawaz Khan, G.S. Dhillon and P.K. Shahgal" H. Nilamani Singh wrote: "We were taken from Rangoon Cental Jail on 13-04-1946 by Ship in the Bay of Bengal and arrived at Calcutta at about 8.00 pm where we were accorded a warm reception with band parties by the INA. Relief Committee and Bengal Red Cross Society with Capt. Rijbir,

ADC to Netaji."[20] Shri H. Nilamani Singh reached Imphal in the morning of 7th May,1946.

Shri H. Nilamani Singh as a Social Worker

Sooner had he arrived at Moirang than Shri H. Nilamani Singh plunged himself into the service of the people of Moirang. He was not a man to sit idle doing nothing. Long before his joining to INA he started his career in the service of people. He rose into prominence with the opening of branch office of Seva Samithi at Moirang which was founded in 1916 under the leadership of Lalita Madhava Sharma, a multi-faceted leader of Manipur. Till then, Moirang did not differ much from typical Indian villages. Very few amenities were available. Government offices were also very few in numbers and infrastructures were practically absent. Roads were not metalized, awfully bad and almost covered with long ground local weeds and reeds. The condition of roads were deplorable with countless potholes. Things get worse during rainy season when heavy downpour made the roads muddy and potholes were not visible due to stagnant water. There were no educational institutions. The highest institution was Moirang Govemment LP School where classes up to class II was opened. The school had no building and was conducted under a share roof of Late Konjengbam Komol Singh, Moirang Ningthou.

The main activities of Seva Samithi, Moirang Branch were to cover the dusty road with harvested local weeds and reeds grew along the roads making walkable during dry season; to construct make-shift bamboo bridges during rainy season; making separate seats for males and females with the help of (dividing) rope fencing during feast and festivities, particularly during Lai Haraoba etc. Shri H. Nilamani Singh wrote: "I took up the work of spreading Rastrabasha Hindi by organizing Hindi schools, started organizing educational institutions (L.P. Schools, N.E. Schools, High Schools) to provide facilities for education of the rural people, organized many co-operatives (consumers, agricultural credit, marketing and banking) for the economic upliftment of the rural poor."[21]

Notable among the educational institutions are existing Moirang College, Moirang Multipurpose Higher Secondary School, Mukta High Schooi, Moirang Girls High School etc. These schools were constructed on the generous donation of the people of Moirang and under the supervision of the construction committee constituted for the purpose. Shri H. Nilamani Singh served the construction committee in all capacities, the President/Chairman, Secretary orTreasurer. He was known to his friends and influential people for his marked sincerity, honesty, integrity, dedication and commitment. Like Subhas Bose, he used to keep records neat and clean and maintained important historical records of every event and sequences at stake in an orderly manner with tips of valuable information. He was accountable to every query of the construction work expenditures and other philanthropic activities of the committees. Shri H. Nilamani Singh was very instrumental to bring one B.S. Guha, a Bengali, all the way long from Calcutta to Moirang. His coming to Moirang was an epoch making event in the educational history of Moirang. Every inch he was a teacher. He was the driving spirit for establishing numerous educational institutions at Moirang. The first generation of the galaxy of academicians, intellectuals, officers. Educationists, medical and engineering professionals etc. of Moirang are almost all his products and contributions. He had become the most celebrated man of his time. The people of Moirang are much indebted to him and his family. Shri H. Nilamani Singh took the key role in the construction of INA Martyrs' Memorial Complex, Moirang dedicated to the unsung patriots who laid down their lives and everything for Independence of lndia." He wrote:

> "I spared no labour in my effort to construct a building in memory of the INA at Moirang by organizing a committee of which I was the (Convenor, later) Secretary. I visited several places for this purpose with Shri Sheel Bhadra Yajee; Ex. MP."[22]

This is the monumental work of Shri H. Nlamani Singh, Shri M. Koireng Singh, Shri M. Manindra Singh, Shri L. Ibomcha Singh, their close associates and the people of Moirang at large. They received donations. Shri H. Nilamani Singh pioneered co-operative movement in Manipur. Under his chairmanship, he founded the Azad Cooperative Society, unlimited at Moirang in 1946. He envisioned a progressive and welfare Manipur state under the cooperative society movement. He was the founder of numbers of Co-operative Banks, Marketing and Credit Societies. Many of them are still existing today. He actively participated in establishing Manipur Women Co-operative Bank, Imphal in 1974 and served as chairman of Apex marketing Cooperative Society, Imphal from 1958-1960. While he was in Rangoon Jail, he learnt Hindi during a period of three months. It turned into one of the most important and memorable event in his lifetime. He started loving Hindi and took pairs for popularizing and propagation of Hindi in the state. In the jail, he subscribed a Daily Hindi Newspaper, *Prachi Prakash* and used to listen to Hindi news bulletin, mainly proceedings of the Red-Fort Trial. After he had returned to Manipur he started a school, The Thambal Smitri Hindi Mahavidyalay in sweet memory of his mother. In recognition of his service for popularizing and propagating Hindi in the state he was awarded "Hindi Sevak". Shri H. Nilamani Singh also joined politics. He wrote: "I was the president of the Tiddim Road Congress in 1950 and also a member of the Manipur State Congress Committee. In the year 1972, I was elected from Bishnupur Moirang Constituency to the then territorial Council of Manipur on the Congress ticket. In the year 1972, I was elected as an MLA from Moirang Constituency and became the Deputy Education Minister. I was President of several Political Organizations in Manipur from 1974 to 1978."[23] In spite of tight and hectic schedule in the service of the people of Manipur he took the responsibility to serve as president of the Manipur Unit of All India Freedom' Fighters organizations since 1974 and the Convenor, Freedom Fighters Cell since 1982. It was he who prepared the list of the freedom fighters in Manipur.

Did Netaji Come to Manipur?

He delivered number of talks and Seminars on INA and Netaji at State and National functions. These talks furnished valuable information of historical importance. Mention may be made of one such talk delivered on 23rd January, 1957 at 8.45 pm through All India Radio, Delhi, which was broadcasted as one of the programmes enlisted on the Birthday Celebration of Subhas Chandra Bose in the same year. In that talk, he divulged the coming of Netaji to Manipur. For years, the people of Moirang narrated the unconfirmed report of the coming of Subhas Chandra Bose in Manipur. But, it remained as tell atale stories and nothing as such could not be established. The same was accounted in the writings of Santhang Haokip, Assistant Professor, History Department, Moirang College in his Ph.D. Thesis submitted to Manipur University, Manipur. Prof. Lal Dena, a historian and scholar also recounted in his article "In Search of ldentity". It is furnished in one of the interviews with Ramlanthang, the son of Kolvella, an INA veteran. According to Ramlanthang, the youngest son of Kolvella, his father (Kolvella) greatly assisted the Indo-Japanese forces; they felt at home at Saikot due the abundance of food grains and livestock, and may be due to the friendly attitude of my father (Kolvella). Pu. Ramlangthang, further stated that, his father's co-operation was appreciated by Subhas Chandra Bose. He further stated that, Subhas Chandra Bose promised not to forget Kolvella's good works. One ofthe high ranking INA commanders came and met Kawlvel (Kolvella) one evening and thanked him profusely, saying "I am so thrilled and particularly grateful to you for what you and your villagers have done for my soldiers. In fact, it is only because of your help and co-operation that my soldiers could survive till today. But many of them are suffering from malaria and dysentery. So we are leaving soon. When India achieves her freedom, you folks will never be forgotten." Who was this officer? Kawlvel (Kolvella) claimed that this officer was no other than Netaji Subhas Chandra Bose."[24]

Shri H. Nilamani Singh also shared the same opinion. In one query of the interview, he was asked:

Q 1: Manipur mein Subhas Chandra Bose Pahlebarkab aaye? (When did Subhas Chandra Bose come to Manipur for the first time ?)

Ans.: *Manipur mein Netaji Subhas Chandra Bose Prithvi ke dwityabadi ladai ke samay, San 1944 ke June maah ke madhyon (dwitya) saptah ke antim charan mein Burma se Tiddim Road hote huye Churachandpur tak gupta roop se pahunch chuke the. Eisa hi batayajata hein.* (It is said that during Second World War, Subhas Chandra Bose came to Manipur along the Tiddim Road and reached Churachandpur in the last leg of the middle week of June, 1944 in disguise).

People are at cross-road whether to believe the theory or not. To many, it appears to be a theory—too good to be true. But, there are many stories about his coming to Manipur. At Phek a villager said, "Indian officers led the Japanese into our village and when they spoke to our elders, they did not sound threatening" (Robert Laymen, End of Empire, 2014: 79). Sipohu Venuh of the same village said, "I saw men of Black race (INA) who came with the Japanese. When the battle of Jessami was raging, Sato, Bose and Phizo were reported to have camped at Layne River Valley for few days wherein villagers who when to meet them said Phizo met them with his palm covering the side of his chin apparently to hide his distort chin."[25] The temperament of Subhas Chandra Bose deserved to be reckoned with. Subhas Chandra Bose was unstoppable. Usually, he remained steadfast and uncompromised. None of the officers could check him from his burning passion of going to Manipur or to the war front, Shah Nawaz Khan, one of his trusted Generals, stated that there were several instances of Netaji going to the war front. Such stories and oral narrative of the villagers are still flouted in remote areas of Manipur. In-depth research activities and micro-level studies are still required to be conducted to the veracity of the statement.

Often, Nilamani was exposed to many military skirmishes and depredations of Allied irregular warfare and guerrilla fighters. On one occasion, he was nearly killed by Allied bombing at Rangoon. Subhas Bose himself was also reported to be involved. Netaji was survived in the incident Bomb splinters hit his car but the target missed him.

Like Subhas Bose, Shri H. Nilamani Singh too left his family. Little did Emilie Schenkl and her daughter Anita Bose, hardly knew that the moment at Kiel, Germany—would be their last to witness the face of Netaji. Subhas Bose did not return and had become a legendary figure. But Shri H. Nilamani Singh survived the war and retuned home. His sons and daughters could enjoy the sharing and caring of their beloved father. In pre-Independence, he fought for political freedom of India and in post-Independence; he fought for economic emancipation of the nation. Regarding his Mission of Life he said "I started my career as a social worker and wish to fade in the same capacity."

NOTES

1. Subhas Chandra Bose (Ed). *An Indian Pilgrim*, www.hindustanbooks.com, p. 49.
2. *Ibid.*, pp. 48-49.
3. H. Nilamani Singh, *H. Nilamani Singh, INA: A Self-Narrative*.
4. Madan Gopal (Ed.). *Subhas Chandra Bose, The Quest of Freedom*, p. 300.
5. S.K. Bose, Alexander Werth, Sh. Ayer (Ed.). *A Beacon across Asia*, p. 176.
6. H. Nilamani Singh, *op. cit.*
7. *Ibid.*
8. *Ibid.*
9. Derek M. Salmi Lt. Col. USAF (Ed.). Slim Chance, 'The pivotal Role of Air Mobility in the Burma Campaign', *Drew Paper No. 15*, Air University School of Advanced Air and Space Studies, p. 38.
10. P.R. Pillay (Ed). *The Indian National Army in the imphal Offensive*, p. 12.
11. H. Nilamani Singh, *op. cit.*

12. Hemant Singh Katoch (July-September 2014). "The Battles of Imphal", in *Journal of Defence Studies*, *8*(3):101-120.
13. *Ibid.*
14. Shah Nawaz Khan (2016). *My Memoirs of INA and Its Netaji*, p. 132.
15. H. Nilamani Singh, *op. cit.*
16. Madan Gopal (Ed.). *Subhas Chandra Bose, The Quest of Freedom*, p. 416.
17. *Ibid.*
18. M. Manindra Singh (Ed.) (1995). *80th Birth Anniversary of Shri M. Koireng Singh*, Moirang, p. 5.
19. H. Nilamani Singh, *op. cit.*
20. *Ibid.*
21. *Ibid.*
22. *Ibid.*
23. *Ibid.*
24. Sonthang Haokip (2012). *Anglo-Kuki Relationship (1777-1945)*, A Doctoral Thesis submitted to Manipur University, Canchipur, Imphal.
25. Zhokhusheyi Rhakho, 'Subhas Chandra Bose and the Trail of INA in Naga Hills during the battle of Kohima', *Eastern Mirror*, June 1, 2077.

REFERENCES

Hemant Singh Katoch (2019). *The Battles of Imphal*, New York.

K. Sobita (Dr.) & Mrinashree Mairembam (Ed.) (2010). *Manipur Ke Azad Hind Fauz-Ek Shradhanjali*, Imphal.

K. Sushila (Dr.) (Ed.) (2015). *INA through the Lens of History*, Imphal, 2015.

M. Manindra Singh (Ed.) (1993). *Souvenir, Golden Jubilee Celebration of Provisional Government of Azad Hind*, Imphal.

Madan Gopal, *Subhas Chandra Bose, The Quest of Freedom.*

Mrinashree Mairembam (Ed.) (2018). *Souvenir,* Platinum Jubilee Celebration of Provisional Government Free India, Imphal.

M. Sanjiv Singh (2010). *M. Koireng Singh gi Punshi Amasung Thabak*, Moirang.

N.G. Jog (1969). *In Freedom's Quest*, Poona.

Proceedings of theNational Seminar on Netaji and INA, Moirang, 1985.

Professor Lal Dena (2008). *In Search of Identity Hmars of North East India*, New Delhi.

Shri Hemam Nilamani Singh in Rangoon Jail.

Shah Nawaz Khan, *My Memoirs of INA and its Netaji.*

S.K. Bose (Ed.) (1973). *A Beacon Across Asia*, New Delhi.

Sonthang Haokip (2011). *Anglo-Kuki Relationship, 1777–1947*, a doctoral thesis submitted to Manipur University, Canchipur, Imphal.

Virender Grover (Ed.) (1991). *Subhas Chandra Bose*, NewDelhi.

22

Potsangbam Tomal Singh (1903-1999)

His Contribution to Political and Socio-Economic Life in 20th Century Manipur

Aheibam Koireng Singh

Shri Potsangbam Tomal Singh, son of Late P. Tomba Singh was born in the year 1903. His birth and death were at the same place at his ancestral residence in Singjamei Chingamakha Ningthoujam Leikai, Imphal of Manipur state. He breathed his last on 21 November, 1999. He was decorated and honoured with an award of Tamrapatra in 1972 by the Government of India for his outstanding contribution in the fight for freedom of India from the British colonial rule. In addition to his active political life, he was a man with multifaceted personality 'having inventive skill in various fields of crafts and designs. His name was enshrined as Freedom fighter in the INA Memorial Complex at Moirang. His life spanned almost a century which covers almost all the political events of Modern Manipur. In Fact, it would not be an exaggeration to say that he was one of the makers of Modern Manipur.

Right from his youthful days, he enthusiastically took part in the issues that concerns the land and its people. He joined Nikhil Hindu Manipuri Mahasabha in 1938. His role in the

Second 'Nupilan' which translates as the Women's War of 1939 is noteworthy. In consultation with Yuvaraj Bodhchandra, he along with the volunteers led by him brought those women agitators who received bayonet injury on 12 December to the hospital. The following day on 13 December, he presided a meeting at Police Lane with a mass gathering of women. In the said meeting, a resolution of 'Civil Disobedience' was adopted for the first time. Immediately, after the said meeting, women in large number came out and dismantled many rice mills and successfully prevented the vehicles from plying and transporting rice to outside the state. During those days, where Nikhil Manipur Mahasabha was there as the only one political party in Manipur, major differences emerged between the group led by Khogendrajit and the one led by Lalita Madhop while the party president Hijam Irabot was away at Cachar. In it, he played a major role in intervening and mediating the crisis. In the year 1938, he was kept in detention at the prison for three months for writing an article condemning the imprisonment of Rani Gaidinliu, an illustrious freedom fighter. He was a working Committee member of Manipur Praja Sanmellani founded in January 7, 1940.

Netaji Subhas Chandra purportedly send a letter addressed to the political parties of Manipur for a quicker success of the on going war of Indian independence. The brief summary of the letter is as follows:

> "My friends from political parties of Manipur! The war is being waged against the British and the Americans for the Independence of India. Therefore, I invite the Manipuris to join the war."
>
> Yours
> Subhas Chandra Bose
> Supreme Commander of the INA

He was among those few political workers of Manipur who responded to the call of Netaji. In the year 1941-42, during the

Japanese War in Manipur, he went to Moirang (presently comes under Bishnupur District) and was there for about four months to join the Indian National Army (INA) led war of Indian independence. As confirmed by his fellow INA veteran, Late Hemam Nilamani Singh, while he was Deputy Education Minister to the Government of Manipur, Potsangbam Tomal joined the INA led movement along with him in the last week of 1944, on which Moirang was captured by the INA. He left Moirang for Rangoon in the first week of July 1944 along with Colonel Shaukat Ali Malik when the order of the retreat was received. Col. S.A. Malik was well-known and credited for commanding a unit of the Bahadur Group in the capture of Moirang during the early phases of Imphal World War II campaign. Bahadur Group, also known as the Special Services Group was a unit that was tasked with frontline intelligence as well as subversion and sabotage operations behind enemy lines. He met Netaji Subhas Chandra Bose at Rangoon and was administered oath by the Netaji to fight against the colonial British Government. Uthonten Sharma, founding President of the Manipuri Paona Independence League confirmed that he was declared wanted by the British Government of Burma and announced a cash reward for providing information leading to his arrest. "He went underground along with us on 1-5-(19)45 while we were searched by the British Government of Burma under Rule 26, Defence of Burma Rules of the Defence of Burma Act, 1940 after the recapture of Burma by the British army", Hemam Nilamani stated. The said rule 26 decrees, "Notwithstanding anything contained in this Act, a Deputy Commissioner may continue and is empowered to retain in custody any person who has been detained under Rule 26 of the Defence of Burma Rules pending the orders of the Governor, if he is satisfied that such person is a dangerous criminal." He was brought to Calcutta (present Kolkata) under an arrangement made by the then British Government of India and returned to Manipur in the second week of April 1946." In the year 1946-47, he was elected as the President of the Manipur

State Congress and worked as a faithful disciple of Gandhi. He also served as the President of Manipur Pradesh Congress Committee (MPCC) in the year 1951-52.

In addition to his active political life, he was also a skilled master craftsman with lot of innovative ideas, an artist who believed in the dictum, 'work is worship'. From the year 1930 onwards, he as a craftsman practiced the brass and bell metal and aluminium works. He also made a pioneering and dedicated effort in ushering Sericulture industry in Manipur. During his MPCC presidentship term (1951-52), he was very much keen and concerned about the sericulture industry in Manipur. Accordingly to uplift and promote sericulture industry in Manipur, he sought support and patronage from Bimala Prasad Chaliha, a freedom fighter and leader of the Indian National Congress who later on became Chief Minister of Assam for three five-year terms. His effort proved fruitful as Assam government extended their helping hands by providing training to the natives of Manipur about the new technologies and methods of sericulture and also by facilitating in the registration under Registrar Office of the Society, Manipur and establishment of the first ever Sericulture and Weaving Co-operative Society of the state with him as the Chairman. He made a reeling *charkha* (spinning wheel) known as 'Tomal Charkha' and with the help of his self-made *charkha*, he started imparting training to the young and unemployed women of Manipur. Then after, sericulture in Manipur began to be rapidly developed winning the confidence and appreciation of the government and the Central Silk Board thereby leading to the establishment of separate Sericulture Department of Manipur.

Though he played key roles in many of the intense political struggles, he was selfless and never did anything for self-gain. He got enchanted and took delight at the thought that he was able to contribute at least something for the betterment of the people. One thing which he very often said which is thought provoking and worth pondering is reproduced herein below:

> *In original Manipuri Manuscript*
> Manipur pikcharabasu mahousa lairembina watana pibiba wata padaba lamni.... .
>
> *Free English Translation by the author*
> Manipur is a self-sufficient land blessed bountifully by the mother nature .... .
>
> *In original Manipuri Manuscript*
> Manipur Bihargi Leikai amana henna chaowi adubu eikhoina ekhutna suba tandrabadi asengba sanaleibak oigani.
>
> *Free English Translation by the author*
> A gramin (village) of Bihar is even bigger than Manipur, even then it would surely be a golden land if we are not lazy to toil and labour by our own hands,
>
> *In original Manipuri Manuscript*
> Yariba makhei mingondagi tangdana esana suja nomja duna hingadabani.
>
> *Free English Translation by the author*
> As possible as it could, one should live by relying on themselves with their own effort without depending on others.

In terms of holding constitutionally elected post, his political career was not that noteworthy. But people respected him as a skilled craftsman and an artist. He never deserted his love for motherland even at the last moment of his deathbed. In the twilight of his life, he seemed very much troubled with the outward appearance of Manipur which overwhelmingly move towards pretentions and duplicities. So he often used to utter with discontent:

> *In original Manipuri Manuscript*
> Eikhoigi Sarkar pairibasingna wakhal khanthaba watpadagi Manipur na lairaribani sotharibani.

> *Free English Translation by the author*
> The poverty and underdevelopment in Manipur continues to prolong due to thoughtlessness and insensitiveness of those in power at the government.

Though he had departed more than a decades ago, the sacrifices he made, the selfless service he rendered, his spirit of nationalism, his cherished dream of self-reliant and self-sufficient Manipur should not be gone into oblivion and deserves to get the attention of those in the echelons of power. Notwithstanding his association with the INA, his concern for the interest and welfare of the state of Manipur clearly illustrates his rootedness as the true son of the soil. His contributions and ideals needs to be recollected and retold and brought to public notice so as to remain fresh and stay relevant to people's memory.

REFERENCES

Application petitioned by PotsangbamTomal Singh to the Chief Commissioner, Manipur Administration for allowing to have the Political sufferer rewards, dated, Imphal, 1959.

DIPR, GoM. *Manipur Today: Golden Jubilee Celebration Issue,* DIPR, GoM, 1992. *http://serimanipur.nic.in/modernizing-of-manipur-sericulture-industry/*

L. Ibobi Singh (1999). "Freedom Fighter PotsangbamTomal Leikhidaba" [tr., Obituary Note on Freedom Fighter PotsangbamTomal], *Newspaper article.*

Priyadarsi Mukherji (2009). *Netaji Subhas Chandra Bose: Contemporary Anecdotes, Reminiscences and Wartime Reportage.* Har Anand Publications, New Delhi.

Ruhinikumar and Sanatomba (1999). "Leibak Ningba Khutnaiba Sinmi amada Sradhanjali Shri PotsangbamTomal Singh (1903-1999)" [tr., Tribute to a patriot craftsman Shri Potsangbam Tomal Singh (1903-1999)].

Testimonial Certificate of P. Tomal Singh, signed and issued by S. Gourahari Singh, Secretary, Government of Manipur, May 31, 1965.

Testimonial Certificate of Shri PotsangbamTomal Singh, signed and issued by H. Nilamani Singh, Deputy Education Minister, not dated. *Defence of Burma Act, 1940.*

Tongbram Gouramani Singh (2011). *Prithibigee Anisuba Laljao* (tr. The Second World War), Imphal.

Wairakpam Mangol Singh (1984). *Prithivigi anisuba Lanjao amasung Manipur Party* (tr., Second World War and Manipur Party), Author is the publisher, Lairikyengbam Leikai, Imphal.

Theme IV
SECOND WORLD WAR AND MANIPUR

23

Ringshi Keishing

A Profile of INA Veteran

Daniel Chabungbam

Ringshi Keishing is one of the last surviving veterans who fought in Subhas Chandra Bose's Indian National Army (INA) against the British. A native of Bungpa Khunou under Phungyar Sub-division in Ukhrul district of Manipur. Keishing Ringshi was born on 7th March, 1920. He has 3 brothers and 5 sisters.

At the age of 94, Keishing Ringshi attended the Annual Reception of freedom fighters hosted by the President on the eve of India's Independence Day celebrations at the Darbar Hall of Rashtrapati Bhavan in New Delhi along with a Kuki war veteran Thangpu and a Meitei war veteran Joykumar hailing from Thangmeiband on August 9, 2013. This was his 7th presence at the annual reception at the Rashtrapati Bhavan and he even said that this may be his last trip to Delhi.

Recalling how he became a part of the INA, Ringshi said that he was captured by the Japanese near Myanmar border along with three other friends in 1943. He along with the others were taken to a village in Burma (now Myanmar) where the Japanese and INA established their headquarters.

Lieutenant Harold of British Army and Prem Bahadur and Dil Bahadur of Gorkha Rifles respectively used to recruit soldiers from Ukhrul area in those days and were arrested with Ringshi along the border by the Japanese troupes. Ringshi was arrested by Japanese and Indian National Army from Chowchu area in Myanmar while travelling in the Burma border areas. They took Ringshi to Kontong in Myanmar where he met Japanese and INA officers.

On learning that Ringshi knows English and Hindi and also learn that he knew the border area well, an INA officer asked him to join them as a guide while his other friends were released. Ringshi was not given any kind of training in joining the INA. He then worked as a guide for a few months. Later, he was given a Tommy gun and this made him a regular soldier and was given the rank of Lieutenant in the Indian National Army.

Ringshi Keishing never met Subhas Chandra Bose but served under Lieutenant Colonel Shah Nawaz Khan who was a close comrade of Subhas Chandra Bose. Shah Nawaz was one of the three defendants in the first of the Indian National Army trials in 1946.

In the month of March in 1943-44, Ringshi was the only freedom fighter among the Nagas of Manipur.

During those days, the British army use to recruit people from Manipur as a volunteer force and was given a monthly salary of Rs. 35 to a soldier while a group commander was given Rs. 60 as their monthly salary, said Ringshi Keishing. This was told by one Captain Khathing of volunteer force to Ringshi to join the British. The volunteer force used to work as a guide for Assam Rifles.

The Japanese force and INA asked anyone from the Tangkhul community who worked for the British army and told him to write a letter as Leiutenant Ringshi and asked for help. Thereby, Ringshi wrote a letter to Khating and Saiza (father of Yangmaso Shaiza) and asked them to help the Japanese force.

As an army man, Ringshi Keishing first fought in a battle at Schakok Camp in Ango Ching hill range. And his second experience of war was at Finch corner then at Kangkhui area and later on at Sangshak. By winning various battles, Ringshi recalled that the Japanese troupe will surely win the war. Indians who were held captive in Burma jail by the Japanese force for supporting the British Army were released and made to join the INA force in the battles against the British Army.

Showing a wound on his head incurred while trying to escape from the hands of the Japanese force and INA soldiers when they were arrested by at Chowchu, Ringshi Keishing said that at this age of 94, he finds difficulties to survive. He has recently undergone heart transplantation with a pacemaker. No assistance has been received from anyone for the transplantation. He wanted his children to cherish his small contribution to India's fight for independence but as of now none of his children is employed. Ringshi now has more than 50 grandchildren.

With the recognition to his contribution to the independence movement, Ringshi Keishing has joined Annual reception at New Delhi by the President's office seven times. He enjoys a monthly pension of Rs. 15,000 from the Central Government while the State Government gave him Rs. 500 per month as pension for freedom fighter. The pension which he gets from the State Government is very less comparing to other states, so, he wants increment in this regard.

In the year 2009, when India's President Pratibha Devi visited Manipur, Ringshi Keishing met her and urged for a gas agency as well as a petrol pump within the discretionary powers of the President, especially because there is a provision of two per cent reservation for freedom fighter category. But despite the exchange of information and letters between Ringshi, the President Office and Ministry of Petroleum and Natural Gas but it did not materialise in his lifetime. He passed away in January 18, 2015 at the ripe age of 94 years.

24

Japanese Bombing of Imphal

M. Ranjit Singh

It was foretold in the Manipuri *Puran* that the years 1939, 1940 and 1941 would be years of trouble in Manipur. The first part of this prophecy turned out to be very much truer than the second. The "Nupi Lan" had disturbed the peace of Imphal in 1939-40 but by February 1941 everything was quiet.

The second half of the year 1941 saw the abdication in September and the death in November of Maharaj Churachand after reigning for exactly fifty years. Then in December 1941 Japan entered in Second World War. This last event was at first taken quietly in Manipur, no one realizing how soon Japan would reach the frontiers of Manipur.

Japan dropped the first bomb on Imphal on Sunday, the 10th May, 1942 and again on Friday, the 16th May, 1942 heralding the beginning of Second World War in Manipur. That was before I was born and exactly 69 years ago.

I am sure all the generations, born after Second World War or Japan *lan* as more popularly known in Manipur, would like to know what actually happened during those bombing days and subsequent war days in Manipur.

But, I must confess here that all the details on bombing days in Manipur have been collected from various Military History books I had studied for my Part D examination during my Army service and, well supplemented by narratives heard from many Manipuri elders during the last fifty years or so. Burma Campaign was Military History subject for my Part D examination.

Maharaja Bodhchandra's accession to the throne almost coincided with the coming of the Second World War to Asia. The War had already commenced in the West in 1939. In 1940 and 1941, the war, however, had no direct impact on Manipur, which still remained one of the world's peaceful beauty spots. Senior British officers present in Manipur in those days were Mr. Christopher Gimson, the Political Agent in Manipur, Mr. T.A. Sharpe, the President of Manipur State Durbar, Mr. L.T. Wilson, S.P. of Manipur and Lt. Col. Hurrel, Commandant of 4 Assam Rifles.

These officers and others when they met in the Club used to discuss strategy and schemes for defeating the Germans, and sometimes they wondered whether their pensions were safe, but otherwise the war seemed very remote. Not until, the Japanese attacked Pearl Harbour on 7th December, 1941, did the possibility, of war reaching India emerge, and even then it seemed improbable. But not for long. Within ten weeks all of Malaya and even Singapore had fallen to Japanese onslaught.

By 7th March, 1942, their conquest of the Dutch East Indies was complete. By second week of May 1942, Lt. General William Slim's (later Field Marshal Sir William Slim) Burma Corps defending Burma consisting of 17 Indian Division, 1st Burma Division and 7 Armoured Brigade duly supported by V & VI Chinese Army were rushing back to India and China to avoid their three enemies, Japanese, hunger, and monsoon. The monsoon was expected to reach Manipur by 20th May, 1942.

It must, however, be noted that Burma Corps' Division were too ill-found, hurriedly collected, and inexperienced Divisions, of which one had been trained for desert warfare and the other contained a large proportion of raw and unreliable Burmese troops.

The retreat of Burma Corps to Manipur was for preservation of maximum force and to rest and recoup to fight Japanese again when the opportunity arises. Of the 150 artillery guns of all kinds that Burma Corps had possessed at one time, but of these only 28 had crossed into India. The total vehicles of Burma Corps on arrival at Imphal were 50 Lorries and 30 Jeeps. No tank could be brought to India. The casualties suffered by the Corps had been some 13,000 men killed, wounded and missing.

The retreat almost coincided with the bombing of Imphal by Japan. In January and February 1942, refugees began to reach Imphal in their hundreds from Burma and were housed on their way through camps at Tamu, Sita and Koirengei; all manned by troops from 4 Assam Rifles. Refugees by April 1942 increased to thousand per day. Altogether 1,90,000 approximate refugees passed through Manipur during these periods. It is widely believed, Helen, famous Bollywood actor of yesteryear escaped through Manipur as a refugee in one of the refugee colony.

The Allied Air Force available during March 1942 in Burma was of two mixed wings, one at Magwe and another at Akyab, both big towns in the central Burma. The British squadrons had Buffaloes and Hurricanes fighter planes, mostly worn out Mark I's and Bomber squadron had Blenheim. The American Volunteer Group Squadron had P 40 Tomahawk fighter planes. Generally, all the Japanese fighters were inferior in performance to the Hurricanes and the P 40 with the exception of their Navy O (zero).

The Navy O of Japanese Air Force was, however, more vulnerable as neither it nor their bombers had self-sealing tanks nor armour for the Pilot. The Navy has one distinctive advantage in range. It had a radius of two hundred and fifty miles or five hundred miles with jettisonable tanks compared with the one hundred and thirty five miles of the Hurricanes II.

On 21st March, 1942, Magwe airfield was suddenly attacked by Japanese fighters and bombers in overwhelming strength. In all

Japanese employed two hundred and fifty aircrafts. The Japanese repeated their Magwe attack on Akyab, with the same results. With Akyab and Magwe abandoned, there were no other British airport/airstrip near Imphal which can protect its sky.

Thus, the Japanese had complete air superiority in the sky of Burma and Manipur during that fateful month of May 1942. The nearest airport available to Allied Force in Burma and Manipur was at Dinjan near Dibrugarh. The six airports/airstrips in Manipur used in later campaigns came up after 1943.

With the Japanese now so close to Manipur, the threat of air raids had become an ever increasing danger. Certain precautions had already been taken by Manipur Government and a black out imposed on Imphal and the nearby villages. Manipur State's Air Raid Precautions Service was formed in early 1942 to dovetail with the Military Passive Air Defence Scheme.

Imphal was divided into sectors each containing a Military Passive Air Defence aid post and a civil ARP aid post. Each such post contained a leader, three helpers and a chowkidar under the control of the Civil Surgeon, Dr. S. Kundu, MB and AMS, who gave instruction in first aid. In addition each sector had one Warden, a Darbar Member or other leading State Servant, and a number of Assistant Wardens, all unpaid volunteers. These volunteers generally briefed people regarding precaution to be taken in case of bombing like closing of ear with cotton swabs, dashing to the nearest fire trench, sticking of glass window panes with sheets of paper etc.

At 4th Assam Rifles base at Kangla, there was hectic activity in implementing plans for Passive Air Defence against Japanese air attacks, which were daily expected after the evacuation of Rangoon in March 1942. Every available man was put to digging trenches and building shelters for his own protection as well as for other inhabitants of the Battalion area. The Manipuri householders had also been told to dig their own trenches. The public slit trenches were dug around Khwairamband bazaar and along the main roads. The public, however, really did not take it seriously.

At Nambol, a section of 4 Assam Rifles was stationed to wait and watch the Japanese aircraft. They were to heliograph a message to Headquarters of 4 Assam Rifles at Kangla on seeing any aircraft, where upon the siren warning would be sounded. Since April 1942, the Japanese reconnaissance plane began to fly near the Manipur sky almost everyday. For the Manipuris who had never seen aeroplane in their life, it was a nice entertainment to watch the flying planes.

The only complaint of Manipuris was that the planes were flying rather high and they were deprived of seeing the aeroplane in detail. The frequency of siren sounding increased, but never a bomb dropped. After a series of false alarms the warnings became little more than tiresome interruptions to the day's leisurely routine, and soon they were regarded with scant respect.

Sunday, the 10th May, 1942 was like any other Sunday in Imphal. Few hours ago, the devoted elderly persons had already come back to home from Govindaji temple after participating "*Dhoop Aarti*" ceremony there. School going children had finished their morning study. Many women were carrying out their weekly chores of washing household clothes in the nearby river banks and ponds.

The professional idlers have already commenced their "*Duri*" (a popular card game of Manipuris) playing session after early lunch. Those groups who can afford played with "Great Moghul," the most popular playing card of those days which was imported from USA. Others played with Indian made playing cards.

Few people had made programme to go to one of the cinema hall existing on that day, i.e. Manipur Talkies, Diana Talkies, and Ram Kumar Talkies. Those women from Imphal who had fanned out across the outlying villages for purchasing vegetables for resale in the evening at Khwairamband bazaar have, however, not returned to their homes. Generally, everybody was in a holiday mood on that Sunday morning.

Mr. Gimson, the Political Agent recalls that when the siren from 4 Assam Rifles sounded around 9.30 etc. on May 10th, he said to his assistant: 'I must remember to tell Hurell (CO 4 AR) to stop these silly signals.' An hour later the Siren wailed again. 'Damn!'

exclaimed Gimson on his verandah. 'I forgot to tell Hurell.' These were almost famous last words. At the same moment two flights of 18 Japanese Bombers bombed and strafed Imphal.

Bombs fell at Residency (present Raj Bhavan), Khoyathong, 4th Assam Rifles location at Kangla, present PWD area, Majorkhul, Thangmeiband, and Mantri Khongnang. Since, the Japanese had complete Air supremacy and there being no presence of anti-aircraft gun at Imphal the Japanese as usual used pattern bombing, coming over in faultless formation, giving themselves a leisurely dummy run, and then letting all their bombs go in one shattering crump.

The bombing at 4th Assam Rifles location was accurate but the air-raid precautions taken by the Battalion stood the test. Casualties were light but unfortunately the incident claimed two key personnel. Subedar Major Sukraj Limbu received grievous wounds during the bombing and they eventually caused his death; the Battalion Panditji was the other person to be wounded. The only direct hit recorded was on the Unit Canteen building with all its stock of Rum. One bomb fell near the Battalion School. The Assam Rifles School was closed being Sunday.

Otherwise the casualty figure would have gone very high. A Military lorry with 11 occupants was blown up in front of the present PWD office. One person was killed while crossing on a fallen tree over Naga River. Lamabam Iboton (Kalki), a clerk in the Foreigner's office also died in the bombing.

Many houses were burnt, many vehicles destroyed and many cattle died in this bombing. War cemetery in Imphal has one plaque of Private E Owen of The King's Regiment and the date of his death is given as May 12th, 1942. In the same cemetery there are also five plaques of British Privates where dates of their death are given as May 13th, 1942. All these British soldiers may have died due to Japanese bombing on May 10th, 1942.

Maharaja Bodhchandra was not present at Imphal on the bombing day as he was away to Thanga. Mr. Sharpe, the President of Manipur State Darbar with Mr. Duncan, Assistant to Political Agent was also away to Ukhrul to receive Lt. Gen. Joseph Warren

Stilwell, Commanding General of the American China-Burma-India Theatre. Gen. Stilwell was on retreat from Homalin on foot hotly chased by Japanese troops till he was received by Mr. Sharpe's group at Chamu, Ukhrul on May 16th, 1942 at 12.45 p.m.

Many Tangkhul Headmen came out at each village with a bottle of rice wine, to welcome General Stilwell. The General described Pushing village as "something which has touch of Alaska. The side walls of the houses have upright boards carved like totems. The trees at the top are all cut in notches, with the top branch cut off."

At Imphal within a few hours of bombing, almost every house in Imphal was abandoned by 1,10,947 residents generally leaving a male member of the family for guarding their properties and fled for safety to outlying villages. For people owning bullock carts and fleeing from Imphal, the loads changed from Phou Bora (sacks of grain) to the household goods and chattels of some family which had fled; and their carts were piled high with furniture, cooking utensils, with mattresses and huge Kangthons (bedsteads) fastened above.

The women and children walked gloomily in the dust, or sat aloft among their belongings, while father whacked the lazy bullocks and gazed placidly forward. In the villages the family had to 'double up' with friends and relatives. Two, three and even four families might live together and they took the inconvenience and upheaval in excellent part and there was minimum grumble.

As a result of the raid, the civil administration of the State ceased to function. For the rest, the State Departments, the Doctors, the clerical staffs and the menials all fled to a safe place. After the bombing most of the police force of 1 Inspector, 4 Sub-Inspectors and 69 Constables deserted their posts and the SP was forced to issue an order on 11th May suspending the functions of the Police. In the centre of Imphal, almost the only civilians remaining were a few pilferers and looters.

At 4 o'clock in the evening, the idol of Lord Govindaji was shifted to the residence of Aribam Anou Pujari at Bamon Leikai. Lord Govindaji was shifted to Uchekon on May 12th again when Maharaj Bodhchandra returned from Thanga.

For several days there was no one to burn or bury the corpses of man and beast alike. And almost the only cheering fact was the Japanese radio claim that they had bombed Imphal Airfield—none existed at the time—and had destroyed between forty and eighty planes—there was not one aircraft within a hundred miles! The Germans went one better, declaring with resonant pride that their Japanese allies had bombed Imphal railway station, when the nearest railway station lay one hundred and thirty miles to the north.

The second bombing raid took place on May 16th, 1942 at around 10 am. The bombs fell at Residency, 4th Assam Rifles area, Khwairamband Bazar, Keishampat and Wahengbam Leikai area. The front of the residency was damaged by a near miss and a bomb landed on the main gate of the jail and demolished it. The main bazaar had been gutted after the second raid and Khwairamband bazaar remain closed.

Some dangerous criminals slipped away from the Jail and indulge in widespread dacoity until recaptured. In fact, a number of them returned on their own accord, as soon as Mr. Sharpe announced that slit trenches had been dug in the Jail. Twenty five bomb craters were counted in the Residency garden. Lt. Gen. Slim was spending the night of May 15th at the Residency.

Whether the Japanese were trying to kill him or the bombing was carried out just to destroy the remnants of Burma Corps will never be known. At 4 Assam Rifles location, the only casualty was the Civilian Medical Officer who had to be evacuated to the Hospital in Kohima. The material damage was again light but, again, the building in which the Canteen stores had been shifted received the direct hit, destroying among other things whatever was left of the Rum—a coincidence that provided much humorous comment among the jawans of 4 Assam Rifles.

The total casualties in both the bombings were 71 killed and about 80 wounded. In addition at least 50 refugees were killed, some in the European refugee camp and some in Lorries on the road. Major N.B. Callan of 10th Baluch Regiment, 2nd Lt. D.R.

Lemerton of Royal Engineers and 2nd Lt. R.Y.S. Stewart of Royal Signals died on the second bombing day and their plaques are there in Imphal War Cemetery. There were altogether 17 bombing raids in Imphal during the Japan war duration.

This does not include dog fights by both sides which formed an integral part of military operations. The next largest casualty during bombing in Imphal took place on Tuesday, the April 20th, 1943 at the temple of Chingangbam Gulab at Khurai where 90 persons died and 49 injured. Kshetrimayum Bidhu Singh had organised a *Gopichakkhang-bal* grand feast (*Utsav*) at the above temple. The dead includes Samurailatpam Nityai (Iboton) Sharma, Bishnupriya, Radhe, Amusana, Angangmacha, Lairenmayum Eka, Khuraijam Angou Singh, Mani's wife and many others.

Imphal remained comparatively quiet during rest of 1942 and the whole of 1943 except for occasional Japanese air raid. The offensive for capture of Imphal began by Japanese 15th Army of 3 Divisions on 6th March, 1944. By March 30th, 1944, Imphal was cut off by land. The complete 4 Corps of Allied Force consisting of 3 Divisions and one Tank Brigade later reinforced by one Division and a Para Brigade were concentrated around Imphal to fight back the Japanese. The entire troops of Allied Force numbering around 1,00,000 in Imphal were supplied by air for four months making the longest and largest air supply operation in the history of war.

The most fiercely contested battle of the Burma campaign, the battle of Imphal which, if for no other reason, will go down in history as the greatest military defeat ever suffered by the Japanese on land. Japanese 15th Army suffered around 30,000 casualties in Battle of Imphal.

This is out of their total strength of around 1,00,000 troops. The British and Indian casualties were around 13,000. Had the fortunes of war gone the other way, there is no knowing how serious would have been the repercussions. With the issue of instructions for withdrawal of Japanese 15th Army from general area Imphal to Tiddim and the line of Chindwin on 20th July, 1942, the Battle of Imphal came to an end.

The common people suffered the most during the war period. In 1942 and 1943, there was a bad harvest at a time when good harvest was most needed. The price of rice rose from about Rs. 1.50 to Rs. 7 and then to Rs. 10 per mound (approximately 38 kg) and was extremely scarce, *atta*, *dal*, flour and sugar being almost unobtainable.

Cigarettes were almost unavailable, though an occasional packet of "Ten Players" found its way to the market at Rs. 5 or 6. One must remember that in those days money was scarce as there were very few Government jobs available and average pay of Government employees were less than Rs. 30 per month.

Throughout the war period the main pre-occupation in Manipur was economic. The Army was employing large numbers of labourers and paying them handsomely. Unskilled labour in the valley and in the hills, which before the war time had earned 4 *annas* (25 paise) per day, was earning Rs. 1.25 as a daily wage.

In the year October 1942 to September 1943, Army purchased locally 78,044 *maunds* of vegetables, 3,17,744 *maunds* of firewood, 31,77,126 pounds (7,94,282 kg) of milk, 6,22,313 pounds (1,30,578 kg) of fish, 26,963 *maunds* of potatoes, 1,34,940 eggs, 10,991 *maunds* of fruit, 11,435 *maunds* of charcoal and 82,322 ducks and chickens. Enterprising persons earned lots of money through various Contract and Supply businesses.

The legacy of this "contract" business is still carried on by many persons in Manipur. The brighter side effect of the war has been the conversion of Dimapur-Imphal-Moreh cart road to an all weather two way tarmac road. This road was constructed under the supervision of Brigadier Michael Gilpin and then of Brigadier Grand, the Chief Engineer of 4th Corps in a record time with thirty thousand coolies from the tea estates of Assam.

One can frightfully imagine the possible fate of this road in case there was no invasion by Japan in 1942. Tulihal airport was made four thousand yards long, owing to a mistake. The Americans always talked in feet, not yards, and one of them asked the British Engineer officer for an airstrip about four thousand long, so down it went as British yards! This error, however, proved of great value for us till date. White sugar introduced during war period has become an indispensable diet of all Manipuris.

I conclude my article with a line borrowed from Field Marshal Slim, "For any inaccuracies and, of course, for its opinions I only am responsible."

NOTE

In British Army, One Army consists of two to three Corps; a Corps is made of two to three Divisions; a Division consists of three Infantry Brigades and one Artillery brigade; and an Infantry Brigade has three Infantry Battalions. However, a Japanese Army has only three Divisions and is like a Corps in British Army.

25

Koirengei Airfield

British's Bulwark Against Japanese Siege

Sunzu Bachaspatimayum

The airfields in Manipur and the history of the Second World War are linked inextricably. If it were not for the several airfields built in North East India by the British, the unprecedented Japanese offensive into North East Indian in 1944 could have bear fruit and the course of history altered.

It was vital for the British Army to build airfields in North East India to counter and defeat the Japanese who occupied British Burma. As many as 200 airfields were commissioned to be built in the whole of northeast India and at least 10 of these were planned in Manipur alone. Before the Japanese incursion, only nine airfields were completed, which included 'fair weather' airfields as well as 'all weather' airfields. Of these, six airfields were scattered around the Imphal Valley, the airfield at Koirengei, also known as the Imphal Main or the Imphal ALG (Advance Landing Ground) was the British's bulwark against Japanese siege of Manipur during the battle of Imphal/Kohima. Today, it is a key part of Manipuri collective memory.

Christopher David Johnson, the British war historian who wrote 'Forgotten Army's Boxes of Lion', a book which details the true account of the defence and evacuation of the largest supply depot on the Imphal Plain during the Japanese siege of Imphal in 1944, explains "had it not for the Koirengei airfield, the outcome of the whole Burma Campaign during World War II would have been very different. When the Japanese Imperial Army began their "march on Delhi" in early 1944, the Imphal Plain and the whole of the British IV Corps were besieged for three months with the only way in or out for men and materials being by air. The lives of thousands of British, Indian, African and Gurkha troops depended on tons of airdropped supplies carried out each day. Rationing was also adopted when the Siege began to bite. This allowed the Allied Commander, General William Slim, to hold out while the Japanese lines of communications faltered and ultimately failed to supply their war efforts and lead to the British breakout on 22nd June, 1944."

The war historian whose father was one of the British soldiers who was evacuated from the Koirengei airfield, further added, "During this period not only were fresh reinforcements and materials flown in but also many thousands of wounded men were flown out to safety in the hospitals in India. Additionally, thousands of troops whose work could not continue like the Engineers and labourers who were involved in building roads and infrastructure were also flown out to reduce the daily consumption rate."

People's Memory

After opening salvo on Pearl Harbor in December 1941, the Imperial Japanese Army advanced through East Asia with the objective of creating what was called the Greater East Asia Co-Prosperity Sphere, an Asian economic and political block sans western influence. In January 1942, Japanese troops advanced into British Burma, gaining control of the whole country in matters of just five months.

With the total occupation of Rangoon (now Yangon), the Japanese had secured almost the entire areas envisioned as the Greater East Asia Co-Prosperity Sphere. The retreating British and Indian forces fled to India *via* Manipur.

To consolidate their control of Burma and to mount pressure on the British, the Japanese set up the Burma Area Army with General Masakazu Kawaba as its commander. With a design to further inspire the on-going freedom movement in India, the Japanese granted Independence to Burma in August 1943 and aided the formation of the Indian National Army with Subhas Chandra Bose as the Supreme Commander and got them involved in Burma. To further break the British defence, Japanese resorted to bombing Imphal valley.

"The Japanese would fly at very high altitude in a certain formation where only one plane could be visible. As it drew nearer, suddenly they would break the formation, revealing a multitude of fighter planes and start dropping bombs," recalls 93-year-old, Yaikhom Rabeinya Singh who narrowly escaped falling prey to a Japan bombing, hiding in a ditch while he was ploughing his paddy fields in 1942. Rabeinya remembered the war in Manipur as horrid times. "Imagine a packet of salt used to cost Rs. 15-20. Starvation, looting, refugees were the norms. The people residing in Imphal were the main sufferers. They had to evacuate their homes in Imphal and seek shelter in the suburbs with their relatives to escape the Japanese bombing. Each home dug v-shaped trenches for cover. Whenever we see or hear Japanese planes approaching, we used to run for cover. On the average 8-10 fighter planes would fly by daily," recalls the frail, World War II survivor.

Another World War II survivor, 85-year old Nimaicharan Khuraijam who lost his father to Japanese bombing at the Chingangbam Mandap in Imphal on 20th April, 1943, the worst civilian casualty that claimed over 100 lives, was awestruck when he and his two friends saw the first landing of Allied fighter planes in Manipur at the Koirengei airfield. "I was in Class 5 when I saw it. We were awestruck watching planes land one by one. A British pilot who got down from the plane saw us and called out. "Come here ! check out !" We went and the pilot asked us one by one, "can you speak English? None of my friends knew ABC but I had picked up the language while conversing with a Nepal soldier who stayed with us at our home". So I stood up and said "I don't know much. Since that day, I became very close to the allied forces and roamed their camps," Khuraijam reminisces.

March to Delhi

Contrary to the Imperial Japanese Army's prideful slogan that it had not lost a single war, Japan suffered a series of defeats in the pacific to US forces and the war fronts were drawing closer to the homeland. Japanese Army Commanders were desperate to reverse their misfortunate. Lt. General Renya Mutaguchi, the Field Commander of the Imperial Japanese Army who commanded the battles of Imphal and Kohima felt that an offensive operation against India was the most effective plan to turn off the tide of War. Plan was to capture a strategic British Army base in India.

Battle of Imphal/Kohima

In the spring of 1944, Japan launched an unprecedented offensive into North East India—code-named U-Go. Japanese troops crossed the mighty Chindwin river, which ran 600 metres wide at several places, trekked the rugged Arakan mountainous region, with peaks as high as 2000 metres, in a 470 kms march. Their aim was Imphal, an allied base, located on a plain surrounded by mountains. To thwart reinforcement, the Japanese plan included a simultaneous attack on Kohima. A successful attack on Imphal would delay any British move back into Burma and give the Japanese a forward base for attacks in India. If Imphal was captured it would create a solid defensive line for the Japanese.

Japan's Most Reckless Battle

The fighting took place in what is considered to be the wettest place on earth. The strategy, aimed at a short decisive battle of three weeks, extended by several months. The Japanese attack on Imphal began on 8th March, 1944. By early April, the Kohima Garrison was cut off but the food position in Kohima was desperate. The Japanese expected a quick decisive campaign but the British carefully planned to draw them into a protracted battle by fighting power and supplies. Through allied coordination, supplies of ammunition, food and medicines, weighing over 250 tons were air dropped on the front lines by undertaking over 200 sorties everyday to count the Japanese siege of Imphal that began on 28th March, 1944. A relief force arrived and bitter fighting continued throughout April and May.

The Failed Siege

Through meticulous planning of logistics, the allied soldiers were properly fed, cared and the injured quickly transported to field hospitals. This logistics boosted the morale of the allied force. The Japanese on the other hand, were running short of supplies and its troops were dying of starvation, disease and faced limited supply lines.

British Army overwhelmed the Japanese with their firepower and efficient logistic planning. By the beginning of May, successive Japanese attacks had failed to defeat the Indian and British defenders. Despite the onset of monsoon rains, the Allies launched a counter-offensive. Due to poor logistical planning, Japanese soldiers succumbed to disease and starvation in the jungle. In the ferocious fighting and disastrous retreat, about 30,000 Japanese soldiers lost their lives.

For many others, the loss on both sides became visible much later. "It was the eclipse of the Rising Sun," says 94-year-old war veteran A.S. Ninglam, who retired as a Subedar of the 4 Assam Rifles, described the Japanese defeat in Manipur. Ninglam hails from Ukhrul, the district from where the Japanese began their march towards Imphal. "The Japanese were mysterious people. They were mostly hiding in the jungle or in the hills. One of our village elders who was presented with an overcoat by a Japanese officer, told me he saw them hiding in the tall trees, jumping from one tree top to another with ease. During the war, very little was known of them. But after the war, we came to know that they had suffered a lot in the jungles of Manipur during their retreat and died of starvation and diseases," Ninglam says.

Manipur on War Tourism Map

Despite being one of the most brutal campaigns in military history, which eventually ended the Japanese era of aggression, the battle of Imphal/Kohima has largely been a forgotten war. Fortunately, since 2013, after the British Army's Central Museum, the National Army Museum, voted it as Britain's greatest battle over the battles of D-Day and Waterloo, it is gradually coming into world focus.

Around the same time, war relic diggers, under the banner of the World War II Imphal Campaign Foundation, became active in Manipur and started identifying battlefields, digging up trenches, excavating war artefacts, recovering human remains and crashed aircraft. The Foundation even succeeded in setting up a private World War II museum, attracting global attention.

Today, Manipur and Nagaland are on the World War tourism map with hordes of war tourists visiting the Imphal War Cemetery and the Kohima War Cemetery maintained by the Commonwealth War Graves Commission. Manipur attracts a lot more Japanese war tourists every year with the Nippon Foundation of Japan assisting in setting up the Imphal Peace Museum at Maibam Lokpa Ching, nicknamed as Red hill, where many Japanese soldiers fell at a decisive battle that led to their retreat from Manipur.

The number of war tourists visiting Manipur is most likely to swell once the Koirengei airfield is made accessible, says Rajeshwor Yumnam, the president of the World War II Imphal Campaign Foundation. "I always dreamt that the state government will take possession of the Koirengei airfield and develop it into a major Wordl War II heritage site, just as France has done with the Normandy landing sites that have become a huge tourist spot," a hopeful Rajeshwor said.

According to British war historian Christopher David Johnson, who says the outcome of the whole Burma campaign would have been very different had it not been for the Koirengei airfield, said that the unique airfield, with two runways perpendicular to each other, should be kept intact and utilised for war tourism with a fitting memorial to those gallant airmen and defenders of the garrison.

Sources in the Defence Ministry confide that the ministry is considering the state government's proposal on the transfer of the historic airfield to Manipur in a positive manner. With things as they stand, the chance to preserve the Koirengei airfield as the World War heritage should not be lost.

26

Indo-Japanese Soldiers in the Khuga Valley of Churachandpur, April to August 1944

Lal Dena

Indo-Japanese forces entered the Khuga Valley of Churachandpur in Manipur and stayed for five months during Second World War beginning from April 7 to August 29, 1944. Much has been written about their military encounters and battles at Imphal, Ukhrul, Kohima and elsewhere. A comparatively less known yet equally important historical theme is the untold story of the Indo-Japanese occupation of the Khuga Valley and the nature of the local people's response to it.

Well aware of the rapid penetration of Indo-Japanese forces deep into Indian soil on the eastern side of Manipur bordering Burma, the local officials hurriedly convened an emergency meeting with the tribal chiefs of Churachandpur at Gangpimuol near old Churachandpur mission headquarters in March 1944. In this meeting, it was decided that all the civilian population residing within the radius of about seven kilometers from Tiddim road should immediately be shifted *en masse* to Guwahati and some other places in the Brahmaputra Valley of Assam.

The American missionary, Rev. Paul Rostad, and his family, had already evacuated the mission compound leaving behind a typewriter, harmonium and many other precious belongings and gone to Nainital, U.P. But a majority of the tribal people fled to the interior parts of south-west Manipur and Mizo hills. Perhaps, not because of their bravery, but because of their equanimity and ignorance, some tribal chiefs and their villagers decided to stay on to face any possible consequences that might come.

Coming of Indo-Japanese Soldiers

As anticipated, just after morning meal on April 4, 1944, four Japanese soldiers in civil dress suddenly intruded into Saikot village (Churachandpur), enquiring where the village soncho (chief) was. They forcibly whisked away Kawlvelthang, then chief of Saikot, to an unknown destination. No one expected that Kawlvelthang to come back alive. On his return late in the night, he reported that he had been taken to such places as Saidan peak, Kaprang, Bijang, Gangpimuol and other places in and around Churachandpur town which had recently been evacuated.

Three days later, on April 7, hundreds of Indo-Japanese soldiers, their faces covered with branches of green leaves, suddenly streamed down from the deep jungle of Lentlang ranges into the Khuga Valley and then encamped in several places with Saikot as their headquarters. Zema Hmar, son of Kawlvelthang, said that the Commander of the Saikot camp was Bujia Musta Hasbe who was a very good and kind-hearted man with whom he later on became close friends. Soon they constructed an observatory post at the Saidan peak from where they could have a good view of the Imphal valley. Below the peak was the Saidan village which had already been evacuated earlier.

Behaviour of Indo-Japanese Soldiers

The immediate problem for the Indo-Japanese leaders was how to get the support and confidence of the local people. For the people, supporting the Indo-Japanese soldiers meant being an enemy of the

British and *vice versa.* To get local support, the Japanese commanders initially adopted two methods—intimidation and friendship. To prove that they meant business, they captured nine local men who had gone to Bijang village (now district headquarters) to enquire about their abandoned properties there on mere suspicion.

Of the nine, three persons miraculously escaped; but the rest were tied against standing trees near the village and were all shot dead. On another occasion, a patrolling party caught two chiefs but released them on the promise of regular supply of arum (sato imo in Japanese) at least twice a week.

Response of the Local People

The Japanese conversed with the local people through the Gurkhali sepoys serving with the Indian National Army (INA). Later on, (late) Vungthanga (retired head clerk, Lamka College, Churachandpur), was caught and forcibly used as the official interpreter for four months till his escape to Silchar in July 1944. Vungthanga practically lived and stayed in the army camps and his main duty was to make known the orders of Japanese officers for requisitioning ration in the form of rice, arum and chicken to the chiefs within the occupied areas.

A week after their settlement, commander Hasbe opened a school at Saikot where common Japanese vocabularies were taught. It was compulsory for those attending the school to memorize the Japanese national anthem. Some of those who attended the school remember the anthem as (as retold by (late) Zema who succeeded his father Kawlvelthang as chief of Saikawt):

Aronga Khitah,
Aronga Khitah,
Kokhoni Khitah:
Jammani Khitah
Nanimo Khitah

But, because of frequent bombings on Churachandpur town and its surroundings not less than two times everyday, the school could not be continued for long. At the same time the Japanese commanders were aware of the fact that some local people were acting as informers of British army intelligence. One evening, the Japanese patrolling party shot dead three British sepoys who probably came from Sugnu, within a few kilometres from the eastern side of the Khuga valley. Again, indiscriminate bombings on Churachandpur, Gangpimuol and the hills surrounding Saikawt village continued unabated.

Unable to get continuous supply by air, the Japanese and INA personnel had to depend more and more on the ration and livestock of the local people. An eye-witness account maintains that all the male folks and young women in the occupied villages were engaged in pounding rice day and night to feed the soldiers. At other times, the male folks also served as coolies and porters carrying ration and ammunition to different camps. Zathuoi, who was a volunteer, also testified that he and his two friends one day carried a wounded Japanese soldier whose leg was completely torn asunder just below his knee, from the Saidan peak to the Saikot camp. Deeply impressed by his forbearance, Zathuoi further stated that not even once did the soldier groan.

Surprisingly, some of the occupying soldiers were Christians. According to Zema, one Sunday evening in the month of August 1944, thirteen Japanese soldiers not only joined the Church service, but also presented a Christian hymn led by one soldier called Nihei Khome and the second stanza of the hymn in English runs thus,

> How sweet the tie of hallowed love,
> That binds our heart in one;
> We gathered on the blessed name
> Of Christ, the Father's Son,
> And though the parting soon may come;
> Yet in His word is given,

The blessed hope that by and by;
We all shall meet in heav'n.
We all shall meet in heav'n.

What a befitting hymn! Zema nostalgically recalls, "We knew the hymn and its tune. As they were singing the hymn, tears were rolling down our cheeks." Rev. (late) Lerthansung, a well-known pastor in the United Pentecostal Church in North East India, who happened to preach at the Kyoto United Pentecostal Church on one of his visits to Japan, met an old man after the church service who apologetically said, "Reverend, I have been to Imphal, Jessami, Shangshak (Ukhrul) Kohima, Churachandpur and Saikawt. I still have maps of the places I visited with some photos of the people. We ate a lot of arum at Churachandpur and Saikawt, you know. But we caused a lot of harm to you people. Please forgive us." At this, Rev. Lerthansung replied "The British officials told us that you are our enemy. But when we see your faces, we realize that we are one and brothers."

Sayonara!

Things rapidly turned against the Indo-Japanese army in Manipur. To make matters worse, many of them started suffering from malaria and dysentry. This told heavily upon their morale. As they had sung in the church service, the time for parting soon came. One of the top-ranking INA commanders came and met Kawlvelthang one evening and thanked him profusely, saying, "I have come all the way from Rangoon and met many people who have been supporting us. I am so thrilled and particularly grateful to you for what you and your villagers have done for my soldiers. In fact, it is only because of your help and co-operation that my soldiers could survive till today. But now many of them are suffering from malaria and dysentery, we are leaving soon.

"When India achieves her freedom, you folks will never be forgotten." Who was this officer? Kawlvel that claimed that this officer was no other than Netaji Subhas Chandra Bose. It might not have been possible for Subhas Chandra Bose to visit

Churachandpur at such a crucial juncture when the Axis powers were on the retreat. This much is clear to us that the officer might have been one of the top-ranking INA leaders. The next day, the officer went to Thingkangphai and hurriedly left for Burma.

Soon after this, the painful yet inevitable decision to leave Manipur was taken and the Indo-Japanese soldiers left bidding, "SAYONARA" to their newly found friends with tears in their eyes! Even in defeat, the Indo-Japanese soldiers earned the respect and admiration of the simple tribal folks. Their unfathomable patriotism, their spirit of sacrifice and their long forbearance are still the talk of every household in the Khuga valley of Manipur even today.

27

The Matric Examination in Manipur during the Second World War

Manindra Konsam
(Translated from Manipuri by Pebam Nganthoiba Mangang)

On 6th November, 1941, Maharaja Churachand took his last breath at Nabadwip in West Bengal. The very next day, after the demise of Maharaja Churachand, his eldest son, Prince Bodhachandra Singh, succeeded to the throne on 7th November, 1941. The coronation ceremony of the new Maharaja of Manipur took place during the Second World War period.

The Second World War began in 1939 and ended in 1945. Britain joined the Second World War on 10th May, 1940. However, the Japanese defeated Britain on many war fronts in the Pacific and South East Asia. As a result, Britain lost its administrative control over such colonial countries positioned in Pacific and South East Asia. The Japanese advanced towards British Burma far longer, and simultaneously, the British government stationed at Manipur also began a huge war preparation to face the battle with the Japanese soldiers who were coming towards Manipur.

Before the completion of six months of taking charge as a King by Maharaja Bodhachandra, 2000 British soldiers arrived in Imphal on each consecutive day on 7th and 8th January, 1942. These soldiers stayed at Johnstone High School, Churachand, Tombisana, and other schools in Imphal. Students stopped attending school as the soldiers occupied the classrooms. However, headmasters and teachers of these schools tried to maintain the academic calendar during the war. The teachers arranged the classes in their individual capacity, particularly for the class X students who were to be given matric examinations.

It was sure that the Second World War would reach Manipur also. Many were aware of the consequences of the imminent war that would bring the sky filled with sounds and smoke of gun firing and bombing. The hue and cry of people and the pain and suffering of innocents' lives would be witnessed soon breaking the peace of the land. People began preparing for the undesirable event, which was uncertain if it would occur at any time in a day or two.

In April 1942, Manipur witnessed a sudden price hike of rice, and the price of a half sack of paddy was increased from Re. 1 to Rs. 20. It is also mentioned in the Cheitharol Kumbaba as follows:

> "Taimajam Hemgi Koom Sak 1864....—29 ni Leibakpokpa da (April 14,1942) Sajibu gi palok oiye | Kalen tha (1942, April 16- May 15) Sagon senna halley| Chaak yam na taang e| Phou sangbai amada lupa 20 piye|" (Cheitharol Kumbaba).

The main reason for the hefty price hike was the uninterrupted arrival of large numbers of soldiers stationed at schools and open spaces in and around the Imphal area.

Finally, Manipur witnessed the Second World War on 10th May, 1942. In the evening of that day, many Japanese warplanes were seen in the sky and bombarded places like Kangla, Puleiromba Khongnangkhong, Major Khun, Khoyathong, Thangmeiband, and Chingmeirong areas. Many people were killed, and houses and vehicles were damaged. People were running for life towards the countryside, leaving the Imphal area, including Sana Konung and Government offices.

On the other hand, the Indian National Army (INA) declared war against Britain and America on 23rd October, 1943 at the headquarters located in Singapore. It may be recalled that INA was founded on 14th December, 1941 under the leadership of Netaji Subhas Chandra Bose at Malaya Jitra Jungle with the help of the Japanese to eliminate the Britishers from the soil of Bharat. After the declaration of war, under the command of Major Shah Nawaz Khan of INA, the Subhas Brigade approached Manipur from Burma and occupied Ukhrul of Manipur on 18th March, 1944. On 19th March, 1944, INA hoisted the Indian National Flag, singing the National Anthem at 'Kenedy Peak' of Ukhrul on British Indian soil. Then, the INA reached Moirang from Tiddim Road and hoisted their INA flag at Moirang Kangla on 14th April, 1944, witnessed by the Japanese Official and general public. This fateful occasion made Moirang occupy an important space in the history of the Indian freedom Struggle Movement.

The Matric Examination of 1943 in Manipur was conducted during the Second World War. The Examination commenced on Monday, 19th April, 1943. In the previous year, the students could not attend classes because militaries occupied the schools. In the case of Johnstone High School, students who were going to appear in the Matric examination were taken regular classes by Headmaster Konjengbam Gouro Singh at his residence located at Kwakeithel. Sometimes, the students were made to stay at his house, and he also provided food.

The total number of students appearing in the Matric examinations was only 7 in 1943: Rajkumar Jaljit, Nepram Sukumar, Potsangbam Tombi, Thokchom Benimadhav, and Maibam Haricharan from Johnstone School (In later years of their lives, they all became a successful person and occupied an important space in the society). Ibomcha Singh from Churachand High School and Kadambini, the only girl from Tamphasana High School were also appeared in the Examination. The details of Ibomcha of Churachan High School had not been explored further after his school life. However, Kadambini, the female student from

Tamphasana High School, later in her school days, became the life partner of the first IGP of Manipur, Shri Laishram Gopal Singh. Rishang Keishing, the then Chief Minister of Manipur and Member of Parliament of both Lok Sabha and Rajya Sabha, was supposed to appear in the Matric Examination of 1943, but he could not write the Examination due to the prevailing Second World War situation.

The Centre for Matric Examination, 1943, was allotted at the residence of the First B.A. of Manipur, Shri Sougaijam Samarendra Singh. He was also a member of Manipur State Darbar and was assigned the duty of In-Charge of the Matric Examination by Calcutta University. The Examination was conducted in the drawing room of his residence located at Moirangkhom Sougaijam Leikai.

On Tuesday, 20th April, 1943, at noon on the second day of the Examination, while students were writing the examination papers, the Japanese dropped the bombs beginning from Khurai Telepati to Khomidok Pangan. There were many casualties and chaos everywhere. At one mandap of Khurai Chingangbam Leikai, around 100 people were killed at one time as the Japanese bombarded the areas while they were having a feast.

On Wednesday, 21st April, 1943, the Japanese dropped bombs at Kangla, Sanjenthong, Residency (Present Raj Bhawan), Wahengbam Leikai, Keishampat, Tera Keithel etc. Many lives were lost and properties were damaged. Despite the war, the Examination was not cancelled. Seven students took the examination in the entire Manipur. Whenever the warplanes were seen flying in the sky, the warning sounds of sirens were given to take precautions. The students appearing in the Examination managed to hide, kneeling inside a big pit dug out at the place of the examination by the person in charge, Shri Sougaijam Samarendra's residence. Once the siren stopped, they were moved out from the pit and resumed the writing, giving extra time to make up the time spent at the pit for hiding. The same procedure was continued whenever siren sounds were heard while writing the Examination.

Despite taking the Examination in such a horrific environment, all the students passed the Matric examination except the female student. Ibomcha from Churachand High School passed in the 3rd Division, and the rest of the students from Johnstone High School passed in the 2nd Division.

If we look at those days of the milieu where Rajkumar Jaljit and his classmates appeared in the Matric Examination at Calcutta University in 1943, it is quite contrary to the present situation of Manipur, where schools and colleges are often closed due to strikes, people's movements or any protest.

28

Second World War in Manipur with Special Reference to Kakching

Nongmaithem Pramodini

The Second World War (popularly known as *Japan Lan*, an exclusive term coined by the Manipuris), spread in many part of Manipur. In fact, the state was one of the major battle fields of this war. The Japanese forces in alliance with the forces of the Indian National Army (Azad Hind Fauz) led by Netaji Subhas Chandra Bose who aimed at the liberation of India from the British colonial rule advanced up to Manipur. The British, an ally of the Allied group was ready to defend against the combined forces. The victorious campaign of the Japanese and the INA forces against Burma heralded their invasion of Manipur. The conquest of Burma resulted to the influx of many refugees including Indian immigrants, British traders etc. in the state. At their impending danger of war the British from the Burma Front, i.e. IV Corps under Lt. General Geoffry Scoones was stationed at Imphal and ready for both defensive and offensive missions. The sudden bombing of Imphal in 1942 and 1943 were followed by other air raids in some villages. These air strikes made by the Japanese Air Force planes marked the arrival of the Second World War in an isolated region like Manipur, a native state under British Paramountcy. Hence the British and Allied force was in a state of preparedness and constructed the airfield of Tuhihal Kakching (popularly known as Pallel to the British), Koirengei and Kangla. Construction of National Highways No. 39, roads connecting Sengmai River to Langathel *via* Kakching Mamangching (the hill ranges on the eastern side of Kakching) and Langmeidong to Tentha *via* Maningching (the hill ranges on the western side of Kakching) as well as construction of barracks, bridges, culvert etc. were worth mentioning.

The Royal Chronicle, *Cheitharol Kumbaba* records that the first bombing of many parts of Imphal, the capital town of Manipur were Nungijungbi, Khuyathong, Mantri Khongnang by the Japanese Air Force planes and the raids occurred on Sunday the 10th May, 1942.[1] According to their source there was a lots of civilian casualty. Shri Govinda was shifted to the residence of Aribam Anou Pujari of Uchekon. The members of royal family also left the Palace and stayed there. All the works of government officers ceased to function. The bombing caused damage to vehicles and killed many cattles. Most inhabitants of Imphal town fled to rural areas. On the next day, Maharaja Bodhchandra Singh has returned from Thanga. Such sir raids took place in many areas and created panic situations. In short, the first bombing of Imphal affected the life and property of the state. Another air raid of Keishampat Wahengbam Leikai on 16th May, 1942 disturbed the normal life of Imphal town. In this catastrophic attack many houses were burnt and lots of inhabitants were forced to seek refuge.

Other records of bombing that of 20th and 21st, 9th November, 15th March, 16th March and 9th April of 1944. The affected areas were Khurai, Teliaptiu, Khomidok, Koirengai, Kakching, Sagolband, Kongan Heinoubok Khsman, Heigang, Heirok, Changangei and so on. These series of air raids made catastrophic effects that burnt many houses including the residency of Christopher Gimson, the then Political Agent of Manipur, killed many people and cattle,. Cheitharol Kumbaba records that Japanese bombing on 20th April, 1943 killed one hundred people who participated in a grand feast at the Mandap of Chingangbam Gulap and many cattle at Porompat.[2]

Thus the so called "Japan Lan" made Manipur a battle field damaging the economy, life, resources, production and so on. The climax of the war scene took place following the arrival of 31 Division under Lt. General Sato and 15 Division led by Lt. General Yamamuchi of Japanese force crossing Chindwin on March 1944 and 33 Division under Major General Yanageda who marched from Tiddim to Manipur chasing the 17 Division of British Army under Major General Cowan. The 31 and 15 Division of Japanese forces fought bloody battles against the British forces at Ukhrul, Kohima, eastern part of Imphal Valley as well as the capital town. The 33 Division could occupy Churachandpur, Moirang, Ningthoukhong, Potshangbam and Bishnupur. The war between these two rival forces at Maibam Lokpa Ching (Red Hill) was dramatic. At first the Japanese occupied the Red Hill but was beaten back from there. Then a fierce battle was fought at Bishnupur. Through the war Manipur was in favour of the Japanese forces, in early stage, it ended with their collapse by July 1944. The above mentioned royal Chronicle records the war fields of Moiranf, Naran Sena, Ningthoukhong, Phubala, Potsahngbam, Irengbam, Lotpaching in the south; Sekmai, Ukhrul in the North; Andro in the East; and Kakching in the south-west.[3]

During the Second World War, Kakhing also became a battle field. Kakching is a flourishing Municipal town and headquarters of Kakching District. It is located in the south-east of capital Imphal with a distance of 44 km. Its real connotation is a community belonging to the Loi groups of Manipur with Scheduled Caste status rather than a distinctive geographical region. In fact, the so called Kakching is derived from the community name. History witnesses that the community was assigned the duty of iron works and compelled to provide iron products to the state. Through majority of the population adopt Hindu cult, many Umanglais like Ibudhou Khamlangba, Irum Ningthou, Naaohalai, Ithok Ningthou, Sengmai Ningthou, Nongda Lairen Pakhangba,

Phousupat Lairembi, Kabui Lai, Singgrong Lairembi, Panthoibi as well as household deities; Laningthou Sanamahi, Ima Leimaren Sidabi are worshipped as popular deities. Imoinu Irat thouni (rites and rituals of Imoinu Lairembi) is also annually performed. Kakching market is the main commercial centre and there are also some local markets; Naodam Bazar (popularly known as Keithel macha), Laithagol Keithel, Khongnang Meira Phangba Keithel, Ningthou Leikai Keithel, Kakching Garden Chingkhong Keithel, Wairi Khongi Keithel, Sumak Leikai Keithel Macha etc. Kakching Garden, Angan Eco Park, Mamang Ching Pukhri, Wangkhei Meiraba Complex, Ithei Maru attract many tourist, students and scholars. There are fifteen temples of Hindu god like Lord Krishna, Nityainanda, Shiv Mahadeva, Gouranityai and that of fifteen traditional gods and goddesses; Ibudhou Khamlangba, Ithak Ningthou, Nongda Lairen Pakhangba, Sengmai Ningthou, Phousupat Lairembi, Senggrong Lairembi, Chumnang Lairembi, Kabui Lai, Lainingthou Sanamahi, Panthoibi Lairembi.

According to both written and oral sources, when Kakching was in the state of village life, many villagers became the victims of the Second World War. Prior to the actual fighting between the Allied forces and the combined army of Japanese and INA forces, there were air raids on the village killing some people. The impending danger of the said 'combined forces' invasion of the allied power made war preparations in Manipur which was extended up to Kakching. The construction of airfield of Kakching (popularly known as Pallel airfield to the foreigners) was taken up with rapid progress. In the book entitled "*Lousipat*", Mayanglambam Ibohal Singh highlighted the narratives collected from the local elders. It is laid down that after the completion of the airfield, a fighter plane landed there for seven days. Not only were the Kakching people the neighbouring villagers amazed by the fighter plane. In that time the road of Lousipat passing through the foothill was not in favourable condition. It is said that in the beginning of 1942, Allied force took initiatives in the improvement of the road.[4] One of the remarkable task coincided with the Second World War was the constriction of

National Highways 39. According to the above mentioned text, it was very difficult for ten wheeler vehicles to run on the phumthi (floating water weeds) that the construction work was delayed. So Major Meke planned to make the water ways by cutting the western hill into two portions so that the water from Lousipat could be drained towards Kharungpat. The work was started under a non-Manipuri contractor. Unfortunately, he became a victim of the war and dozer was used in the works of the construction of the National Highway 39. Thus the cutting of hill could not be carried on for many years.

The road from Sengmai River to Langathel *via* Kakching Mamangching (Eastern hill) and from Langmeidong to Tentha *via* Maningching (western hill range) were constructed. Regarding the construction of Pallel Bridge over Sengmai River, it is asserted that it was completed on 15th June, 1942.[5] The villagers also took up protective measure among which the digging of *Lalkom* (war pits) inside the house or homestead are worth mentioning. History witnessed that Manipur fought a number of wars with Burma (Myanmar) in which Kakching was the main theatre. In 1758 Meidingu Maramba *alias* Gourshyam led the Manipur force in a campaign against Awa force. The war was fought at Kakching and the Manipuri force could defeat the Awa force. In other war fought during the reign of Meidingu Chingthangkhomba *alias* Bhagyachandra, Meidingu Labanyachandra, Meidingu Chourjit, the village was one of the remarkable battle fields. Cheitharol Kumbaba records that the Manipuri force under Meidingu Chourjit fought for eleven days at Kakching Panjao which resulted to their defeat of Manipur force and flight of the King to Cachar.[6] During the Seven Years Devastation of Manipur (1819-1826) there were battles between the guerrilla force led by the revolutionary leader Ibungsija Herachandra (a prince) and Awa force.

During the Second World War Kakching people met lots of sufferings as the village was also a war field. N. Gandhar Singh, in his book entitled "*Kakching*" gives a brief account of the war preparation of allied forces in Manipur.[7] He asserted that as soon as Maharaja Bodhchandra ascended the throne of Manipur on 7th November, 1941 there was arriving the impending danger of Second World War in the State. The conquest of British Burma by the combined forces of the Japanese and Indian National Army under Netaji Subhas Chandra Bose resulted to the influx of a large number of refugees who looked for their destination to India through the route of Manipur. They thronged into the refugee camps set up by the Government of Manipur. In earlier wars with Awa some hill routes nearby Kakching, Heirok and Pallel villages had been used as main roads. The allied forces had already built war camps at Pallel. As a defensive measure two battalions under Capt. Sher Bahadur and Kali Bahadur had been stationed in the eastern side of Sengmai River. Moreover, one police outpost and a telegraph office had been opened. He also mentioned of the Kakching aerodrome in the western side of Kakching Leingang Loukon (paddy field of Leingang pat (Leingang Lake). This aerodrome was popularly known as Pallel Aerodrom as Pallel was a well-known village which has been used as the gateway since early times. During the course of the war, Kakching became the sheltering village of many refugees from neighbourhood villages. The construction of the highway from Pallel to Tummu was started from March 3, 1942 and it was completed on June 10. Prior to the arrival of the above mentioned three divisions of Japanese force in Manipur the Kakching people met disastrous air raids of Japanese fighters planes. Cheitharol Kumbaba records that the bombing of Kakching on Tuesday, November 9, 1943, caused a lot of civilian casualties. Another bombing in December also made heavy losses. These air attacks killed many people including women who worked in the agricultural field, labourer, even including one contractor.

There were also dock fights between the fighter's planes of both sides as the Japanese fighter planes attach the airfield of Kakching. There are oral narratives transmitted from the forefathers that the Japanese plane stole seven fighter planes of the allied force from the said air field. According to *Cheitharol Kumbaba* the war ended in August.

The people of Kakching suffered a lot due to the war. Large number of people was compelled to evacuate from their houses to give accommodation for the army. It is said that nearly four hundred houses of Kakching Khullen Sumak Leikai were evacuated. They took shelter to other Leikais—Makha Leika, Pat Leikai, Khumjampat etc. Still today there is one family of Yengkhom clan in Makha Leikai who left their original home, Sumak Leikai. N. Gandhar Singh asserted that Naorem Thanil the then Kakching Nigthou supplied cattle to the Allied Force.[8]

In the midst of the dreadful war scene the women flock of Kakching suffered a lot. They felt panic of facing sexual assault by the African soldiers. During the course of the war the II (East African Infantry Division) under the Major General Charles Christopher Fowkes of Allied force was deployed at Kakching. Some of these African soldiers were notorious and sometimes they gave threat to the normal life of the villagers. Some women were sexually harassed by them. Such happening created discontent among the villagers. It was very shocked to hear the story of such incident narrated by local grandmothers some years back. The story runs as: one day a couple worked in their paddy field, at that time some African soldiers came and raped the wife in front of her husband who was helpless to protect her. She was shocked and her heart was broken that he cried and told him, "I don't like to live in this condition. Kill me, please."

Thus some women became rape victims and these provoked the anger of the villagers. Women could not go outside and work freely. In some places they gathered inside some selected houses and they were guarded by the menfolk. However, the barbaric nature of some soldiers remains the same. As a consequence some of them were killed by the angry mob. It is also said that two African soldiers who targeted three women who were working in the field were killed. Thus the Kakching people taught a lesson and the said heinous crime against women had been discontinued.

Regarding the role of Kakching people in the INA movement in Manipur, it is difficult to reconstruct the facts due to the lack of ample sources. According to reliable sources some of Manipuris, Nagas, Kukis extended both moral and physical support to the Indian National Army. Dr. Priyadarshini M. Gangte, in her "*Revisiting Netaji's Role in the Freedom Struggle of India, INA and Manipur Perspectives*—Part 2, asserts that some thirty two Meitei who earned livelihood in Burma joined the INA under the leadership of L. Guno Singh and thirteen of them reached Pallel where they sought the support of local people. I had a friend of Gangte family from Churachandpur in my University days. Her father was a freedom fighter pensioner; she told me that he was one of the INA volunteer who worked in Manipur. N. Gunadhor Singh remarks that the Kakching people were aware of the INA and Netaji Subhas Chandra Bose whose divisional headquarters was at Tengnoupal which led to the advancement of the force up to Pallel and Kakching. The INA propaganda campaign sheet and speech of Netaji Subhas Chandra Bose recorded in the gramophone were circulated to the people. Those who knew the language interpreted all these into Manipuri. It helped the people to aware of the role of Indian National Army under the said leader in the freedom struggle of India. This some people of Kakching might have supported the movement in spite of the fact that major population remained non-committal.

An interview with a local woman named Kshtrimayum Ibeni Devi, a resident of Kakching Khullen Mayanglambam Pareng, Ward No. 10 highlights the happening of the Second World War at her early age. It is said that her elder brother named Mangi and his friends brought the photos of Netaji Subhas Chandra Bose. They gave the photos to her and other girls. Sometimes, they brought groundnuts also. The allied soldiers tried to snatch the photos as they noticed about that. But, they did not give the photos. Thus two photos were kept in the box. But, these had gone missing some years back. She also narrates that they feared going outside to feel that they might have been sexually assaulted by the African soldiers. Their parents, guardians and other elders did not allow them to go outside to avoid the danger of such happening.

A Book titled "*Prithivigee Anisuba Lanjao Amasung Manipur Party*" by W. Mangol Singh gives information about the role of Manipuris in the liberation movement of India led by INA. The Manipur Party under the leadership of Laishram Guna Singh (Lairikyengbam Leikai) and Laikhuram Mukh Singh (Thangmeiband) actively worked for the INA mission. The volunteers who headed for Churachandpur were Ballav Sharma (Bamon Leikai), Salam Yaima (Soibam Leikai), Mairenbam Ahanjao (Moirang), Takhellambam Chandrasing (Khurai), Mutum Chaoba (Keirao), Laishram Ningthemjao (Kendat), Tomba (Kendat), Kshtrimayum Babu (Tera Keithel), Oinam Maipak (Chanrangpat), Ningthoujam Gulap (Heirok), Laishram Tollamu (Kendat), Tomba Singh (Kendat), Manggi (Kendat), Nongthombam Amu (Huikap), Chanam Amu (Thoubal Wangkhem), Sanajao (Thoubal), Kongkham Angou (Wangkhei), Sapam Angou (Kabo Wakching), Thouroijam Tomba (Moirang). The volunteers under Guna and Mukh who headed for south- east border for Manipur were Loukrakpam Mukh (Keirao), Aribam Atombau Sharma (Thangmeiband), Amu Singh (Keirao), Nongthongbam Amu Singh (Kendat), Laishram Jugindro (Kendat), Bamao Sahrma (Mandalay), Shougaijam Khondon Singh, Iboton Singh (Kakching), Maibam Thagoi (Kendat). Among the INA volunteers Ibeton Singh of Kakching is worth mentioning. One local elder mentioned of another volunteer, named Nila Singh.

In the midst of chaos and sufferings of the war many villagers including grown-ups and even the boys engaged themselves in wage earnings. They washed the clothes of the soldiers for soaps, cigarettes, biscuits, soaks, shoes etc. sometimes the soldiers gave them salt cakes known as Sambor in exchange of eggs and bananas. Some people collected stones from Laipham Loknung (the hill ranges in the eastern side of National Highway No. 39) for crushing. These were supplied to the contractors of the construction works. At night they went for film, Chinese circus offered by the Allied Army.[9] The people met hardships of the shortage of food and price rises. Many people were engaged as wage labourers in the construction works and other development works. Some of the villagers became contractors. The people were compelled to supply food, cattle and other items to the Allied force. N. Gandhar Singh highlighted a related story, after the war was over Maharaja Bodhchandra made royal visit of Kakching Market, salt mine of Waikhong as well as worship of Wangbren by the end of 1945. When he arrived at Kakching Market, Maharaja rebuked the village elders as well as dignitaries. He insisted that they should give the reason why the Kakching people supplied cattle to the army for consumption. As the cattle was worshipped by the Hindus, the King felt angry to think that the people disregarded Hinduism. The village authorities and elders totally bewildered by the angry mood of the King remained silent. But, one person Lanjingba kneeled down in front of Maharaja and sought permission for saying few words. As his request was granted, he highlighted the hardship met by the villagers during the course of the war. During the Second World War Kakching was a great battle field.

A large number of soldiers of the Allied force were deployed in the Kakching airfield. As Manipur was a native state under British Paramountcy, the people has to obey the order of the government. Hence, the villagers supplied rations and other items for the army through the contractors. Though they had no intention they did so under compulsion. The officers also announced that the soldiers would met difficulty without food and the urgent need of the hour was food and victory. The people could not convey the situation to the King as there was lack of communication due to the closure of offices. His delivery impressed the King that he forgave the Kakching people and headed for Waikhong salt mine, an abode of Wangbren.

There was fragment of war weapons, vehicles tools, implements and many other articles. The tools and implements were collected by the villagers and used in various purposes. The war brought a great change in the socio-economic and political activities of Kakching. The contact with foreigners and growth of knowledge of using Western technology had witnessed a change in the vision of the people. Housing roads, bridges, market had been improved to a great extent. Though majority of the people faced the problem of economic deterioration during the course of the war, the contractors and traders got benefited. N. Gandhar Singh mentioned of one trader name Khumukcham Ibobi Singh who benefited a lot from the war.[10] It is said that Ibobi collected the fragments of vehicles, weapons, tools and implements as he knew the value of those articles. Besides, he purchased many houses auctioned by the official and army outbidding others. He opened a workshop and engaged many skilled mechanics. In this way, he becomes a rich person. The villagers received compensatory payment for their losses and damaged during the war.

One of the most remarkable impact of the war was the progress of formal education in the village. One upper primary school was established near Naodam Thingel in the eastern side of Loujai Lambi (the road from Khongnang Mari fangba to Laimanai Chingjin Passing Naodam Bazar). But the academic activities of the school have been ceased due to the war. But post-war scenario of education in Kakching was in favourable condition. M. Sanggaai Singh remarks that after the Second World War Kakching had been gradually developed with rapid progress of education.[11] Many private LP ME schools for each locality had been established by public efforts. N. Gandhar Singh highlighted that the Allied were victorious over the Axis power in Europe with the surrounding of Germany.

> It is probably on May 8, 1945, they were in the school. A Madraji Lt. crossed the canal and to his great joy he informed that Germany had surrendered last night, May 7 and war ended in Europe for which they could enjoy holiday to celebrate the war victory. Thus the day was announced as holiday. Japan surrendered on September 2 and the day was also announced as Holiday.

Thus, the Second World War brought great changes in many spheres of Kakching village. In fact, the post-war Kakching marked the progress of both material and intellectual aspects of this village.

NOTES

1. L. Ibongohal Singh and N. Khelchandra Singh (2nd Ed.) (1989). *Cheitharol Khumbaba*, Imphal, p. 641.
2. *Ibid.*, p. 642.
3. *Ibid.*, p. 644.
4. Mayanglambam Ibohal Singh, *Lousipat*, Kakching, p. 17.
5. Mutum Ibohal Singh (2016). *Pallel Ithihas*, p. 19.
6. *Cheitharol Kumbaba*, p. 211.
7. N. Gandhar Singh (2003). *Kakching*, pp. 18-19.
8. N. Gandhar Singh (2014). *Khunganggi Wari*, p. 29.
9. *Ibid.*, p. 59.
10. N. Gandhar Singh, *Kakching*, p. 20.
11. M. Sanggai Singh (2003). *Educational Survey*, Kakching, p. 24.

REFERENCES

Gangmumei Kamei (2016). *A History of Modern Manipur* (1826-2000), New Delhi, 2016.

J. Roy (1999). *History of Manipur* (Second revised), Calcutta.

Laldena (Ed.), *History of Modern Manipur* (1826-1949).

W. Mangol Singh, *Prithivi gi Anisuba Lanjao Amasung Manipur Party.*

29

My Childhood Memoir of Second World War in Manipur

Khuraijam Nimaicharan Singh

The Shadow of War

After 1941 was just over, the early days of 1942 were occupied with a common talk of a dreaded war which was likely to come soon to Manipur. To my thinking, menfolk in my locality, perhaps everyone and all in Manipur were anxious of the war. They used to sit and discuss things on many such troubles and difficulties that the coming war would surely bring to their lives. Wherever and whenever they meet; their conversation turned into the topic of a war which was about to come into this region of Manipur; and they felt worried on what to be done and where to go for their shelters.

We learnt from their conversation that the coming war was not the kind of a fighting to be taken place at a particular place with swords, spears and any such things like daggers and clubs etc., but a kind of a war using what was called flying balloons from which a dangerous object called bombs would be dropped down causing a thousand deaths in a moment. It was also heard that thousands of men, women and children were killed in Burma by a poison-bomb—causing havoc and destruction on the land. "Mandalay has been captured by the Japanese, and Manipur will be reached soon." "Where shall we rush to protect ourselves, and where to hide? What would be done to our belongings and properties etc.? Such were the unsettled state of things that occupied elders in those days. They were sad and helpless in waiting what might be fallen them. In the meantime, whether a rumour or fact, there were also news of certain happenings of odd events known as UPADRAP (happening of unusual things) in Manipur somewhere and even in the royal temple of Manipur where Govindaji was worshipped. These all meant something a bad omen of the region creating terror in the minds of all.

Often, we could hear talks on what is called bomb and its power of destruction by killing thousands when it explodes. Along with that, there was also the saying that the deafening explosion of a bomb could even kill a young babe causing it to ooze out blood from the ears. Hearing those worried discussion of the elders, our minds were weakened, we could not utter a single word but sitting dose to our father's knees. So, the early part of 1942 was a period of restlessness accompanied with fears and misgivings. Very often, panic stricken men and women came rushing to their homes from the big market in Imphal. Such a happening was becoming frequent as and when someone spread the news of an instant coming of the war. Breaking up a market from such a rumour or news is called KEITHEL KAIBA in Manipuri and when such a melee occurs, people in the market ran helter-skelter giving advantage to thieves on one side also.

As the situation aggravates, the then British Government in Manipur was sending out precautionary pamphlets in public places in Imphal. On them, detail instructions were given letting all to understand on what to be done and how to take care of themselves at the time of bombing from aeroplanes. According to the pamphlets, the things we understood from our elders were—when a bombing was to happen, a loud siren will be given beforehand. At every home, a 'V' shaped trench or ditche should be kept ready for hiding ourselves during bombardment. We should close the ears with our fingers and hold breath, it was also advised.

Since we had not already experienced the nature and impact of a bomb, we had also a belief in somebody's saying whether right or wrong that it would be safer for us to hide ourselves under our bedsteads during bombing. So many varied opinions whether true or not were beginning to spread everywhere, and we could not ascertain a definite idea as to what would be done at the time of bombing from above. Day by day, fears and panic increased in the minds of all. Loud warning sirens, as was already announced in the pamphlets, were beginning to blow out from the 4th Assam Rifles Cantonment as a practice to be followed when a sudden airraid was to happen. This was a warning signal of alertness given to all and everybody who could hear it. Whenever the siren was blowing out as a regular practice from the 4th Assam Rifles Cantonment, most people could not understand it to be a practice, so they were frightened by it all the more and what to say, we could hear parents calling about their children; and even at school also we were made to jump down and kneel into those trenches specially dug out for the purpose. The Thangmeiband U.P. School where I was then a student of Class III had also six or seven such long ditches where we used to jump down whenever a siren was heard.

So, when we had not already experienced what a bombing was, we came to learn beforehand that we should keep ourselves hiding in a pit or trench. But we children had such a false belief of hiding ourselves in an unseen comer of a place, or in a bush or under our bedsteads at home to be the better and safer place for our protection. Now, the day of first bombing was sure to come one day but when that would be, was not known to all. Everybody grew anxious day by day and every household used to have their dinners and suppers quite earlier than before to keep themselves alert for a sudden coming of the war. Elderly people put their heads together with the fear conscience of an unknown calamity to be faced by them sooner or later.

The First Sight of a Flying Balloon (Aeroplane) and Imphal Bombing

In those days, aeroplanes were known as balloons by most of the people in Manipur. We hadn't seen any one of them before, but heard of it very often as the news of the war was approaching day by day. On some casual occasions, there was news of balloons (aeroplanes) coming in the sky, but most of us couldn't have a clear view of them, as they were flying so high above the clouds. Hearing the sounds of the planes, we looked up at the sky, but it died down in the far distance among the clouds while we were so trying to locate the object. A few people could locate them instantly, however, it was lost from sight while one was trying to find it out. So, many things were on the lips of people of the time with overwhelming fears.

Trepidation and anxieties increased day in and day out. On one such a day in the morning at about 8 etc. we could have a clear view of what was much talked about "A Japanese plane". It was only one that was circling in the air again and again above the places of Imphal town, the capital of Manipur. At last, it came to our knowledge that the pilot of the plane flying not so high above the ground must have taken photographs of the important places of their bombing targets in Imphal.

From that day onwards, Khwairamband Bazar, the biggest women market in Manipur was under the stress of disturbances and breaking up repeatedly through such rumours of an instant Japanese attack from the air. The loud siren from the Assam Rifles too was blowing more often giving tensions to everybody. All were on the alert of a coming war. The time was in the beginning of May 1942 and most schools in Manipur were not yet starting their summer vacations. No sooner had we seen a low flying Japanese plane one day as was mentioned above, then came the day for the first bombardment on Imphal to be carried out by the Japanese on a day when most of the civilians and students would be at home.

In the early morning of that particular day, at about 8 or 9 A.M. etc. there came a plane in the sky, very bright in the sunlight and not so high above the treetops. Most people in that morning could see it well. Perhaps it could be a prior observation carried out by the plane some hours before the coming of their group of fighter planes to bomb Imphal for the first time in the history of the great world war.

It being in the month of May, the sun was also extremely hot at the time of noon. It was at this time that I went with some of my friends to play in the water of the Imphal River. The spot of the river where we went to, was known to most of us as Yaikhom Hiden, towards the south-western side of Lamlong Bazar, and at a distance of about 200 metres from my home. The easy going life of children as it was, we almost forgot the fear of planes and bombing in that moment, and we were all in a frolic splashing water to one another. The river bed was full of the noise of our shouting and laughing. While the mind got so indulged in such a happy mood of ecstasy, we could not at all hear the 'rumbling sound of the aeroplanes' flying above. In that very moment, one Ta Tomei, a brother, few years older than us, while he was sneaking up the river bank had apparently seen the planes. Instantly he, in a trembling voice called all of us to come up and see the planes. We ran up and looked at the sky all wet. The planes were many and the rumbling sounds from them seemed to be inside our body. Panicky as we were, we counted the planes instantly. They looked to be only four at first; but in a moment, they, from above the other were spreading out; and in a second, as we counted, they were twenty-four or so. This must have been their formation of flying, six planes each in four groups flying one above the other in the same position and speed so as to be looked upon as only four from below.

Now, the sight of those planes was looked like a swarm of bees flying above the Imphal area the then capital region of Manipur. Those who could have a view of that occurrence on that day will hardly forget it for ever. Then we, being fear stricken, ran to our homes all wet and half naked, closing the ears with our fingers. Oh! what an ordeal it was! Noise of calling their children by nervous parents filled the surrounding atmosphere. We felt as if we were being chased by the planes, and instantly we could hear thunder-like sound of explosions at places not so far away, along with the whirring of the planes from above.

It was on this day, the 10th of May, 1942 (Sunday) at noon time that the Japanese had for the first time, bombed on the plains of Imphal the only Town of Manipur, and with that, the great Second World War had its first landing on the soil of this region. It will for ever remain a Red Lettered Day in the history of Manipur and particularly in the course of the Second World War in the Asian front. My house was at a distance of about 200 metres from the river and that also by a short cutting through two homesteads in the neighbourhood. I ran panting with my friend Gopalmacha to reach our home. His home was farther away from mine, so we both took shelter under our bedstead inside the house. Breathless, we were closing the ears with our fingers and uttered the holy name "Hare Krisna, Hare Krisna", in our mouths. After a while the planes seemed to have gone back towards the southern sky and silence prevailed everywhere. Not so long after that, the atmosphere was again awakening with the noise of calling children by elders from all directions. From our hiding place, my friend Gopalmacha too has rushed away to his parents. Those were the moments that engulfed everybody in fear and it seemed as if the planes would be coming back to strike us again. Everybody looked puzzled, not knowing what to do.

We, four of us (two elder sisters, a younger one and myself) remained sitting in the veranda without a word. We looked at our father who stood by. "Calm down, Calm down, control your fears", said my father to us. He had several things in his mind, we knew, but he did not know what to decide in that moment. Thus, no sooner had the first bombing occurred in Imphal than we could see lines of men and women going on the Ayangpalli Road, just in front of our house with whatever they could carry in their hands or on the heads. There were also bullock carts carrying huge pile of materials like boxes, bedstead, bundles of utensils etc. Such a row of people leaving their homes for a distant destination was ceaseless in my thinking in that afternoon. My bewildered father asked us, "Where shall we go my children? Do you like to go to your uncle's place at Napet Village or at Kanglasifai, the place of your aunty?" At this, we quickly replied in a single voice, "At our aunt's home to Kanglasifai."

Refugees from Burma

An endless stream of men, women and children was, in that period pouring in from Burma. They were known as Burmese refugees and they became the topic of those days everywhere. They had been traversing long distances through mountain tracts, jungles and swamps only to reach a place of their shelter. Apparently most of the people were Indians and Nepalese who were already living in Burma (now called, Myanmar), and driven out by the war when the places were completely overrun and seized by the Japanese army causing several damages to civil life and property. Particularly those non-Burmese people could no more find places to live there, and as such they escaped from the war in Burma either by the sea route from Rangoon to Calcutta (Now Kolkata) or cutting through jungles and mountain areas towards the north to reach Manipur the border land of India. So the refugees, exhausted both in body and mind came passing through hilly tracts of many miles on foot only to reach India.

The refugees, on their reaching Manipur were looked like people who were already dead. They famished with thirst and hunger could scarcely balance their body. They were staggering, stumbling as they went and dragged their pact heavily on the road. Many of them were lying or sprawling on the ground almost dead like and seemed co forget cares and anxieties of their belongings, near and dear ones. Most of them were separated from the company of their own families, either strayed, lost or dead along the long stretch they had been pushing through. Some of them were not only wearied but also bore in their hearts the agony of separation from their loved ones whom they had left dead far behind as they came. Those fellows had to submit to their evil destiny by dragging themselves just like dying lunatics with everything lost in their visions. They came eating or chewing anything they could find on the way; and no water to drink except the little available on the roadside, no matter dirty or clean. We had heard that the number of those who were fallen dead on the Imphal-Dimapur road was so large that the tractors and Bulldozers brought here for war purposes had to push the corpses down into large pits to be buried collectively.

Among those refugees, there were also men who were still strong in health and with enough money in their pockets. Those were the people who on their request, were said to have been transported for certain distances on the road or up to Dimapur in private lorries or trucks on payment. But, on the other hand, there were groups of miserable fellows who could not afford to pay for such a transportation of themselves for they were pennyless and almost deadlike. It was also learnt that at Koirengei, a place on the northern outskirt of Imphal, a camp was organised under British arrangement for those refugees coming out from Burma. Those wretched people reached the camp in thousands, and most of them were sick and ill with no food and sufficient clothing on them. Even though they were comfortably sheltered at the camp, they thought, they were yet to reach India and so their minds were anxious and could not be reached there. At Kanglatongbi, a place on the Dimapur road, about 7 miles from Koirengei, another camp was also made by the Britishers for those refugees, it was learnt; but the refugees were not willing to stay there, and instead, they marched on and on causing hindrance to the line of vehicles coming from the opposite direction. It was but a few lucky ones who at last could reach Dimapur after passing through several hardships and untold miseries and sufferings on their long traverse.

One Year's Full after the First Bombing and Preparation

Ever since the first and the second bombings in Imphal on the 10th and 16th of May, 1942, there had been no Japanese attack from the air or on the ground for about one year up to April 1943. It may be recalled that during the period of a long stretch of one year, almost every household in Manipur, even most of the town dwellers who took refuge in distant villages, could live peacefully by working in different fields of activities. On the other hand, it was a lime for this plate called Manipur to see and enjoy the view of several activities of all the allied forces in their building up strong defensive positions everywhere to fulfil all their requisites of a fierce war to be fought here within a short time. Every day and night, thousands of different vehicles, quite a strange to this place were ceaselessly coming in, carrying soldiers, guns, technicians, other equipments and foods etc. Thus, the grand preparation of the war was soon taken up in Imphal and at other places of Manipur as they thought it necessary under certain strategic points of view. For transport facility, new roads were cut through villages and open fields and they were made serviceable for army vehicles. Bridges were spanned on rivers to connect roads and places. Constructions of air fields too were taken up soon one after another; and among them, the then Imphal airfield, better known as the Koirengei Air-field was the first among those so far made and used by the Anglo-American forces during the war. After which, came the Tulihal and the Kangla Airfields, the Wangjing and Sapam and the Pallel. All the airfields six in number were first made by surfacing large areas of open fields with bulldozers. Along with such developments, big sized anti aircraft guns (cannons) were also installed with bunkers of sand bags around them almost in the vicinity of all airfields and at roadsides.

In these grand task of all sorts of constructions requiring services for both technical and manuals etc., it may be mentioned that majority of the workers was from Manipur and the rest from outside; and as such, many ordinary workers also could earn a handsome amount as wages per day, so a famine which would otherwise have been occurred, was itself checked and prevented. Many a literate people from Manipur had worked as overseers, surveyors, SDOs, contractors and suppliers etc. by extending their best help on a war footing towards fulfilling all those objectives as envisaged in the plans of the Britishers. On the other side, the

Japanese, had they continued further attacks in Imphal just after their first air-raid in 1942 without creating such a lull of one year's time, Imphal would have been in their hands easily, but contrary to that, while they were making army bases in Burma and Singapore with a plan for a large-scale attack of Imphal, an ample time was so given to the allied forces of the Anglo-Americans, Indians, Africans and Canadians etc. to complete in advance all those defensive positions as well as strong bases in Imphal.

Now, an interesting account on the first making of Tulihal Air-strip, better known as Changaangei Aerodrome, as was recorded in Imphal the celebrated war story of that period compiled by Anthony Brett James and Geoffrey Evans, reveals the fact that at the time of its first surfacing the field for an airstrip, an American officer in charge of aerodrome construction was said to have been asked by one British engineer about the length of the fields to be surfaced with bulldozer. At this the American officer replied in brief "4000 (four thousand) only." As he did not distinctly tell the British engineer whether it was in terms of feet or yards, the British engineer took it for yards and went on surfacing the fields up to a distance of four thousand yards in length. In truth, the American meant it in feet but the Britisher took it for yard, as yard was used in England in measuring length and distance. Though it looks a little horrendous at first, it became so useful of course, and of a far reaching importance afterwards; the story goes. In the thick of the war, it was a pleasant sight to see the landing of two planes with heavy loads from different sides or taking off to different directions simultaneously right from the centre of the air-strip; and specially in a moon-lit night it was a picturesque sight to see the planes landing and taking off at the same time; records the book.

The glimpses of those days that I, as a young boy, had seen and experienced were so many to describe. Not so far away from the newly made Air-strip at Kangla, places for parking aeroplanes were carefully arranged in a line just near the borders of nearby villages, and these parking sites were connected with broad ways (road) specially surfaced and linked with the Air-strip so that the planes, after their landing could be parked at those sites where their engines were checked and refueled. The reason why I am giving these details was that, luckily in my boyhood I lived nearby such an Air-strip during the war. To continue again, those parking sites of planes (one for each plane) spacing about 50ft × 30ft were surrounded with high bunkers on three sides leaving the front side open for planes to drive in and out.

To us, (we children) those days were the times of happiness and found a lot of pastime wherever we looked at. At any time, whenever we looked out, everything was found surprisingly interesting and enjoyable to us. Hardly we remembered our personal sorrows in the midst of all that grandeur of the war. At places, big anti aircraft guns were placed pointing their heads or nozzles upwards. A scientific machine called Radar was also installed nearby the Airstrip. Over and above this, the sight of thousands of different army men, not only from India but also from other countries, had attracted our attentions with delights.

Furthermore, everyday, throughout day and night, the deep humming of the engines of those transport vehicles which were coming in a never ending line to Manipur could be heard from the distant Imphal-Dimapur Road. Task for improvement of the roads which would become awfully muddy or slippery in the rainy season was soon taken up by dumping stone boulders or shingles on them and even some important ones were also tarred upon. Incidents of sinking the wheels of trucks or Jeeps in certain pools of mud or in ditches, occurred very often at places. In such a time, when the driver found it helpless to move his vehicle, surely "he would call and request the Manipuri bystanders for help". Readily, when the required help was extended, the pleasing driver drove up his vehicle and went away saying o.k, to all. The very popular word 'o.k.' was first heard from English and American army during the war.

It is to be said that most of the various arms and ammunitions, guns and other implements such as food items, clothing and medicals etc. which were brought to Imphal were at first stocked in Imphal itself and then a large quantity of which was again shifted to

Moreh and Tamu to be kept ready as their preparation in advance for their defensive posts. That was the time which was termed as a period of Zig-Saw Puzzle on both sides. The Japanese too, on one side was making grand plans as to which of the directions, their army would advance first and under whose leadership etc. Similarly, on the side of the Allied forces too, every arrangement was kept ready to defend and counteract any massive attack from the Japanese as and when the moment comes.

Army in the Vacant Private Houses in Imphal

Several Indian Army platoons had already been stationed in the vacant houses in Imphal. Such occupation of the vacant civilian houses by platoons of Indian army was arranged mainly at places situated along the sides of highways in Imphal or at other places; but majority of the army camps was made with tents specially put up and arranged with amenities needed for the time. Also in our homestead at Khurai Thoudam Lelkai, Ayang Palli Road, Imphal, there were some Gorkha armies of the Kali Bahadur regiments occupying the vacated outhouses in our compound except the main dwelling house where my father along with me was staying for a time.

One evening, when my father and I were sitting in the verandah, I was simply looking out towards the backyard of ourhouse. In the very moment, I could see with surprise the coming of two white men, very tall and with rain coats over them. Breaking a small part of the bamboo fencing at the backyard, the two white men were approaching us. On seeing them, I was overwhelmed with fear, and the moment I informed my father of their presence, they stepped up the verandah and stood looking around. They seemed to utter something in their mouths, then they asked my father about something. On being heard from my father, the two fellows moved away again through the next compound of our neighbour. On their disappearance, I asked my father who they were. "They are Gora, the whites", said my father, "They all speak English and they were just looking our places." That was the first day that I had ever seen the kind of people known as Gora in those days. Not so long after that, men of their group were to become familiar with me in my after days during the war.

One afternoon again, there came a line of soldiers on horseback with all their belongings on the Ayang-Palli road. They were all Gurkhali soldiers and their temporary destinations were to be in our locality. They entered in the vacant homesteads one after another and thus made a camp of the platoons there. In our compound too, some of them entered and lived in the two Sangois (out houses) and also at the vacant house of our Tajou, the fostered brother of whom I had already accounted in former parts of this book. The said places along with the adjoining ones of all neighbours too were fully occupied by those army men who came with their horses bringing all their requisites. As they were people like us in appearance, I did not feel so much fear of them. Most of them talked with my father on several things. They looked pleased and very friendly with us. They used to ask our wants, particularly for kitchen menu like dals, ghees, salts and oils etc. everyday. They liked to share with us all that they had in their stock. They were angry if we refused to take anything what they liked to give us.

So, after spending a few days with those army men at our home at Khurai Lamlong, we came to know that they were a part of the Nepali regiment under the command of Kali Bahadur the famous leader of the brave Gurkhas of the Second World War time. Then, after the war, the very shocking news that pierced my heart was the misfortune that had been suffered by the whole regiment of Kali Bahadur at the battlefield of Shangshak where they all had been killed without a single survivor, it was learnt.

The Unforgettable Fierce Bombing

It was the full-moon day of Shajibu month of the Manipuris, the 20th of April, 1943. Almost all inhabitants of Imphal area had, due to the compelling circumstances of the war, taken shelter in different and distant villages in Manipur. But particularly, in a place of Khurai area in Imphal East, a few close friends who got parted and settled at scattered places had so arranged a feast by communicating themselves to attend it at Khurai Chingangbam Mandap a religious place. The feast was especially meant for a get-together of their old friendships as well as to revive a Cultural Natya Society which they had already formed before the war in Manipur. True, it was during the period of the war, but they, like other human beings, were all eager to meet and see one another. In that arranged feast on the 20th of April, 1943, many had participated, it was learnt. The feast was said to have been attended by about 200 persons including those family members living nearby the mandap and who, till the time were staying still at their homes, the head and inmates of the Brahmin's family (owner of the mandap) boys and girls and those invited persons from distant places etc. But it so happened that the day was a fatal day to be coincided with that grand feast of those innocent people who gathered there.

So, it was noon when we could hear the deep, rumbling sounds of unseen planes flying so high in the distant stray clouds above the southern sky of Manipur. By this time, it could be presumed that the particular innocent civilians who had already gathered for the arranged feast at Khurai Chingangbam Mandap, a religious place, might have possibly started enjoying the grand feast without any such an inkling of what might become on their lot by getting themselves entrapped in a fatal bombing accident within a few minutes to come in their lives. Now, as the planes were approaching Imphal, the distant heavy sounds were becoming louder and nearer, and grew all the more heavy and fearful than what it had been a few minutes before. Soon, the deafening, thunderous shots of the big anti air-craft guns from different positions began firing up from the grounds; and along with that, we could also hear the roaring of the planes swooping down for their bombing targets on different spots. For some minutes, the deafening sounds of the guns firing up, and the explosion of the bombs anywhere along with the noise of the fighter planes in action, rented the sky. We could not make out which of the deafening sounds were from bombs exploded on the grounds or from cannon balls exploded in the air from the anti-aircraft guns. People in fear and frantic rushed into pits, ditches and ponds, wherever they could find at the moment. The impact of the Japanese bombing from their planes on that day was so fearful and powerful that it would remain ever remembered by anybody who had personally involved or engulfed in it. The moments made all think as if they were all dead and killed by the bombing. That was really a fearful occurrence that created a trauma and a nightmare in the daylight for quarter of an hour in the atmosphere.

As for myself, it was while I was just playing and roaming along the western bank of the Iril River at Kanglasifai when the sudden bombardment came to happen quite surprisingly. Hearing the gun shots and the explosion of bombs accompanied with the roaring of the fighter planes above, I was overwhelmed with fear and rushed down hurriedly to the river-bed and hid myself in a sunken part on the side of the bank just near a bamboo groove. I felt breathless and was panting throughout the moments of the bombing that continued for a while and I began to think of my father who had been away to Imphal on that day.

As the planes have gone back, the bombing also ceased and no more shots from the anti-aircraft guns could be heard. The atmosphere was calm again. We could not say if any of the invading planes on that day was or were shot down somewhere in Manipur. The Japanese bombing on that day was said to have directly targeted and dropped bombs along the regions from Kongba Bazar to Chingarel on the Ukhrul road where many of the armies of the allied forces were already encamped. Along the lines of the bombing, many private houses were burnt and damaged, buildings destroyed and pedestrians, carters and a lot of civilians (men and women) were killed or mutilated. Of all the bombings in Manipur so far carried out by the Japanese during the great Second World War, the bombing on the 20th of April, 1943 was the most terrific and the one in which a great majority of innocent civilians was said to have been wounded or killed and victimised and on one side, the bombing caused no killings and damages to British Camps and their armies so far, it was learnt.

After a while, no sooner had the bombing ceased than I ran hurriedly back to the house of my aunty where we had been staying since the outbreak of the war in Manipur. There, I could see my sisters also waiting for the return of my father with anxieties on their faces. Everybody at my aunt's home appeared to be restless with the agony of what might befallen to my father. In that moment, there was no means for any information from the Imphal side where the bombing had just rocked and obviously destroyed everything there. We could also see the column of distant smoke that raised up in the south-western sky. All the while, I was restless to think of my father who had gone to Imphal in that morning. Everybody at the house could not escape the fearful anxiety for the unknown whereabouts of my father. In that melee of grief and anxiety my aunt was heard to utter die words, "Oh God! What could be the fate of my brother? Let him return safe and sound, I pray!! What are all these! Rush to Imphal, anybody of you." She told her sons and suggested it better for them to immediately rush to Imphal and trail the whereabouts of my father. When all the inmates and neighbours were thus flustered and nervous of the unexpected turn of the sad event; we, four children being unable to control the upsurge of emotions began to sob one after another. Somebody consoled us not to weep saying our father would surely return. Some villagers who had been to Imphal in their daily errands, were then coming back, and from them we could hear the news that none of the participants of the feast at Khurai, Chingangbam Mandap could survive the bombing.

Then the saddest news made us unconscious and felt that the world around us was suddenly lost from us. The day was such a day of so much sorrow and sadness that my words failed me to express the agony of it in full. It will only be known to any boy or girl if he or she happens to experience such a stroke of misfortune of parting their parents as it happened so immediately in my life. I did not cry calling my father aloud but I couldn't bear the pangs in me, it was too hard a blow to suffer. I bowed and put my head down to the shawl that my father had used in the morning of that day, and on it I tried to bloat my tears but I couldn't check the flow or it. Being unable to believe myself, I came after a while, to the edge of the pond which was at the backyard of my aunt's compound, and at that spot I remained gazing towards the western direction with such a firm belief of my father's return from the place.

Every second, I scanned the images of those persons appearing out in the distance from the bend of the small hillock called Laiching. At this time, some of our sympathisers had rushed to Imphal for accurate information of our father. Every moment the vision of persons who were returning towards the village on their bicycle made me to utter these words in my mind "Oh, would that be my father!" Now it became evening, the colour of the atmosphere was fading. There was no more sight of any person coming back past the bend of the small hillock; and my father had never returned. I stood up and looked at the distant sky that seemed to be above the Imphal plain. I couldn't check the tears that rolled down from my eyes. I, started sobbing bitterly in that stilly hours and nothing else could console me. Now most of those people who had rushed to Imphal were returning home, and from some of them, we could gather the news that from the bombing site, the wounded victims of the accident were learnt to have been carried away somewhere in military vehicles, and the civilian relatives were not permitted to accompany the wounded ones. At this, the few sympathisers standing around us were of the opinion that our father too would certainly have been included among those who were transported elsewhere, possibly to a military hospital. In my heart, I prayed that God might save my father. Soon after this, the two sons of my aunt were also returning from the bombing site in Imphal with the clear news of the bombing that had fatally dropped just on the top of the mandap killing most of the people participating the feast under that Mandap. It was also clear that not a single civilian relative of the wounded victims was allowed to enter the spot while the victims were to be carried off in military ambulance.

Almost all the people gathered at the house of our aunt shared our grief and they too felt moved and cried as we were doing helplessly. It was an ordeal of a fateful day, and the saddest one of all days in my childhood. We felt it as if it was a sorrowful dream and we couldn't bear the sudden and unexpected blow of fate on the lot of my father and us. We remained crying and crying as we were consoled by some of those elderly people in the house. Night came and unknowingly the goddess of sleep seemed to embrace us. We fell asleep and forgot the event for a time till we awoke again in the morning of the following day.

In the early morning, the Tajou (the big brother like person of ours) who had been staying for some days looking after our homestead in Imphal, arrived at our place with a bundle of the clothes that our father had worn on the previous day when he went to participate the feast in Imphal. At the sight of those clothes, 'shirt and *dhoti* etc. fully smeared with blood all over them, we burst in tears and cried again inconsolably. Our Tajou gave us the news that our father got seriously wounded in the bombing and he was subsequently transported with the wounded ones to the military hospital at Sanjenthong where my father too was lying under medical care and nursing. But it was unfortunate, in the early morning of the next day, when Tajou with some men went to the hospital, they could not see my father in the hospital bed rather they could only find out that my father had indeed breathed his last in that previous night.

Our Tajou detailed the sufferings and the plight of our father when he first found him rolling on the ground. On seeing Tajou, our father was said to have told him about us in brief "those children". All these were narrated with tears in his eyes. He further said that before the bombing, when our father was coming on his bicycle past our gate in Imphal, he called out to Tajou from the road asking if they had had their day's meal, also informing that he too was going to join a feast at Chingangbam Mandap. It was from this previous knowledge that after the bombing was ceased, our Tajou hurried to the Chingangbam Mandap where by the side of a ditch and close to the Mandap destroyed by the Bomb, he could see my father rolling and sighing in a pool of blood. He also said that our father could still speak to see him but soon all the wounded ones were being lifted up in military ambulance and then were carried away to somewhere. At the moment when our Tajou was about to accompany my father while he was being lifted up, he (Tajou) was not permitted, we were told. The only words that my father reminded him were "Go, those my children", he said.

In the early morning of the next day, my eldest sister took the blood stained clothes of my father to the river and washed them. While she was washing the clothes in the running stream of water with tears in her eyes, I, by this time, remained sitting near the edge of the stream and saw the flowing down of the bloods from the clothes of my father. To me it was unbearable to see the blood washed out from the clothes and its flowing down the stream mixing with the bluish water of the Iril River. I couldn't check my tears and wept bitterly sitting on the bank of the river. So we parted our father when the Great Second World War was in progress taking its terrific turn of ravaging the north-eastern regions of India. War had thus made me an orphan.

One Afternoon of the First Landing of Fighter Planes at Kangla Airfield

One afternoon, in the month of September/October 1943 there came a line of a very swift and red-tipped fighter planes known as Spitfires flying in the sky from the southern direction of Manipur, presumably from Burma. Seeing the strange sight of the planes, I, with my friends rushed out to the open and remained gazing at them intently with excitement. The planes that came flying in a line were at last making a round for a time apparently to observe the air-strip and the places of the surroundings. How soon we liked them to land on the newly made air-strip at Kangla and how curious we were of seeing them on the ground, particularly those men (pilots) who would be inside as drivers. After making rounds three or four times above the surrounding areas of the newly constructed air-strip, we could see wheels sliding down from the planes. We were sure that the planes were landing soon.

With a thrilling experience we rushed up to the place nearing the border of the air-strip and stood, all in a group with our palms in front of our foreheads shading our eyes and waiting to catch a clear sight of those planes lowering from the northern sky for their first touchdown on the strip. It was surprising to see the size of the planes that they looked to be just a foot long when they were flying above but how big they were when we saw them on the ground. Now, all the planes were parked for a time in the available spaces of the southern end of the air-strip. The actual size of the fighter planes may be about twenty feet in length and the two wings of about thirteen feet on both sides. The planes were of smoke colour with a propeller in the pointed front, and the pilot's seat was just in the middle of the two wings and covered with a movable glasshood. There are neatly painted round marks just below the wings and on the sides of the planes. How thrilled we were to see the fighter planes stationary on the ground just a few yards away from us.

Some of us wanted to go closer to them, and look at the aircrafts well, but we couldn't, as we were afraid of the unexpected strange situation. So we remained gazing at them from a little distance. Pushing back the window-like hood that covered the seats of the pilot, there came out the English men from inside those planes, and they bore a fearful look to see at first. The oxygen mask on their heads, made their heads look like the trunks of young elephants; and when they removed it from their heads, it was revealed to us that they were the white and tall English people with red hairs. Getting out from inside their planes, they were making a mental survey of the surrounding places of the air-strip on which they were just flying down. As they were looking around, they caught a view of us suddenly, and for a moment, they seemingly fixed their attention to us. We, being afraid, were about to run back and stepped a little backward. One from amongst them called out to us saying— "Ye, Chacko—Chacko ...!" Soon afterwards, we came to understand that we boys were addressed by them as Chacko. Being aware of own fright, the pilots smiled at us saying—"Come on-Come on."

Stepping a few steps forward and stepping a little backward again, we were closing at them. By this time, the pilots in a group, went on talking heartily on something we couldn't understand. Then, someone from the group told us to sit down in a line and as we were doing so, he took out chewing gums from his pocket and went on distributing it to each of us. But as we did not know at first what a chewing gum was, we remained looking at them only holding the chewing gums in our hands. In that moment, another one from the group took out the same from his pocket and showing it to us he tore the wrapper and threw it inside his mouth and chewed. Then we also did likewise and tasted the flavour of chewing gum for the first time in our childhood.

The pilots wore black jackets and trousers of soft leather. The cap or the oxygen mask they were putting on was also black. On the shoulders and breasts of their shirts, a badge of a flying bird was beautifully knitted with the insignia R.A.F. below it. They looked to be very smart and strong indeed. It is to those people that we remained looking at for a short while with a mixed feeling of happiness and fears. They knew, we were afraid of them, and to dispel the fright from our minds, they made their look and demeanour to be very friendly. Then, one of those pilots made a query by pointing his finger to each of us one by one, and went on asking "Can you speak English? Can you speak English?" 1 knew what he was asking. Ah! How I liked to answer his question! I had to wait my turn with a little trembling.

Now, on such a rare occurrence as seeing the planes and the pilots for the first time in our lives, a mention may be made regarding the difference of ideas between my friends and me. The other boys (friends) I was accompanying with, were not school going ones, and they had not yet learnt what ABC is. So, on that day, theirs was to enjoy the sights of the occurrence only, but mine was the eagerness to communicate anyhow with those pilots on certain things for the day with nervous excitement as well as to enjoy the sight and the short company with them, so that an everlasting memory may be impressed in the mind. Here, the very incident made me to remember what my father had told me once when I requested him to let me know a short answer to be given to any army man on their asking me if I could speak English. At that, my father had told me, "You are to say, Sir, I don't know so much." Now, these words were moving up on my lips as I was waiting for the query from that English pilot. But what to do if he went on asking me many further questions, I felt excited with pleasure and fear; and while I was in the said mood, the pilot moved up to me and smilingly pointing his finger, said "O.K. Can you speak English?" Immediately, the sentence that was already moving on my lips went off from my mouth saying "Sir, I don't know so much." Hearing me saying this English sentence, the pilot was wonderstruck. He looked straight in my eyes, then called out to his friends with surprise and said, "He can speak English."

Instantly they all collected around me and with a surprise, went on asking me several things which 1 could or could not make out. To me, it had been a rare moment of an unexpected experience of a surprising occurrence of pleasure, pride and fear, all mixed up with nervous feelings. The day may rightly be called the first of all days in my boyhood to have acquainted and converse in English with those pilots who came from England. Their jolly mood, friendliness and their fun loving nature had created in me a courage to gather all that wits and knowledge I had, and tried to answer them anyhow. Some of them asked my name and where I was from. Taking out a piece of paper from his pocket, one another pilot asked me to read the words printed on it. To the young pilots, it was a great pleasure to find me, an untidy boy who could speak certain English words and structures quite beyond their belief in such a remote corner of the world and thousands of miles away from their homeland across the seas.

From the next day onwards, many white soldiers and technicians in uniforms were seen arriving from other places to the new air-strip. And as such many, Anglo-Americans, Canadians and others had started pouring in for encampments in the surroundings. In this way, my own pleasurable chances and opportunities of making friends and acquaintances with so many of those white people either from Europe or America had begun to occupy a place in my day-to-day life enabling me to forget my own loneliness of being an orphan. How much I loved them and how much I was loved. Their memory still lingers in my heart and the remembrance of them is only the example of my love and regard for them. Almost all of them were from far-off places of the world, they were all human beings. Who knows who went back to their parents at home or who might have been killed where. Nothing was heard and known of them after. This is the culture of war, this is what War does.

The First Plane Accident before the Eyes

Now, a period of two and half years was elapsed since the great Second World War had its first landing in Manipur. The sky above the regions could not remain in peace even for a single day. All day and night, one could hear the loud nerve racking shots of anti-aircraft cannons producing loud explosions two times up, renting the sky. And along with that, the sounds of aeroplanes flying in all hours were becoming the parts accompanied with our daily life. The noisy flight of aeroplanes of all kinds throughout hours everyday, was not only due to arrivals of British planes from outer regions, rather, it was mainly due to the existence of airstrips that were made with emergence on the plains of Manipur for immediate purposes of the war. There, planes were landing and taking off keeping the airstrips busy for twenty-four hours every day. Planes like Spitfires, Beau fighters, big bombers and lighter planes were, in all times flying up from the strips and went on doing their works, like practicing, patrolling and transporting and other works as their errands, or doing reconnaissance throughout hours everyday. The aerobatics of fighter planes were wonderful to look at from below. Sometimes, they fly up vertically so high until they are not visible from the ground and then dropping downward in a nose dive as if they were about to crash, but suddenly in moments they fly off aside with the wing pointing up. Sometimes, they also roll down from the sky above as if the engine was out of function. But, soon the engine sounded and flew so fast away over the tree tops to reach the mountain side at the distance. It was thrilling to see them doing all that creating miracles before the eyes. So, we young boys had a specially enjoyable time when seeing the grand feats and aerobatics of those fighter planes, and what we admired most were particularly the pilots who were doing all that. Sitting in an open space, we enjoyed the wonderful show of the planes at times without changing our views.

One afternoon, in the middle of summer and autumn, a lone fighter plane, probably a spitfire the fastest of all planes during the war, was practising high up in the sky performing all the skills and aerobatics that the pilot could do with his machine. He dropped down, flew up and whisked aside, put out the engine and restarts in the sky. All these lie did as a wonderful spectacle to the eyes of all. So, as a fish does in the water, while the plane was playing for half an hour in the sky, we could hear a long loud sound up in the sky and along with that, the plane was seen flying down slantwise towards the south eastern direction leaving behind a long line of bluish smoke as it flew down. In a moment the sound of the plane was no longer heard but the line of smoke it just left, remained clear up in the sky as it was drawn by a big coloured pencil downwards. We knew it to be an accident of the plane and shuddered to think as to what might have been the fate of the pilot who drove the plane. Wonder struck, while thus looking up at the line of smoke drawn slantwise towards the horizon of south-eastern sky, we could suddenly see a small ball-like object floating just beneath the line of smoke above. Immediately, we came to know that it was the pilot who had luckily jumped out of the seat of his plane that has just fallen crashed somewhere down.

We gasped and stood looking up, as the ball-like parachute was floating down slantwise towards the site where the plane crashed down. As the parachute was lowering down, the form of a man looking like a tiny doll, could also be seen with the parachute strings above his head. Running and running, we too followed him on the ground keeping our gaze at him upwards. Reaching the eastern side of the river, we cut our way past the fields of Moirangkampu just only to see the pilot's landing on the ground with his parachute. But we couldn't see him as he had already landed there. When we reached the Yaral Lake, we found a throng of army and air force personnel coming in their trucks and jeeps for rescuing their friend. The crashed plane was seen burning by the hillside, whereas the pilot, who just landed nearby, could not be traced out for some time. The Yaral Lake, was a swampy and full of bogs and also covered with reeds and undergrowth of wild plants and shrubs in those days. So the rescue party could not immediately find him out. It was only when the pilot, who was sinking up to his waist in mud, was waiving a red handkerchief to his men, and only then he could be given an instant help by throwing a long rope to him to pull him up. When he came up the road, he was surrounded by his colleagues and comrades showering congratulations upon him.

The Second Accident

The occurrence of the accident was in the year 1944. It was in the month of April or May when the fields were parched and cracked with the heat of summer months with no rain till then. The ill fated plane was seen flying down just from the height of tree tops and cutting over the field northwards only a few feet above the ground in front of me. At the sight, I stood up amazed with a start and was about to run back for fear of the unusual sight and action of the plane. Suddenly, I could realize that something was wrong with the engine of the plane and that was why it was spearheading down towards the air strip on the western side of the river. Apparently, it was his grim attempt to reach the air strip which was about one or two hundred yards away on the western side of the river. Alas! The plane had no time but to strike with its whole impact against an elevated earth bund of the paddy field below. The moment, it struck the place with its frontal portion, the plane was overturned with fumes and flames raising up the sky with an explosion. Villagers of the place were rushing out with large pots and jars of water to put out the burning plane but as they couldn't proceed nearer to the site of the crash, they remained standing with no chance to help, but gazing at the tragic sight of the crash in which the pilot too would have been surely killed. All uttered in their mouths. "Oh, The pilot would be inside the burning!" In a moment, there came a number of British and American airforce personnel and medical group for extending their ready help to the pilot who, if he had luck, could otherwise survive. They also could do nothing, for, the crash of the plane had already been completed minutes ahead of their reaching the place. The time, there was no bridge on the river. So they had to cross the shallow water of the river on foot to reach the other side. Some of them, ran up from their bathing in the river with no shoes on their feet and as such the parched paddy fields handicapped them to tread upon it. They brought a stretcher and with it, some of them made their way nearer to the burning site, and soon we could see them carrying out the pilot on the stretcher covered with a white sheet of cloth.

Now, it was clear that the pilot, knowing the failure of his engine, had apparently made an instant attempt to jump down with his parachute while he was still high up in the sky, and the moment he had loosened off the straps from around his body, the plane suddenly got lowered down uncontrollably arid as his favourable time had so rushed out, he, having no alternative was to be inside the plane till it fatally crashed against an elevated portion of the vast field. The moment when the plane got overturned with a great force the pilot was possibly thrown out and died a few feet away from the burning site of the plane itself. Thus, it was in that unfortunate accident that the life of a young pilot was lost. What a tragic moment it was! Presumably with full of spirit, he had so come out from his far away home to join the air force and with a cherished hope to return home after the war. But the young man, after his coming from his distant home across the seas, was made to lose his life in an accident as this in an unknown place. Surely, the sad end of this young man must have been felt in the breath and pulse of his dear parents at his distant home. Recollecting the incident, still the mind can't help making a guess whether it could be for the young unfortunate pilot that a father from England has made an inscription on a bronze plate in the war cemetery Imphal, with the words as "Your father's mind often travels to this grave far away from Leeds England."

The Third Accident

Another accident which may also be called the third of the kind we had seen was of a big cargo plane, better known as bomber in those periods of the war. It came to happen quite unexpectedly one winter morning. To everybody's belief, the accident was not due to any failure of the engines of the air craft, but a matter of carelessness on the part of the man who piloted it. The morning was cold and foggy and for quite a long time there was no sunshine. The whole atmosphere around, appeared to have been enveloped in misty clouds everywhere. Generally in all times, Cargo planes, like the one I have just mentioned, used to fly to and fro daily between and among the six airstrips ever made in different places on the plains of Manipur. Perhaps they were transporting men, ration or ammunitions, we can't say.

On such a daily or casual errand, the coming of the said Bomber plane was heard in the sky in that winter morning. Maybe it was coming from Changangei, another airstrip in the southern side of Imphal, and it was heading its way for landing at the Kangla Air strip on the north. Usually, in all landings of aeroplanes on the Kangla airstrip, they would surely make a round from the north-eastern sky of this particular region, and then turning on the left, they would begin lowering down and down to land from the northern boundary of the strip. One important feature of the surrounding places of the Kangla Airstrip is the big hill that stands prominently on the near east of the airstrip. So most of the planes bound for landing on this strip were to fly past above the hill or to lower themselves than the hilltop and fly on its side as and when they approached for a normal landing on the airstrip.

In that morning, the top of the hill too could not be visible because of the foggy weather and even the plane when it came flying above our heads, it was not visible. When it was nearing the hill, we thought that the pilot by himself, would surely aware of the rising hill top with the help of die indicators in his cockpit. The location of such a hill or otherwise must have been known to a frequent flier on such a hilly and mountainous regions of Manipur. On the other hand we suppose whether he was a first comer to this airstrip. Straight, as the plane flew against the side of the hill top, or mountain side, a loud bang from chat direction reached our ears. Certainly, the plane has met with an accident as we had doubted for, it was an unseen accident of the bomber plane which had just flown past our heads above. To this accident nobody rushed up to the spot, for it was cold and chilly morning with fogs even up to the hill top, and one could not find out where the probable site of the accident would-be.

When the fog sparred with the light of the sun coming through the clouds, we caught a sight of the ill fated plane at a distance on the mountain side without burning. The bomber plane had just struck against the mountain wall and was rolling down scooping a large quantity of loosened earth as it slid. Usually, in those days, most cargo planes, used to keep their side door wide open while they were flying, and at this particular time too, it was presumed that the few men or the things inside, must have been automatically ejected out from inside the plane at the moment when it collided against the hard mountain side and overturned. As was mentioned above, when the plane was falling down from the mountain ravine, one of its wings too was broken off, and a huge quantity of earth was pushing down in it, the few people if there could be any, were apparently buried without any trace. As for the pilots who were inside the cockpit, would have died the moment when the plane in its flying speed struck against the mountain with a bang. A few days later, some woodcutters of the village who went up the mountainside were said to have seen a lot of potatoes, onions and small tins of milkmaid brand and canned fruits etc. scattered here and there in the woods. For many years after the war had ended, the broken body of the plane could well be seen from a distance as a picture left behind by the ravages of war.

Kanglasifai, the Village During the War

In the narration of this imperfect story, I think it a must to describe something in detail about the location, life and features of the village known as Kanglasifai of which a repeated mention was made in the course of the story. In the beginning of the war, there was a common saying among peoples of Manipur that the safest or the best place of our protection would be at places of any names having the sound of K, in the first syllable of the word. Giving reference to it, most people believed that hiding in a pit (*Kom* in Manipuri), was the right place during an air raid. As the word Kom begins with the letter K, it also became a truth according to *Purana* the sacred book of the Manipuri. But to my own boyish imagination of the time, Kanglasifai the village where we took refuge during the war, has also got the sound of Kin the first syllable of the word, and as such, it was testifying a fact that during the whole course of the war, there had been no damages from bombings in the village. So far as the possible bombing targets from Japanese planes were to be concerned, there were the big aerodrome with planes in all comers and directions all around in particular, and various army camps, artillery stores and all those needed for the war, were installed but nothing like bombings etc. had happened so far and never for a single day did any Japanese plane approach in the air space above.

Kanglasifai, the village in particular, is situated to the north-eastern part of Imphal the Capital of Manipur. It is about nine kilometres away from Imphal proper itself. From Chairenthong, the short bridge on the Imphal-Ukhrul road, we should take a right tum on the inter-village road (Turel Ahanbi) eastward. By this route we come to Angom village on the western side of the Iril River. Then after traversing a short distance near the foothills of a small hillock known as Laiching, we shall again have to follow the path that runs through an expanse of paddy fields to reach the village (Kanglasifai). The first spot where the path or the road touches the village was known as Kyamlei Makhong on the western bank of the Iril River where a ferry service was also flourished for peoples on both sides of the river. But, at present, a modern suspension bridge has been spanned there across the river.

To the north of Kanglasifai, there are villages called Faknung and Sawombung, and on the west of the Kangla airstrip running parallel with the Imphal-Ukhrul Road on the western side. On the east, stands the Chingkhei hill, rather a small portion of a mountain with all its glory. In days of so restless time, it may be mentioned that anything bad had never happened to interrupt the normal ways of life of the village so far. The village had its cultural and religious festivals observed annually as usual and with no hindrance because of the war. Even though, it was a period of the great Second World War, the famous Jatra plays, Nat Sankirtans of renowned artistes of the time, Rasa dance and Gauralilas etc. were not totally lost from the life of this village and those were very often arranged with pomp and grandeur by most elderly people of the place.

The number of households on both sides of the river which flows down southward through this village, may approximately be one hundred and fifty. The habitations along the western bank of the river are known as Sangomsang as per settlement record of the government, whereas the another on the east of the river, as Kanglasifai, but to everybody, both the places here on both sides of the river are known as the same single village 'Kanglasifai' and as Kangla in short. In the real sense of the term, the word Kangla is the name given to the ancient royal citadel of Manipur; and the reason why the particular village came to be known with a rather strange prefix "Kangla" can be traced back to those olden days when Chandrakriti Maharaja was the reigning king of Manipur about three hundred years back. Many soldiers or Sifais who guarded the royal palace of the Maharaja were made to live in this village on the riverside, and henceforth the said place came to be known as Kanglasifai afterwards. Then, Shangomsang the habitation on the west of the river was also said, to have been so named for their supplying milk to the royal kitchen everyday. The word Shangom is milk in Manipuri and Shang is the shed. As the village had a lot of cowshed and produced a large quantity of milk enough to serve the royal homes, the place came to be known as the place of milk sheds which in Manipuri, is the word Shangomshang. The clue to this factual account was collected from aged people of the village. But the two villages, taken as one, the popular accepted name is Kanglasifai or Kangla in short as was mentioned above.

Thus, the name of Kangla will for ever remain unerased from the pages of the history of Second World War, since the Kangla airfield that had been constructed at the backside of this village was found vividly described in 'IMPHAL the celebrated war' story compiled and written after the war by Geoffrey Evans and Anthony Brett James. So, Kangla being the name of an important place during the period of the great Second World War, will ever remain in history even generations after.

30

My 'Japanlan' Memoir after Four Score Years

Irengbam Mohendra Singh

On August 15, 1947, India got Independence. On August 8, 1942 the Quit India movement was launched in Bombay by All India Congress Committee, led by Mahatma Gandhi. But, it was the beat of a distant drum in Manipur, muffled by the sound and fury of World War II or Japanlan. In Manipur in 1942, far removed from the concerns of posterity, the mighty Japanese began their relentless pursuit of a Japanese Empire in Asia. This 75-year old episodic memory of Japanlan with crumbs of British rule in Manipur will be portrayed through the looking-glass of dominant historical approaches in four columns. Manipur, the last place on Earth with its secluded capital Imphal, wedged between Burma and India, and under British suzerainty only for 56 years, was unknown to the world until World War II. In this weird land lived seven clans of Meiteis in the valley, and thirty six tribal communities in the hills, in harmonious coexistence. Rustic Manipur of those days would not have been anywhere near as amazing in another country.

Imphal combined the benefits of a town with the beauty and fresh air of the countryside. The majestic tree lined nine ranges of mountains with their peaks dipping in the white cloud, acted as security barriers for Manipur. During Japanlan, Manipur gloriously stood the test of time against the Nippon Army that ploughed as a whirlwind from far-away Japan. History destined Manipur to be guarded by the Allies rather than by Manipuris. Meitei primitive innocence had a knock on the head when the Japanese Army that tasted victory in Southeast Asia met its Waterloo in Manipur. Japanlan arrived in Manipur on May 10, 1942 with the promise of destruction it was going to wreak. It ended on August 15, 1945 as suddenly as it started, after the Japanese surrendered to the Allies on August 6, 1945. It was a simple matter of Americans dropping two small atom bombs over Hiroshima and Nagasaki.

After the Anglo-Manipuri war of April 27, 1891, ending in a British victory, the beginning had begun for frustrated Meitei alpha males in Imphal town. Illiteracy deprived them of the power of imagination to question the received wisdom of the time. They became *laissez-faire* without a calling. Not because they were lazy, but most of them were unemployed as there were no suitable jobs for them. Egotistical Meitei men shunned blue-collar works. Meitei women became breadwinners for the family as beta females. The dysfunctional monarchy had no powers to call up able-bodied men for customary unpaid annual royal service (in lieu of taxes) or enlist them up for soldiering in wars with neighbouring Naga Hills and Lushai Hills, as well as with Awa, Ahoms, Casaries, Tripuris and the British. So they indulged their free time in leisure generated by their indigenous sports and gambling like dog-fighting.

The villagers were occupied with and contentedly subsisted from their farming. Meiteis were functionally literate because of their Hindu philosophy. They enjoyed Hindu myths and their indigenous culture as stairways to Heaven, while keeping the British as their guard dogs, paying an annual tribute of Rs. 50,000. Meiteis had not felt being ruled by the British as they had not been interfered with in their daily living. The British presence was minimum. Just before World War II as far I knew, there were only 5 or 6 Sahibs, who were hardly seen except when they came out to play polo at the Mapal Kangjeibung on Sunday afternoons in winter, sometimes with memsahibs.

The great turning point of World War II in Asia began in Manipur on May 10, 1942 when the Japanese first dropped their bombs over Imphal and were routed in late 1945, when all the remnants of the Allies Army left Imphal. This account is based on a penumbra of my memories as a young boy, and what I heard from my father. It will thus be less than a theatre of images as it is a formulation of less than the requirement for a textual score, without its precision and normative. It is also punctuated with some satire as it cannot be written without some digress and at the risk of being jejune.

As Manipuris had always appreciated British fairness in administration, there had been shortages of antipathy to them unlike to Meitei kings, who, living in Manipur that time forgot, became despotic. Freed from lethal insecurity of their throne and strategically inhibited from the suffering of their poor peasants they heaved upon them burdens of unjust taxes to replenish royal coiffeurs, with Brahma Sabha as cheerleaders. The oft-written Chandon shelkhaiba, i.e. taxation for putting chandon (Vaishnavite sect mark) on their foreheads attracted vitriol from the four corners of Imphal valley. Levy of Mangba-Sengba tax, i.e. 'pollution tax' caused extreme misery to impecunious Meitei men, whose family would be expelled from participation in the community until the individuals were purified, shengdokba (clean) by Brahma Sabha, on payment of a sum of money that the people could ill-afford. My father was maliciously picked as a victim when his 3-year old son died at a time when he needed his community.

Manipuris remained loyal to the British during the war. They admired the Japanese for their cleverness and bravery, but did not like them because every item they manufactured and brought to Imphal like bicycles and fountain pens were very cheap but third class in quality. A fountain pen I had for five paisa, would always leak staining my fingers. When the Japanese planes dropped the first bombs over Imphal, one midmorning of Sunday, May 10, 1942, I was walking back home from Khwairamband keithel (bazaar) about 4 minutes' walk from the Maharani thong bridge across the Naga River that connects Uripok Road. I went there to buy raspberries on a Khongnangmana (papal leaf) for a half a paisa.

Rows of tin-roofed Ima Keithel (women's market) of Khwairamband Keithel were on the far side of the bridge with a large stone statue of Keithel Lairembi (Market goddess) facing north. At its northern was the fish market next to Pangal market selling eggs, chicken and ducks. Between Ima Keithel and Majorkhul was a tiny Hao Keithel for hill dwellers.

Khwairamband Keithel was divided into two blocks by a road running from the west gate of Kangla, joining Uripok Road to Kangchup Hill, where the water refinery tank was located. Sadar Bazaar in the north was separated from Johnston High School on its eastside by a high brick wall. To the east of the school was the Civil Hospital. The south block was Maxwell Bazaar, the present choke-a-block Paona Bazaar. There were three cinema halls, one at Sadar and two at Maxwell. There was a tiny-winy mosque by the Nambul River, opposite Wahengbam Leikai, but without 'Allahu-Akbar' evening muezzin calls. As I walked home I heard a big bang as the bomb crashed upon the bazaar full of people or, the cantonment at Kangla Fort in the British Reserve. As a child I was non-plussed.

At the cantonment was stationed the 4th Assam Rifles Battalion of 600 soldiers, mainly Gurkhas with a leavening of a handful of Khongjai, Tangkhul and Lushai. My father took me there once to see *Bali* (animal sacrifice) on the day of Dashera when the priest of the Kalimai Temple at the Cantonment would slaughter buffaloes and goats. The battalion was to fly the British flag and to discipline any Manipuri tribal uprising, such as the Jadonang/Gaidinliu Revolt or the Kuki Rebellion.

After half a century's association with these very disciplined Gurkhas, Meitei town's people became quite homely with them. No Meitei would be recruited in the battalion as the British did not trust them. It had units stationed at Churachandpur, Tamenglong and Ukhrul. Showing British authority, when the replaced detachment from Tamenglong came marching down Uripok Road from Kangchup to a light infantry quick step, it was led by their Band playing a marching song.

The entire population of Uripok would rush out to the road to see the 'pageant'. The band was uniformed exactly as the present Assam Rifles Band that entertains spectators at the Manipur International Polo Tournaments. In tiny Manipur everything was produced. It had no beggars and no homeless people like those in Mumbai, London or New York. None died of starvation. During World War II there was no famine in Manipur as was in Calcutta.

The popular phrase Manipur Sana leibak (golden land) is a key to unlatch and lift the lid on Manipuris' fortitude to go through tragedies and triumphs and still survive. The "Battle of Imphal", I learnt later, was actually the fighting in the regions surrounding the present city of Imphal, especially for four months in 1944.

It began in May after the Japanese launched several air attacks on Bishnupur village. From August it took place along the dozen miles of the Old Cachar Road between Bishnupur and onetime suspension bridge over the Leimatak River. During the next two months, Potsangbam and Ningthoukhong were the scenes of ferocious battles. The brave Japanese were only 16 km from Imphal. General Slim commented: "Whatever one may think of the military wisdom of thus pursuing a hopeless object, there can be no question of the supreme courage and hardihood of the Japanese soldiers who made the attempts. I know of no army that could have equalled them."

Before I begin this write-up, I would like to express my tender emotions like poetry drawn from the prose, to see online, the images of Krishna Janma celebration at Mahabali on August 15 this year, as I remember going there as a little boy just before World War II. Equally touching is the group photograph of North American Manipuri Association Convention 2017, US, with 200 membership of Manipuri diasporas, including one from my school days. As I recall I was one of the first three Manipuris who have ever settled in the West.

I've just dusted through my brain and got rid of all the gauzy cobwebs. I can remember that fateful day of May 10, 1942, though not as clearly as a cube of sunshine, when the town's people of Imphal were jolted with intermittent, as yet unimaginable, sounds of bombs exploding over the town centre. The chilling truth flashed across their mind that the Japanlan had indeed arrived after all. Having switched off the chatter of everyday talk of the coming war, most people fled their homes as news quickly spread from words of mouth that, it was indeed Japanese bombs.

Manipuris remained uneducated even in their own vernacular. Yet the last English-educated Meitei rulers preferred to keep the masses uneducated, as if wanting them to cultivate wisdom out of ignorance, like extracting blood out of stone. The British were uninterested. Only James Johnston started a school to teach Manipuris enough English to work as their pen pushers. So Manipuris had never seen an aeroplane before, nor had an idea of what it looked like.

When the Japanese reconnaissance planes were flying silently in the azure Imphal firmament for a few days before the bombing, people didn't know they were aeroplanes. Sirens from the British Cantonment in the ancient Manipur capital of Kangla, were whining. But everybody thought they were practice runs. There was no way of knowing that the Japanese were round the corner as Imphal had no daily newspapers, radio, or telephone to contact with the outside world except by telegram from the infamous Telegraph Office of Nupilan-2 connection.

My father was quite friendly with Christopher Gimson, the Political Agent (Boro Sahib) from 1933 till the end of the war in 1945. After he went back to England I called at his house in Leicester with my girlfriend Margaret in 1967. My father knew about the sirens.

On a hilltop in south of Imphal, a section of 4th Assam Rifles was stationed to watch the sky during the day, with orders that as soon as they saw or heard an aircraft, they were to heliograph a message to headquarters at Kangla, whereupon a siren would be sounded from the top of a metal pole. In the good old days the siren was sounded everyday exactly at 12-noon from this contraption near the west gate. Imphal dwellers then knew it was *numit yungba*.

As I walked home, our Uripok Road was weirdly quiet. In our house my father, cool as a cucumber, was directing everybody to pack bags and bundles with essential goods that each person could carry. We left the house after locking it up in a couple of hours and walked up the Uripok Road towards Kangchup for our new life in the village. The Road was jostled by men, women and children, fleeing the town in all directions to outlying villages for safety.

Imphal in those days had no automobiles. The rich had pedal bikes like Raleigh's and Humbers. Most transport from outlying villages to Imphal was by bullock carts grinding the dusty main roads especially in winter, bringing paddy in gunny bags. Some inter-Leikai (between dwelling blocks) lanes were knee-deep in mud during the rainy season. Shoes were non-rainy season accessories. There were only 3-4 lorries that I saw plying.

There was a government red-painted truck Dakgari that carried post to and back from the 'Imphal Railway station' at Dimapur, the metre-gauge single track Railhead in Assam. Another passenger bus called Moiranggari with galvanised metal sheet body, was parked by the Nambul River near Wahengbam Leikai. It carried passengers from Khwairamband Bazaar to Nambol, Bishnupur and Moirang.

King Bodhchandra had a small black car. During the War in 1944, he succeeded his father Churachand who lived at the new palace that was built for boy Raja Chandrakriti on November 4, 1910, on time for his return from Mayo College in Ajmer. It was designed by a British architect in a pseudo-Rajput style; probably because Manipuri rajas were Hindus with Rajput surnames as Singh and their wives, Devi. Bodhchandra stayed put in Imphal during the war and was appreciated by the British Army that took control of Manipur's administration.

The palace had a carriageway from the north main gate into its low brick-walled compound. It was neatly surfaced by crushed red brick chips with a couple of small fountains with sprinklers by its sides. The tiny Durbar Hall was located in the west near the gate. The main building was painted off-white. I've been inside the palace compound once before the war with my sister-in-law Ibemhal when she went to sing for Jalakheli (water sport) festival at the Govindaji mandab, and a couple of times inside the building after the war, through the good offices of a couple of young Ranis.

The palace gate was guarded by armed Meitei police known as State Military Police (SMP) garrisoned at the present 1st Manipur Rifles Cantonment, armed with downgraded 303 rifles with their magazines taken out and sealed. I remember two well-known havildars promoted to jamandars in the new 1st Manipur Rifles. The battalion was formed by Captain Priyobarta as Chief Minister of Independent Manipur (1949) after recruiting Gurkhas from Shillong.

I knew Captain M.K. Priyobrata, and his younger brother M.K. Joy—a dashing Army Captain. Both brothers volunteered to join the Indian Army to fight for Britain during the war. They were our pride and joy. I also knew their younger sister, one and the only one, Princess M.K. Binodini. I saw her last as she came to give her condolence to my father when my mother Mani Devi died. The Palace, one of the very few Meitei historical edifices, had not been improved after the war.

When my wife Margaret, son Neil and I went to meet the regal-looking titular king Leishemba Sanajaoba a few years ago, it was shamefully dilapidated as the succeeding Ibobi Congress Government took no interest. In 1942, the British administration had been warning Imphalites about the Japanese bombing with slit trenches dug up in the bazaar area and along the main roads like Uripok and Sagolband. Householders were told to dig up such bomb shelters. We had one in our garden.

My father Irengbam Gulamjat Singh was a civil engineer, qualified from Dacca. Later, he was sent by the Administration for training in Electric Engineering to Shillong. He was running the Electrical Department of Manipur after the State British Civil Engineer C.F. Jeffrey, with no experience of Electrical Engineering, left to retire in Australia. He was running the hydro electric powerhouse, which he and Jeffrey built at Sanahal Lokchao.

Jeffery built a nice bungalow for himself by the Indo-Burma (IB) Road, near the PWD office that was situated near the present Hotel Classic. The site of the powerhouse was scenically very beautiful, a bit like the Lauterbrunnen Fall, Bern in Switzerland (Sangam film starring Raj Kapoor and Vijayanthimala) with a waterfall and diaphanous water of Leimakhong River meandering down with its booming flow sound, as the running water hit or rolled large boulders and rocks along the river bed. It was full of trout fish (Sana Nga). The whole setup of the powerhouse existed until the early 1970s when it was completely destroyed by a landslide.

My father kept the powerhouse running during the war and after. As Chief Electrical Engineer, he constructed his post-war office Near Keisampat, now opposite the Manipur State Archives Complex. My orthodox father wouldn't dine with beef-eating Sahibs but would eat biscuits with a cup of tea. Jeffery respected his orthodoxy to the extent that when I was going out with Margaret, now my wife, he, having been informed by Gimson, wrote to a friend of my father in Imphal, about the possible disaster of my marrying an English girl.

Gimson had told my father about the imminent arrival of the Japanese to Manipur. So he had made arrangements for us to flee Imphal the same day as the bombing, and stay with a family in the village of Senjam-Chirang near Koutruk, the site for Manipur Sports University. It's about 19 km from Sanahal Lokchao through Khurukhul village. My father had already hired a lorry that was owned by the Kangabam family in our neighbourhood, to take us to the village in the afternoon. But as the bombs exploded over Imphal at noon, we fled on foot. I vaguely remember that day. I was told, as I could not walk far I had a piggy-ride on the backs of my two sister-in-laws. The village was about 25 km from our house. But it took an eternity.

The evening was closing in by the time we arrived in the village. We settled in our prearranged dwelling place, which my father had rented and converted as our family home with adequate lighting with kerosene lanterns. The next morning, my two brothers cycled to Imphal to see that our home was not looted. My father went to see Gimson, who told him that almost everybody had left Imphal except some looters in the bazaar area. Assam rifles Gurkhas were posted. All Marwari merchants had also left on foot along with a large number of refugees from Burma, who had been staying at makeshift accommodations at Koirengei in north Imphal, where the military later built the first aerodrome.

The apocalyptic modernity of World War II made Imphal town look like the Hollywood ghost town in Santa Fe in the Old Wild West. After the second bombing over Imphal on May 16, 1942, six days after the first, Gimson told my father during one of his visits that, a few bombs fell on his Residency compound. One demolished the main jail gate. Many prisoners escaped. Thousands more of the refugees, mostly Indians including Helen of Bollywood, and a handful of Europeans, who had tracked along the old trodden path over the mountains from Tamu in Burma to Moreh in Manipur, and been staying at Koirengei, had left on foot for Assam.

This tortuous mountain path was later made a two-lane tarmac road in 1942 by the British Army, on time for evacuation of retreating British troops from Burma. It was named Indo-Burma (IB) Road.

Gimson told my father that all the policemen had deserted. He made a request for two Burma Police officers to come and organise policing at Imphal. His liveried servants had also fled home to Assam. He gave my father a twisted metal shrapnel that made a hole in his gramophone inside his bungalow.

Before Japanlan one could see Gimson's Residency compound (now Raj Bhavan) while walking past the two front gates, open day and night without guards, like the gates of Heaven. Imphal was the safest place to live in India. One could see the beautiful drive (Gimson had no car), surfaced with red crushed brick chips, neatly lined on each side by manicured green lawns. A solitary brick building, the Treasury, stood next to the northern gate (to keep government money). It was guarded by a lone Gurkha sentry.

It was exciting when I first went inside the Residency compound with its vibrant English garden flowers, just before Independence in 1947. The late Moirangthem Gojendra, father of Shantikumar, and I went to see the last political agent Mr. Pearson (he had a car) to seek theatre tickets when the British Shakespearena Theatre Company came to Imphal and performed at the Manipur Dramatic Union Hall at Yaiskul.

I chanced to see the interior of the Residency Bungalow when I went as a doctor to attend to Chief Commissioner Baleswar Prasad in 1963 or 1964. Another smaller bungalow had been built for the President of the Manipur State Durbar (PMSD) or Chhota Sahib, the second highest administrative officer, usually young ICS Britons. This residence has, since Independence, been occupied by succeeding Chief Ministers of Manipur. I've been inside it for some time during its occupation by Mairenbam Koireng, the first Chief Minister.

Flashed back, our village was peaceful with a crystal clear shallow stream running on a bed of pebbles, right through the middle of it. Though the hosts in the village were very welcoming, tension gripped the refugees in the way storm clouds gather when there's going to be rain. It exploded in a month, not from Japanese bombs, but from malarial parasites. Three or four people were cremated everyday by the riverbank. Our family including me survived as my father knew about malaria and procured the bitter liquid quinine. As a boy I thought I wouldn't survive to be an adult.

A year later, my second brother Yaima took me to Imphal on a bicycle to watch a Tarzan film with Johnny Weissmuller at MNB Cinema hall in the town centre, which became operational for soldiers. The town centre was deserted with most buildings in ruins. A few Meitei traders under temporary shades at Maxwell Bazaar, the present Paona Bazaar, were vending vegetables, fish and other knick-knacks to various multiethnic soldiers: brown, black and white.

In our village, Indian army foot patrols and Gurkhas in armoured cars, reminded us of the war. Outside the village, at a grazing field, there was a small British radar station with the personnel wearing British Air Force Khaki uniforms. The village boys would make bamboo beds for them to sleep in their tents. We would take them in exchange for nice things to eat, communicating in broken English. There were intermittent firing practices of big guns from a location between our and Khurukhul village, aiming towards Ingourok Hill in west Imphal valley, south of Leimakhong, 20 km from Kangla.

At the foothills of Leimakhong there was a large military establishment in 1943-44, between the Leimakhong River and the present headquarters of 57 Mountain Division. There, one day I saw a Pathan soldier with long cropped hair at the back, stabbing an English Captain to death in front of everybody.

Hear about the present-day (2017) Number 183 [Indian] Military hospital at Leimakhong, there was in 1943-45, Number 41 Indian General Hospital with Australian nurses of Queen Alexandra's Imperial Military Nursing Service. This large base hospital was separated into two by a slip road for ambulance cars, running from north to south from the uphill main road to the power house.

The smaller one on the west side was for white soldiers and the bigger one in the east for non-white soldiers. It was a very big hospital complex with European doctors attending to the wounded or ill soldiers evacuated from the frontline. There was an enormous canteen. My father used to take me there to buy chocolate and canned food stuffs, such as garden peas, pears, condensed or evaporated milk and Kraft-K cheese.

I often went to the powerhouse with my father on his bicycle, and stayed for a few days at a time at his little bungalow. It was quite an excitement. The powerhouse was guarded by a small unit from the 4th Assam Rifles, who used to give me a *paratha* every morning for breakfast.

The back-end of year-1942 was lucrative for many Meiteis as labourers and *thikadars* (contractors). General Slim was widening the IB Road for transporting troops and equipment to Moreh from Dimapur. He was among the first batch of British soldiers that walked haggard and jiggered all the way from Tamu to Imphal *via* Moreh.

The War gave unemployed Meiteis work in road-building with so much inflated money to finance the war, something that had never been seen before. Most women were glittered with gold. Meitei *thikadars* from our village and adjoining villages made pots of money from contracting for road-building, involving tedious carving of the hills of a small stretch of the IB Road passing the hilly Feidinga area where now, DGI Memi's 'The Great Escape' garden is situated. The *thikadars* lavished money like dirt. Hilarity prevailed over their lack of prudence. Those *thikadars*, rendered comic by their own travesty, became targets of comedians like Khutamacha, who appeared in a *shumanglila* (outdoor drama) with a heist of comedies. He made the second ever long-playing vinyl record from Gauhati studio, in which he sang a hilarious song with the lyrics: *thikadar Meitei macha apumbasinkamgitennapalladu na mamaida maihing kare* (all these Meitei contractors are now having melasma—dark irregular skin patches on their faces, as they are now hit by the arrow of income tax).

The entire IB Road stretched 320 km from the Dimapur railhead in Assam to Moreh town in Manipur at the Burma border, running right through the centre of Imphal through Thoubal to Palel, 30 km from Imphal, where during the war the Allies built another airfield, and where the only known battle involving Netaji Subhas Chandra Bose's Indian National Army (INA) took place during the night of May 2, 1944. Only a few Gurkhas guarding the airfield beat them back with over 200 casualties. By May 4 they withdrew to Khanjol, their base.

General Slim conducted the war with his Allies troops battling the Japanese around Imphal and in Kohima, as well as in the Burma Campaign, from a bungalow at Kangla, which is now preserved as "Slim's Cottage". Luckily, when my wife Margaret, son Neil and I were invited by the MHRPA to the 10th International Polo Tournament in Imphal in 2016, I was taken one day, along with foreign polo players for a tour of Kangla, including the Slim Cottage, guided by Suranjan Lairenjam and Nanjest Thongjam.

The war was excitement for Meiteis who didn't take part in it. We were suddenly thrown in a cauldron containing all human races. The population shift from Imphal town to the periphery brought out thriving markets, such as Lamshang bazaar on Kangchup Road, providing various commodities for neighbouring villages. Meiteis in the villages, continued to enjoy the old slew of pastimes, such as *Laiharaoba, khubakishei*, circus and magic shows, oblivious of the raging war.

One educated Meitei girl Chandrakala from Lairikyengbam Leikai became famous for singing Meitei "opera song" at *Ras Lila*: Gauriya Vaishnav classical musical. She and other girls gave a stunning performance at one organised by my father at our village in the winter of 1944.

The venue was lit up with electric lamps from a generator by his electricians. Four or five Gurkhas from the unit guarding his Power House, acted as security guards. My little sister Rupobati, probably played a *Gopi* (cowgirl) and her cousin sister Nungshi played Radha. The first Manipuri vinyl record was made by Chandrakala. I am very glad that, she in her 90s, is still active and healthy by the time I am writing this memoir.

After the Japanese gave "Britannia ruled the waves" a nasty shock in Southeast Asia with their lightening attacks, they sneaked through the jungles of Burma, infested with malaria, cholera and dysentery, right to the outskirts of Imphal. Imphal thus became the nerve centre of the British Commonwealth soldiers fighting the Japanese simultaneously at Imphal and Kohima fronts. It was as if the whole universe was connected with Imphal in a state of gibbering excitement.

Japanlan was the greatest discovery of the world for Manipuris without having to travel since the earth's formation 4.5 billion years ago. Manipuris were lucky to be part of the pioneering British generation furthering the experimental method of jungle warfare that was not in the old war game books.

The history of the Japanese cutting off the 4th Corps of the British Army in Manipur from the rest of the world in early 1944, is a gripping tale of their courage and endurance. Imphal became a warzone with crumbling buildings, rubbish heaps and all kinds of military trucks packed with soldiers passing through it *en route* to other parts of Manipur, and to the Burma border.

In mid-1944, young American transport pilots flying their Dakotas to Imphal Koirengei and Tulihal airfields to bring military men, equipment and supplies, brought some glamour to the war. Their easygoing character, smart dress in light Khaki poplin trousers without pleats, matching shirts and matching cotton belts, with a fag of lucky Strike dangling from one corner of their mouth or chewing gum, wearing aviator RayBan glasses and driving their jeeps, made a quick impression on young Manipuris as they did everywhere.

At the backend of 1944, my eldest brother Gokulchandra, a civil engineer, had to come and live in Imphal as the State Public Works Department (PWD) began to function again. As our home was occupied by the military my brother had to stay with a Brahmin family at Bamon Leikai. He brought me to go to school. This is where I met the late R.K. Maipaksana, father of R.K. Dilip, as my private tutor.

Schools were open in 1944 as most people had returned to Imphal and people from outer Imphal did not flee at all. Singjamei and Kongba Bazaars took the place of Khwairamband Bazaar that was still deserted. The only private Bengali School for children of Bengalis living at Babupara was vacant as they had gone back to Bengal. It continued to serve as a big military canteen where we used to buy novelties.

I went to a middle school at Moirangkhom hillock that had seen the worst side of the war. In the school we had bamboo benches to sit on. Teachers used the backside of wooden windows that were painted black for the war, as blackboards. The teachers were very good though. They helped me to qualify with a merit scholarship in 1946 for Johnstone High School in the old building. R.K. Dorendra Singh, ex-Chief Minister of Manipur and Dr. Elangbam Kuladhaja Singh, ex-Principal of RIMS, were my class fellows. Churachand High School was open. Tombisana High School was bombed out.

In 1945, we boys from Bamon Leikai used to walk to the war-torn town centre to see children's films like Hunter Wali and Passing Shaw. It had a few Indian military policemen patrolling on foot, perhaps to keep an eye on the remaining Indian troops in the bazaar area. Curiously their revolver holsters had no guns inside.

Japanlan ended elsewhere on August 15, 1945. Manipur was still a battlefield with pockets of Indian sapper units still left after the British and most of the Indian and Gurkha troops had been evacuated. Many Meitei families from the centre of Imphal could not still return as their houses like ours, were occupied by the remnants of the unarmed Indian army.

When our family did return home in the beginning of 1946, there was a Muslim unit in the homesteads near the main Uripok road. I used to go to brush my teeth at the old toti (drinking water stand pipe) by the road every morning at seven O'clock. When I came back I would go past their langer (Urdu, kitchen) hoping that the cooks would give me a *paratha*, which they did.

Following the war, boys in Imphal including me, began to feel the impact of the war, especially of the Americans, in dress and manner. Young Meiteis, who were innately mechanical and quick to learn, soon reassembled many trucks, jeeps and motorbikes that, by 1947 Imphal was full of them. My eldest brother had a jeep with which I learnt to drive.

The war bewitched the Meitei nation. The immediate post-war Imphal was the equivalent of peeling onions, removing the unpalatable coverings, unearthing the generations of hopes and regrets. Its tranquil surface belied soul-swelling depths. Literary biopic paterfamilias began to riposte to common social and cultural topics.

There was a natural movement towards modifying traditional beliefs in accordance with modern ideas and deliberate rejection of the styles of the past, such as an increasing adoption of wearing trousers instead of pheijom (*dhoti*) and a change in unmarried girls' Mangka-style haircut to the universal. There was liberalism and relaxation in religious orthodoxy, such as allowing Muslims and tribal people in Brahmin-run restaurants and Meitei homes.

Even my father had done away with the pre-war orthodoxy of his conventional creed. He cordially accepted my English wife Margaret as his daughter-in-law. Because of the war and his liberalism I've become an agnostic as have my daughter Anita, my son Neil, and my wife Margaret.

Before the war, mostly Bengali films were screened in Imphal cinema halls, as Meiteis were fluent in Bengali because it was the medium of instruction in schools. Odd Hindi films were also shown like Bandhan starring Ashok Kumar and Lila Chitnis, which I went to see with my brother. From 1944 onwards, no Bengali film was shown because of Hindi/Urdu speaking soldiers. By 1945 many Meiteis including me, had a working knowledge of Hindi because of the war, to enjoy Hindi films. From 1946 Cinema halls screened Hollywood films. I saw Romeo and Juliet with Norma Shearer at the MNB Cinema Hall.

Exposure to Hindi and English films helped Manipuris to develop an ebbing consciousness that the world is vast with different races, religions, politics and cultures. Manipuris have experienced the exceptional, which wouldn't have happened without Japanlan.

The post-war period seemed to promise greater equality and diversity among the Manipuri people. It was a time of enormous social and economic upheaval. Education began in earnest in 1944 with the opening of various high schools. There was an engagement and a willingness among parents to fight for their children's higher education. They began to embrace richness and complexities of life.

The educated Manipuris saw a new dawn of modernity and began to harbour a neo-political frame of mind. The resurgence of Imphal began in 1946 with the reconstruction of Imphal town centre. New buildings have come up very fast with shops at the Maxwell and Sadar Bazaars with goods imported from Calcutta, all run by inexperienced Manipuris born without business acumen.

Three cinema halls and three drama halls have provided relaxation for the Imphal residents. The town has worn the image of a modern Indian town with paved roads and automobiles. More and more hilldwellers have come down to live at the town centre and so have many high school tribal students.

There was an educational renaissance for all Manipuris, who were until then politically naïve and educationally backward as they lived a cloistered existence. It was not like watching a favourite movie in high definition. It was original. It was a fascinating window on a lost Manipuri civilisation. As a consequence, some educated Manipuris about this time, began to put politics into their heads and dabble in it. And, because they were novices they couldn't 'turn the pumpkin into a coach' like Cinderella's.

By 1947, Calcutta-printed newspapers like *Amrita bazaar Pratika, Hindustan Times* and *Statesman* were available daily in Imphal. Modern sports became regular events. By 1950, 'Birla Airlines' introduced daily flights to Imphal and back to Calcutta *via* Gauhati, keeping Manipuris more in touch with the rest of India. Most families by this time, owned a radio to listen to daily news and Manipuri songs broadcast from Gauhati. There was more reliance on science.

Manipuris owe a great deal to Japanlan. Without it Manipuris (Indians) might still be struggling for a while for independence. It's a piece of quasi-fiction that the behaviour of the Manipuri youth, who are now in their 80s, formed the first phalanx in a major character upheaval of Meiteis. These young Meitei brains shaped and defined a new Meitei culture by their personal experiences but also by those of our ancestors and by environment.

Exploring the impact of the Japanlan on Meiteis 75 years ago with the end of British colonial rule; new geopolitical events; social and economic consequences; the mythological, philosophical and psychological effects of the war, one could see their craving for freedom with a relaxed attitude towards a secular worldview.

For hill-dwellers there was an intense arousal for a belonging, dreams of equality, fairness and justice, and to be able to freely choose Jesus Christ and follow his ways.

31

Reverberations of a War Before Time*

Khuraijam Surjalal Singh

"There's no war that will end all wars."

–Haruki Murakami

Before the Second World War, Manipur was a quiet corner of the Raj with very few links to the outside world. Natives thrived within a rich history of Monarchy, and both inter- and intra-state wars that had soon lost their historical niche. Then, the Second World War reached and was felt in India and Manipur with the Japanese bombing of Imphal on 10th May, 1942. The aggression that the Japanese unleashed in Manipur, greatly affected the life of the natives in Imphal and the far-flung regions of Manipur. Manipur became the part of India that was mostly affected by the war and the Burma campaign of the Axis forces.

Burma (now Myanmar) had fallen to the Japanese in early 1942, and thousands of refugees fleeing from Burma had flowed in hordes into Manipur. With this, Manipur became a buffer state and a frontline between the Axis forces and the then British India.

The present write-up is based on the recollections from the memories of RK. Tamphasana of Sagolband Tera Sapam Leirak and Maibam(o) Tombimacha Devi of Patsoi Salam Mayai Leikai.

At Koirengei Airfield, a large refugee camp was set up. By April 1942, Japanese planes were seen surveying Manipur from her skies. To the people that had never seen an airplane in their life, it was an enthralling sight to see 'man-made dragonflies' hovering high over their fields. No one felt the gravity of the impending air raids.

The older people who were slightly aware of the situation told the young ones that the Japanese were coming to fight the British and that they were going to drop bombs on the Sarkar. The people carried swords to 'cut the wick' of the bombs.

In the months that followed, Manipur turned into an operation base, and people and soldiers of all sorts of race and religion thronged in.

The Bombings and the Relocations

The first bombings of Imphal were on May 10th and 19th, 1942 resulting in a lot of casualties. Residents of areas that were bombed fled from the city and relocated to remote areas of the state. The folk that was daring enough to remain back dug trenches and bomb shelters, and dove in each time they heard sirens wailing and planes flying overhead. As per British records, 84 Manipuris died as a result of the bomb explosions on the fateful day of 10th May, 1942.

R.K. Tamphasana, a resident of Sagolband Tera Sapam Leirak, Imphal West recollects that it was Kalen Tritiya, the third day of Kalen the Manipuri month of May on a Sunday when she saw a huge plane flying low for surveillance at around 8 AM. She was 19 years old at that time. By noon, she heard of an air assault at Koirengei. "There was a single file of Jets, then one by one they separated, 1-2-4-8. There were 17 bomber jets in total, white and ashy like dragonflies. They said the pilots were all 15 years old Japanese girls. 6 days later, another air raid struck again. Khwairamband, Kangla, etc. were all bombed."

In the city, areas like the North AOC, the Khwairamband Bazar, Nagamapal, Khuyathong etc. were bombed. Civilians and vendors who were unaware of the danger lost their lives. Goras (white soldiers) in the area, died in their vehicles. In a matter of seconds, the streets that were filled with the everyday lives of the people reeked of death and havoc.

"We were a small family of three. The day the bombs dropped for the first time, my husband was down with fever. I had bought a *Ngakra* (catfish) from the bazaar and my child of 9 months was slung on my back. While I was cooking, I heard the sound and saw bright flames eastward. I was so scared that I ran inside with my child and prayed for dear life. Soon, Dr. Gopal's family from Waheng Leikai came running to seek refuge in our home as their locality was bombed. My husband's aunt belonged to Dr. Gopal's family. They shared the food I had cooked for the day. Dr. Gopal's father came running through the muddy streets with her aged mother slung on his back.

My husband's younger brother was tilling his plot of land at Leitong when the bombs struck. After the bombing, he came riding the bullock-cart with the *ghumti.* As soon as he reached the front porch, he made no sound and hurried inside the house. He came out with the beds and my wardrobe and placed them on the bullock-cart. He then took me and my child to his aunt's home at Patsoi Khunou near Leitong. On the way there, I saw many war refugees at the Langjing Achouba area with shackles on their wrists and ankles. I saw people in such a state for the first time in my life. As soon as we reached his aunt's home, he left me and my belongings and rode off to pick my ailing husband whom we left at home. There we took refuge for many days to come. My neighbours from our locality all left their homes in fear of the bombs and fled to Patsoi Khunou area. I remember people from the Bijoygovinda area took refuge at Patsoi Khunou.

Three days later after the bombing incident, soldiers thronged the streets of Khwairamband with camouflaged wreaths on their heads. They camouflaged their bodies with ink to hide from the Japanese bomber planes.

Within a short period, soldiers of all races thronged in. The Goras (whites), the Koktumbis (Afghans), the Negros (Africans), Pathan Punjabis (Sikhs), and others.

"A year later, on a Sajibu Purnima, in Khurai Konsam Leikai, at Chingangbam Gulap's mandap, when *Gopi Khujon* was being performed, another air raid struck and 300 people gathered in the mandap died. Only my maternal uncle and the *pujari* survived as they both jumped into a pond when the bombs fell. For 5 days, my maternal uncle collected wood from the locality and cremated the victims."

The Struggle for Survival Against The Japanese Air Invasion

The Allied soldiers stayed in almost all parts of Manipur. They stayed in almost all the localities of the greater Imphal area and the adjacent areas. In the outskirts of Manipur, they stayed in areas where the Japanese soldiers were very likely to thread through.

The displaced refugees came unprepared. They had to take shelter in the Shangois (outhouse). Most of them slept on the ground with a strip of cloth. Some had to sit and sleep in a corner to accommodate the others who were also seeking refuge. Some drove away cattle from cowsheds and cooked food there among the filth.

People ate whatever was available to them and survived with items that were not consumed before their displacement. Those who sought refuge in localities near ponds and rivers went fishing and collected vegetables from the water bodies. Near military camps, people begged for Sambar from the soldiers, and at times, the soldiers gave it off freely for the people walked long distance just for food.

Tumai (rice variety) *grains, heibong mana* (fig leaves), *phunil* (Anaphilis Concorta Hook), *leibak kundo* (common purslane) became common vegetables and food grains during the displacement. Some owners of homes where the refugees settled shared their foodgrains, vegetables, and household items with the refugees.

Others were not very helpful for they were hesitant in sharing their food grains with the refugees. Well to do refugees bought land and stayed there on their own. Despite staying away from their homes, the displaced people often came to their homes to collect rice and other necessary items. But it was a time of war and unattended items were quickly stolen. Many reached their homes to find unknown people hauling off their food grains from their storehouses.

"We took shelter in a Shangoi in my husband's aunt's plot of land. Her husband's name was Bokul. The Shangoi was very big and many people took shelter together with us. We made partitions with cloth, mats, or any available material. We shared whatever we had with her family and she shared whatever she had with us. We were allowed to set up our kitchen by their's and we enjoyed the same luxuries as them.

We took refuge at Patsoi till the month of Wakching (December). Then we came back home. We found Goras (English) living in our home and the other houses of the locality. My neighbours also had returned slowly found their houses used as barracks by the Goras. They had written barrack numbers on the pillars and had hollowed out the mud walls to make entry points for their vehicles. They wrote pillar number 9 on the pillar of Khuraijam—Dinamani's home. Brahmin Mandaps in my locality—Chingtham Mandap, and Bamon Leirak Mandap were used as Mess halls by the soldiers. They used to bring cattle and goats for their meals. The Goras liked beef. Each day was a tale of a different aroma from these setups.

I didn't know the language they were speaking. I only know a few words like '*dushmon*' (enemy) and '*sathi*' (friend). The Goras in my locality were nice people. They gave us biscuit tins, bread, and fragrant hair oils. They also wanted to hold our children but I was always hesitant.

The small kitchen gardens we had tended to and the vegetables that flourished before we left were driven over by their vehicles and the land was unusable. One day, my aunt and I went to meet the Goras to tell them that they were our '*dushmons*' for ruining our kitchen gardens. The young Goras called me '*rajkumari*' and gave me a plate of *chappati* with mutton and *dal*. They were friendly people. We were getting used to life after forced refuge."

Heavy artillery was utilized to face the Japanese Air Raids. R.K. Tamphasana recollected seeing soldiers manning the heavy artillery. She narrated her first encounter of Canon firing. On a Thursday, from the southern side of her house, she heard an unfamiliar sound in the air. "I thought I heard a kitten crying for its mother from the air."

She later came to know that the sound was of a cannon firing from the Ningthemkol area near the present Little Flower School. Ever since that day, she said there were sounds of Cannons fired by Allied soldiers every Thursday. The localities call this continuous incident the Thursday Firing and people did not leave their homes on Thursdays.

"But after 8 days of resettling down at home, a cigar-smoking Gora came riding a Chobilet (Chevrolet) and scattered pamphlets. He spoke in broken Manipuri and told us in the locality to vacate our homes in a week or we will lose our possessions. So we ran again, this time to a vacant house in Sukham Locality of Sagolband Sayang Pukhri Mapal.

Right in front of the house under the thicket of a Nongang hei (Longan) tree, they dug a V-shaped trench. A few days later, around mid-day, we heard the sirens wailing. I strapped on my child and ran into the trench for cover. I saw the bomb as it came crashing down the sky, a flaming ball of fire, into a pond a few metres away from the trench. We survived only because the bomb exploded in the pond. Elsewhere people weren't very fortunate, for later in our journeys I saw massacred bodies in trenches.

Bombs and sirens became a normal thing. We were instructed to take cover or go into v-shaped pits with the first sound of a siren and come out with the second sound of the siren. If the siren sounded hasty (uu-uu-uu) three times, we had to take cover. If it was sounded only once and long (uuuuuuu), it meant the danger was over.

We stayed at Sayang locality for three months from Wakching to Sajibu Purnima. During the stay, my brother-in-law married a lady from Kwakeithel. After the marriage, we left for Sorok Keithel at Lamsang."

The shifting and moving affected the people and many struggled to find spaces to stay and food to eat. People longed for the comfort of their homes and their beds and broke down often at times. Many died during the constant moving. R.K. Tamphasana's brother fell to Jaundice during the relocations.

Maibam (o) Tombimacha Devi from Patsoi Salam Mayai Leikai, who had housed with displaced people from Imphal in her land during the Japanese Invasion of Manipur said, "Before the war, we saw airplanes in the sky that looked like small *Pangandems* (power loom spindle). Word soon spread that a war was coming and we had to dig trenches and bomb shelters. We had pounded the grains earlier. When the air raid struck, the refugees came running with their belongings slung to their backs. When asked about what had happened, the only words which came out of their trembling lips were that bombs had destroyed their homes.

People from Moirang Leirak, Keishamthong, and Keishampat came to seek refuge in my locality. From Keishamthong, B.A. Angou and Aribam Tomba's family sought refuge here. My grandmother was from Keishampat Kangabam Leikai, so their whole family stayed here in a shangoi in the locality. At that time, my family only had a Yumjao (traditional Manipuri House). So the front porch and the sides were used up to house the refugees.

We shared all the luxuries of our home with the displaced people. We gave them our food and we shared the beds for the ladies those came with them. Our men slept in the barns and haystacks with the menfolk of the displaced group.

The refugees came running in the heat of the moment. They had no time to pack their belongings and stock up on their share of food during their stay. They were all good-natured people. When they left, we bid tearful goodbyes to them. Their old folk was cremated here in our locality during the displacement and to this day, we still visit each other on family occasions."

Days of War, Death, and Despair

Villages were bombed. The houses that had only experienced the faintest of candlelight were destroyed in the maelstrom of the bitterest conflict the world had experienced. Manipur's indigenous population was suddenly exposed to people from different parts of the world and intense propaganda of both the Allied and the Axis forces. Manipur and her populace had to change for ever.

Japan found itself on the wrong side of the war with its ties to the Axis and their military ambitions. Thousands of Allied forces fought to defend British India from the Japanese conquest. As the war went on, despair and death followed. Bodies piled rotting in the streets. Flies, rats, and crows appeared in scores and the smell of decay filled the air. With the vermins came the diseases: Cholera, *laijao thokpa* (smallpox), *eshing pukchatpa* (diabetes), Jaundice etc. Food and drinking water became a huge issue, and the dry summer added to the misery.

R.K. Tamphasana recollects stories of the Japanese soldiers that she heard from her elders and friends who experienced them first hand. "The Japanese soldiers were stationed at Moirang. We heard that the Japanese were very fair complexioned but spoke like birds. They were said to be so adept that they sailed the Loktak with a sheet of tent cloth. People from Kumbi told me that the Japanese started begging and snatching the food of the locals."

Tales of Japanese soldiers, their cruelty, and their thievery are still told to this day in many parts of Manipur. Yet, many who had seen and spoken to the Japanese beg to differ. To them, the Japanese soldiers were young slaves in a war run by the old. Incidents of women and child harassment were rare and the soldiers were briefed before the campaign not to harass people. Japanese doctors treated the sick and old in the localities where they were stationed.

> "The Goras told the people living in Moirang and Nambol to leave their homes for a battle was to be fought soon. They said the young Goras waived their caps as they left. Then a great battle was fought

> at Maibamlotpa Ching between the Goras and the Japanese."

The Aftermath

After the war and displacement, Manipur faced near-famine conditions after the war as no farming had been possible during the two years of the war and people consumed their food store dry. Many civilians died as a direct result of the war and thousands more perished due to disease outbreaks like Cholera epidemics that followed after the war ended.

The defeat in the battles of Imphal and Kohima combined is considered the largest defeat on land for the Japanese Army. Around 30,000 Japanese soldiers lost their lives and around 23,000 were injured in the battles fought between the Japanese Fifteenth Army and the British Fourteenth Army. These numbers include those who died in battle, those who succumbed to diseases, and those who perished in the disastrous retreat back to the Chindwin River in Burma. In 1944, the British Fourteenth Army won a decisive victory over the Japanese forces at Imphal. It was on 22nd June, 1944 when the Japanese forces finally withdrew. Soon life in Manipur came back to normalcy.

The people slowly came back to their localities. They rebuilt their homes destroyed by the war and tilled the land for agriculture. The soldiers died and those who survived went home to their families. They left unerasable memories of war, cruelty, and the massacre in people, and others, memories of sharing, of respect, and gifts untold.

It was as John Parratt stated in '*Wounded Land*', "By the time the war ended, Manipur had been forcibly dragged into the modern era." Manipur's experience in the war brought fast-paced changes in the socio-economic lives, culture, and economy of the people. This gradually ushered in a broader mindset and stronger social forces that paved way for economic and political changes in Post World War Manipur.

Present Day

In 2019, former adversaries Britain and Japan came together to inaugurate the Imphal Peace Museum at Maibam Lotpa Ching to commemorate the 75th anniversary of the 'Battle of Imphal'. Today, the museum stands as memorabilia of the old saying, "As long as greed is stronger than compassion, there will always be suffering."

Sagolband Tera Sapam Leirak, Khuraijam Kollup (community) where the Goras stationed and drove their 'Chobilets', is teeming with the life and sounds of the local folk. The homes where the Goras stayed and wrote their barrack number have now been swallowed up by bigger concrete structures. The Mess hall Mandaps have resumed their usual morning *aartis*. Now and then when digging a deep pit for a concrete foundation, people still recover old war memorabilia; bullets, rusty bayonets, shell splinters etc. R.K. Tamphasana had aged gracefully to a ripe, old 98 and tells tales of her journey and life during the war. Her hearing and sight had betrayed her but her mind is still fresh as the old days of her youth.

Likewise, Maibam (o) Tombimacha Devi of Patsoi Salam Mayai Leikai, now 100 years and 9 months old still recollects those days when she saw people running with bags and anguish moist on their foreheads trembling with fear. The fields that remained barren during the days of war are filled with golden paddy husks today. The Shangois house no more refugees.

The city of Imphal is home to two cemeteries maintained by the Commonwealth War Graves Commission. 15 minutes ride down the Tiddim Road takes us to Maibamlotpa ching (hill) where two Japanese War Memorial stands today at the base of the hill to tell the tales of the Japanese soldiers and their war exploits.

The people have lived through war and peace, through famine and plenty. They have heard the sirens and the wails of war and also the sounds of laughter and merry. Wars have no more place in today's society. People who had experienced the war firsthand are no more amongst the living and the descendants had soon forgotten the Japanese Invasion of Manipur.

The Forgotten War only remains a thing of human memory and the battlefield where the Goras and Japanese once fought got reclaimed by nature and echoes with the songs of cicadas and would like to end with a quote once stated by Winston Churchill, "*Old men make war, young men fight and die.*"

REFERENCES

Hemant Singh Katoch (2018). *Imphal 1944: The Japanese Invasion of India,* Osprey Publishing.

Maibam (o) Tombimacha Devi, *Interview by the Author,* Patsoi Salam Mayai Leikai, Imphal.

Singh, J.W. (September 2014). 2nd Displacement of the inhabitants of Manipur during the World War II. *Socrates, 2*(3): 6-17.

_________(July–August, 2014). "Types of Soldiers that came to Manipur in World War II", *SRJIS. II/XIII*: 1599-68.

_________ (2014). "Soldiers in the Localities of Manipur in World War II", *IJHSS, 4*(3): 253-56.

Tamphasana, R.K. *Interview by the Author,* Sagolband Tera Sapam Leirak, Imphal, not dated.

Yaiphaba Meetei Kangjam (2019). *Forgotten Voices of the Japan Laan the Battle of Imphal and the Second World War in Manipur,* INTACH Intangible Cultural Heritage in Association with Aryan Books International.

32

Japanlan and Imphal Peace Museum

A Personal Reflection

James Khangenbam

Legendary filmmaker Aribam Syam Sharma, in the introduction of his autobiography, 'Eigi Paodam' (My Account) wrote—"It was before lunch on a Sunday morning of May 10, 1942, Japan dropped a bomb from the sky which marked the advent of the Second World War in Manipur." He also wrote that after the war many changes were witnessed in terms of the appearance of an individual and their dress pattern. Similarly, "G.C. Tongbra, an eminent playwright of Manipur, took shelter at Nambol as his locality in Imphal experienced heavy bombings during Second World War", wrote Tayenjam Bijoykumar in his article entitled, '*Life Sketch of G.C. Tongbra compiled by Bijoykumar Tayenjam.*" Late G.C. Tongbra revolutionized the theatre movement in Manipur just after the Second World War. The end of the war had brought enthusiasm and a new wave of plays. Manipuri plays were rejuvenated, according to the article.

The Battle of Imphal as the people of Manipur often call "Japanlan" (war) took place from 15th March to 18 July, 1944. Fought between Allied Forces and Axis forces particularly Japan plus the Indian National Army (INA), the Battle of Imphal has often been regarded as one of the fiercest battle of the Second World War. The Imperial Japanese Army suffered huge casualties. It has been estimated that the majority of the 90,000 soldiers died or were severely injured and most of these losses were caused by a serious logistic failure in terms of food supply and decision-making from their end, leaving many sufferings by starvation besides illness. On the other hand, the Allied Forces' side suffered almost entirely in the battle, leaving around 12,000 soldiers dead. The Japanese army marched through Myanmar and invaded Manipur and Nagaland. They entered Manipur from three sides to fight against the Allies who were already holding a strong position under the then Colonial British India. There are other stories that the then Indian National Army, led by Subhas Chandra Bose in collaboration with his team of Japanese soldiers, also joined the war with their own agenda of liberating India to fight against the British army.

Eyewitness Stories from the Locals

Other than documented stories of soldiers and their movement from the war diaries written by war veterans, we have also been hearing stories about the war in the form of the oral tradition of storytelling from our grandparents, such as how they had to flee Imphal for survival, how they offered help to soldiers, and so on. Though there have been not many civilian casualties compared to other battlefields in Asia, Imphal suffered quite a few air raid attacks in May 1942 and April 1943, among which the Khurai area experienced the most fatal attack leaving many people dead at a ceremonial meal at a community hall, according to Khuraijam Nimaicharan, a Sahitya Bhusan Awardee. Indeed, people of Manipur have also equally gone through a lot of sufferings due to the war, as indicated by Professor Naorem Lokendra, former Dean, School of Social Sciences, Manipur University.

Manipuri people are always inquisitive about the battles that took place in Manipur during the war. Stories about the war from eyewitness revolve around in the community and it is being passed on from one generation to another generation. On the technicality, say about the speed of the war planes are all but speculations. The call for a just knowledge is yet to be ascertained. Perhaps the unearthing of the same from the diaries of the soldiers on the understanding of the region and how the soldiers laid their ammunition and set out for the battles would be of great help to the inquisitive researchers and story tellers of the region. The records of how many war planes flew above the sky could all be traced in the war diaries and beyond the stories of the battles we could even delve into the stories of how the soldiers perceived about the places and the people which would be of immense interest and understanding of the bygone days from the eyes of a visitor.

From the local war survivor stories, it is also learnt that some Brahmins when they ran for life has to carry along their Gods wrapped in clothes, while some hide them to recover later. M Gourachandra, the owner of People's Museum, Kakching use to tell stories of what he witnessed in his locality at the time of war, according to him the foothills surrounding Kakching were parked with war planes which took off and returned after accomplishing their mission. The World War II museum he runs with the collection of war relics is contemporized with other handicraft work collections by different communities living in Manipur. He has written a book about the war he witnessed in Manipuri language.

Another witness who is an elderly man in his eighties from the locality of Maibam Lotpa Ching also known as Red Hills narrated about the gun fight that took place in his locality. His family could not have escaped the war and has to crawl inside their home for couple of days until the gun fight gets over. It was learnt that the Japanese soldiers arrived in their village during midnight and took positions to fight the British soldiers who were camped at an adjacent hill top. The localities moved away quietly during the mid-night but the family of the elder man whom I met could not have escaped than to wake up in the middle of a gunfight. He narrated that the Japanese soldiers dug pits in the hill slopes and took positions. The British soldiers were well positioned, after huge casualties the Japanese soldiers lost their ambition of capturing the hilltop. Local witness claimed that the Japanese soldier advanced at a certain point of the hill, as they advance further they dug pits in the hill to create bunkers and fight the enemy. The elderly man also claimed that the Japanese soldiers were looking weary.

At another place surrounding the Red Hills I was shown by my local guide that Japanese were also well equipped with tanks which were positioned in the plain area away from the foothill and there was also heavy exchange of fire around the area. A small memorial centre for the departed soldiers constructed by voluntary donations from the localities of Maibam Lotpa Ching also tells a story of empathy by the locals towards the victims of war. The centre is adjacent to the India Peace Memorial, Maibam Lotpa Ching. A local volunteer who is also a handicap man in his sixties with a register book usually takes around people visiting the India Peace Memorial, Maibam Lotpa Ching providing information about the battle that took place in and around the Red Hills.

The stories of battles are also the stories of survival. How skilfully people have to survive and escape death during war? How to tolerate and live with hope for survival in the uncertain time? How much a square meal has meant to them? What goes in the mind when you crawl under a dug-up pit opting safety than comfort? How one would have breathed safely thinking that splinters of bomb would not cut their body while crawling under a dug pit? How the story of losing communication might have generated fear to the family members and how the individual stories would have unfolded after the war be it grief or joy of losing or finding their near and dear ones. The civilian stories need to be retold and a dedicated centre for civilian lost during World War II and survivor families would serve the right reason to console the loss in its true sense for complete peace. Peace always begins from the home and a peace measure to the locals is peace initiative for the whole world. Forgiveness and understanding is the key to a wholesome peace.

It is very encouraging for the nations who once fought in Imphal are coming to shake hands in Imphal as commemorations of World War II is being hosted by a voluntary organization in Manipur and the government of Manipur. The inquisitive stories of World War II also mature with reconciliations and acceptance of the mistakes. This being the current message also sends a message to avoid war in future.

The Untranslated Stories of Imphal Campaign

There are authentic books about 'Imphal Campaign' by Japanese authors but most of them are written in Japanese language. During our study tour at Japan for the Peace Museum initiatives, we were addressing a group of journalists in a press conference at the Sasakawa Peace Foundation's office and I witnessed the enthusiasm among the journalists in publishing the news story of an announcement of the Foundation's initiative in calling volunteers for translating some of the books on 'Imphal Campaign' into English language. I hope the initiative must have been started by now and in the days to come, we will be able to read books by Japanese authors on 'Imphal Campaign'.

Reconciliation Initiatives and My Study Visit to Japan

There has been lots of reconciliation initiatives taking place among the warring nations including India after the Second World War. Manipur-based volunteer organizations particularly the Manipur Tourism Forum have played significant roles in inviting delegates from different countries to commemorate the war at the memorial sites in Manipur. They have also been actively engaging with other important initiatives, such as excavating war remains voluntarily so as to tell the stories of the past incidents to the next generations in collaboration with war veterans, victim families or the ministries from the respective countries.

In July 2018, as a video archivist, I was lucky enough to take part in one of these reconciliation initiatives where a group of people from Manipur, who have been associated with the peace museum project in Maibam Lotpa Ching, to study and understand at how the Second World War related museums in Japan are telling stories.

This study tour programme was funded and organized by the Sasakawa Peace Foundation (SPF), a Tokyo-based philanthropic organization.

Travelling to Japan—The Land of Reflection and "the Start of Our Moral Awakening"

Before I move onto share my experience from the peace museum initiative visit, I would like to share a news story I came across from a television news channel related to Japan and War. When Barrack Obama, the former President of United States of America, visited Hiroshima in 2016, an atomic bombing survivor who was about to meet Obama was questioned a day ahead by a journalist enquiring if he would ask for forgiveness from the American President. The gentleman answered, "No, I would not ask for his forgiveness. Mankind has made a lot of mistakes and I have forgiven him."

It was a huge reconciliation and a bold step by Japan to invite the President of U.S. to a memorial commemoration in Hiroshima. When Obama landed in Japan and delivered a speech in Hiroshima, he concluded with, "The World was for ever changed here, but today the children of this city will go through their day in peace. What a precious thing that is. It is worth protecting, and then extending to every child. That is a future we can choose, a future in which Hiroshima and Nagasaki are known not as the dawn of atomic warfare but as the start of our own moral awakening."

War and its horrifying tragedy have taught mankind enormous lessons. However, are we learning it the right way, is the learning a continuous process, perhaps a museum remains as a mirror reflecting the flaw mankind has committed in its past actions? Museum curators, contributors and researchers associated with museums have kept polishing their insightful updates like a living entity. It is the effort of these dedicated people that we are able to see our past more clearly to reflect on our present.

How Okinawa Island recovered from the devastation of World War II

After the Second World War defeat, Japan went on to sign an agreement with the US allowing the US military to rule Okinawa until 1972. At present the island is still heavily militarized by the US Military who believe in serving their country by being stationed there. Protests by civilians to remove the US bases have been going on for many decades, which is considered one of the longest peace protests in the world. On the other hand, it is recently reported that the people of Okinawa are sharply divided over the US base issue as it has become extremely politicized in the country.

When it comes to the struggle of the Okinawan people after the battle of Okinawa (World War II), they had to start their lives from scratch. The remains of military uniforms and empty bottles were not even spared by the people as they cut the bottles to make flower vases and re-stitched the military jackets and trousers to make school uniforms and sell them on the streets. Many of them were compelled to work in the US military camp to earn their livelihood until they managed to support themselves. Individual and industrial ventures started to exist in abundance over a period of time. On top of that, the island has also become a favourite destination for holidaying where many people from other parts of Japan and neighbouring countries started visiting the islands for its charm.

We also found the people extremely warm hearted, wearing broad smiles every time. In addition, there are rich traditions and cultural practices are evident, such as folk songs they sing and play with their musical instruments. I would like to share my experience about visiting one museum from among eight other museums, I visited in Japan.

Haebaru Town Museum Okinawa

A very significant part of this museum run by the town council is that it blends with the war stories and the socio-cultural outlook of people living in Haebaru town. The museum also offers variety of programmes and events for their residents. When we visited, programmes for children were taking place outside the museum. The Museum is quite educational as the traditional lifestyle of the community, housing and cultural practices are well depicted besides the war time stories. Not only literature on the soldier's stories but also even cooking utensils, drink bottles and cans are on display, including cigarettes in vogue at that time.

In response to our query, the curator explained that the display in the museum has never been changed since its inception. Most interestingly, it has restored a cave for visitors to give a sense of how those caves looked like and were relevant during the time of war as a hideout or a place where wounded soldiers were treated. A very captivating section of the museum is the representation of tunnel hospital displaying life-size figures of wounded soldiers being treated on hospital beds within. The museum has a whole lot of researched information on display.

It is also saddening to learn that Haebaru town has also suffered post war casualties following unexploded ordinance. The danger still lurks in the towns according to the curator of the museum.

Bringing a Unique Peace Museum to Imphal

Coming back to the purpose of our visit, during the peace museum study tour in Japan, some of the museum curators expressed their willingness to support the Peace Museum on the Second World War at Maibam Lotpa Ching, Red Hills. The Sasakawa Peace Foundation, who took the initiative to take us to Japan, and the Nippon Foundation, the main sponsor of the museum project, have also shown a strong interest in supporting a knowledge sharing initiative by bringing those peace museum curators from Japan to Imphal. The Nippon Foundation, the parent organization of the SPF, later funded the construction of the peace museum in Maibam Lotpa Ching, following a request from the 2nd World War Imphal Campaign Foundation and the Manipur Tourism Forum through the Embassy of Japan, New Delhi. Imphal Peace Museum, Maibam Lotpa Ching was inaugurated on 22nd June, 2019.

War has brought tragedies and the process of reconciliation is adorned with the realization of the past mistakes. The journey to peace building is worth every step. How can a State like Manipur recover from the impact of the Second World War remain untold to and unheard by the present generation? We have been listening only to personal stories of our grandparents. The philanthropic foundations in Japan wish that the stories from the natives of the State should come out. They wish to tell the next generation through the peace museum initiative of the mistake of war to learn from it and not to repeat it.

Conclusion

Coming to the conclusion, most importantly, are the stories of war teaching us any lessons. Practically, war tourism generates revenue to the tourism sector. Leaving aside these factors, Manipur has been actively engaging themselves in commemorating the anniversary of World War II annually by giving condolences to the departed soldier who laid down their lives in the soil of Manipur. Are the events taking place in Imphal unique and impactful? Is Manipur contributing to global peace? Are the affections by the locals creating a warm environment for the participating nations to make friendships meaningful and cementing a healing message to the World? Will Manipur stand tall in hosting such similar events in future?

Are the impacts of World War II to Manipur discussed in the contemporary society? Are the victims of the war being consoled officially in the present era? Do we have a dedicated memorial centre where we pay homage to the war victims of Manipur civilians during World War II?

33

JAPANLAN

Life in Kangla Sangomshang and Siphai

Bramhacharimayum Sadananda Sharma

As Air-raid sirens sounded the warning during the Second World War. It became an almost daily part of life in both the capital and villages. When people heard the siren they would stop what they were doing and make for a safe shelter. At the same time Japanese planes came for air raid, sounds of those planes were quite loudly heard; many of us hide in a pit (Kom) in Manipuri. As narrated by Ngangbam Tocha Singh, 92 years old elderly man from Kangla Sangomshang who is once a care giver of the colonial "Sepoy" during the Second World War. When it comes to Second World War the name of Kangla will for ever remain unerased from the history. Kangla being the name of an important place during the period of the great Second World War will ever remain in history even generations after generations.

The very village of Tocha, Kangla Sangomshang lies on the western bank of the Iril River which flows down southward through the village, whereas on the east of the river lies Kangla Siphai. Kangla Siphai is situated to the north-eastern part of Imphal, the capital of Manipur, around 9 kilometres away from Imphal itself. From Chairenthong, the short bridge from Imphal-Ukhrul Road, taking a right turn on the inter-village road eastward. As per settlement record of the government, both the places here on both sides of the river, Kangla Siphai and Kangla Sangomshang are known as the same single village as "Kangla" in short.

The word "Kangla" can be traced back to those olden days when Chandrakirti Maharaja was the reigning King of Manipur about 300 years back. Many soldiers or Siphais who guarded the royal palace of the Maharaja were made to live in this village on the riverside, and hence the place came to be known as "Kangla Siphai" afterwards.[1] According to old aged people "Kangla Sangomshang" was also said to be have been so named for supplying milk to the royal kitchen during those times. The word Shangom is milk and Shang meaning shed. It is said that the village had a lot of cowsheds and produced large quantity of milk which is enough to serve the royal homes; hence the place came to be known as place of milk sheds.[2]

Very near to the east of the village, stands the great Chingkhei Ching (a small mountain) as a protector of the people of this village. The place of the mountain is also regarded as the abode of the legendary King Chingkhei Ningthou. The relation between the lives of the people on both sides of the river and the Chingkhei Hill is very close that the hill itself is a good source of several things which the villagers need in their day-to-day life. The hill provides them with fire woods, bamboos, trees and many edible herbs and vegetables. In simple word Chingkhei hill may be called the life of the villagers.[3]

During the time of Second World War, as narrated by Ngangbam Tocha, the colonial Sepoy took shelter in Kangla Sangomshang and set up their camp in Tarakonjin, a hill in Kangla Sangomshang where they kept Sten-gun, bombs, and even anti-aircraft gun etc. They captured the area from Chingarel (a small hill situated near Ukhrul Road, which is currently Assam Rifles camp) to Ningthoubung for constructing their camp. Planes are kept hidden in bushes covering by black tent, grass and leaves to protect from enemies air raid. He works for 7/8 years for the colonial Sepoy assisting them in guarding the plane and camps protecting from cattle and intruders. He even took care of their horses cleaning and feeding in returns as a monthly salary they paid some amount and it was huge during those times, he said.

One memorable and witty moment for Tocha is that being a teenager he was interested in how an airplane work and fly. So, he keeps a close watch on how the armies handle all those control and procedure to fly. Not so long to his boyish imagination he thought he acquires enough knowledge to fly an airplane, out of curiosity and desire one fine day seeing a situation, narrating the story suddenly Tocha exclaimed that he had no clue how come he was inside the airplane then he started the engine, and he pushes a paddle the plane started moving slowly, but he got panic and shout for help, meanwhile, all the armies came out and stop the plane, one of the flying commander even slap him but didn't get any severe punishment, Tocha made a soft smile.[4]

During those times when the Japanese bombed Imphal town on Sunday, the 10th May, 1942 there was no airport in Manipur. In fact, the only airport in the North-eastern Region of India at that time was at Dinjan, near Dibrugarh. Koirengei Airfield was constructed during 1942-43 with the help of American Engineers. The other two main all weather airfields constructed in Manipur during World War II were the Tulihal and Pallel airfields. Three other fair weather airfields were also made during this period at Thoubal, Sapam and Kangla Siphai.

All these airfields did play a big role in saving Manipur from the clutches of the invading Japanese Army. Tocha added, there were many army resided in Kangla, foods were supplied by army aeroplanes sometimes through air drop. They sometimes eat our indigenous food but being a spicy food they could not take it often. He continued, during war time many villagers fled to other neighbouring villages specifically in Tumukhong, Moirangpurel, Sabungkhok, Pukhao etc. and settle there by doing agricultural work for survival. Not only were those, villagers from Kangla

Sangomshang also displaced to the other side of Iril River (Kangla Siphai) so as not to injure when bombing. He said, even though there were many bomb explosions near the village, there was no report of casualty only one cattle was injured in bombing.

In those days, the primary occupation of the villagers mainly depends on agricultural work. Among the villagers, one or two were employed in Government Departments in the post of "*ameen*" (one who demarcate lands) and clerks. It will be hard for us to visualise the situation of that time, there were big airfield with planes in different directions and many army camps, arms and ammunitions were stored which are needed for war. Amidst war zone life was simple for them few stalls of women vendors can be seen selling *pans*, sweets, cigarettes etc.

One unique performance which they saw first time during war time is that many armies from camps of Indian armies along with workers were there performing drills every morning which is quite new for them.[5] Their special moment during that time lies in the grazing field located at the southward of Kangla village that links with the northern outskirt of the Angom village. It was also the grazing ground of the time, being a vast grassy plain, was made into a sports complex by the British Army and as such different games like football, athletics, rugby, volleyball, softball and Indian *kabaddi* etc. were played and practiced there everyday by Indian and British armies.

Besides army men, a few interested young men of the villages too joined the game. According to Ngangbam Tocha he also participated in the practice of certain games like football in which he acquires a lot of skills and tactics, one day he was playing with the armies and he kicks the ball with all five toe and he got injured, there the army gave him first aid and necessary treatment. During those times many tournaments of different games were held and conducted by the Anglo-Americans which encamped in and around the Kangla airfield. On the western boundary of this field, lies a small hillock known as Tarakonjin, a popular playing place for all youth. During war time, there stood a big tent on that hillock, said to be the camp of a general and in it many big British and American officers held meetings and discussions.[6]

Recalling the past, eyes misted over with tears he continued that, after the war, as a token of appreciation for his work, the colonial "Shipoy" presented a certificate and also ask him to visit their country independently and presented a pistol along with a Sten Gun. But those entire precious certificates were thrown in river where many were arrested for keeping those things at that time. The old aged Ngangbam Tocha recalled his memory in a sweet voice and said those days were quite a troublesome time compared to today's situation. But with the grace of god we survive and those sweet and troublesome memories become our source of happiness. People were generous and kind helping each other, sharing things between friends and neighbours were a part of life. Most of my childhood's friends are not with me anymore, "I missed them a lot" were his words wiping his eyes filled with tears, with his khudei (a single piece of cloth Meitei men used to traditionally wear around their waist with its end tipped end tucked in the back usually when they are at home or are at family feast and other specific occasions).

NOTES

1. Kh. Nimaicharan Singh, *The 2nd World War in Manipur & My Childhood*, Kh. Ratankumar Singh, Imphal, pp. 116-19.
2. *Ibid.*, p. 119.
3. *Ibid.*, pp. 119-20.
4. Lt. Col. M. Ranjit Singh (Retd.), "Koirengei Airfield: From airfield to a historical site or a parking space?", *e-pao.net.*, 1 May, 2017.
5. Kh. Nimaicharan Singh, *op.cit.*, p. 117.
6. *Ibid.*, pp. 123-24.

Index